Governance and Human Capital
The 21st Century Agenda

Governance and Human Capital
The 21st Century Agenda

Editors

SHARIF AS-SABER
RUMKI BASU
RAZA AHMAD
RFI SMITH
AHMAD MOHAMMAD MARTADHA

STERLING PUBLISHERS PRIVATE LIMITED

STERLING PUBLISHERS PRIVATE LIMITED
A-59, Okhla Industrial Area, Phase-II, New Delhi-110020.
Tel: 26387070, 26386209 Fax: 91-11-26383788
e-mail: mail@sterlingpublishers.com
www.sterlingpublishers.com

Governance and Human Capital: The 21st Century Agenda
©2011, *Editors and Contributors*
ISBN 978 81 207 5778 3

All rights are reserved. No part of this publication may be reproduced, stored in a retrieval system or transmitted, in any form or by any means, mechanical, photocopying, recording or otherwise, without prior written permission of the original publisher.

PRINTED IN INDIA
Printed and Published by Sterling Publishers Pvt. Ltd., New Delhi-110 020.

Acknowledgments

We acknowledge with gratitude all those who ensured the success of the NAPSIPAG International Conference 2009 on the theme, " Human Capital and Good Governance" at the Universiti Utara Malaysia (UUM). The conference was organised jointly by NAPSIPAG (JNU), the Ministry of Higher Education (Malaysia) and the College of Law, Government and International Studies (COLGIS) at University Utara Malaysia.

For their invaluable personal and institutional support we wish to extend our thanks to, YB Dato' Saifuddin Abdullah, Deputy Minister, Ministry of Higher Education, Tan Sri Shamsudin Osman, Chairman, Employees Provident Fund, Tan Sri Dr Nordin Kardi, Vice-Chancellor, Universiti Utara Malaysia, Associate Professor Dr Asmah Laili Hj. Yeon, Assistant Vice-Chancellor, University Utara Malaysis , College of Law, Government and International Studies, State Secretary General's Office, Kedah Darulaman.

For their energy, commitment and gracious hospitality we extend our thanks to Associate Professor Dr Ahmad Martadha Mohamed, Director, NAPSIPAG 2009 Conference, all members of the Organizing Committee, College of Law, Government and International Studies at Universiti Utara Malaysia and the staff at the Executive Development Centre, University Utara Malaysia.

For their focused and timely key note speeches we extend our thanks to Professor Chris Nyland, Department of Management, Monash University, Professor Ian Marsh, Australian Innovation Research Centre, University of Tasmania, Professor Tan Sri Dato' Dzulkifli Abdul Razak, Vice-Chancellor, Universiti Sains Malaysia, Dato' Dr Muhamad bin Hamzah, Director, Institut Tadbiran Awam Negara (INTAN), Dr Sharif As-Saber, Monash University and Prof. Amita Singh, Secretary General (NAPSIPAG) and Chairperson Centre for the Study of Law and Governance, JNU, Delhi.

This publication would not have been possible within the deadline without the knowledge driven steering role of the NAPSIPAG Secretariat located at the Centre for the Study of Law and Governance Jawaharlal Nehru University. The able leadership of Prof. Amita Singh as the Secretary General of the Group and Ms Sylvia Yambem as the alert Executive Research Coordinator successfully managed the authors as well as the publication demands. Ms Seema Mudgal, Office Assistant and Mr Jhumman Yadav, Office Attendant willingly worked overtime to see the project book completed in time. Ms Rizwana Shamshad, Monash Asia Institute, Monash University provided the long distance support to publication.

Finally, for their enthusiastic and thoughtful participation we wish to thank all conference participants.

Contents

Acknowledgments   v

Section 1:
STRATEGIES FOR DEVELOPING HUMAN CAPITAL

Chapter 1	INTRODUCTION	3
Chapter 2	HUMAN CAPITAL INDICATORS: Towards Achieving a Knowledge Society in Malaysia *Norsiah Abdul Hamid and Halimah Badioze Zaman*	10
Chapter 3	STRENGTHENING RURAL GOVERNANCE: Farmer Field Schools as a Strategy to Build Human Capital in Conflict affected Jaffna District of Sri Lanka *D.L Chamila Jayashantha and Puvaneswary Ponniah*	23
Chapter 4	STRENGTHENING HUMAN CAPITAL THROUGH CITIZENSHIP VALUES EDUCATION *Eleanor E. Nicolas*	33
Chapter 5	NEW BANTAYAN BARANGAY DEVELOPMENT PLANNING: A Blended Learning Approach *Aristeo C. Salapa*	41
Chapter 6	STRATEGY FOR IMPROVING HUMAN CAPITAL IN BANGLADESH AND NEPAL: Does it help for Women Empowerment *Tek Nath Dhakal and Faraha Nawaz*	52
Chapter 7	DOES INTERNATIONAL MIGRATION INDUCE HUMAN CAPITAL INVESTMENT AND KNOWLEDGE TRANSFER? Evidence from the Philippines *Eduardo T. Gonzalez*	63
Chapter 8	AN EXAMINATION OF AUDIT FUNCTIONS IN INSTITUTIONS OF HIGHER LEARNING *Mohd Raime Ramlan, Mohamad Naimi Mohamad Noor and Raudah Danila*	77

Section 2:
HUMAN RESOURCE MANAGEMENT AND CAPACITY BUILDING

Chapter 9	ACADEMIC STANDARDS VERSUS POLITICAL LOYALTY IN HIGHER EDUCATIONAL INSTITUTIONS IN BANGLADESH: The Case of Rajshahi University *Ishtiaq Jamil and Pranab Kumar Panday*	89

Chapter 10	BUILDING SELF EFFICACY AND RESILIENCE IN CREATING POSITIVE GOVERNANCE Lipi Mukhopadhyay	103
Chapter 11	EMPOWERMENT OF WOMEN THROUGH EDUCATION: Innovative Policy Interventions in Rajasthan Sheila Rai	111
Chapter 12	PREPARING HUMAN RESOURCE FOR E-GOVERNMENT: Some Evidence from Bangladesh Civil Service Shah Mohammad Sanaul Hoque, and Fatema-Tu-Zohra Binte Zaman	121
Chapter 13	VOCATIONAL EDUCATION AND PARTICIPATORY DEVELOPMENT IN THE NORTH EASTERN REGION OF INDIA Sylvia Yambem	134

Section 3:
ISSUES IN HIGHER EDUCATION AND POLICY REFORMS

Chapter 14	CIVIL SERVICE RECRUITMENT POLICY IN BANGLADESH: An Agenda for Reform M. Abdul Wahhab	149
Chapter 15	HIGHER EDUCATION: Recent Reform Initiatives In India Suman Sharma	159
Chapter 16	REVAMPING HIGHER EDUCATION IN THE CONTEXT OF KNOWLEDGE ECONOMY: Perception of Academia Baiju K.C., Faculty and Asha J.V	171
Chapter 17	IS HIGHER EDUCATION A PUBLIC GOOD? Policy Dilemmas in a Democratic State Rumki Basu	180
Chapter 18	THE HUMAN RIGHTS BASED APPROACH AND GOVERNANCE PRINCIPLES – A Higher Education Perspective Maria Clarisa R. Sia	191
Chapter 19	STUDENT MOBILITY IN ASIA: An Appraisal A.K. Malik	201
Chapter 20	REVISITING THE BANYAN TREE CLASSROOM A Prognosis for Future Amita Singh	213
	About the Contributors	219
	About NAPSIPAG	223

Section 1

STRATEGIES FOR DEVELOPING HUMAN CAPITAL

CHAPTER 1

INTRODUCTION

According to Mahbub Ul Haq, the founder of UNDP's famous Human Development Index, "The objective of development is to create an enabling environment for people to enjoy long, healthy and creative lives" (UNDP, 2010). Necessary levels of skills, knowledge and health are therefore, needed to be achieved in a society through investment in the people, which in turn, may contribute to creating a knowledge-based society. Collectively known as 'human capital', it is an essential precondition for improving governance and fostering growth and human wellbeing. As the global population is growing fast with mounting pressure on the provision of essential services and social security, the focus is gradually shifting towards the efficient utilization of human capital through the creation of a knowledge-based society ready for taking up the challenges of the 21st century.

It has been observed that countries that have been experiencing persistent growth in income have also been showing enhancements in the education and training of their labour forces. For instance, the outstanding economic growth of Japan, Singapore, Taiwan and other emerging Asian countries in recent years shows the importance of human capital growth (Becker, 1993; 2002). Appropriate policies in enriching human capital and their effective implantation, therefore, are essential for a country's sustainable growth and development.

Governance, on the other hand, has become a new buzzword of the twenty-first century (Chatterjee, 2004; Jessop, 1998). Kjaer (2006) defines governance as the capacity to define and implement policies. Rhodes (1996) suggests six different uses for the term 'governance': corporate governance, the new public management, good governance, socio-cybernetic systems, and self-organizing networks. According to World Bank (1992), which suggests the term 'good governance' as a mandatory component for its lending policy to developing countries, good governance involves

> an efficient public service, an independent judicial system and legal framework to enforce contracts; the accountable administration of public funds; an independent public auditor, responsible to a representative legislature; respect for the law and human rights at all levels of government; a pluralistic institutional structure, and a free press.

In the Asia-Pacific, especially within its developing region, governance is fraught with a lot of problems including the lack of efficiency, transparency and responsiveness. It is argued that a knowledge-based society can be instrumental in combating these problems. Enhanced skill levels among public employees would be able to improve efficiency, whereas an educated and knowledgeable society would create awareness about the society's needs and aspirations and the accountability of the public service to the society. Therefore, a clear understanding of causal links between enhanced human capital and good governance is imperative.

It is not easy to capture a comprehensive picture of the various issues that are likely to affect human capital and its relationship with good governance. From an Asia-Pacific perspective, this book has compiled a set of outstanding papers that have dealt with a number of key issues pertaining to human capital and good governance. The book is divided into three major sections. The first two sections deal with strategies for developing human capital and human resource management and capacity building. As higher education is increasingly becoming an instrument of advanced skill-development, countries around the world are increasingly emphasizing the enhancement of this important sector and constantly looking for avenues in improving this sector's national as well as international competitiveness. In this light, the third section of the book is dedicated to issues in higher education and its associated policy reforms. The book argues that an effective human capital policy which includes reform of the education system and the development of skilled human capital under the umbrella of good governance is likely to foster economic growth and enhance human well-being.

The first section of the book introduces several strategies for developing human capital from a selection of Asia Pacific countries. Norsiah Abdul Hamid and Haliman Badioze Zaman's paper looks at the Human Capital Indicators from a Malaysian perspective. The paper discusses the importance of these indicators in the development of a knowledge society. The authors argue that these indicators can be used for the development of a Malaysian Knowledge Society and act as a guideline for the government to streamline policy implementation, specifically in the context of human capital development. The study employed a survey questionnaire as an instrument for data collection. The study involves 450 respondents from three stakeholders in Malaysia, particularly officials from the public sector, the private sector and the NGOs. A total of 44 human capital indicators were proposed based on the review of literature and qualitative studies. These indicators consisted of four sub-dimensions, viz., education and training, skills, research and development, as well as knowledge sharing and dissemination. Results show that 15 indicators are perceived to be extremely important, while 29 indicators are relatively less important. The authors consider these indicators to be able to represent the human capital dimension in the development of Malaysia's Knowledge Society.

D.L Chamila Jayashantha and Puvaneswary Ponniah's paper deals with an interesting issue on the role of farmer field schools as a strategy to build human capital in the conflict affected Jaffna district of Sri Lanka. The paper starts with the introduction of a project called, "Local Initiatives For Tomorrow (LIFT)" implemented by CARE International in Sri Lanka. The paper tells a success story of creating human capital in a conflict affected region through this project. The project intended to strengthen community-level institutions supporting economic activity, employment creation and provision of basic social services in 32 villages in Jaffna district of Sri Lanka by 2008. Jaffna was directly affected by a three decade long ethnic war and the impact of the conflict is prominently visible in its socioeconomic, political and infrastructural domains. CARE expected to have an improved level of community participation in decision making and management of resources pertaining to their own development, while fulfilling service requirements and livelihood needs. CARE believed that this could only be achieved through human capacity building and social empowerment. The Farmer Field Schools approach was adopted as the key strategy. The project ensured a wide array of training for the community ranging from basic agricultural training as a direct support for their main stay, agriculture, and also training for conflict resolution which aims at social empowerment. Despite numerous institutional and policy challenges, Farmer Field Schools now perform well not only to fulfil agricultural extension requirements within their communities, but also as effective conduits dealing with rural governance priorities. The paper examines the importance of identifying alternative human capacity building strategies to be implemented to restore livelihoods and subsequently to increase community involvement in resource management and decision making in conflict affected areas.

The third paper of this section is contributed by Eleanor E. Nicolas. Nicolas' paper underpins the important role of citizenship values education in strengthening human capital. The paper argues, as the value system of a society is inextricably intertwined with democracy and development, in a country where corruption and lack of trust and public confidence in its institutions are perceived to be pervasive, citizenship and values education could work as an antidote to these challenges. From a Filipino perspective, the paper emphasised the formation of multi-sectoral groups to identify and disseminate the idea of systemic and holistic approach to strengthening national values through measures that promote value formation and civic/citizenship education. This group convened three national congresses on good citizenship to generate a critical mass of advocates of good citizenship values. A significant number of people from academe, business, religious groups, and civil society organisations have become actively engaged in promoting citizenship values.

Aristeo C. Sapala's paper provides an overview of a blended learning approach based on the new Barangay development planning in the Philippines. Blended Learning (BL) is a combination of approaches to learning that promotes the readiness of graduate students to elevate knowledge to higher levels. This presents a challenge for professors teaching at the graduate level. Theory and direct application of such learning in a given span of time is a hard task to realize. The syllabus, in this regard, plays a vital role. Well-planned course curricula measure the output of the exercise at the end of the semester. This blended learning system is applied by graduate public administration students of the University of South-Eastern Philippines. The author considers such an innovative learning strategy to be able to positively impact on human capital and its use in improving governance.

T.N. Dhakal and Faraha Nawaz's paper deals with the strategy for improving human capital in Bangladesh and Nepal and its impact on women's empowerment. The paper argues that every nation needs to have its human capital developed to generate employment contributing to socio-economic transformation. Empowering women is an important component of this strategic objective. In two South Asian countries, Bangladesh and Nepal, governments have adopted inclusive policies to empower women by ensuring effective women's participation in the formulation, implementation, coordination, monitoring and evaluation of relevant policies and launching women targeted special programs. But in reality the findings show that despite government initiatives in these countries, women still lag behind in mainstream development. This paper discusses the major factors that are hindering the enhancement of human capital necessary for women's empowerment in these countries.

The paper by Eduardo T. Gonzalez poses a question on the ability of international migration to induce human capital investment and knowledge transfer. The paper scrutinizes the impact of international migration on human capital accumulation in the Philippines as a source country. As recent evidence suggests that international migration generates net fiscal and social benefits on those remaining behind, the paper finds a mixture of favourable effects and smaller gains. Remittances posted by Filipino migrants contribute to investments in health and education sectors. Greater competition for the "emigration slots" leads to increases in the country's stock of human capital. But the Philippines is clearly struggling with underdeveloped diaspora networks and inadequate support for returning migrants. The paper concludes with a note that the institutional environment of a "soft state" in the Philippines makes it hard to deal with these issues.

In the final paper of this section, *Mohd Raime Ramlan, Mohd Naimi Mohamed Noor, and Raudah Danila* have attempted to examine audit functions in institutions of higher learning. As financial statements are accepted as major sources of a company's financial position, the auditor is expected to enhance the quality of the financial report; its reliability, credibility and comparability through a proper and competent audit process. This study has selected students of higher learning institutions in Malaysia to examine how respondents actually view the audit functions in terms of their importance and effectiveness. The descriptive technique employed statistically indicated that all audit functions were perceived as important and effective. For perceived importance, the findings indicated that the students expected auditors to enhance the reliability of financial statements and ensure that reports are prepared in accordance with Generally Accepted Accounting Principles (GAAP) and sufficiently carry out valuation of company liabilities. In terms of effectiveness, they agree that the auditors have effectively delivered audit functions such as performing an independent opinion of the financial report.

The second section of the book appraises issues concerning human resource management and capacity building. The first paper of the section by Ishtiaq Jamil and Pranab Panday examines an important issue pertaining to the impact of political loyalty on academic standards in higher education institutions in Bangladesh. The paper highlights the negative impact of undue political influence on higher educational institutions in Bangladesh. The paper analyzes how politics impedes academic standards and quality through nepotism, lobbying, and other political activities under different political banners. Findings from the study of a public university – Rajshahi University – reveal that recruitment of fresh teachers as well as career advancement is an occasion where political loyalty of candidates plays an important role in the recruitment process. Candidates with strong affiliation to the political party in power have greater chances of recruitment than candidates with only excellent academic records. Political loyalty reigns over academic qualifications compromising the quality of staffing and service delivery and negatively affecting knowledge creation and dissemination.

The paper by Lipi Mukhopadhyay emphasizes the importance of building self-efficacy and resilience as a catalyst to create positive governance. The author argues that positive emotion and resilience may systematically enhance human capabilities. From the social-cognitive perspective, one's sense of self-efficacy, which is determined by an array of personal, social, and environmental factors, may be changed not only to influence one's level of self-efficacy, but also to affect subsequent performance on significant tasks. Accordingly, resilient people need to be able to solve problem with a calm, confident sense of being able to overcome adversity. They need to approach challenges with learning agility: the ability to learn from each experience, positive or negative. These characteristics, according to Mukhopadhyay, could be identified and utilized in creating a positive atmosphere for development of good governance.

Sheila Rai, in her paper, "Empowerment of Women through Education: Innovative Policy Interventions in Rajasthan", highlights the non-negotiable nature of education for women and its importance in transition towards knowledge based development and well being. As a critical component of the Millennium Development Goals, it is increasingly important to consider what must be done to help women and girls not simply to get by, but to emerge empowered and thrive. The paper strongly pleads for greater investment by governments and international development agencies in enhancing girls' education to achieve gender equality and women's empowerment. Based on Rajasthan, this paper attempts to assess the interventionist role of the state and its resultant impact on the actual status of women's education.

The paper by S.M.S Hoque and Fatima-Tu-Zohra Binte draws on an interesting topic for discussion. Based on evidence from the Bangladesh civil service, the paper highlights how human capital in e-government techniques and literacy is achieved in a country such as Bangladesh. The authors argue that, as public servants are the main drivers to implement e-government as a critical element on the 'supply side' of e-government applications, they need to accrue appropriate skills to understand, learn, use and disseminate such knowledge . The skills of public servants are also key to planning, designing and implementing any e-government initiative. Therefore, necessarily the workforce must be equipped with the right aptitude (skill) perception (understanding), attitude (desire) and to move with changes. In light of these criteria, the paper investigates the preparedness of the Bangladesh Civil Service (BCS) for e-government. In particular it deals with the groups of entry level, mid level and senior level public officials working in the BCS. The study reveals that regarding preparedness, members of the BCS show considerable strengths for e-government with respect to their interest and adaptability to new technologies. However, despite their levels of awareness and positive attitudes towards e-government they have low levels of ICT aptitude. Authors suggest more intensive and robust training and motivational programs within the civil service to provide efficient e-government services in Bangladesh.

Sylvia Yambem's paper deals with vocational education and participatory development in the North Eastern region of India that comprises the eight Indian states of Arunachal Pradesh, Assam, Manipur, Mizoram, Nagaland, Sikkim and Tripura. Home to about 3.9% of the total population of India, the region boasts of a literacy level higher than the national average of 68.5%. The state of Mizoram with 88.49% has the second highest literacy rate in the country, after Kerala. However, this high literacy level does not translate to higher productivity or higher employability. To counter this dilemma, the North Eastern Region Vision 2020 proposed the adoption of vocational skill building and training based education within the framework of participatory development. The paper looks at two issues: the prevailing state of education and the participatory, development based vocational education and technical programme framework advocated. The paper highlights the paradox that a positive correlation between improved human capital and higher productivity and growth is not observed. It attempts to address the reasons behind this situation.

The third section of the book deliberates on issues in higher education and policy reforms. The paper by M. Abdul Wahhab examines the civil service recruitment policy in

Bangladesh and its reform agenda. The paper reveals that a sound and appropriate civil service recruitment policy does not exist in Bangladesh. Executive orders govern recruitment policy. Instead of merit, the existing recruitment policy gives emphasis to quotas and reserves the majority of posts for preferred groups. Likewise, ad hoc appointments also dominate civil service recruitment policy. Through quota and ad hoc appointments, the government politicises the civil service. The paper recommends the introduction of the principles of merit in civil service recruitment. It proposes the abolition of all types of quotas except for the tribal peoples. It also proposes the need to avoid ad hoc appointments. Since a single Public Service Commission is unable to hold competitive examinations regularly and on time, the paper suggests the establishment of more than one Public Service Commission. It also proposes to reform competitive examinations to avoid lengthy selection processes; and to minimize political pressures and corruption.

Suman Sharma's paper addresses the recent reform initiatives in the Indian higher education sector. Sharma, in her paper, has highlighted the critical importance of education in building human capital. She, however, argues that despite the historical ruling by the Indian Supreme Court in 1993 making the right to education inherent in the right to life, a serious and deep crisis still exists. This paper has made an attempt to evaluate India's efforts in reforming the higher education sector. However, it has not ignored the controversies that are going on surrounding the current and the future structures and agendas of the regulatory authority in shaping the higher education sector.

Based on perceptions of academia, the next paper deliberates on mechanisms to revamp higher education. In this paper, Baiju K. and Asha J.V highlight the importance of improving education and learning paradigms in light of new knowledge and information. Against this backdrop, this paper focuses on perceptions in academia of the key aspects of education which help in enhancing human capital through skill-building and knowledge-development leading to economic growth. The data were collected from 80 college teachers selected from two representative districts of Kerala, India through a questionnaire. The major challenges identified include difficulties in guaranteeing quality and the need to preserve national culture and identity, ensure that the government sets national policy objectives for higher education, and ensure equity of access to higher education.

Rumki Basu's paper encompasses an interesting dilemma within the higher education sector in India and poses a question as to whether higher education could be considered as a public good. While tertiary education is undergoing extensive expansion and diversification creating a large pool of educated people worldwide, India is facing an enormous shortage of employable talent and skills in diverse sectors of the economy. The biggest challenge the country faces is to impart marketable skills and competencies to the young so that they can meet the needs of a rapidly expanding economy. It is argued that the higher education policy agenda in India is judgmentally clouded in its policy imperatives by avoiding any systematic and strong measures on issues such as 'equality vs. quality', or 'merit criteria vs. 'social justice'.

Maria Clarisa R. Sia, in her paper, has drawn a higher education perspective on human rights based approach and governance principles. Sia argues that in a true democracy, effective governance and societal improvement are considered to be the core strategies in achieving development and enhancing standards of living. Mainstreaming and the application of a human-rights based approach to governance and development are considered to be important strategic tools to implement these strategies. Based on the evidence of the University of the Philippines, the paper highlights the role of such institutions in building greater trust and confidence in political and administrative leaders.

In an intriguing paper, A.K. Malik has examined the issue of student mobility in Asia. Malik identified the phenomenon of increased student mobility from the developing world to the developed. However, he argues that in recent times intra-regional student mobility is also increasing. In East Asia and the Pacific, increased numbers of students are remaining in their own region. Foreign students are admitted for both educational and economic considerations. Keeping this in view, this paper explains the effects of home and host countries on institutions of higher education and of mobility of students. This is highlighted independently, describing factors determining the mobility, objectives and reasons for studying abroad and benefits of student exchange and exchange strategies across Asian countries. Finally, the paper discusses strategies to stimulate, maintain and widen intra-Asian educational interaction as a central feature of university level cooperation.

Finally, Amita Singh, in her stimulating and scholarly article, provides a dismal picture of the social and human conditions of the world's poor and disadvantaged and proposes necessary measures to alleviate poverty and inequality through imparting knowledge and skills among the downtrodden. She argues that without achieving equity and justice while enhancing human capital, the realisation of the Millennium Development Goals will be impossible.

Sharif As-Saber, Monash University
Rumki Basu, Jamia Millia University
RFI Smith, Monash University
Raza Ahmad, Pakistan Policy Group
Ahmed Martadha Mohamed, Universiti Uttara Malaysia

References

Becker, G.S. 1993. *Human capital: A theoretical and empirical analysis, with special reference to education* (3rd Edition), The University of Chicago Press, Chicago
—————— 2002. Human Capital. *Revista de Ciencias Empresariales y Economía*, Vol. 1, pp. 12-23
Chatterjee, P, 2004. *The Politics of the Governed*. Columbia University Press, New York
Chazan, Naomi, 1992. Liberalization, Governance and Political Space in Ghana, in Goran Hyden and Michael Bratton, eds. *Governance and Politics in Africa*. Lynne Rienner, ,Boulder, CO, pp. 121-142
Jessop, B. 1998. The Rise of Governance and the Risks of Failure: The Case for Economic Development, *International Social Science Journal*, vol. 50 (155), pp. 29-45
Kjaer, A. M. 2006. *Governance*. Cambridge: Polity Press.
Rhodes, R. 1996. The New Governance: Governing without Government. *Political Studies*, vol. 44 (4), pp. 652-667
UNDP, 2010. The Human Development Concept, http://hdr.undp.org/en/humandev/, accessed on 21 October.
World Bank, 1992. *Governance and Development*, Washington DC, The World Bank.

CHAPTER 2

HUMAN CAPITAL INDICATORS:
Towards Achieving a Knowledge Society in Malaysia

NORSIAH ABDUL HAMID AND HALIMAH BADIOZE ZAMAN

Abstract

This article discusses about a study which attempts to determine the important indicators that represent the human capital dimension in the development of a knowledge society. These indicators can be used for the development of a Malaysian Knowledge Society and act as a guideline for the government to streamline the policy implementations, specifically in the context of human capital development. The study employed a survey questionnaire as an instrument for data collection. The sample population involves 450 respondents from three stakeholders in Malaysia, particularly officers from the government sector, the private sector and the NGOs. A total of 44 human capital indicators were proposed based on review of literature and qualitative studies. These indicators consisted of four sub-dimensions namely education and training, skills, research and development, as well as knowledge sharing and dissemination. The general public were required to rate the importance of the indicators based on their perception. Results show that 15 indicators are perceived as extremely important, while 29 indicators are relatively less important. These indicators can represent the human capital dimension in the development of Malaysia's Knowledge Society.

Introduction

Vision 2020 is a long-term plan which is a guide towards achieving a developed society by the year 2020. This vision, which was introduced in February 1991, aims to transform the Malaysian society into a knowledge society 'in its own mould' (Mahathir, 1991). The 'mould' here means it is endogenously developed within the society, without duplicating any other country and taking into account a holistic approach which covers various aspects of economy, social, political and cultural norms as well as spiritual values and psychology (Mahathir, 1991). All these aspects are critical in ensuring that the development of a Knowledge Society (henceforth KS) is on the right track. In a KS, the important inputs are technology, knowledge as well as research and development (R&D), which are known as a quartenary industry (Abdul Rahim & Zulikha, 2005), while industrial society used the traditional inputs consisting of land, labour, capital and entrepreneurship, known as tertiary industry. Moreover, in order to strengthen the planning and implementation of Vision 2020, the Malaysian government under the current Prime Minister, Dato' Seri Mohd Najib Tun Razak has introduced a model called New Economic Model (NEM). In parallel with the nine central strategic challenges of Vision 2020, the main goals of this model are that Malaysia will become a high income advanced nation with inclusiveness and sustainability, which together will translate into a high quality of life for the citizen by the year 2020 (NEAC, 2010). As shown in Figure 1, citizens were the main target of the model and this is tightly related to HC. This model emphasised that top priority must be given to human capital policies, as they will be crucial in reducing income inequality (NEAC, 2010).

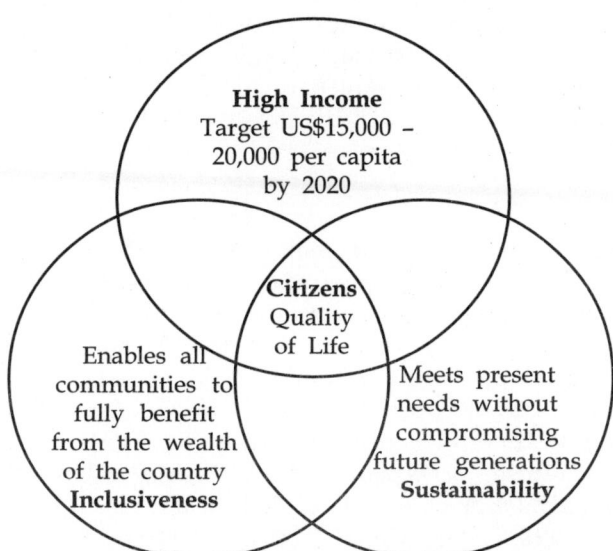

FIGURE 1: Goals of Malaysia's New Economic Model
(National Economic Advisory Council, 2010)

The development of a nation will never be successful without human beings as major players, and therein lies the concept of 'human capital' (henceforth HC). Naisbitt, Naisbitt and Philips (1999) opined that technological and knowledge growth are not beneficial unless related to human beings. The essence of their idea is to balance the material wonders such as technology with the spiritual demands of human nature. In any KS, not only the technologies need to be taken into account, but also the ends value-based which will make it effective (Communication Rights in the Information Society, 2002). During the first phase of the World Summit on the Information Society (WSIS), UNESCO emphasised that the concept of knowledge societies is more all-embracing and more conducive to empowerment than the concept of technology and connectivity itself, which often dominates debates on the information society (UNESCO, 2005).

The HC dimension is undoubtedly crucial in the development of a KS. HC means empowering humans with all the knowledge and skills needed to survive in a society that continuously changes. There exist myriad approaches and a countless number of ways to define HC. HC is a concept that encompasses many dimensions which make it quite a complex phenomenon (Natoli 2008). The Commission of the European Communities (2003) stated that HC consists of "knowledge, skills, competencies and attributes embodied in individuals which facilitate personal, social and economic well-being". HC has certain underlying characteristics, since it is embodied in humans (Natoli 2008). HC is non-tradable and no market exists that would permit the exchange of HC assets (except in the case of slavery); has both qualitative and quantitative aspects; can be either general or specific; and contains external effects from the social environment and the institutional context in which they live, which continually shapes its acquisition (Laroche, Merette & Ruggeri, 1999; Natoli 2008). Key skills and personal attributes relevant to HC may be conceptualised as communication, numeracy intra-personal skills (e.g. motivation/ perseverance, learning to learn, self-discipline, problem solving, capacity to make judgements based on a relevant set of ethical values and goals in life) and inter-personal skills (e.g. teamwork, leadership). Human capital as employed by the government of Malaysia refers to "individuals who are knowledgeable, confident, possessing noble values and high morality, ethical, well-mannered, disciplined, dynamic, innovative, creative, healthy, patriotic, just, progressive, resilient and competitive" (Prime Minister's Office of Malaysia, 2007).

HC in the context of this study is viewed from a few different angles, including inter-related elements of knowledge, skills, competencies, and attributes, and its significant activities such as education, training, research and development (R&D), various knowledge activities, and support from the government and private sector. Education implies the transfer of knowledge and the expansion of the learner's mind, while training involves inculcating skills in all manner of operations (Ungku A. Aziz, 1991). Some empirical studies of growth and its related documents have attempted to assess the role of HC as a determinant in long-term performance using measures of HC based on, among other things, literacy rates (Mansell & When, 1998; Archibugi & Coco, 2004; 2005), school enrolment rates (United Nations, 2000; ITU, 2003; Halimah, 2004), tertiary enrolment (Abdul Rahim & Zulikha, 2005; UNDP, 2001), tertiary attainment (Sharma, Ng, Dharmawirya & Samuel, 2010); expenditure on education and training (Halimah, 2004; Ahmed, 2008), years of schooling (Archibugi & Coco, 2004; 2005; Halimah, 2004) and level of education of the labour force (Halimah, 2004). However, these measures are subject to considerable data limitations and only capture certain aspects of HC (Laroche, Merette & Ruggeri, 1999).

In discussing the concept of KS, it is necessary to focus on the term 'knowledge' as this element is an integral part in the development of such a society. The nature of knowledge which is abstract and usually lies in the human mind makes it difficult to conceptualise and/or measure it. Moreover, the concept of knowledge is dynamic, flexible and interactive (Shariffadeen, 2008; Sayed & Cheng, 2004). Although there are many definitions of KS and Knowledge-based Economy (KBE) by different scholars and organisations, all these definitions revolve around the new growth theory of an economy, based on production, distribution and utilisation of knowledge (Kwong, 2008). Romer (1986) proposed a new theory called Endogenous Growth Theory (EGT) where he introduced a model of economic growth which is driven by the accumulation of knowledge. He argued that knowledge is the basic form of capital and knowledge is different from physical capital. Romer (1990) proposed a model of endogenous growth that contains four basic inputs: (i) capital (measured in units of consumption goods); (ii) labour (skills available from a healthy human body); (iii) human capital (activities such as formal education and on-the-job training); and (iv) technology (an index of the level of technology). EGT focuses on knowledge and technological progress, emphasising that the knowledge and technological progress should not be regarded as an exogenous variable, but as having taken place within a country, that is, as an endogenous variable. Among the reasons for the development of this theory are first because the output of industrialised countries is so much higher now than it was a century ago, and second, there is growth in HC (i.e. the development in education and technologies) (We, 1994).

In determining a nation's holistic growth, many existing models and measurements focused on the development of HC. The emphasis of HC dimension is not limited to social growth measurements, such as Millennium Development Goals (United Nations, 2000), but also adopted by economic growth measurements (Chen, 2008; Natoli, 2008) and technological growth measurements such as the Technology Achievement Index (TAI) (Desai, Fukuda-Parr, Johansson & Sagasti, 2002), the ArCo Technology Index (Archibugi & Coco, 2004; 2005), Digital Access Index (ITU, 2003) and Digital Divide Index (Husing & Selhofer, 2004). Table 1 shows some models which adopted the HC variables in measuring human, economic, technological and social development.

TABLE 1: Some Models which adopted Human Capital Variables in Measuring Growth

Model	Dimension/Variable	Indicators of Human Capital
INEXSK model (Mansell & When, 1998)	Technical Graduates Index Literacy Share	Graduates in Computer Science and Mathematics plus all levels of Engineering Population - Percentage of population that is literate
Millennium Development Goals (United Nations, 2000)	Goal 2: Achieve universal primary education	Ensure that, by 2015, children everywhere, boys and girls alike, will be able to complete a full course of primary schooling: 2.1 Net enrolment ratio in primary education 2.2 Proportion of pupils starting grade 1 who reach last grade of primary education 2.3 Literacy rate of 15-24 year olds, women and men
	Goal 3: Promote gender equality and empower women	Eliminate gender disparity in primary and secondary education, preferably by 2005, and in all levels of education no later than 2015: 3.1 Ratios of girls to boys in primary, secondary and tertiary education

Oh (2000)	Manpower Index	- Staff in telecommunication services per 100 inhabitants - Research staff per 100 inhabitants
Technology Achievement Index (Desai, Fukuda-Parr, Johansson & Sagasti, 2002)	Human skills needed to create and absorb innovations	- Mean years of schooling - Gross enrolment ratio of tertiary students enrolled in science, mathematics and engineering.
Digital Access Index (ITU, 2003)	Knowledge	- Adult literacy - Combined primary, secondary and tertiary school enrolment level
Digital Divide Index (Husing & Selhofer, 2004)	Education	- People who finished formal school education at an age of 15 years or below
ArCo Technology Index (Archibugi & Coco, 2004; 2005)	The development of human skills Creation of technology	- Tertiary science and engineering enrolment - Mean years of schooling - Literacy rate - Patents - Scientific articles
Abdul Rahim & Zulikha (2005)	Literacy and enrolment	- Level of adult literacy (% in cohort aged 15 years and above) - Ratio of total enrolment in primary, secondary and university (% in schooling age cohort)
Knowledge Assessment Methodology (World Bank, 2008)	Education and skills of population Innovation system	- Adult literacy rate - Gross secondary enrolment rate - Gross tertiary enrolment rate - Total Royalty Payments and Receipts - Patent Applications Granted by the US Patent and Trademark Office - Scientific and Technical Journal Articles
Sharma et al., 2010	IP regime Higher Education R&D	- Patents; Share of Citations - Tertiary Attainment; Percentage of GDP invested in HE - GERD / BERD; R&D; Employment per Capita

With regards to the existing models, it can be summarised that the HC dimension has been emphasised in the study of growth and development. Furthermore, among the most important indicators in the above mentioned models is adult literacy rate, school and tertiary enrolment, mean years of schooling, patents and articles in scientific journals. All these indicators are therefore considered critical in HC development. In addition to the activities mentioned earlier, the need for knowledge generation is also critical in the development of a knowledge society. This can be achieved by active participation of government and private sector in R&D activities. This includes the funding and expenditure for R&D, cooperation between government, private sector and university, award of grants for local researchers, patents and copyrights. In Malaysia, there are few studies which focus on the economic aspect, ICT and knowledge content (i.e. Shapira, Youtie, Yogeesvaran & Zakiah, 2005; Abdul Rahim & Zulikha, 2005), but there is a lack of research on KS development (Norsiah & Halimah, 2008). This study therefore attempts to develop and propose a list of indicators which could represent the HC dimension in order to achieve the KS status in Malaysia. It should be mentioned that the discussion on Human Capital in this article was derived from a broader research scope conducted previously on the topic of KS, of which the aims of the research was to determine the significant dimensions and important indicators of Malaysia's KS. A general model of Knowledge Society proposed and validated earlier is shown in Figure 2.

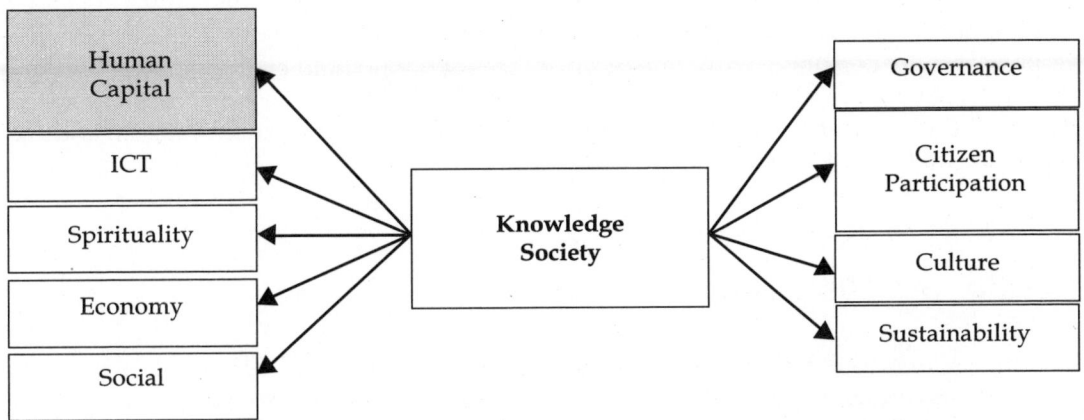

FIGURE 2: Malaysia's Knowledge Society Model

Methodology

The instrument for data collection was a survey questionnaire which was distributed online via an online service provider for the duration of two months. The questionnaire was developed based on a review of literature and existing models, and qualitative studies done previously namely: the five-round modified Delphi technique involving ten experts and semi-structured interviews with two prominent experts. The two experts involved in the interviews were a former Prime Minister of Malaysia who initiated Vision 2020, and a member of National IT Council (NITC). The findings of the Delphi technique and the interviews with the experts had contributed tremendously towards the design and development of KS indicators (for further readings, please refer to Norsiah & Halimah 2009a; 2009b). The survey was conducted to determine the perceived important indicators of Knowledge Society by the general public. The questionnaire consisted of two parts. Part A was about the demographic profile of the respondents and Part B listed 44 items as Human Capital indicators in which the respondents were asked to rate their perception based on a five-point Likert-type scale of importance, ranging from 1=extremely unimportant to 5=extremely important. The data were analysed using descriptive statistics comprising of frequency and percentage. These were done using SPSS v.16 software.

This study employed a purposive random sampling in which the targeted respondents were identified prior to the questionnaire distribution based on the availability of email addresses. For the government sector, the respondents were selected randomly based on staff directory in the ministry/agency's Web site. Due to the broader scope of the private sector throughout the country, the personnel for the private sector were selected only from the list of companies in Cyberjaya, where they were actively involved in knowledge and R&D activities. Lastly, for the non-government organisations (NGOs), the list was acquired from search engines and the personnel were contacted either via email or telephone call to invite them to participate in the online survey. All the targeted respondents are personnel with university degrees and who hold executive positions and above. The invitation to participate in the online survey was sent via email and supported by an official letter and two web site links, one for the Malay language version, and the other for the English version.

Results and Discussion

The survey involved 450 respondents, comprising 235 males and 193 females; while 22 respondents did not report their gender. The age of the respondents ranged between 20 to 60 years and above (mean for age is 37.74 years). The majority are Malays (78.4% or n=353) and in this group the majority works with the government sector (77.3%, n=348). The majority of the respondents have a Bachelor's degree (56.7% or n=255), and some of them hold a PhD (6% or n=27). The majority of the respondents have working experience between 1 and 10 years (mean=13.83). The demographic profiles of the respondents are summarised in Table 2.

TABLE 2: Demographic Profiles of the Respondents (n=450)

Demographic Details	f	%	Demographic Details	f	%
Gender			Race		
Male	235	52.2	Malay	353	78.4
Female	193	42.9	Chinese	36	8.0
Not reported	22	4.9	Indian	26	5.8
Age			Sabah/Sarawak Ethnic group	10	2.2
20 - 29 years old	82	18.2	Not reported	25	5.6
30 - 39	143	31.8	Highest Level of Education		
40 - 49	71	15.8	PhD	27	6.0
50 - 59	64	14.2	Master's	128	28.4
60 and above	2	0.4	Bachelor's	255	56.7
Not reported	88	19.6	Not reported	40	8.9
Mean: 37.74			Working Experience		
Employer			1 - 10 years	184	40.9
Government	348	77.3	11 - 20 years	89	19.8
Private	61	13.6	21 - 30 years	73	16.2
NGO	6	1.3	31 - 40 years	22	4.9
Not reported	35	7.8	Not reported	82	18.2
			Mean: 13.83		

Table 3 shows 44 indicators which were proposed to represent the HC dimension in the development of a Malaysian KS. The indicators can be classified into four sub-dimensions namely: education and training, research and development, skills, as well as knowledge sharing and dissemination. The survey was conducted to determine which indicators were perceived as important by the general public. Some of the indicators proposed here were quantitative in nature, while some were qualitative.

The majority of the respondents perceived 15 indicators as 'extremely important' [indicators i1, i2, i4, i5, i6, i7, i8, i16, i17, i20, i21, i23, i24, i25, i27]. These indicators include elements of education, such as adult literacy rate (55.3%), total expenditure on education (50.2%), pupil-teacher ratio at school (49.3%), school and tertiary education's role in fulfilling societal needs (both 58%), number of school enrolments (45.6%) and number of pupils completing school education (54%). As such, the respondents also perceived the rest of the items as 'important' [indicators i3, i9, i10, i11, i12, i13, i14, i15, i18, i19, i22, i26, i28 to i44].

Among the most important indicators as perceived by the respondents in terms of skills and competencies are 'communication competency' [i23] (62%), 'intra-personal skills' [i24] (58.4%) and 'inter-personal skills' [i25] (53.8%). In contrast, there is no indicator scored 'unimportant'. Similarly, the majority of the respondents perceived the indicator pertaining to the quality of knowledge acquired by citizens [i27] as extremely important with a score of 56.9%. The respondents also perceived proficiency in Malay and English languages [i20 and i21] as extremely important (45.6% and 54.4%) while the majority of the respondents (55.6%) perceived proficiency in foreign language [i22] as important.

Another indicator which was perceived as extremely important by 56% of the respondents is 'fair and equitable distribution of information and knowledge sources among citizens' [i17].

In addition, the R&D activities were also perceived as important [i28 to i37]. Among the R&D indicators perceived as important are the number of research institutions/centres [i30] (57.3%), the number of patents awarded to local researchers [i33] (56.2%) and the number of copyrights awarded to local researchers [i34] (56%). The knowledge sharing and dissemination indicators are also perceived as important [i38 to i44]. These include the number of publications and the preservation of local and indigenous knowledge. The overall results proved that all the 44 indicators proposed are either perceived as important or extremely important by the public.

TABLE 3: Human Capital Indicators and Scores (n=450)

Code	Description	Extremely unimportant f	%	Unimportant f	%	Less important f	%	Important f	%	Extremely important f	%
Education and Training											
i1.	Adults literacy rate	-	-	3	.7	17	3.8	181	40.2	**249**	**55.3**
i2.	Total expenditure on education	-	-	-	-	24	5.3	200	44.4	**226**	**50.2**
i3.	Total expenditure on training	1	.2	-	-	30	6.7	**250**	**55.6**	169	37.6
i4.	Ratio of pupil-teacher at school	-	-	2	.4	18	4.0	208	46.2	**222**	**49.3**
i5.	School education fulfils societal needs	-	-	-	-	6	1.3	183	40.7	**261**	**58.0**
i6.	Tertiary education fulfils societal needs	-	-	-	-	17	3.8	172	38.2	**261**	**58.0**
i7.	Number of school enrolments	-	-	3	.7	37	8.2	205	45.6	**205**	**45.6**
i8.	Number of pupils completing school education	-	-	2	.4	23	5.1	182	40.4	**243**	**54.0**
i9.	Number of tertiary enrolments	1	.2	1	.2	34	6.9	**250**	**55.6**	167	37.1
i10.	Number of tertiary graduates	-	-	1	.2	38	8.4	**246**	**54.7**	165	36.7
i11.	Tertiary students in Science, Mathematics and Engineering	-	-	4	.9	65	14.4	**239**	**53.1**	142	31.6
i12.	Number of professional workers	-	-	3	.7	31	6.9	**241**	**53.6**	175	38.9
i13.	Number of training courses for workers	-	-	3	.7	54	12.0	**250**	**55.6**	143	31.8
i14.	Number of workers attending training course	1	.2	1	.2	56	12.4	**240**	**53.3**	152	33.8
Skills and Competencies											
i15.	Number of local professional workers migrates to other countries (brain drain)	2	.4	22	4.9	104	23.1	**190**	**42.2**	132	29.3
i16.	Number of local professional workers coming back to work in Malaysia (brain gain)	2	.4	5	1.1	59	13.1	186	41.3	**198**	**44.0**
i17.	Fair and equitable distribution of information and knowledge sources among citizens	-	-	-	-	14	3.1	184	40.9	**252**	**56.0**
i18.	Application of electronic learning	-	-	1	.2	41	9.1	**239**	**53.1**	169	37.6

i19.	Application of mobile learning	-	-	1	.2	59	13.1	**251**	**55.8**	139 30.9
i20.	Malay language proficiency as a national language	-	-	10	2.2	69	15.3	166	36.9	**205 45.6**
i21.	English language proficiency	1	.2	1	.2	8	1.8	195	43.3	**245 54.4**
i22.	Foreign language proficiency	1	.2	9	2.0	101	22.4	**250**	**55.6**	89 19.8
i23.	Communication competency	1	.2	-	-	9	2.0	161	35.8	**279 62.0**
i24.	Intra-personal skills (e.g. motivation/ perseverance, problem solving, self-discipline, capacity to make judgements based on goals in life)	-	-	-	-	17	3.8	170	37.8	**263 58.4**
i25.	Inter-personal skills (e.g. teamwork, leadership)	-	-	-	-	17	3.8	191	42.4	**242 53.8**
i26.	Consider experts' opinion in particular fields/areas	-	-	-	-	35	7.8	**231**	**51.3**	184 40.9
i27.	Quality of knowledge acquired by citizens	-	-	-	-	9	2.0	185	41.1	**256 56.9**

Research and Development

i28.	Total expenditure for R&D	-	-	-	-	28	6.2	**235**	**52.2**	187 41.6
i29.	Number of researchers in R&D	-	-	-	-	36	8.0	**224**	**49.8**	190 42.2
i30.	Number of research institutions/centres	-	-	2	.4	54	12.0	**258**	**57.3**	136 30.2
i31.	Number of research projects awarded grant locally	-	-	1	.2	72	16.0	**251**	**55.8**	126 28.0
i32.	Number of research projects awarded grant by foreign/ international agency	-	-	2	.4	79	17.6	**249**	**55.3**	120 26.7
i33.	Number of patents awarded to local researchers	-	-	3	.7	50	11.1	**253**	**56.2**	144 32.0
i34.	Number of copyrights awarded to local researchers	-	-	2	.4	50	11.1	**252**	**56.0**	146 32.4
i35.	Number of awards received by local researchers	1	.2	4	.9	79	17.6	**239**	**53.1**	127 28.2
i36.	Effective protection system of intellectual property	-	-	-	-	42	9.3	**221**	**49.1**	187 41.6
i37.	Research cooperation between university-private sector-government	-	-	1	.2	27	6.0	**232**	**51.6**	190 42.2

Knowledge Sharing and Dissemination

i38.	Number of locally printed educational books sold	-	-	3	.7	53	11.8	**243**	**54.0**	151 33.6
i39.	Number of locally published journals	-	-	2	.4	47	10.4	**231**	**51.3**	170 37.8
i40.	Number of journal article by local authors	-	-	2	.4	43	9.6	**241**	**53.6**	164 36.4
i41.	Number of printed newspapers sold	-	-	12	2.7	115	25.6	**235**	**52.2**	88 19.6
i42.	Number of local educational magazines sold	-	-	4	.9	73	16.2	**250**	**55.6**	123 27.3
i43.	Number of libraries (public and university)	-	-	2	.4	53	11.8	**248**	**55.1**	147 32.7
i44.	Preservation of local and indigenous knowledge	-	-	2	.4	43	9.6	**227**	**50.4**	178 39.6

Bold *Indicates majority score*

The importance of the HC dimension in a holistic development of a society has been emphasised by various parties in various fields (i.e. Ahmed, 2008; Halimah, 2004; ITU, 2003; Mansell & When, 1998; Romer, 1990; United Nations, 2000; UNDP, 2001; World Bank, 2008). Ahmed (2008), in addition, stressed that all the variables in HC are significantly related to economic growth variables represented by the Gross Domestic Product (GDP) in Malaysia. There has been a significant increase in the number of population having access to education at all levels for the past decades, while the total enrolment at the tertiary level in local public educational institutions has doubled in the past few years (Ahmed, 2008).

Indicators pertaining to skills and training also show significant importance in the development of a Malaysian KS. This is parallel to the findings of Frietsch and Gehrke (2006) who stress that education and skills are of growing relevance, both from an entrepreneurial and from the individual point of view. Higher levels of qualification induce higher productivity and therefore higher earnings and a lower unemployment risk. Training and professional development are deemed priorities in the KS (Gilomen, 2002). These include infrastructure for training, training of teaching staff and adult education. In order to develop and sustain the knowledge of humans, there is a need for continuous training and it is considered as crucial to developing human skills (UNDP, 2001). It is therefore evident that the education, skills, training and competency indicators are critical to the building of a K.S.

R&D activities are crucial in the development of HC since it produces quality researchers and scientists. This leads to the creation of good innovation and output. R&D activities, however, require a holistic participation from the government, the private sector and the research institutions. The Malaysian government is undoubtedly active in promoting R&D activities by providing funds and infrastructure. Recently, the government has established many grant schemes to enhance private sector involvement and commitments in R&D activities and to accelerate the rate of commercialisation of R&D findings within the public sector (Shapira et al., 2005). Moreover, cooperation between university-industry-government (also known as 'triple helix' relation) is critical to the production of quality research, great innovation and wealth generation.

Knowledge sharing and dissemination activities are also critical in the development of HC. Publication of scientific materials through books, journals, magazines and newspapers need to be encouraged in order to share and disseminate the information and knowledge among citizens. As stated by OECD (2005), scientific publishing has an important role in the production and diffusion of knowledge, which can disseminate research findings and this diffusion drives economic growth, further research and increase the level of knowledge of people. Moreover, there is also a perception that local and indigenous knowledge needs to be preserved. This kind of knowledge is important to be documented and recorded in archives for future reference by the younger generations.

Conclusion

Human Capital (HC) is an important dimension in the development of a Knowledge Society. Any country wishing to enhance its societal development needs to take into account the development of HC as part of the growth measurement. HC dimension covers inter-related elements of knowledge, skills, competencies, and attributes, and its significant activities such as education, R&D and knowledge activities. This article has discussed a study that attempted to propose HC indicators which are crucial for the development of a Malaysian KS and to identify the perceived importance of the indicators proposed. A total of 44 indicators were self-rated by 450 respondents, consisting of the general public of three major stakeholders in Malaysia. Results indicated that the majority of the indicators

(66%) were perceived as important, whilst 34% were perceived as extremely important. These findings also support the earlier findings from the Delphi technique and the experts' interview, in which most of the statements pertaining to HC scored high consensus, while the two prominent experts in the interview also emphasised the critical needs for HC in achieving the Knowledge Society (Norsiah & Halimah, 2009a; 2009b). The study concludes that the proposed indicators can be used as a guideline in the development of a Malaysian Knowledge Society.

References

- Abdul Rahim A. &Zulikha, J. (2005). *Agenda ICT ke arah pembangunan k-ekonomi Malaysia*. Sintok: Penerbit Universiti Utara Malaysia.
- Ahmed, E. M. (2008). ICT and human capital intensities effects on Malaysian productivity growth. *International Research Journal of Finance and Economics*, (13), 152-161.
- Archibugi, D. & Coco, A. (2004). A new indicator of technological capabilities for developed and developing countries (ArCo). *World Development*, 32(4), 629-654.
- Archibugi, D. & Coco, A. (2005). Measuring technological capabilities at the country level: A survey and a menu for choice. *Research Policy*, 34:175-194.
- Commission of the European Communities. (2003). Building the knowledge society: Social and human capital interactions. Available at: http://www.einclusion-eu.org/ShowCase.asp?CaseTitleID=49&CaseID=98&MenuID=156.
- Communication Rights in the Information Society (CRIS). (2002). The 'information society' a useful concept for civil society? (1). Available at: http://www.wacc.org.uk/de/content/ pdf/641.
- Desai, M., Fukuda-Parr, S., Johansson, C. & Sagasti, F. (2002). Measuring the technology achievement of nations and the capacity to participate in the network age. *Journal of Human Development*, 3(1), 95-122.
- Frietsch, R. & Gehrke, B. (2006). Education structures and highly skilled employment in Europe - A comparison. In U. Schmoch, C. Rammer and H. Legler (Eds.). *National systems of innovation in comparison*. Dordrecht, The Netherlands: Springer.
- Gilomen, H. (2002). Education in the new economy - A statistical framework. In *IAOS Conference 2002*. London, UK: Office for National Statistics, UK. Available at: http://www.statistics.gov.uk/IAOSlondon2002/presentations.asp.
- Halimah, A. (2004). Human capital and technology development in Malaysia. *International Education Journal*, 5(2), 239-246.
- Husing, T. & Selhofer, H. (2004). DIDIX: A digital divide index for measuring inequality in IT diffusion. *IT&SOCIETY*, 1(7), 21-38.
- International Telecommunication Union. (2003). Gauging ICT potential around the world: ITU releases the first Digital Access Index. *ITU News*, available at: http://www.itu.int/ITU-D/ict/dai/material/DAI_ITUNews_e.pdf.
- Kwong, H.C. (2008). Being critical on ICT and development. In proceedings of *The 6th International Malaysian Studies Conference (MSC6)*. Kuching, Sarawak: Malaysian Social Science Association.
- Laroche, M., Merette, M. & Ruggeri, G. C. (1999). On the concept and dimensions of human capital in a knowledge-based economy context. *Canadian Public Policy/Analyse de Politiques*, 25(1), 87-100.
- Mahathir, M. (1991). *Malaysia: The way forward*. Kuala Lumpur: Centre for Economic Research & Services, Malaysian Business Council.
- Mansell, R. & When, U. (1998). *Knowledge societies: Information technology for sustainable development*. New York: United Nations Commission on Science and Technology for Development.
- Naisbitt, J., Naisbitt, N. & Philips, D. (1999). *High tech high touch: Technology and our search for meaning*. London: Nicholas Brealey Publishing.

- National Economic Advisory Council (NEAC). (2010). New economic model for Malaysia 2010. http://www.neac.gov.my/content/download-option-new-economic-model-malaysia -2010.
- Natoli, R. (2008). *Indicators of economic and social progress: An assessment and an alternative.* Doctoral thesis, School of Applied Economics, Faculty of Business and Law, Victoria University, Melbourne, Australia.
- Norsiah, A. H. & Halimah, B. Z. (2008). Preliminary study on knowledge society criteria and indicators: A cognitive informatics approach. In Halimah B.Z., Sembok, T. M. T., van Rijsbergen, K., Zadeh, L., Bruza, P., Shih, T. & Taib, M. N. (Eds.). *International Symposium on Information Technology 2008,* Kuala Lumpur: UKM/IEEE.
- Norsiah, A.H. & Halimah, B.Z. (2009a). *Defining Malaysian knowledge society: Results from the Delphi technique.* In Lytras, M.D., Ordóñez de Pablos, P. Damiani, E., Avison, D., Naeve A. & Horner, D.G. (Eds.). Proceedings of The 2nd World Summit on the Knowledge Society, Springer Communications in Computer and Information Science (CCIS) Series, Vol. 49, pp. 179-189. Organised by Open Research Society, Crete, Greece, 16th – 18th September 2009. http://www.springer.com/computer/general/ book/978 -3-642-04756-5.
- Norsiah, A.H. & Halimah, B.Z. 2009b. *Framework of Malaysian knowledge society: Results from dual data approach.* Proceedings of the World Academy of Science, Engineering and Technology, Vol. 58, October 2009. Venice, Italy.
- Oh, J. (2000). The role of the new media in information society. *Korea Review of International Studies,* 3(1), 131.
- Organisation for Economic Co-operation and Development (OECD). (2005). *Digital broadband content: Scientific publishing.* [cited 27th July 2007]. Available at: http://www.oecd.org/ dataoecd/ 42/12/353 93145.pdf.
- Prime Minister's Office of Malaysia. (2007). *Human capital development.* Available at: http://www.pmo.gov.my/humancapital/index.html.
- Romer, P. M. (1986). Increasing returns and long-run growth. *Journal of Political Economy,* 94(5), 1002-1037.
- Romer, P. M. (1990). Endogenous technological change. *Journal of Political Economy,* 98(5), 71-102.
- Sayed, H. & Cheng, M. Y. (2004). *An introduction to knowledge economy: Concepts and issues.* 2nd ed. Kuala Lumpur: McGraw-Hill.
- Shapira, P., Youtie, J., Yogeesvaran, K. & Zakiah, J. (2006). Knowledge economy measurement: Methods, results and insights from the Malaysian knowledge content study. *Research Policy,* 35(10), 1522-1537.
- Shariffadeen, T. M. A. (2008). Personal communication. 26th December 2008.
- Ungku A. Aziz. (1991). Human resource development: The key towards a developed and industrialized society. In *National Seminar "Towards a Developed and Industrialized Society: Understanding the Concept, Implications and Challenges of Vision 2020.* Kuala Lumpur, Malaysia: Socio-Economic Research Unit, Prime Minister's Department.
- United Nations Development Program (UNDP). (2001). *Human development report 2001.* New York: United Nations. Available at: http://hdr.undp.org/en/media/completenew1.pdf.
- United Nations Educational, Scientific and Cultural Organization (UNESCO). (2005). *UNESCO World Report: Towards knowledge societies.* UNESCO Publishing. Available at: http://unesdoc.unesco.org/images/0014/001418/141843e.pdf.
- United Nations. (2000). *United Nations Millennium Declaration.* Available at: http://www.un.org/millenniumgoals/bkgd.shtml.
- We, G. *What is endogenous growth theory?* (1994). Available at: http://www.sistemasdec onocimiento.org/English/e100mty/inputs/General_KBD_inputs/kbd_files/ 005_endogenous_growth/3_gladys_what_EGT.pdf.
- World Bank. (2008). *Knowledge assessment methodology.* Available at: http://web. worldbank.org/ WBSITE/EXTERNAL/WBI/WBIPROGRAMS/KFDLP/EXTUNIKAM/ 0,,menuPK:1414738~pagePK:64168427~piPK:64168435~theSitePK:1414721,00.html?

CHAPTER 3

STRENGTHENING RURAL GOVERNANCE:
Farmer Field Schools as a Strategy to Build Human Capital in Conflict affected Jaffna District of Sri Lanka

D.L CHAMILA JAYASHANTHA AND PUVANESWARY PONNIAH

Abstract

"Local Initiatives For Tomorrow (LIFT)" project implemented by CARE International in Sri Lanka intended to strengthen community-level institutions supporting economic activity, employment creation and provision of basic social services in 32 villages in Jaffna district of Sri Lanka by 2008. Jaffna was directly affected by a three decade long ethnic war and the impact of the conflict is prominently visible in socioeconomic, political and infrastructural domains. CARE expected to have an improved level of community participation in decision making and management of resources pertaining to their own development, while fulfilling service requirements and livelihood needs. CARE believed this can only be achieved through human capacity building and social empowerment. Farmer Field Schools approach was adopted as the key strategy. The project ensured wide array of training to the community ranging from basic agricultural training as a direct support for their main stay, the agriculture, and also training for conflict resolution which aims at social empowerment. Despite numerous institutional and policy challenges, Farmer Field Schools now perform well not only to fulfill agricultural extension requirements within their communities, but also as effective conduits dealing with rural governance priorities. The purpose of this paper is to examine the importance of identifying alternative human capacity building strategies to be implemented to restore livelihoods and subsequently to increase community involvement in resource management and decision making in conflict affected areas. The paper will explain the key processes utilised in the project and also review the impact of the intervention.

Introduction

The majority of the world's poor live in rural areas. According to IFAD (2001) 1.2 billion extremely poor people live and work in rural areas in the world. This situation demands a greater focus on rural development. Hence, many international institutions such as UNDP, the World Bank and the Asian Development Bank have paid considerable attention to strategizing rural poverty alleviation approaches, e.g. Millennium Development Goals. As a new trend a significant attention on improving community and rural governance has emerged after modern discourses on rural poverty alleviation. CARE International in Sri Lanka, through one of its development projects called Local Initiatives For Tomorrow (LIFT) implemented in conflict affected areas since 2002 to 2008, used Farmer Field Schools (FFS) as the principal strategy for building human capital and social empowerment with the effective use and management of the resource base on which the rural people depend. LIFT was funded by Canadian International Development Agency (CIDA). The purpose of this paper is to review the outcomes of this intervention which did not, merely restrict the role of FFS for agricultural matters. The paper explains the performance of FFS against various functions pertaining to rural governance and the impact made on local decision making processes.

Community Governance in Focus

Governance can be simply defined as institutions, mechanisms, and traditions through which the authority in a territory is exercised. Kraay (2006) includes the process by which governments are selected, monitored and replaced; the capacity of a government to effectively formulate and implement policies; and the respect of citizens for the institutions that govern social and economic interaction as key integral areas of the concept of governance. The advent of new rural development strategies such as "Reaching the Rural Poor" of World Bank (2001) has suggested a distinct focus on rural areas, to redress the causes of persisting rural poverty and environmental degradation. Corner (2005), states that the links between governance and poverty are not yet well understood & further points out "the governance and poverty reduction agendas have increasingly converged as a result of a rethinking of the nature of well-being and human development that recognises the multifaceted nature of poverty and deprivation, and as a result of a broadening of the concept of governance to include political accountability and participation".

Suan-Pheng (2002) remarked that such strategies aim at fostering broad-based rural growth by increasing productivity and improving the competitiveness of both agricultural and non farm rural activities. In order to achieve the aforesaid objective, rural development strategies stress the need for policy and institutional reforms to build rural social capital to govern their resource base. Therefore the present demand on improved rural governance is greater than ever, because that relate to judicious management of rural resource bases. Today rural governance should be able to provide services ranging from timely market information for producers to education, health and social well being which are crucial to human productivity and assistance to cope with disasters. Therefore rural governance goes beyond mere public administration to becoming a seamless extension of planning and management of entire rural spaces for creating a conducive sphere for community driven development. Nixon (2008) states that community-driven development refers to programmatic interventions that emphasise community participation, empowerment, local contributions, and the development of community capacity or social capital in providing resources for development projects at community level. Richardson (1999) suggests that community governance does require good mechanisms for vision building and conflict resolution at the community level, such as effective use of community boards and informal mechanisms. Rural governance possesses the unique ability of addressing specific needs of communities that are diverse from location to location (in environmental and ethno-cultural differences) like emergence and evolution of the village Panchayat system in India.

Richardson (1999) defines community governance as a concept that recognises the "ownership" of the "wicked issues" resting with the community as a whole. Effective ways forward will require the cooperation of many participants each of whom has a part to contribute to the solution. Epstein et al (2005) points that the effective community governance model recognises *engaging citizens, measuring results,* and *getting things done* as three "core community skills" that help people and organisations make decisions about what actions to take in a community and help them measure the community's performance in achieving results. Nixon (2008) quotes UNDP's definition of community governance as "a set of institutions, mechanisms and processes, through which citizens and their groups can articulate their interests and needs, mediate their differences and exercise their rights and obligations at the local level". Kraay (2006) suggests measuring governance as important given the demonstrated strong links between good governance and good development outcomes. This situation urges the need of building social capital in order to enable the rural poor to play a significant role in governance.

Community Capital Building to Improve Community Governance

Nowadays community development programmes are being formulated in an integrated manner, aiming the development of key subsectors such as natural resources, infrastructure, economy, social conditions and human resources. In terms of improving rural governance, building the human capacity is crucial provided that gives voice to the poor and enables their participation and entry not only in national economic development but also in the participation of decision making processes. It ensures the bottom-top approach to create a conducive environment for the rural poor with aforesaid core community skills. In order to form strong community networks, social capital building has also become an emerging priority to promote community participation in governance, especially in the context where people are vulnerable to natural and human made disasters. Carter (1999) portrays social capital as embedded in the structure of social relations, and encompasses norms and social networks which facilitate social action, thus enabling individuals to act collectively.

It is observed that various strategies and approaches are being employed by government, private sector and civil society actors to ensure citizens' engagement in the process of community governance. Basically, it is vital to *engage citizens* in deciding what to do and to engage them in deciding what results to measure or what performance goals or targets to measure against. Governments tend to widely use decentralisation as a measure to enhance efficiency of governance through improving community participation. Sri Ranjith (2007) argues that the existing capacity-building of the local government through decentralisation of power is a necessary policy reform, but this is not a sufficient condition for creating a new form of good governance. The lack of local governments' capacity is identified in four major areas, i.e. fiscal powers, access to financial resources, legal authority and professionally qualified personnel. This impairs accountability, transparency, management efficiency and the active role of civil society groups in governance.

In this backdrop, civil society agencies active in poverty alleviation are often seen as using alternative mechanisms such as community based organisations in order to empower local communities to fulfill their role in governance. Nevertheless these interventions have proved the vital role of human capital building strategies, provided that well informed, knowledgeable communities can lead in decision making particularly with respect to allocation of development resources in any context. With regard to rural governance, human capital building approaches and strategies exceed the boundaries of mundane vocational or technical training, and such strategies should be able to build community capacity for integration, strategic management of resources through shared understanding of opportunities issues and problems. Atchoarena (2006) points out that the role of education is not to 'train' people in a narrow sense for the existing rural occupations. According to him human capital building is about more than earning a living, and has multiple aims and benefits that includes the opportunity to assist people in their social and economic mobility, and contributes to cultural and political identity and participation. People not only suffer high incidence of poverty and inequality due to lack of resources and skills but also they are deprived from access to judicious management of resource bases, in an era when the community ownership and effective management of resources has become a key priority of the poverty alleviation campaigns taken place across the developing world.

Jaffna: Backdrop of a Conflict Affected District

Jaffna district which is situated in the Northern Province of Sri Lanka is directly impacted by the armed conflict subjecting its 632,463 residents mostly of Tamil origin to repeated displacement, severe economic hardship, and multiple social and political constraints. The district is divided into 15 divisional secretariats. Jaffna to date also remains one of the heavily militarised areas in the country. The only land route to the peninsula was closed for years. It restrained all human and economic relationships with the mainland and impacted on all socioeconomic aspects of civic life in the peninsula. The district has been hotly contested in the civil war between the Sri Lankan Army and the LTTE (Liberation Tigers of Tamil Elam). Jaffna has substantially destructed infrastructure; in terms of community and economic perspectives. Democratic structures and processes had been abandoned for a long time and the district experienced human rights violations that are common to any conflicting situation. Not only Jaffna residents have experienced displacement for more than one time, but also the area has hosted internally displaced people from time to time. The conflict tremendously disturbed livelihoods, for example fishing sector experienced severe restrictions. Access to agricultural lands was also curtailed because the most fertile land continue to be designated as high security zones where civilian access is either not allowed or closely monitored by the military. The situation has now started to improve.

Jaffna was also affected by the tsunami in 2004 resulting in almost 3700 deaths and severe damage or loss of property and assets. Despite the impacts & threats of natural and human-made disasters, Jaffna continued to receive considerable development support from various development actors including the government. The positive impact of development interventions always depends on the communities' capacity to judicious management of the aid & assistance received. Such a situation demands high level of community participation & representation in the process of local governance; the existing systems may have to be improved or replaced with more pragmatic and productive approaches. Clarke (1999) stressed, that community leadership and community governance cannot simply be tackled with the existing structure and ways of working in government. He argues that radical changes will be needed if the roles in community leadership and community governance are to be properly reflected.

The nature of issues in a locality which is severely affected by an ethnic conflict is always complicated. So human and social capacity building is necessary to ensure the efficiency of community development as well as establishment of democratic processes. Carter (1999) points out that building community capacity for change requires developing stronger human and social capital. Human capital is embodied in individuals' skills and knowledge and can be created through educational opportunities. Given the complexity of the situation, community capacities need to be developed to handle issues which cross boundaries and the management of complex set of relationships. Organisation development and the training and development of community leaders is crucial. As the LIFT project aimed to strengthen community-level institutions supporting economic activity, employment creation and provision of basic social services among those whose unfulfilled aspirations have fueled the conflict, the project selected 32 villages in 05 divisional secretariats. Selection of divisional secretariats and then villages for intervention was done after a thorough consultative process with key stakeholders and community leaders.

Farmer Field Schools (FFS) as an Effective Approach to Build Human Capital

It is observed that different actors involved in improving rural governance in Sri Lanka tend to select various community based structures ranging from farmers organisations, rural development societies to women's societies and sometimes special committees called "*Janasabha*". Selection or formation of suitable structures depends on socio-cultural or economic factors such as livelihood sources. The FFS approach was originally developed as an extension and education approach based on principles of Integrated Pest Management and sustainable agriculture. Pontius et al (2000) state the historical context out of which FFS approach emerged as dominated by the agricultural projects of the green revolution. FFS was a response to contextual, location specific challenges faced by rice farmers in the tropics; secondly as a recognition of the need for farmers to identify indigenous solutions to location specific problems. Early rice based field experiments with the FFS approach was conducted in the Philippines in the mid-1980s and around 1990 FAO started promoting FFS on a bigger scale in Indonesia which today by many is considered the cradle of FFS. The main technical foci of the FFS included Low External Input Rice Production, Integrated Pest Management (IPM), Insect management, Vegetable cultivation, Rice fish, Balanced fertilizer doses, Organic manure etc.

FFS approach has gradually spread to other countries, particularly in the Asian region. Though FFS is still used widely as a term, it has undergone and continues to undergo significant changes to accommodate specific needs of different contexts. As mentioned, the FFS approach and scope has been adopted by other non-agricultural activities over recent years. These include Water management, Household Livelihoods Security, linking up with local institutions, service providers and local government; improved access to public information by farmers; marketing networks, water and sanitation, rural infrastructure development, social protection, savings and credit group facilities and even prevention of HIV/AIDS etc. The FFS approach can be used in many different situations. Though it originated in the agriculture sector, it is fundamentally a participatory group approach for collective action and social mobilisation by the local community.

The Process: Farmer Field Schools in LIFT Project

The Farmer Field School (FFS) approach was the overarching method for the majority of the components in the LIFT project. FFS approach has its foundations in adult, non-formal education principles, and emphasises group learning by doing and empowering farmers to actively identify, critically analyze, make informed decisions and solve their own problems. Remarkably, this approach has many similarities to psychosocial support approaches; both promote skill development and empowerment and adopt participatory methods towards achieving restoration and development. In the LIFT project, the challenge was for the FFS approach to extend itself and become a tool for addressing wider livelihood issues beyond agriculture and to promote local institutional development through the formation of strong Community Based Organisations. The LIFT project employed the following consecutive steps to form & strengthen FFS, though which the human capacity building requirement was addressed. The project formed 32 Farmer Field Schools in Jaffna.

First, the project approached the village to build the rapport and trust with designated communities. The Project was able to get a basic understanding about the location, history, culture, the political environment of the area, and so on. The second step was the community meeting. It was used to inform the community in greater detail about the project, discuss the scope of the project, major strategies, and to know whether the community was interested in participation. The third step was the most critical in the entire process. After the community meeting and community consultation commissioned to screen the eligibility of beneficiaries, the FFSs were formed. At the end of this meeting held to explain the anticipated roles from the leading individuals and members, the FFS was asked to enter into a learning contract with the project and other relevant stakeholders. A typical learning contract includes, objectives of the contract, time frame of the contract, roles and commitments from stakeholders and finally establishment of the principles and norms of the FFS. Objectives of both fourth and fifth steps namely resource mapping and participatory needs assessment was to identify all possible resources of the community as well as identify the problems that the FFS members have been encountering. Various techniques such as Participatory Rural Appraisal (PRA) methods were adapted during these phases. Karanja (1988) remarks that Participatory Rural Appraisal is an excellent tool to bring together development needs defined by community groups on the one hand and on the other hand resources and technical skills of government donor agencies and non-governmental organisations. In so doing, it integrates traditional skills and external technical knowledge in the development process. Rather than importing and imposing foreign technologies, Participatory Rural Appraisal utilises and enhances locally conceived sustainable approaches. However, during the fifth step, the participatory needs assessment did a proper problem analysis which helped the group to identify learning needs for the year, depending on the learning cycle.

The sixth step was planning. Clarke (1999) states that community planning is seen as a means of giving expression to the role through a process drawing together all the stakeholders in local governance. During this phase FFS group members prioritised needs and developed an action plan for the year. A brief scanning on available local institutional & service support in the area was also included as a part of the planning process. The seventh was the training session to build community capacity. During the initial cycles of learning contract, technical training was prioritised. Later as aforesaid, the scope included other non-agriculture related activities, like creating the FFS as an effective conduit which is able to fulfill various service needs of members and manage local resource bases while influencing key decision making processes. LIFT ensured wide array of training for the members of these FFSs such as Community Leadership, Conflict Resolution, Financial and Non Financial Recordkeeping, Social Responsibilities and Rights, Negotiation Skills, Time management, Gender and Development. The final step was another typical ingredient of FFS. By the end of a year or a crop season FFS did a reflective assessment evaluating successes and failures and shared experiences within the FFS and also with an adjacent FFS. As a part of the FFS self-evaluation process, an evaluation of the capacity building of FFS facilitated after the first year learning cycle stated; 1) Organise meetings without assistance from the project, 2) FFS have own plans for the season/ year, 3) Collectively address problems beyond the scope of a traditional FFS, 4). Functional links with other institutions, 5) Contact organisations for services, 6) Evidence of collective decision making, 7) Members actively participate in FFS meetings and 8) FFS members conduct sessions as trainers or experts.

Results and Discussion

Half way through the stipulated project period, it was observed that very important impacts especially relevant to the needs of conflict areas, have been made by this approach. The Interim evaluation report reveals that, the project has forged functional linkages with government and other service providers; developed social capital through ownership, motivation, leadership capabilities and confidence; expanded social safety nets through enhanced village unity; local funds for lending; increase in community self help activities; and decreased local level interpersonal and intercommunity conflict. However, in order to review the present performances of FFS, a series of focus group discussions were held and few secondary data sources were also utilised. Table one illustrates that all the field schools have started to address community issues by launching various interventions.

TABLE 01 - Responsiveness of field schools to various community requirements

Community Development Interventions	Number of FFS involved
0-5	9
6-10	10
11-15	7
16-20	4

By the end of the project, as a result of improving the analytical ability and decision-making power of field schools which required technical skills, recognition as community representatives, ability to develop relationships and the power to influence decisions were all seen to be significantly enhanced with various functional linkages. The effort of field schools to influence the implementation of policy in their communities is perhaps the most considerable impact of the project's support. Table two shows the various intervention domains, and it is conspicuous that field schools have significantly broadened the scope of interventions, not merely restricting them to agricultural extension purposes.

Table 02 - FFS Interventions by Sector

Sector	Number of Interventions
Infrastructure Development	10
Conflict Resolution	18
Microfinance	25
Advocacy at Local Level	17
Linking, Convincing Service Providers	144
Community Strengthening	04
Awareness Raising and Training	50
Resource acquisition	06
Disaster Response	22

It was seen that Farmer Field Schools have leveraged additional development resources for their communities because of their high level and visible performances. They have also facilitated increased level of communication and interaction between villages. As intended beneficiaries and participants (especially women) indicated that social cohesion (or capital) within villages was at least as important a benefit as improved economic status. Remarkably, field schools acted as important coping mechanisms for their communities during disasters, Tsunami for example, and in events like internal displacement due to the conflict. These organisations have also started to play a critical role in restoration of livelihoods through savings & credit facilities provided for members by the FFS or linking the needed with financial institutions such as banks. Facilitating linkages with service providers has addressed longstanding issues such as access to land deeds, postal service, transport service, health facilities such as mobile clinics, and access to better agricultural (extension as well as agrarian development) services from the concerned departments. Leading members of field schools have become prominent civil society activists, while 28% of the field schools have started to represent various divisional statutory forums where major development decisions are taken, for example the Divisional Agriculture Committee (DAC). Puvaneswary (2006) remarks that the executive committees of field schools assist in inter-personal and inter-community conflicts by linking people with local processes that address such issues. In some cases, management committees also act as mediators. These are not only minor disputes that are related to water and agriculture, but also wider community concerns. It was also learnt that 73% of the field schools try to ensure the rule of law within their respective jurisdictions.

LIFT project had a precise gender strategy. So the project ensured that 51% of executive committee positions were held by women, while 42.5% of the membership comprised of women. It was extremely useful to ensure gender sensitive development. For instance, in an area where emergence of women headed households was seen as a significant concern, that application was vital.

Conclusion

Emerging development trends with a special focus on rural poor, suggest that political, social and economic development priorities could be achieved upon a broad consensus in society. These trends indicate that empowered civil society and various interest groups can directly influence and participate in policy decision making, with respect to allocations of development resources in particular. CARE International in Sri Lanka formulated the LIFT project as an alternative approach to fulfill the human capacity building requirements to enable communities to play a central role in their own development. The LIFT Project carried out a series of technical training in order to ensure sustainable management of natural resources by limiting land and environmental degradation, improving water management, and safe exploitation of forest resources in Jaffna where the main livelihood source is agriculture. On the other hand training focused on developing community-level management skills that promotes social empowerment. The aim of this alternative approach was not merely to educate and raise skill levels, but also enhance the problem-solving abilities of community members to enable them to be productive workers in any given industry.

The impact of the LIFT project necessarily moved beyond intended improvements of agricultural extension. Jaffna as an area which experienced decades long ethnic war, contribution of respective communities was vital than the other areas to instigate their own development. Besides enhancing the agriculture, FFS approach facilitated the process of service provision, which was essential in such a devastated area, where neither democratic administrative processes nor community structures can be seen. Community representation was considerably improved in local decision making fora as a result of empowerment through the LIFT project. They also undertook intra and inter community conflict resolution measures while giving due recognition to community development as well as coping with unforeseen occurrences such as disasters. It is to be mentioned that requirement of discovering non-formal but strong human capacity building measures such as FFS is greater than ever in an era, where reaching the rural poor has been prioritised.

References

- Adair Michael & Chandra Coomeraswamy, 2006, Interim Evaluation of CIDA Sri Lanka's Local Initiatives for Tomorrow Project (LIFT), CARE International
- Atchoarena David (2006) The Evaluation of International Cooperation in Education: A Rural Perspective, *Journal of International Cooperation in Education,* Vol.9, No.1, (2006) pp.59 – 70, CICE Hiroshima University
- Carter Carolyn S (1999) Education and Development in Poor Rural Communities: An Interdisciplinary Research Agenda, ERIC Digest, ERIC Clearinghouse on Rural Education and Small Schools Charleston WV
- Clarke Michael & John Stewart., (1999) Community governance, community Leadership and the new local government, Joseph Rowntree Foundation.
- Epstein Paul, Paul M. Coates, Lyle D. Wray, David Swain (2005) Results that Matter: Improving Communities by Engaging Citizens, Measuring Performance, and Getting Things Done
- International Fund for Agricultural Development (IFAD) (2001) Rural Poverty Report, The Challenge of Ending Rural Poverty
- Karanja Mary N (1988) Good Governance and Community Participation as Tools to Make Environmental Enforcement and Compliance Happen
- Kraay A, (2006) *'What Is Governance and How Do We Measure It?'* Outline of Presentation at Workshop on Governance and Development
- Mander H, and Aslif, M., (2004) *'Good Governance'* (Resource Book), Action Aid International
- Nixon Hamish (2008) The Changing Face of Local Governance? Community Development Councils in Afghanistan, Afghanistan Research and Evaluation Unit, Working Paper Series
- Pontius John, Russell Dilts, Amdrew Bartlett (2002) From Farmer Feidl Schools To Community IPM, Ten Years of IPM training in Asia. FAO Community IPM Programme, Jakarta.
- Puvaneswary P.,(2006) Capacity Building of Farmers in the Conflict Affected Areas of Sri Lanka. Symposium Proceedings on Development Initiatives in Water Sector: Lessons Learnt by NGOs, CAPNET, University of Peradeniya.
- Rhodes R.A.W, (1997) *'Understanding Governance, Policy Networks, Governance, Reflectivity and Accountability.'* Open University Press, USA
- Richardson Mike (1999) Community Governance: Resource Kit Christchurch City Council
- Sri Ranjith J. G (2007) Governance and Community Participation: A Collective Approach to Regional (Urban) Development in Sri Lanka, The Peradeniya Journal of Economics Volume 1, Number 1 & 2, June / December 2007, Published by the Department of Economics and Statistics, University of Peradeniya, Sri Lanka.
- Stark N, (2005) 'Effective Rural Governance: What it is? Does it matter?' Rural Governance Initiative, Rural Policy Research Institute (RUPRI)
- Suan-Pheng K, (2002) 'Changing paradigm of rural governance for sustainable development: Defining the niche and role of GIS', Proceedings of 7th International Seminar on GIS in Developing Countries, International Rice Research Institute
- United Nations Development Programme, (2005) *'Pro-poor urban governance; lessons from life 2002-2005'*

CHAPTER 4

STRENGTHENING HUMAN CAPITAL THROUGH CITIZENSHIP VALUES EDUCATION

Eleanor E. Nicolas

Abstract

The values system of a society is inextricably intertwined with democracy and development. In a country where corruption and lack of trust and public confidence in its institutions are perceived to be pervasive, citizenship and values education is seen as antidote to these challenges. Towards this end, a multisectoral group underscored the need for systemic and holistic approach to strengthening Filipino values through measures that promote values formation and civic/citizenship education. This group convened three national congresses on good citizenship to generate a critical mass of advocates of good citizenship values. The academe, business, religious groups, and civil society organisations are actively engaged in promoting citizenship values. They are encouraged to more proactively collaborate or partner with government agencies to carry out measures on citizenship and values formation. Sustaining the initial gains and small victories from these engagements remains a challenge.

Introduction

The Philippines remains steadfast in its pursuit for national transformation. This has become increasingly difficult due to persistent problems of poverty, limited access to basic social services, income disparities, patronage, insurgency and Mindanao conflict, weak implementation, and corruption. At the crux of these problems is the "the state of the Filipino values." The Filipino values system is perceived to be one of the many sources of graft and corruption. Results of periodic surveys conducted by international and national organisations show a worsening incidence of corruption, which, in turn, impacts on the country's economic growth and development. This assertion is corroborated in the Medium-Term Philippine Development Plan 2004-2010 (NEDA, 2003) which states that

Graft and corruption are increasingly viewed as threats to the sustained growth and development of the country. Corruption distorts access to services for the poor, results in government's poor performance and, consequently, low public confidence in government. The culture of corruption in the country breeds the vicious cycles of poverty and underdevelopment.

The overall effect of a failed values system is very alarming since it tends to be systemic and impinges on the core processes and outcomes of the country's national transformation. Further, official government policies and pronouncements, and published studies pointed to the Filipino values system as the weakest link in nation building. Systemic and holistic approach to strengthening the Filipino values is deemed imperative through such institutionalised interventions such as values formation and civic/citizenship education (Adorio, 2005).

Significance of Citizenship and Values Education

The need to promote citizenship and values education is greater that ever before – this was the call for action expressed by five developed countries during their 2008 conference on Education for Values and Citizenship. They assert that citizenship and values education is the lifeblood of democracy and democratic institutions. It is one of society's strongest defences against the rise of cynicism, apathy, violence and all forms of discrimination and intolerance. Its promotion further contributes significantly to social cohesion and social justice (www.nfer.ac.uk/nfer/publications/33303).

In terms of content, Maitles and Gilchrist assert that the meaning of citizenship must cover economic and global citizenship to be relevant in the modern world. They refer to Marshall's definition of citizenship (1950) which comprises three components – civil citizenship, political citizenship and social citizenship. People having a say in the day to day matters that affect their lives is equally important as their formal rights. In this regard, education for citizenship initiatives are bound with democracy and serve as means to develop legitimacy for existing social relations (Maitles, Henry & Isabel Gilchrist, 2005).

The relationship between citizenship and democracry is likewise examined in the Philippine context. Diokno (1997) asserts that where citizenship is not effective, there can be no real democracy. This nexus was traditionally viewed as focusing on government structures and processes. This shifted to a pro-active view which focuses on shared values and understanding through as deliberative process that emphasises the democratizing function of citizenship. The latter are demonstrated in (a) indigenous, day-to-day practices of democracy and decision making in communities where government mechanisms may or may exist (leader selection, consultations, dispute settlement without recourse to court); (b) initiatives by organised groups or sectors who explore other venues of expression or alternative solutions particularly when their rights or interests are threatened (e.g., court system); and (c) citizens to perform obligations and exercise their rights – entail capacity building and organising to effectively negotiate and exert pressure to bring about desired change

Constitutional Provision on Citizenship Values

The 1987 Philippine Constitution has enshrined in its Preamble the ideal values that would make for a good Filipino citizen. These values are Faith in Almighty God; Patriotism; Work; Respect for Life; Respect for Law and Government; Unity; Peace; Promotion of the Common Good; Truth; Justice; Freedom; Love; Equality; Concern for the Family and Future Generations; Concern for the Environment; and Order.

As duty-bearer, the government has to ensure internalisation of these ideal values. It has incorporated values formation as one of the implementation strategies of the MTPDP 2004-2010 in the areas of education, culture, and anti-corruption. The MTPDP 2004-2010 identifies the core values that have to be integrated into the curricula of the formal educational system as shown in the following table.

Core Values in the Curriculum

Day Care Center	Pre-School	Elementary Education	Secondary Education	Higher Education (Values formation in POIs* of National Service Training Program)
Self-respect and self-esteem	Self-respect and self-esteem	Valuing self	Valuing others	1. Faith in the Almighty
Love of family and respect for elders	Obedience to elders	Respect for Country	Respect for others and rule of law	2. Respect for Life 3. Order 4. Work
Honesty, Perseverance, Resourcefulness	Honesty	Truthfulness	Fortitude, Integrity	5. Concern for the Family and Future Generations
	Discernment between Right and wrong	Respect for life	Humility	6. Love 7. Freedom 8. Peace
	Loyalty	Responsibility	Social Responsibility	9. Truth 10. Justice
		Independence	Economic Responsibility	11. Unity
Sharing and Cooperation	Sharing and Cooperation	Equality	Temperance	12. Equality 13. Respect for Law and Government
Love of God and Country	Love of God and Country	Love of God and Country	Spirituality	14. Patriotism
Cleanliness of surroundings	Environment Consciousness	Environment Consciousness	Peace	15. Promotion of the Common Good, and
Sharing/ Thrift/ Frugality	Sharing/ Thrift/ Frugality	Sharing/ Thrift/ Frugality	Sharing/ Thrift/ Frugality	16. Concern for the Environment.

* NEDA. (2003). Medium-Term Philippine Development Plan 2004-2010. Chapter 18 Education, Program of Instructions, pp.205-221.

The government has adopted the inculcation of values in schools and various government institutions as a strategy against corruption. It requires the conduct of lifestyle check and the integration of integrity development review in government agencies. The key agencies involved in anti-corruption are the Office of the Ombudsman and the Presidential Anti-Graft Commission (PAGC). These agencies' efforts are reinforced by the newly formed Presidential Council on Values Formation (PCVF) chaired by President Gloria Macapagal-Arroyo, with eleven (11) members coming from different religious organisations. Moreover, the government declared a Decade (2005-2015) of Good Governance and Good Citizenship to Fight Corruption and Eradicate Poverty (Republic of the Philippines, 2004). The Proclamation asserts that *"the necessity of instilling the Filipino values enshrined in the Preamble of the 1987 Constitution will lead to the making of good citizens, thereby contributing to nation building."*

Initiatives on Citizenship Education

This paper presents the knowledge exchange and experiential sharing of various organisations engaged in the promotion of civic/citizenship values through the National Congress on Good Citizenship (NCGC). A multisectoral organisation composed of the Good Citizenship Movement (GCM) – a civil society organisation, the University of the Philippines National College of Public Administration and Governance, Center for Leadership, Citizenship and Democracy (UPNCPAG, CLCD) – an academe, and the Commission on Higher Education (CHED) – a government agency, spearheaded and convened the NCGC. The CLCD served as the secretariat. The NCGC, held annually from 2006 to onwards for two days each, is intended to be an occasion for a comprehensive and multisectoral review of programs and activities on civic/citizenship education, identify areas of collaborative engagements, monitor implementation of action programs, and recommend appropriate policies and strategies to strenghten civic/citizenship values education.

Overall Goal of the NCGC

As overall goal, the series of NCGC envisions a critical mass of advocates of good citizenship values that would jumpstart the citizenry, individually and collectively, into good governance and actions that would reduce corruption. Participants in the NCGCs came from various sectors, namely, government agencies, academe, nongovernment organisations, religious organisations, local government units and the business sector. They are potential advocates of good citizenship values (GCVs).

Specifically, these congresses served as venues for civil society, government, and private sector to come together to (1) reflect on and celebrate current efforts on values formation nationwide; (2) organise/form or collaborate through partnerships or other forms/modes of engagements that will help in the promotion of good citizenship values and human rights nationwide; (3) contribute to the reduction of problems of poverty and corruption, and the protection and promotion of human rights; and (4) to sustain advocacy for the promotion and strengthening of good citizenship values through the use of appropriate pedagogical approaches to values formation and citizenship education. The three NCGCs examined the discourses, methodologies, measures, activities and practices that would promote citizenship values.

First National Congress on Good Citizenship (CLCD, 2006)

The first NCGC, held on 27-28 October 2006 had as its theme, **Good Citizenship Values: Building Blocks of Development**. It presented the 16 values contained in the Preamble of the 1987 Philippine Constitution as a framework for good citizenship values. The 1st NCGC resulted in the formulation of the national action plan on good citizenship and the formation of a multisectoral council composed of representatives of participants from academe, government, civil society, and business sector who would provide leadership and direction to congress activities. It also paved the way for the implementation of programs and projects, namely: (1) the continuing teachers' training by a joint team of the GCM and the EDSA People Power Commission for teachers of the National Service Training Program (NSTP), using modules developed jointly by the two institutions and distributed by the CHED; (2) Trainors' Training conducted by the Presidential Anti-Graft Commission for participants coming from 24 government agencies; (3) training on the GCVs conducted by the Moral Recovery Officers Foundation, Inc., and their integration into the programs of the Department of Agrarian Reform; (4) implementation by the Union Bank of a P10-million project for informing early-graders on the good citizenship values; (5) implementation of the *Kabanalan at Kabayanihan* (holiness and heroism) parish-based formation program on the good citizenship values by the Catholic Diocese in Quezon City; and (6) integration of the GCVs into the NSTP courses, particularly Civic Welfare (CWTS 1 and 2), for tertiary education.

Second National Congress on Good Citizenship (CLCD, 2007)

The 2nd NCGC, held on August 17-18, 2007 with **"ImagiNation: Art of Nation Building"** as its theme, focused specifically on social artistry as a methodology in values formation and in promoting good citizenship values. It demonstrated the use of contemporary and traditional music, performing arts, visual arts, and poetry. It enabled participants to discover their own creativity and to use their talents in promoting the GCVs.

The 2nd NCGC resulted in the formation of four (4) task forces, namely, (a) education and training, (b) research and materials development, (c) social engineering, and (d) advocacy and information, each of which comprised the congress participants as members; and (2) two resolutions that requested the honorable members of the House of Representatives and the Senate (two houses of the Philippine Legislature), respectively, to (a) enact legislation for the integration of the Good Citizenship Values enshrined in the 1987 Philippine Constitution into the curriculum and training programs of academe, government, business and civil society sectors, and (b) support the implementation of Republic Act No. 9163 known as the National Service Training Program (NSTP) Act of 2001. These were submitted to Senator Alan Peter Cayetano, Chairman of the Senate Committee on Education; Representative Del R. de Guzman, Chairman of the House

Committee on Basic Education; and Representative Cynthia A. Villar, Chairman of the House Committee on Higher and Technical Education. Further, the 2nd NCGC resulted in downstream activities exploring the application of social artistry. These were the (1) Two-day Character First! Program in Bayawan City, Negros Oriental, and the (2) Two-Day Capacity Enhancement on Teaching Good Citizenship Values in NSTP using Deliberate Technique and Social Artistry in Region XI (April 7-8, 2008). The Bayawan experienced focused on the use of social artistry in drawing community values and problems in a local setting. The Davao experience highlighted social artistry as a methodology to facilitate the integration of good citizenship values into the National Service Training Program (NSTP) in Region XI. Both experiences showed the potential of social artistry in demonstrating individual understanding of values expressed through the arts and presented to the community, and in articulating individual and/or shared values and collective/community aspirations.

Third National Congress on Good Citizenship (CLCD, 2008)

The 3rd NCGC focused on the theme **"Strengthening Good Governance in the Public and Private Sectors through Responsible Citizenship** and was convened on 21-22 October 2008. It underpinned the link between responsible citizenship and good governance, and the usage and practices of good citizenship values for alleviating poverty and reducing corruption in public and private sectors. The 3rd NCGC tackled the following: (a) knowledge (i.e., lessons and challenges) on the initiatives of government, civil society, business, and academe in promoting good citizenship values; (b) concrete actions, measures and practices in the public and private sectors that demonstrate the link between responsible citizenship and good governance; and (c) mechanisms for sustaining the practices of responsible citizenship.

The 3rd Congress endeavored to deepen appreciation of the relationship between good citizenship and good governance by setting up mechanism/s or formulating instrument/s that institutionalise GCVs such as a GCV Scorecard. The challenge was how to ensure the institutionalisation of good citizenship values in the workplaces. Further, institutionalisation would require that promotion of good citizenship values must include the dimension of measuring outcomes from work done. Institutionalisation could be facilitated with the enactment of the House Bill No 5156 or "The Good Citizenship Act of 2008," pending at the House of Representatives which is the lower house of the Philippine Congress. Likewise, the 3rd NCGC discussed the measurement concept and tools; and draft, design, and agreed on shared GCV scorecards.

The following were some of the key lessons learned from the initiatives in developing citizenship values from the perspectives of the four sectors, namely, academe, government, civil society, and business sector. The academe's experience in promoting good citizenship through the NSTP has been favorable. The NSTP has been instrumental in imparting individual and collective responsibility for the common good and learning the value of service to others through students' activities and projects in schools and in community immersions. The expected end result of these activities is to replicate the same activities in the context of core values of *Maka-Diyos* (God-centered), *Maka-Tao* (people centered), *Maka-Bayan* (country-centered) at *Maka-Kalikasan* (environment friendly).

The government initiatives were (1) system review, (2) policy review, and (3) change in behavior. The lessons learned that are essential to integrity are in the four core values: (1) MAKA-DIYOS – involvement in ecumenical and spiritual activities for values formation which are concretised by nondiscriminatory provision of free services; (2) MAKA-TAO – refinement of individual government agency's vision, mission, goals and objectives in accordance with the respective mandate and agenda of the present administration, whether on infrastructure, basic social services, or others; or in human resource development or in organizing unions and associations; (3) MAKA-BAYAN – contribution of a government employee to the country's development by patronizing own products, public sector volunteerism during elections, prioritizing public service to personal service; (4) MAKA-KALIKASAN – participation in the different environmental activities, like Earth Charter, tree planting, waste management or segregation for sustainable development.

On the part of the civil society organisations, the lessons learned from the Gawad Kalinga was shared. Gawad Kalinga (GK) is involved in building more than 1,500 communities all over the country and four (4) communities outside of the country. GK is already on its fifth year of operation and has built more than 30,000 homes since it started in 2004. The GK development model is driven by *bayanihan*, which is the Filipino value of volunteerism. Three lessons shared from the GK initiative are "(1) make the work inspiring - this means inspiring people to believe that they are empowered to do thing; (2) make the work inclusive – this means, not alienating anybody regardless of his/her social grouping, socio-economic status in life, religious affiliation or political affiliation; and (3) do the work with the highest integrity factor – this means that given an alienated society and country where corruption is rampant, integrity shines out amidst of all of these problems; integrity simply means that a person has tried as much as possible to walk his/her talk." This means changing the mindset and attitude of the poor from hopelessness and helplessness to confidence of one's capacity and will power.

From the private sector, a bank experience in promoting good citizenship values was shared. It produced the handbook, **As a Filipino,** which is a storybook about the 16 values. The handbook represents the bank's contribution to the promotion of good citizenship values in line with its Philanthropy and Corporate Social Responsibility (CSR). Its CSR program has targeted UN Millennium Development Goals and allocated one percent of its net income to support its social responsibility function.

In February-March 2009, the UP NCPAG-CLCD conducted a field validation as a follow-through on the action/re-entry plans of the participants in their respective workplaces. Concrete activities undertaken by the participants reflected the results of advocacies and the serious efforts of key informants to make improvements or changes in their workplaces. Values-based leadership emerged as the critical factor in initiating and facilitating changes towards a desired goal/objective. Leaders are seen as role models, living exemplars, and practitioners of values they preach (CLCD, 2009).

Conclusion

On the whole, the advocacy of good citizenship indicated positive and encouraging results. The field validation showed renewed and sustained institutional and organisational interests to enliven civic and citizenship values education with the use of varied methodological approaches and to institutionalise responsible citizenship through multisectoral collaboration. Sustaining the gains, however, entails generating knowledge on success or pitfalls of initiatives on promoting good citizenship values in the public and private sectors. These lessons can be shared and replicated. It requires that accomplishments and initiatives are monitored periodically. Likewise, alternative courses of action for institutionalisation of good citizenship values at various tiers of governance and with the public and private sectors have to be explored.

End notes

Adorio, Mercedes P. (2005) *Education for Good Citizenship: From Theory and Practice*, unpublished paper. March 5.

Center for Leadership Citizenship and Democracy. (2006). U.P. National College of Public Administration and Governance. Final Project Outputs, 1st National Congress on Good Citizenship, Submitted to the United Nations Development Programme, Quezon City, Philippines. January 9.

_____. (2007). U.P. National College of Public Administration and Governance. Final Project Outputs, 2nd National Congress on Good Citizenship, submitted to the UNDP, Quezon City, Philippines. March 14.

_____ .(2008). U.P. National College of Public Administration and Governance. Final Project Terminal Report 3rd National Congress on Good Citizenship Project, Submitted to the UNDP, Quezon City, Philippines. January 28.

_____ . (2009). U.P. National College of Public Administration and Governance. Final Report on the Field Validation of Good Citizenship Initiatives: GCV Scorecard and other Outputs, Submitted to the UNDP, Quezon City, Philippines. May 5.

Citizenship and Values Education to the Rescue! Making the Case for a Call to Action - Full Report Ninth Annual Conference - Education for Values and Citizenship in England, Ireland, Northern ... www.nfer.ac.uk/nfer/publications/33303/33303.pdf

Diokno, Maria Serena I. ed. (1997) "Becoming a Filipino Citizen, Perspectives on Citizenship and Democracy," **Democracy and Citizenship in Filipino Political Culture**. Quezon City: Third World Studies Center, pp. 17-38.

Maitles, Henry & Isabel Gilchrist. (2005). 'We're citizens now'!: the development of positive values through a democratic approach to learning. **Journal for Critical Education Policy Studies**. Vol. 3, No. 1 (March). www.jceps.com/

Marshall, J.T. (1950). **Citizenship and Social Class and other Essays**. Cambridge: Cambridge University Press.

National Economic and Development Authority. (2003). **Medium-Term Philippine Development Plan 2004-2010**, Philippines: NEDA. p. 249.

Republic of the Philippines. (2004). Executive Order No. 713 which amended Executive Orders Nos. 314 and 347 renamed the Ad Hoc Council for Values Formation as the Presidential Council on Values Formation; and Presidential Proclamation No. 828 which declared 2005-2015 as the Decade of Good Governance and Good Citizenship to Fight Corruption and Eradicate Poverty.

Chapter 5

NEW BANTAYAN BARANGAY DEVELOPMENT PLANNING:
A Blended Learning Approach

Aristeo C. Salapa

Abstract

Development planning using Blended Learning (BL) is a must for graduate students. A combination of approaches to learning promotes the readiness of graduate students to elevate knowledge to higher levels. This presents a dilemma for professors teaching at the graduate level. Theory and direct application of such learning in a given span of time is a task to realise. The syllabus plays a vital role. A real planned course measures the output at the end of the semester.

A certain instructional and educational strategy must be employed. And this is blended learning as applied by graduate public administration students of the University of Southeastern Philippines, College of Governance, Business and Economics in collaborating to make a Barangay development plan in a chosen Barangay. Further, usable application of planning models transpired and simulated in classroom discussions.

Expanding students abilities not just within the four corners of the room where simulation is best tested but by actual and practice on the ground prepares them for the real work ahead. This is clearly manifested in realisation of the University's four-fold thrust of instruction, research, extension and production. Meshing all these together, the learner and the community reap large rewards.

Graduate students best equipped both in theory and in practice via blended learning are demonstrations of the University's edge for competitive advantage.

Background/Rationale of the Study

> Who dares to teach must never cease to learn.
>
> - John Cotton Dana

The University of Southeastern Philippines (USeP) envisions a modern state university at the cutting edge of academic excellence and at the forefront of research development. It aims to build an institution that provides a harmonious and conducive atmosphere for faculty and students to develop and attain their potential, and becomes an active participant in the promotion of the well-being and welfare of the community and society (Prantilla, University Manual I, 1998).

Over the last 28 years, the university's commitment to producing high quality graduates and relevant researches has been enduring. It is likewise evident that the efforts of the university to respond to changes within and outside its environment have increased tremendously (Strategic Plan, 2007-2021).

The Department of Governance Studies (DGS), one of the departments of the College of Governance, Business and Economics, offers the Master of Public Administration program that aims to upgrade and enhance the administrative skills and professional competence of leaders and practitioners both in the government and non-government sectors (MPA Brochure). This is done via acquisition of advanced knowledge, a thorough mastery of research methods and a spirit of searching inquiry in a multi-disciplinary approach and varied levels through policy making analysis, administrative theory and behavior, human resource management, budgeting and financial resource management, management and research design and analysis so as to be experts in organisation studies, fiscal administration and public policy and program administration (CGBE Brochure).

To heed this call is a noble task for professors. Independent learning is valued so that full and active development learning between professors and students will occur. Academic freedom is practiced within the guidance of academic heads of institutions and the Commission on Higher Education (CHED). This context fosters the development of students in the furtherance of their studies and encourages them to make connections in other related fields.

Three important considerations in teaching graduate students come to the fore. These are: the concept of adult learning, the mode of delivery and activities to test whether knowledge is applied.

Hence, this endeavor.

The Issue, the Theory and the Process

The Issue

The four-fold thrust of the University namely: instruction, research, extension and production are embedded in every curricular program of the University. The syllabus prepared by professors should manifest all of these.

As a graduate program, with a five month scope of coverage[1], the challenge of incorporating theory, practice and the thrust of the University became an arduous task not withstanding other important concerns like security, financial resources and leg working.[2]

For the first semester, classes at the University start during the month of June. It is expected that professors distribute the syllabus at the beginning of class so that participants know what to expect. Careful planning from the professor in charge is expected so that by the end of the semester, products and results are delivered. Best techniques must be used in the delivery of such courses.

Two of the courses offered in the Master of Public Administration program are Management Planning and Control and Strategic Planning for Public Action. These courses have a description of processes and techniques in administrative planning, organisational analysis and control with simulation and actual planning where time and resources are not that openly available in a given semester. Teaching planning, per se, whether strategic or development and the process involved in it, is one major subject in the MPA program that calls for a blended technique so that theory and application is achieve given limited time but at maximum level.

The Theories Employed

Three existing theories are used to solidify the claims. These are the following:
1. Adult Learning- As Malcolm Knowles (1978, 1990) argued adulthood has arrived when people behave in ways and believe themselves to be adults. Further, Burns (1995) has said that by adulthood people are self-directing. Adult learners bring a great deal of experience to the learning environment. Educators can use this as a resource; adults expect to have a high degree of influence on what they are to be educated for, and how they are to be educated; the active participation of learners should be encouraged in designing and implementing educational programs; adults need to be able to see applications for new learning; adult learners expect to have a high degree of influence on how learning will be evaluated; and adults expect their responses to be acted upon when asked for feedback on the progress of the program.
2. Blended Learning- Bersin, (2004) has argued that blended learning is a "combination of different training media...to create an optimum training program for a specific audience... traditional instructor led-training is being supplemented with other electronic formats." The rationale for blended learning is that it addresses the different learning styles and the multiple method of information delivery reinforces the lesson. A major component of the blended learning design is the provision of experiential learning - considered to be the most effective method of delivering instruction.

By applying learning theories of Keller, Gagné, Bloom, Merrill, Clark and Gery,[3] we have identified five key ingredients for a blended learning model: (1) **Scheduled Events:** Synchronous, instructor-led learning events in which all learners participate at the same time, such as in a "virtual classroom."; (2) **Online Content:** Asynchronous learning experiences that learners complete individually, at their own speed and on their own time, such as simulations, tutorials, and exercises; (3) **Collaboration:** Environments in which learners communicate with others, for example, threaded discussions and online chat; (4) **Assessment:** A measure of learners' knowledge. Pre-assessments can come before scheduled events or online content, to determine prior knowledge, and post-assessments can occur following scheduled or online learning events, to measure learning transfer; (5) **Reference Materials:** On-the-job reference materials that enhance learning retention and transfer, including PDA downloads and PDFs.

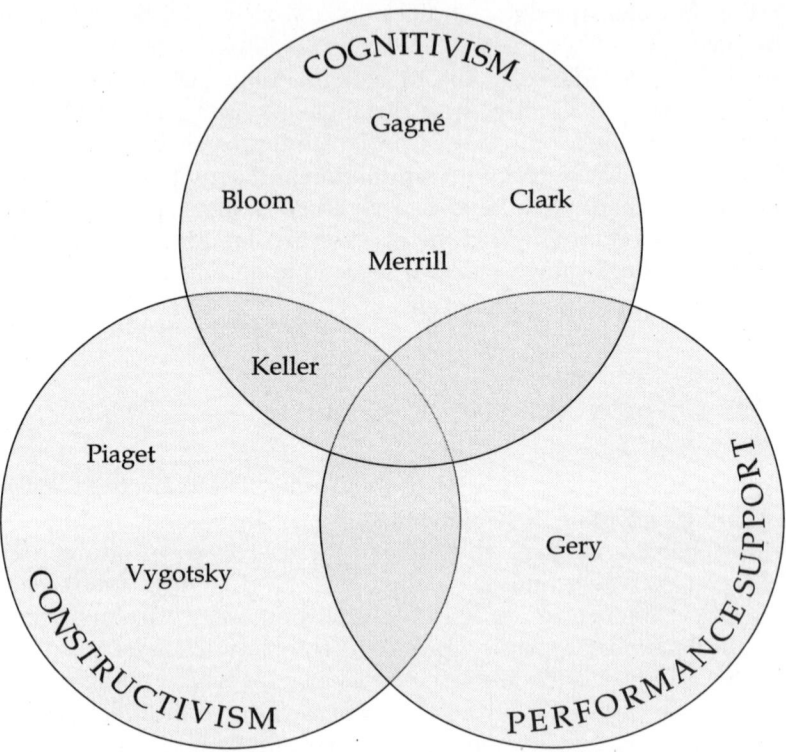

FIGURE 1: Blended Learning Model

Further, the goal of a blended learning course is "mastery" of the subject which is demonstrated by having the student successfully teach the material to another person. Thus, a student of public administration can employ the C's – compare, consequence and connect after comprehending.

3. Action Learning- links the world of learning with the world of action through a reflective process within small cooperative learning groups known as "action learning sets." The "sets" meet regularly to work on individual members' real life issues with the aim of learning with and from each other. Reg Revans, father of action learning, has said that there can be no learning without action and no (sober deliberate) action without learning. He further said, that learning can be shown by the following equation, where L is learning, P is programmed knowledge (e.g. traditional instruction) and Q is questioning insight: ($L= P+Q$). This theory is used as a guide in developing the Barangay development plan of New Bantayan. Participatory planning (PP)[1] was also used.

Below is the process flow and conceptual framework of this study:

```
┌─────────────────────────┐
│   Blended Learning      │
│   Approach coupled with │
│   other theories        │
└─────────────────────────┘
            │
            ▼
┌─────────────────────────┐
│  Phase 1-               │
│  MPA students Acquisition│
│  Of Knowledge           │
│  • Planning Process     │
│    and Model            │
└─────────────────────────┘
            │
            ▼
```

- Barangay Profile
- Secondary Data Analysis

→

- Phase 2- Seminar Workshop
    - SWOT
    - Problem Tree
    - Objective Tree
    - Vision, Mission, Goals Formulation
    - Activities
- Phase 3- Writeshop of the Facilitators and Turn-Over

→ Barangay Development Plan of New Bantayan (2010-2012)

Results

Phase 1- Learning, Equipping and Leg Working[1]

The months of June and July were allotted for Phase 1. Classes were held every Saturday for 3 hours. Guided by the syllabus given to all 14 officially enrolled students, classroom outlines were delivered via PowerPoint presentations, open forums and home assignments using all modes of communications such as mobiles, emails, on line chats, plus tasking[2]. A Gantt chart was maintained to keep things on track as well as monitor progress. Updates were regularly done via texting; Saturday classes served as group meetings prior to the discussion of major topics in class.

The major topics discussed during these months with close guidance and consideration of what will happen in actuality when implemented were the following: background review of RA7160- The Local Government Code of 1991 specifically book 3- local governments with some updates; the preparatory for planning: thorough review of the planning process; training with lecture on the application of the stages of planning-environmental scanning, SWOT[3], problem tree[4], objective tree[5], writing VISION, MISSION and goals, simulating the writing of the plan and analysis of secondary data retrieve from the said Barangay; anticipated activities were seen as well. Clue guides were also given. Moreover, a secondary data analysis was also done on the Barangay.[6] An ocular visit and initial field interview to the residents for a quick snap shot was initiated. This was followed by the conduct of Stakeholder analysis.

On week days, students, amid their tight working schedules, took time to appear in the chosen Barangay to present the proposal for Barangay Development Planning to the Barangay Council. A resolution was obtained for their nod and acceptance. Other team members took time to prepare for their budget and needed contribution for Phase 2. Indeed, well prepared and carefully assigned tasks were distributed to all. Environmental assessment[7] of the Barangay was also done during this phase.

Also included in this two month preparation before embarking on Phase 2 were a series of capability building sessions. These included: how to give effective lectures, how to maintain rapport with participants, how to process activities, how to maintain decorum and order, how to deal with elders, learning action songs and most importantly how to use the vernacular in daily conversations.

A partnership with shared responsibility and certain amount of contributions from both the students and the partner barangay was finalised.

Phase 2- The MPA students (Facilitators) in Practice and the Participants

The Location

The chosen barangay was Barangay New Bantayan at the Municipality of Asuncion in the Province of Davao del Norte. The Municipality has 20 barangays. Of these, only 1 barangay has an existing Barangay Development Plan. The Mayor welcomed the entry to the Barangay by the students of USeP as " a welcome change to the people of New Bantayan". Furthermore, the task, he added, is so noble.

The barangay has around 2800 residents. The main source of income is banana farming. Its Internal revenue allotment (IRA), share from the LGU, is less than 1 million pesos. Many of its barangay officials are newly elected. The barangay has a potential for agricultural development as well as eco-tourism. In one of the meetings of the barangay officials with the MPA students, they admitted that their annual plans and activities were mostly "copy and paste" of the previous year. They need fresh ideas and guidance to view in greater perspective what service in the barangay is all about and be informed of the varied linkages that they can connect to.

The Seminar-Writeshop[8]

On August 5, 6, 7 and 8, 2009, MPA students began work at Barangay New Bantayan. Thirty –two (32) participants as identified in the Stakeholder analysis [9]came with vigor and enthusiasm. MPA students assigned to topics came ready and prepared. It was grace under pressure. The seminar-workshop of 4 days employed a variety of approaches as mode of delivery. In summary, the activities consisted of the following: Day 1- Registration, Expectations, SWOT[10]; Day 2- Problem Tree [11]and Objective Tree[12], VISION and MISSION making; Day 3- GOALS and activities; Day 4- Activity Planning for the next 3 years following this format- barangay development thrust, objectives, programs/activities, strategies, indicators, expected output, time frame, budget, source of fund, person/agency responsible; Day 4- Writeshop for the Goals and Closing Ceremony.[13]

Phase 3- Facilitators Writeshop and Turn-Over

After a week, the facilitators went back to the working table and spent 2 overnights to finally write the 3-Year Development Plan of Barangay New Bantayan from 2010-2012. Key steps included: review barangay profile; consolidate the 3 year action plan; write current situation of the barangay and a plenary session to unify all efforts.

By September 03, 2009, the facilitators went back to New Bantayan and present the first draft of their Barangay development Plan to their Barangay Council. We need strong linked arms for development to happen. After some suggestions and some recommendations, facilitators finalised the 135 page Barangay Development Plan of New Bantayan. The contents included : methodology, schedule of activities, messages, barangay profile, barangay principles and values, vision, mission, barangay development thrusts with current situation, objectives, and the 3 year proposed activities as arranged by the council of New Bantayan. On September 11, 2009, together with officials of the College, facilitators and in celebration of Araw ng Barangay of New Bantayan, a formal turn-over was made. It was witnessed by the Mayor of the town, representatives from the Governor and House of Representatives. A summary of the plan was also presented to the constituents of New Bantayan.

Conclusions and Recommendations

From the theories espoused, three important results come from this research: adult learning and strategies applied and approaches suit the graduate students well. These are manifested in the bond created during 5 months of interaction and hard work, and the values learned. Results come also from concepts learned outside the classroom and learning at their own pace. The combination of hard work and learning contributes to the realisation of making a BDP. The BDP was a bold step in the Master of Public Administration program of the college. Several attempts were made in the past but never pushed through. Through several approaches it led to such realisation. Second, is the application of Blended Learning (BL) among graduate students. Blended learning helps them a lot in closely monitoring developments and filling gaps. BL provides an impact of learning beyond the traditional academic mode. It also paved the way for interaction among graduate students and learning on their own. The classroom environments became an avenue of sharing and follow up. Clearly, technology is an important tool in today's academic environment.

Action Learning defines the application. As future administrations and practitioners of public administration it is necessary to have a clear grasp of how development planning works from pre planning, to planning, selection of participants, workshop, and writing the plan. Graduate students were able to experience the nitty-gritty details involved in writing a plan. Participatory planning is a vital tool where the constituents of the Barangay can claim that it is their plan.

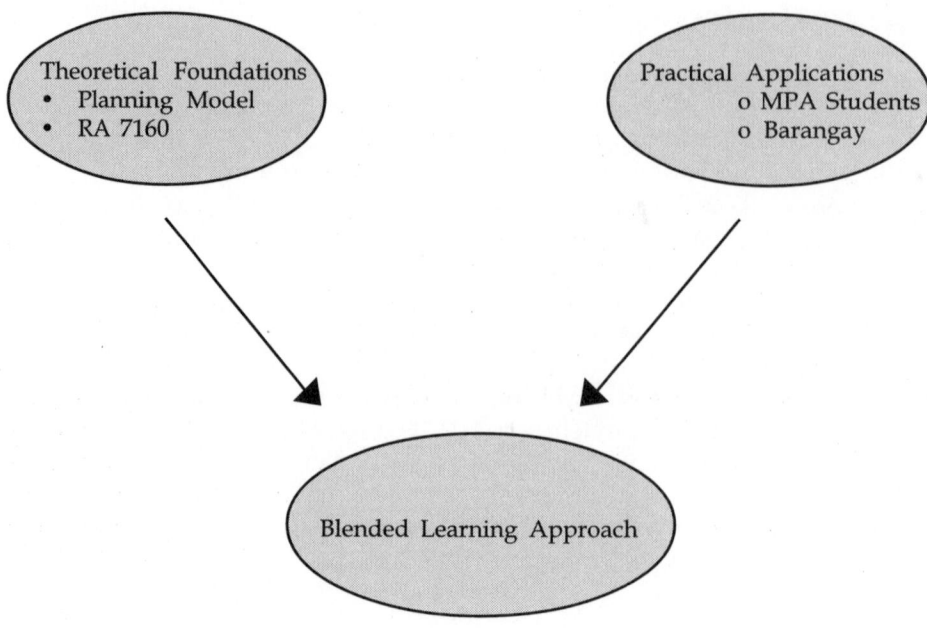

But the job does not end there. After the realisation of this document, monitoring and implementation and evaluation should take place to complete the planning process. Assistance via capability building, linkage and others must be extended to the barangay to sustain the quest for development. The people of the Barangay must claim ownership and contribute towards the full realisation of it. Working hand-in-hand is a must.

It is proposed that the following framework works best for higher educational learning:

The experience brought many insights not just for the graduate students of this institution but for the institution itself. Graduate students were able to realise that theory and practice in the realm of administration must go hand in hand so that tools can be applied with greater ease. Mastery of particular techniques might be the call of the times and versatility demanded in the use of the different tools available for planning. However the actual experience of working in the field gave them the courage to stand and claim that they can do such work in later years. The learning processes gave them the perspective of adjusting and innovating and especially of complementing actual needs on the ground. Experience multiplied the impact of class room learning.

The college now has to think about its real role and sources of academic expertise. It should continue to search for a variety of approaches to fully hone students towards creating for themselves an academic edge and competitiveness.

References

Acosta, R.M.(1991).Local government capability-building handbook. Konrad Adenauer Foundations

Allmendinger, P(2002). Planning theory.New York: PALGRAVE

A manual on the estate/Barangay-level productivity systems assessment and planning(PSAP) Methodology. Philippine Partnership for the Development of Human Resources in Rural Area

Annual Report(2004). University of Southeastern Philippines, Davao City

An introduction to blended learning. Retrieved September 06, 2010 from http://www.amanet.org/Training/articles/An-Introduction-to-Blended-Learning.aspx

Barangay Development Planning(1997). Barangay administration training program. MODULE 2. Local Government Academy. Department of Interior and Local Government

Barangay Profile(n.d.) New Bantayan. Municipality of Asuncion. Province of davao del Norte

Barangay Binancian. Five year participatory land used-based Barangay development plan 2006-2010. Municipality of Asuncion, Province of Davao del Norte

Bersin, J.(2004). The blended learning book: best practices, proven methodologies and lessons learned. San Francisco: Pfeiffer

Blended Learning Design: 5 Key Ingredients. Retrieved September 01, 2010 from http://www.Agilantlearning.com/Instructionaldesign.html

Burns,J.(1995). The adult learner at work. Sydney: Business and Professional Publishing

Burns, S.(1995). Rapid changes require enhancement of adult learning. HR Monthly June,16-17

Chen, C.C.&Jones, K.T.(2007). Blended learning vs traditional classroom settings: assessing Effectiveness and student perceptions in an MBA accounting course. The journal of Educators online,4(1),2-5

Chambers, L.D.& Taylor, M.A.P.(1999). Strategic planning: processes, tools and outcomes. England: Ashgate Publishing Company

College of Governance, Business and Economics Brochure. University of Southeastern Philippines Davao City

Comprehensive Barangay Development Planning Manual(2008). Mindanao Rural Development Program
Dziuban, C.D., Hartman, J.L.& Moskal,P.D.(2004). Blended learning. Retrieved September 08, 2010 From www.educause.ed/ecar
DA-PRISP(1998). Participatory planning:facilitator's handbook. Quezon City, Philippines
Graduate School Code. School of government and management. University of Southeastern Philippines
Graham, C.C.Blended learning systems. Retrieved on September 02, 2010 from http:// media.wiley.com/ product_data/except/86/07879775/0787977586.pdf
General Primer. RA 7160: The local government code of 1991. BOOK III
Husay Balangay(2002). Local Government Academy
Joyce,P.(1999). Strategic management for the public services. Philadelphia: Open University Press
Knowles, M.S.(1990). The adult learner: a neglected series, 4th edition. Houston: Gulf Publishing Company. Book Division
Kooiman, J.(2003). Governing as governance. London: SAGE Publications, Inc.
LGU Facilitator's Manual. Barangay land use planning: resource management component. Upland Development Program in Southern Mindanao
Manual of Operations. The Philippine minimum basic needs(MBN) approach to improved quality of life
Mclendon, B.W.&Catanese, A.J.(1996).Planners on Planning, 1st edition, San Francisco: Jossey –Bass Inc
McGill, I &Beaty,L(1995). Action learning, 2nd edition, A guide for professional, management and Educational development. London: Kogan Page
Prantilla, E.B.(1998). University Manual. University of Southeastern Philippines, Davao City
Preston, P.LE Breton &Henning ,D.A.(n.d.). Planning theory. New Jersey: Prentice-Hall, Inc
RA 7160. Local government code of 1991
Rossett, Allison &Frazee, R.V.(2006). Blended learning opportunities. Retrieved on September 03, 2010 from www.grossmont.edu/don.dean/PKMS_ddean/ET95A/whitepaper_blendlearn.pdf
Strategic Plan 2007-2021. University of Southeastern Philippines, Davao City
William, R.K.& David, I.(n.d.). Strategic Planning and Policy. Cleveland

End notes

[1] The Philippines has two academic semesters in a given school year. This starts on the month of June of a given year and ends middle of October of the same year. Second semester follows after a break. Every semester, a desired 54 hours of academic works is expected for every subject course taken.

[2] This usually refers to a task or action to be undertaken like collection of data, calling offices, training, writing reports and the like.

[3] Known theorists of learning

[4] It philosophises that when the local people take an active role in the development planning process at their respective levels, the entailing development plans and activities will be most responsive to their real needs and consequently be considered most effective.

[5] Refer to footnote 2

[6] Students are assigned to different responsibilities like preparing of tool kits, hand-outs, do marketing of needed materials, approaching people in varied agencies to ask for technical help and the like.

[7] Stands for: STRENGTH, WEAKNESS, OPPORTUNITIES and THREATS; a more deliberate and friendly way of drawing different issues in the Barangay; easy approach for local people not having a technical background on planning.

[8] A process employed by the graduate students to arrange Barangay concerns and issues as identified by the participants into cause and effect relationships but in negative form.

[9] A process employed after the results of problem tree analysis but now in positive form

[10] Smallest political unit of government in the Philippines which also serve as the primary planning and implementing unit of government (local, provincial, regional and national) policies, plans, programs,

projects, and activities in the community, and as a forum wherein the collective views of the people may be expressed, crystallised and considered, and where disputes may be amicably settled.

[11] This includes PEST- political, economic, social and technological analysis of the barangay

[12] It is a mechanism where a combination of lecture and workshop takes place. Specifically as well, a certain amount of time is allotted to write up all the outputs during the workshop.

[13] Applied with innovations in choosing the participants based on secondary analysis, interview and sector represented

[14] Refer to footnote 7

[15] Refer to footnote 8

[16] Refer to footnote 9

[17] These are the methods used during the conduct of the said BDP seminar-lecture-workshop. An agreed planning model was used by the students are guidepost to effectively deliver inputs. It usually follows with lecture and later workshop approaches

CHAPTER 6

STRATEGY FOR IMPROVING HUMAN CAPITAL IN BANGLADESH AND NEPAL:
Does it help for Women Empowerment

TEK NATH DHAKAL AND FARAHA NAWAZ

Abstract

Every nation needs to have its human capital to be developed to generate employment and contribute for socio-economic transformation. Many countries adopt human capital development as a special strategy to empower their people. As the government of Bangladesh has adopted inclusive policies to enroll in the civil service and other sector, the share of women has been increased but not at expected level. Again in Nepal Major strategies developed for empowering the women were to make effective women's participation in the formulation, implementation, coordination, monitoring and evaluation of related sector policy and women targeted programs. But in reality the findings show that the governments in these countries have been trying to empower women by enhancing their capacity and adopting inclusive policies, they still are back from the mainstream development. In this context, this paper seeks the major factor that affect to enhance human capital particularly for women empowerment in these countries.

Introduction

The well-trained and experienced people help to generate employment and contribute for socio-economic growth of the country. So, development of human capital is one of the fundamentals for developing the human resources. Normally, for all types of employment - direct employment, self-employment and also for foreign employment it requires skill hands. So the different governments at national level and different organisations at organisational level try to enhance the quality of human resources. However, developing countries often could not give full fledge attention to develop the human capital, though such countries have abundant labor force. The remittance earning due to using the human capital such as in Bangladesh and Nepal is one of largest national income sources. In addition to this, development of human capital helps for women empowerment. In such countries due to many reasons they could not come forward to complete the masculine section. Though the women section comprises 50% of the total population they are still found mostly in household works or low level of unskilled works. Only a meager number are in the highly skilled and working as professional.

In this context, what strategies have been developed to enhance human capital for contributing to women empowerment in Bangladesh and Nepal has become one of the major objectives of this paper. To understand this, the available materials socio-economic status of these countries, women status, and the efforts made for developing the human capacity have been reviewed. In addition, some thirty key informants those working in the government, NGO and the academic institutions were discussed on different dimension of human capital development, policy aspects and some pertinent bottlenecks that hinders for developing the human capital in relation to the women empowerment. Hence this study tries to analyze the human capital development which helps for empowering human capital especially among the women.

Concept of Human capital

The importance of human capital is not only a new phenomena but also in the ancient days as well. A Chinese proverb says "To plan one year, saw seed; to plan ten years, plant trees; and to plan 100 years, develop human resources". It shows that the development of human capital is not only a short term strategy, but it should be looked from the long term perspective. The definition human capital used by Peter Husz **(1998:9)** is: "By human capital we mean the time, experience, knowledge and abilities of an individual household or a generation, which can be used in the production process". Thus, there is no reason not to believe that human capital consists of a much larger number of components, which may be routine, age, wisdom, self-esteem and so many others. 'Human capital' can also be understood as "..a process of learning, a sequence of programmed behavior. It is application of knowledge. It gives people an awareness of the rules and procedures to guide their behavior. It attempts to improve their performance on the current job and prepare them for an intended job (Mamoria, 1984, 11). Thus, it tries to enhance the capacity by changing the behaviours. It is also concerned with preparing employees to work effectively and efficiently in the organisation (DeCenzo and Robbins, 1998). In general it helps to develop specific type skilled persons in required number; fulfill the demand of skilled human resources; support industrial expansion; strengthen economic growth; increase enthusiasm in working condition; develop desired attitude of the people; and enhance entrepreneurial abilities, etc.

The process of empowerment could play vital role for enhancing human capital especially among the women. Empowerment is perceived as occurring from below or from within, as marginalised individuals and groups become able to organise themselves and their resources to contest unequal structures and define their own place in the wider context of their lives. It is also indicated as an outcome in which a person or group enjoys a state of empowerment, and also as a process that moves a group or person from a lower to a higher state of empowerment (Mette, Bertelsen and Holland, 2006). There are four-features of women's empowerment- resources, relationship, power and perception (Chen, 1990 cited in Haider and Akhtar, 1999). Malhotra et al. (2002: 13) on the other hand considers three important dimensions of women's empowerment such as socio-economic dimension, familial dimension, and psychological dimension. So it is an internal process of women's life. Economic liberation and greater mobility have shaped self-esteem, self-confidence, self-respect, self-reliance and courage to face torment among the women (Khanum, 2001). To be empowered, women must have clear perception regarding their own values and ability. So the relationship between human capital and women empowerment is important.

Socio-Economic Status of Bangladesh and Nepal

In the South Asian Region, Bangladesh and Nepal place at the bottom of the development status. These countries are characterised by high poverty and high population growth. The economy is overwhelmingly agricultural, with the cultivation of rice (in case of Bangladesh) and rice, maize, millet, etc., (in Nepal) are the important source which contribute their economy. In this globalisation era these countries face enormous challenges for competing in the international context. The major impediments of Bangladesh economy include natural disasters such as flood where as Nepal's problem is landslides and flood as well. Both of these countries have weak political structure. Nepal faces even worse due to decade long violence and continued political instability which affect to make aggressive economic plan, program and its successful implementation.

The socio-economic status of these countries gives somehow similar picture as HDI value of Bangladesh is 0.524 and of Nepal 0.530 (see Box A). Nearly half of the adult population is still illiterate and life expectancy just around 63 years. The women literacy rate is only around 60% of the male literacy rate. Due to the fast growing population, the unemployment has also become problem. Of the total unemployed nearly half of the population is underemployed of which two-third are among the agriculture labours.

It is conceivable that Bangladesh is trying to utilise its manpower and even women now play a massive role to make the economy better, which is a major shift in terms of country's socio-economic structure. Bangladesh economic culture is characterised by domination of some major sectors like garments, industries, fisheries etc., and one notable aspects of Bangladesh economy is utilisation of social capital that is also a distinctive feature of Bangladesh culture. But in Nepal, Tourism, carpet, garment, etc., are the major non-farm economic activities. There is no doubt that Bangladesh economy is doing better than ever and there have been some major trends in Bangladesh to compete with outside world to meet the requirements of globalisation. In addition, remittance has become one of the contributory segments in Bangladesh and Nepal. As an agricultural country Bangladesh has also achieved steady increases in food grain production including better flood control and irrigation, a generally more efficient use of fertilizers, and the establishment of better distribution and rural credit networks. In recent decade, Bangladesh economy has been shifted to industrial sector. Bangladeshi garments and knitwear export to U.S. and the EU market has been in the rising trend.

Woman Status in Bangladeshi Context

Women constitute about half of the population in Bangladesh but traditionally, majority of them are disadvantaged, underprivileged, illiterate and poor Though nonagricultural sector has been coming up aggressively in Bangladesh, culture does not permit rural women to go out and work with other people. They need ideal environment in the various garments where they work and make a positive contribution for their families and also for the country. Many new jobs of nearly 1.5 million have been created mostly for women by the country's private ready-made garment industry, which grew at double-digit rates through most of the 1990s (see Table 1).

TABLE 1: Percentage of male/female in each sector and in total labor force in Bangladesh

Sector	% of each sector		% of total labor		Total
	Male	Female	Male	Female	(1000s)
Agriculture	54	46	77	53	32,170
Manufacturing	62	38	7	7	3,782
Services	80	20	40	16	12,156
Total	63	37	100	100	51,497

Source: Khan, Farida C (2005), "Gender violence and development in Bangladesh", International Social Science Journal, Vol. 57, Issue. 02, pp. 219-230)

Bangladeshi women face two-fold realities in their lifetime: one determined by a culture and tradition that tends to keep them inside family homesteads and the other is fashioned by increasing poverty that forces them outside into wage employment like building construction labor work or road construction for economic survival. For social and cultural constraints it has been a great challenge for Bangladeshi women to represent them in various sectors of economy of Bangladesh. However, the women in Bangladesh are relatively low in service sector compared to male section.

Woman Status in Nepalese Context

Nepal has been constrained by low socio-economic development due to various reasons such as traditional social value, primitive farming technology, lack of skill, and meager income level. As a result, people from the low income bracket, including the women, could not come onto the forefront of the development process. It is also conceivable that the women still face some oppression that keeps them inside family homesteads.

The educational statistics show that only 55% of the adults are literate in Nepal, of which women's share is almost half of the male literacy rate. Similarly, women's participation in civil service, Government, Parliament, Judicial system is also very low (see Box B). Despite making bigger contribution to agriculture production, women's share in ownership of property is insignificant. As a general practice, socio-economic condition of women in rural areas is much vulnerable than in the urban areas. However, illiteracy and low level of income are common features among the adult and elderly women in the urban areas as well. To break this situation, both government organisations and NGOs have come forward with synergic efforts following the government's adoption of government-NGO partnership policy in the national development plans since the early 1990s. The aftermath of people's movement in 2006, the inclusion of Women in various governmental positions including in Constituent Assembly have been reserved for 33 percent (Law Book Management Committee 2007). This has bring a change for bringing women in governance process and helpful to empower them.

Discussion on the Efforts of Human Capital Development for Women Empowerment

This study focuses that since the last decade the traditional views of women have been changed quite remarkably and women contribute to a larger extent to Bangladesh economy. However, gender related issues in Nepal and Bangladesh are to equality in job opportunity, equal intellectual opportunity, women exploitation, exploitation against girls, discrimination on legal right, and social and gender inequalities, etc.

Major outcomes

It is conceivable that the share of rural women in total employed population in Bangladesh rose from 9 percent to 13 percent since the late 1980s (Mizan 1994). It also indicates that rural women have been involving themselves in market based economic activities like garments sector at a pace that is growing much faster than that of men. Various non-governmental organisations like Bangladesh Rural Advance Committee (BRAC), CARE are now working in Bangladesh focusing on the empowerment on women. As the government has adopted inclusive policies to enroll in the civil service and other sector, the share of women has been dramatically increased. Participation in different entrepreneurial activities has empowered women in social, economic and cultural fields. Now the power and access in taking decision of their own has increased in economic and household matters for women in third world countries like Bangladesh. They are now much more self confident than before. Women are much organised as they have learned about different rights. But the indicators of women development still show a pathetic picture despite all the rhetoric. Another important indicator of women empowerment is political participation which is not widely seen among Bangladeshi women entrepreneurs. Economic emancipation and greater mobility women can achieve a higher degree of decision-making power in every aspect including our politics.

Since the recent past there has been a great interest in participation in paid employment and within the household and wider society in Bangladesh. Traditionally, women's mobility from home to outside arena is highly restricted by social norms and cultural practices; especially rural women generally have little freedom of movement. Women entrepreneurs are mobilizing their social capital and can found a quarter of all women are self-employed or engaged various activities in urban areas as a result of greater economic opportunities available in the cities. Among informal sector activities, women mostly sell groceries, betel nut, soft drinks, snacks, sweetmeats, country cakes etc., in small roadside shops. These women merely migrated from rural areas engage these economic activities. They also go door to door to sell ash, soap, bangles, etc. It is conceivable that the women earners are disadvantaged in terms of their monthly income. The average monthly income of men was Tk[1]. 2,073 ($30.94) compared to just Tk. 686 ($10.23) for women (Salway, Jesmin & Rahman 2005). However, right now some sectors in urban areas do offer greater monthly income for women that allow women make positive contribution to household and to nation's economy.

In urban areas there are many sectors offering job opportunities for rural women. Rural women do not have text -book knowledge, but they also have potentiality to make contribution to the nation's economy and they also make contribution to reducing poverty from our country through their employment in urban areas. Rural women do not have higher certificates, but they can easily get employment in various garments sector with little training. To promote women's entrepreneurial activities, MIDAS (Micro Industries Development Assistance Society) instituted a Women Entrepreneurship Development Committee headed by a leading women entrepreneur of the country. This committee helps women to start businesses by offering collateral free loans. At monthly meetings, women' entrepreneurs are given counseling on various aspects of business activities (Banglapedia) The Grameen Bank[2] of Bangladesh formally began operating as a specialised credit institution in 1983, although its history can be traced back to an innovative pilot project that began in 1976. The bank gives small-business loans to the poorest of the rural poor on a group liability basis instead of requiring any collateral. Because they have no collateral, the Grameen Bank borrowers do not have access to conventional sources of credit. The loan and the accrued interest are repayable in small weekly installments over a period of one year. The bank also provides comprehensive investment advice to its clients and helps them generate savings for themselves. The most distinctive feature of the Grameen Bank is that 95 percent of its borrowers are women. As of August 1998, out of a total of 2,357,153 borrowers, 2,232,905 were female. Thus Grameen Bank has virtually become an exclusively female-based organisation in Bangladesh. Even though women have shown themselves to be adept at saving and are highly creative entrepreneurs, their access in financial services is often made more difficult gender discrimination. It is plausible that the greatest obstacle women face is the lack of capital required for building the permanent structure of the enterprise, labor savings tool to ease domestic burden, and raw materials and growth enhancing machineries needed to increase productivity in their enterprises (Islam, 2007). It is conceivable that many NGOs along with some financial institutions like Grameen Bank merely work rural women to provide with them all sorts of support to start small-scale enterprises. Now women make up 80 percent of the clients of the thirty-four largest micro lenders (Islam, 2007). These institutions encourage women to take credit without any interest. Since rural women do not have much access to other resources, so they are encouraged by the credit system of these institutions. Rural women can start small scale business with these credit and can contribute to household income that allow them to live a healthy and happily life and it also allow them to spend money for the better education of their children

It is conceivable that the women in Bangladesh now play in dominant role in labor market. Since majority of women live in villages, the agriculture sector has greater percent women workforce. 77% of total female labor force and 53% of total male labor force were absorbed in agriculture in 2000. Bangladesh civil service has a certain quota for women in civil service and even Bangladesh National Parliament has certain seats for women for better representation. The Bangladeshi women civil servants do hold the attitude that indicate that these women can bringing about a transformational rather than a transactional style and consequently, the women represent a number of department of civil service, which in Bangladesh extends to local administration (Wilson 2000).

In early 1980s, the number of women's share in bureaucracy, and other sector in Nepal was less than 10% which rose to around 20% at present. However, they are still far behind than male population. The Interim Constitution 2007 in Nepal made a mandatory provision for having one-third of the Constituent Assembly members should be among the women. It opens the doors for bringing women participation across the country and from among different ethnic minorities and also the *dalits* at the law making apex body. Nepal has also developed a policy to empower women and for making gender equality in different spheres of lives. For this, women empowerment, gender equality and mainstreaming are felt necessary to include in the objectives as well as programs of different line ministries. The 10th Plan (2002/07) aimed to create egalitarian society based upon women's rights by improving GDI and by abolishing all form of discriminations against women for the realisation of economic growth and poverty eradication. More specifically it aimed to raise up to 0.55 GDI, 0.50 GEM and 20% participation in policy development. Major strategies developed for empowering the women were (NPC, 2003):

o   Make effective women's participation in the formulation, implementation, coordination, monitoring and evaluation of related sector policy and women targeted programs;
o   Increase women's participation in every aspects of projects relating to poverty alleviation and income generating;
o   Increase awareness of gender equality at all groups and levels; and
o   Make amendment in the laws discriminating women on the basis of equity and international commitment.

Three areas of programs such as mainstreaming, empowerment and gender quality were designed to empower the women section in Nepal (NPC, 2002: 522-3).

o   <u>Mainstreaming</u> – setting-up gender resource center; formulation of national action plan mainstreaming and development of women, develop reproductive health care service, assessing women's share in agriculture development, and training.
o   <u>Empowerment</u> – increasing women's participation at all levels of political administrative, technical service, and constitutional bodies and committees; establishing coordination with the concerned ministries for arranging special programs, networks develop for training, leadership quality, capacity building, scholarship arrangement, etc
o   <u>Gender equality</u> – improvement in existing legal system, awareness building on their rights, provide compensation, counseling service medical treatment, legal advice and rehabilitation and re-integration for the survivors of domestic violence, trafficking and other types of activities.

Taking into account the women's engagement in informal sector, subsistence and domestic labour, without wage or with low wage the Interim plan (2007/10) aims for reaching Gender Empowerment Measurement (GEM) from 0.520 to 0.556; women receiving delivery assistance from health worker from 23.4% to 35%; women's participation in overall state machinery to 33%; and participation of men and women in labour is 67.6 and 48.9% respectively (NPC, 2007: 100-10). In addition, NGOs are also coming up to with different programs to empower women. Their major programs include training, awareness building, saving-credit, and income generation. Altogether around 3,000 NGOs have been working for women empowerment activities.

To augment the women status in Nepal the Civil Code (11th amendment) in 2003 has been passed in an effort to abolish discrimination against women. This amendment also highlights on right of woman to property, abortion, sexual exploitation, minimum marriage age and marriage and divorce. In addition, formation of high level committee to review all type of legal discrimination against women, setting up the Women section in all the ministries is another important effort to enhance women empowerment in Nepal. Nepal has also constituted National Women Commission and prepared national work plan for gender equality and women empowerment in line with Beijing Work Plan. As a result almost 40,000 women have been elected in the local level election. The present Constituent Assembly comprises to one-third of the members which is considered as a big departure to enhance the capacity of women in Nepal. Similarly, improvement in civil service act to create more job opportunity for women is another outcome of empowering women.

Major challenges

Despite improvement in the human capacity building especially of women empowerment, the sector still faces number of problems. Both social and economic issues contributed to left out from the mainstream development of this section of population. Some of the problems/challenges related to gender development in Nepal are (based on discussion with key informants Sep. 2009):

o   condition of women has become deplorable due to armed conflict and displacement
o   opportunities of livelihood at the local level have been lost,
o   agreement to check cross-border human trafficking still does not exist,
o   labor exploitation by the informal and unorganised sector goes unabated and exposure to such risks in imminent
o   there is an increasing feminisation of poverty,
o   the social status of women still consider is low, and
o   use of women labor for income generating activities is not yet a reality

On the other hand, Bangladeshi societies and culture have some specific issues that increase poverty and consequently make the economy slower. As a result a variety of complexes are found among the potential workers which restrain to do manual labor and an insistence on its own dignity (Ali, Ashraf; Kuddus, Ruhul & Andaleeb, Saad Syed 2003). The impact of such complexes could be seen among the young students could not work in college cafeteria or any other restaurants. Bringing women in such public places is even challenging due to the various forms of complexes and discriminations. Bangladesh's traditional normative family system does not allow women to work freely. Women can get power and status, but they remain dependent on men throughout life cycles (Kibria 1995). The social stigma and the value system often become hurdle to bring them in the forefront of development. In addition, average Bangladeshi people are relatively less productive due to the extreme poverty and inadequate access to health services. Even though the present growth rate is declining, the overall growth rate of population for Bangladesh is alarming. Since most of the rural people of Bangladesh are illiterate, rural people do not know the importance of using contraception, which allows high growth rate. These all factors result low productivity of average people of Bangladesh. Still women in Bangladesh engaged in non-monetised sector and in subsistence activities. This is mainly due to lack of enhancement of empowerment efforts to the women.

Conclusion

The government in Bangladesh and Nepal has been coming up to create more opportunity for women as well in the socio-economic process. Experience shows that the combine efforts of government and NGO intervention have been able to motivate the women into socio-economic activities. As a result the number of women participation in the economic activities and governance has been increasing. The inclusive policies adopted in legal instruments, prioritizing the women empowerment programs and projects at public and nonprofit level such as in Nepal found helpful to bring more women in the development process. It is also evident that girl enrollment at primary, secondary and tertiary level has been increasing in these countries which contributes to develop human capital. Creating more opportunities to access financial and other resources can also be found helpful to empower the women. However, women's skill development, entrepreneurial abilities, and their involvement in organised sectors in Bangladesh are still far behind compared to men. Due to the traditional social, cultural and religious values often restrain the people particularly the women to work freely particularly in rural areas. The efforts at various levels and by different sectors are not enough to make them fully self-reliant and self-sustaining. One of the important aspects to be taken into consideration is that skill and know-how, which are critical for human capital development are needed for empowering the women in these countries. It can be said that promoting the greater participation of women in decision-making continue to be a formidable challenge. As both governmental and non-governmental organisations have been adopting inclusive policy and also programs for enhancing the capacity of women has been slowly getting success which ultimately contribute in enhancing human capital.

References

Ahmed, Erfan Fauzia (2004), "The Rise of the Bangladesh Garment Industry: Globalization, Women Workers, and Voice", *NWSA Journal*, Vol. 16, Issue. 02, pp. 34-45 Ali, Ashraf; Kuddus, Ruhul & Andaleeb, Saad Syed (Eds) (2003), "*Development Issues of Bangladesh II*" (Dhaka) Bangladesh Development Initiative- The University Press Limited. ADB (2001), "Country Briefing Paper: Women in Bangladesh", (Manila) Asian Development Bank, Program Department West.

Alauddin, Mohammad & Hossain, Mosharaff (2001), "*Environment and Agriculture in a Developing economy: Problems and Prospects for Bangladesh*" Journal of International Development, Vol. 16, Issue. 01, pp. 40-45

Bhuiyan, Ali Farhad (2002), "Information Technology for Economic and Social Benefit- Options for Bangladesh", *the International Information and Library Review*, Vol. 34, Issue. 03. Banglapedia: National Encyclopedia of Bangladesh, "NGO",
http://banglapedia.org/HT/N_0204.HTM Retrieved on April 20, 2007

Banglapedia: National Encyclopedia of Bangladesh, "Women",
http://banglapedia.org/HT/W_0067.HTM Retrieved on April 20, 2007

Bernasek, Alexandra (2003), "Banking on Social Change: Grameen Bank Lending to Women", *International Journal of Politics, Culture and Society*, Vol. 16, Issue. 03, pp. 369-385

Cavendish, Marshall (2005), "*Peoples of Eastern Asia: Volume 1: Bangladesh – Brunei*", New York Library of Congress

CBS, 2002 *Statistical Year Book 2002.* Kathmandu: Central Bureau of Statistics

Chowdhury, R. Mahfuz (2005), "Why Developing Countries like Bangladesh Remain Poor", Expatriate Bangladeshi 2000, http://www.eb2000.org/short_note_24.htm Retrieved on February 08, 2007

Dhakal, Tek Nath (2007): "Changing Women Status in Nepal: A Case of Dhalachhe Women Saving-credit Group in Lalitpur Sub-metropolis of Patan District" In: *Administrative Souvenir* Kathmandu: Free Student Union, Public Administration Campus, October, pp. 11-12

Dhakal, Tek Nath (2008): "Government-Civil Society Collaboration to Combat Trafficking in Women and

Children in Nepal". In: Deguchi, Masa, Govind P. Dhakal, Tek Nath Dhakal (Eds.). *Conflicts vs. Social Harmony: Does Nonprofit Sector Matter?* Tokyo: Aggreplanning. pp. 63-84.

DeCenzo, David A. and Stephen P.Robbins 1998, *Personnel/Human Resource management*, 3rd edition

Islam, Tazul(2007), "*Micro Credit and Poverty Alleviation*", Ashgate Publishing Limited

Hossain, Mohammad A. & Tisdell, Clement A (2005), "closing the gender in Bangladesh: inequality in education, employment and earnings", *International Journal of Social Science*, Vol. 32, Issue. 05, pp. 439-453

Mamoria, C.B. (1984): *Personnel Management and Industrial Relations.* New Delhi: Himalaya Publishing House.

Martin Husz, "*Human Capital, Endogenous Growth, and Government Policy*", Peter Lang GmbH, Frankfurt am Main, 1998, pp9

Kibria, Nazli (1995), "Culture, Social Class, and Income Control in the Lives of Women Garment Workers in Bangladesh", *Gender & Society*, Vol. 09, Issue. 03, pp. 289-309.

Kabeer, Naila & Mahmud, Simeen (2004), "Globalization, Gender and Poverty: Bangladesh Women Workers in Export and Local Markets", Journal of International Development, Vol. 16, Issue. 01, pp. 93-109

Khan, Farida C (2005), "Gender Violence and Development in Bangladesh", *International Social Science Journal*, Vol. 57, Issue. 02, pp. 219-230

Law Book Management Committee (2007) *The Interim Constitution of Nepal.* Kathmandu Law Book Management Committee Mette, Ruth Alsop Frost Bertelsen Jeremy Holland (2006) *Empowerment in Practice From*

Analysis to Implementation. Washington, DC: The International Bank for Reconstruction and Development/ The World Bank

Mizan, Nahar Ainon (1994), "*In Quest of Empowerment: the Grameen Bank Impact on Women's Power and Status*", The University Press Limited

Norton, H.K. James (2004), "*Global Studies: India and South Asia,* India, McGraw- Hill/Dushkin Company.

NPC, 2003. The Tenth Plan (2002-07). Kathmandu: National Planning Commission

NPC, 2007. Three Year Interim Plan (2007/08-1009/2010). Kathmandu: National Planning Commission

Onlinewomenplitics.org, "Women's right in Bangladesh", Retrieved April 15, 2007 from, http://www.onlinewomeninpolitics.org/womensit/bd-w-sit.pdf

Rahman, Shahidur(2004), "Global Shift: Bangladesh Garment Industry in Perspective", *Asian Affair*, Vol. 26, No. 01, pp. 75-91, http://www.cdrb.org/journal/2004/1/3.pdf Retrieved on April 13, 2007

Solaiman, Mohammad & Belal, Rahman Ataur (1999), "An Account of the Sustainable Development Process in Bangladesh", *Sustainable Development*, Vol. 07, Issue. 03, pp. 121-131

Salway, Sarah; Jesmin, Sonia & Rahman, Shahana (2005), "Women's Employment in Urban Bangladesh: A Challenge to Gender Identity?", *Development and Change*, Vol. 36, Issue. 02, pp. 317-349

The World Fact Book, "Bangladesh", http://www.cia.gov/cia/publications/factbook/geos/bg.html#Peopleht Retrieved April 20, 2007

CHAPTER 7

DOES INTERNATIONAL MIGRATION INDUCE HUMAN CAPITAL INVESTMENT AND KNOWLEDGE TRANSFER?
Evidence from the Philippines

Eduardo T. Gonzalez

Abstract

This paper scrutinises the impact of international migration on human capital accumulation in the Philippines as a source country. Recent views have suggested that international migration generates net fiscal and social benefits on those remaining behind. The findings suggest a mixture of favourable effects and smaller gains. Remittances posted by Filipino migrants relax constraints on health and schooling investment. Greater competition for the "emigration slots" leads to increases in the country's stock of human capital. But the Philippines is clearly struggling with underdeveloped diaspora networks and inadequate support for return migrants. All these are taking place in an institutional environment of a "soft state", indicating the immense challenges that the Philippine authorities face as they try to install better governance approaches to manage the consequences (especially on knowledge transfer) of migrant flows, and put in place solid policy measures with regard to the strengthening of diasporas, the facilitation of remittance flows, and establishing incentives for highly-skilled returnees.

Introduction

The Philippines is among a number of Asian countries that have engaged in the export of labour. The skill export strategy is presumed to be constructive to the extent that it sets off positive induced and feedback effects, especially in human capital accumulation.

Accordingly, this paper scrutinises the impact of both flows (emigration) and stocks (diasporas) on human capital accumulation in the Philippines as a source country, and the range of governance approaches available to the Philippine authorities to manage the consequences (especially on human capital build-up) of those flows.

Following Brown (2000), each country invests in the development of skills and competencies through training and education and looks ahead to a dividend when the individual becomes economically active and starts paying taxes. But in a context where migration encourages a transfer of human capital from a relatively poor source country to developed receiving countries, especially in key sectors such as education, health, communication and industry, the widely-held view is that the outflow of skilled workers can depress domestic productivity, inflict substantial long-run harm by slowing endogenous economic growth and increase inequality as the earnings of the remaining highly skilled workers rise and those of the less skilled fall (ESCAP, 2005, Todaro and Smith, 2006). However, this "pessimistic" perspective is based on a number of critical assumptions: migrants self-select out of the general population, there is no uncertainty on migration opportunities, and there is complete disconnection after emigration (Rapoport, 2008).

Recent views are more optimistic. Waving the above listed assumptions allows for potentially direct favourable effects and positive externalities to kick-in: migrants may return after a while, embodying a brain grain; the decision to seek education may be made in a context of uncertainty regarding future migration possibilities; and skilled migrants may post remittances—a major source of disposable income that can relax credit constraints on human and physical capital investment (Rapoport, 2008).

Kapur and McHale (2005) propose analyzing four channels—prospect, absence, diaspora, and return, to understand the issue. However, the absence channel, which focuses the "emigration surplus"—the costs on those remaining at home when skilled individuals leave—is not taken up, for lack of data. There is a dearth of estimates of any losses imposed (Lucas, 2001). Instead, the provision channel, which draws attention to the role of remittances, is added in the analysis.

- The *prospect* channel captures the way in which emigration affects the decision-making of people in the sending country, whether or not they truly end up leaving. In particular the prospect of emigration heightens the incentive to acquire more education. This is illustrated by the enormous increase in nursing education in the Philippines (Kapur and McHale, 2005). This channel affects decisions on types of skill acquisition.
- The *diaspora* channel discusses the rise of entrepreneurial migrant networks critical for linking domestic residents to skilled expatriates who use their accumulated knowledge to invest in home-country projects. They are not well developed but are likely to have significant long-term consequences for human capital development.
- The *return* channel looks at how emigrants coming home with augmented capital—financial and human—can affect the domestic knowledge industry differently than if they had never left.
- The *provision* channel checks out how remittance transfers promote access to educational and health services for the recipients, thereby increasing economic and social inclusion.

The purpose of this paper is to look into these key channels through which international skilled migration affects human capital in the Philippines.

Stock and flows of migratory Filipino human capital

Asia hosts one of the world's largest labour exporting countries, the Philippines. Among the most widely dispersed diasporas, Filipino migrants range from the less skilled to the highly skilled. A majority of Filipino overseas workers, as they are called, are under fixed term contracts in the Middle East, while a small number of permanent emigrants tend to go to North America (see Figure 1). Four-tenths of the permanent outflow is college educated, and their numbers go above the net change of skilled workers in the country (Lowell and Findlay, 2001). In 2007, the number of higher-paid and skilled workers such as those working in the medical, healthcare, information technology, food and hotel services continued to rise, notwithstanding the decline in the number of professional workers (Bayangos and Jansen, 2009). The Philippines keeps on exporting its skilled workers despite a very high proportion of the country's workers already being abroad (Yavuzer, 2008).

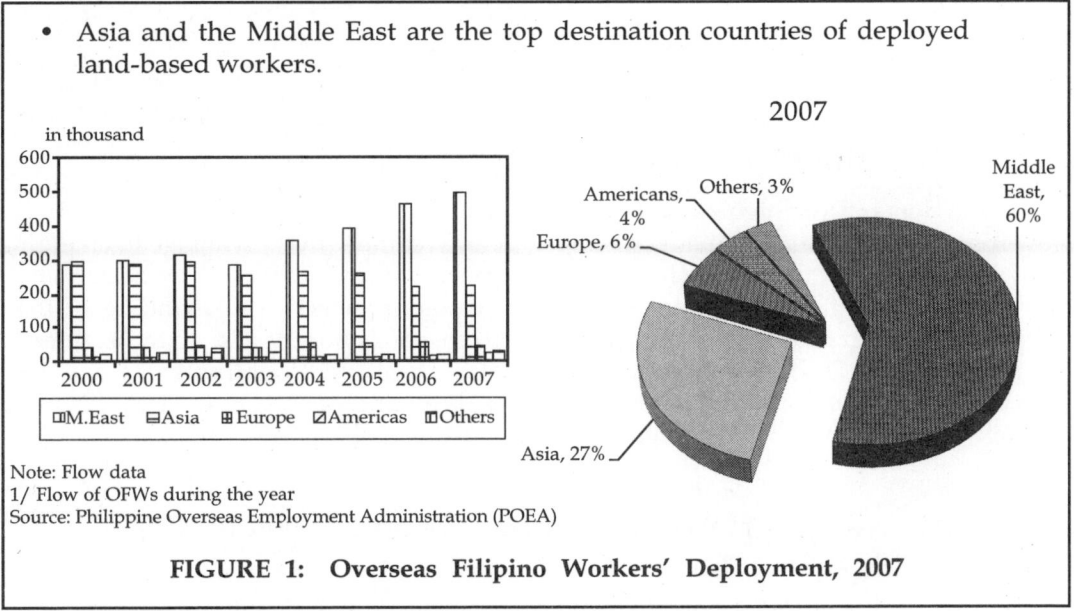

FIGURE 1: Overseas Filipino Workers' Deployment, 2007

As for the stock of Filipinos working outside, their numbers have grown to at least 7 million and upwards of 10 million if unauthorised migrants were counted (see Figure 2). OECD data suggest that among developing countries, the Philippines has the highest emigration stocks of university-educated expatriates (over one million) in high-income economies (Docquier and Marfouk, 2006, Kuznetsov and Sabel, 2006). However, the fraction working in science and engineering occupations is notably low among scientists and engineers from the Philippines. Likewise, presumably because many of the Filipino graduates are trained outside the US, their qualifications do not receive a high level of recognition among US employers (Lucas, 2001). There could even be deskilling as skilled and educated migrants take on jobs that are below their skill levels (Asis, 2006).

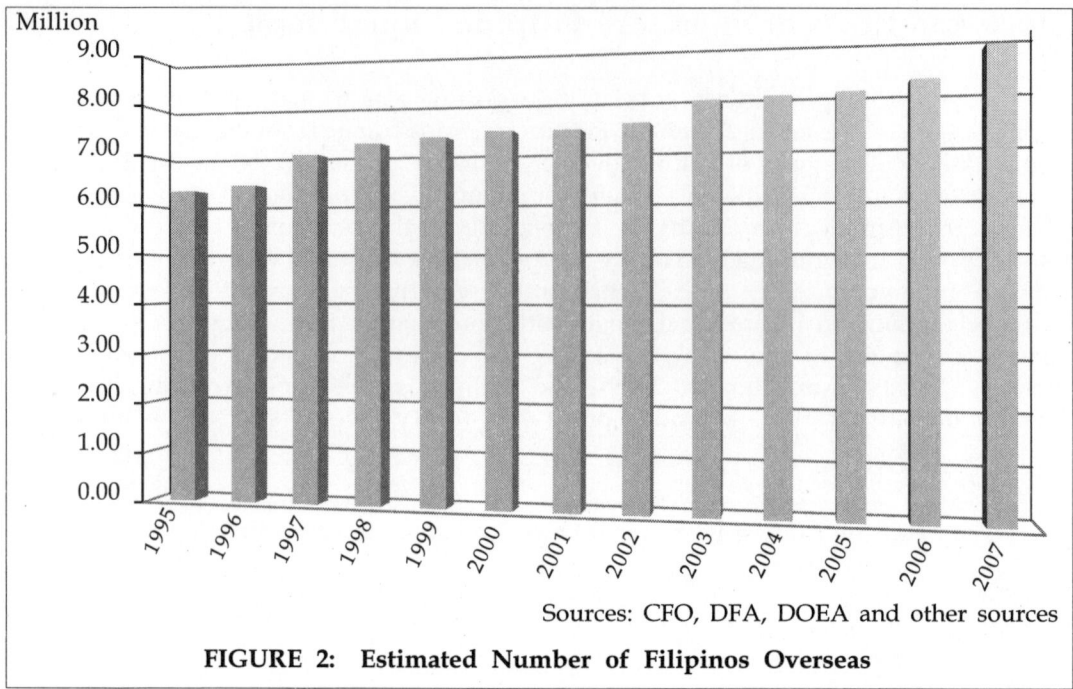
FIGURE 2: Estimated Number of Filipinos Overseas
Sources: CFO, DFA, DOEA and other sources

The demand for high skilled migrants will likely continue. Developed country governments are concerned about creating a national competitive advantage in emerging knowledge-based industries (such as ICT) that face a shortage of workers with specialised skills. As a result, rich countries will likely engage in selective dismantling of their barriers to immigration of the highly skilled from poor countries, despite heightened security concerns (Desai, Kapur and McHale, 2001). Developed countries will also permit a greater scale of immigration to relieve the fiscal pressures of aging societies. This trend is likely to hike demand for service providers (Kapur and McHale, 2005).

Provision: How do flows of remittances and flows of skills interact with each other?

Remittances are an important feature of migration as they provide a considerable share of a developing country's income. Remittances support private households directly; by contrast, official development assistance and foreign direct investment are supplied at the country level (Steinweg, 2006). In the Philippines, remittances from overseas Filipino workers have risen sharply (see Figure 3): as of end-December 2007, they have reached US$14.5 billion, the highest level since the 1980s (Bayangos and Jansen, 2009), making the country the fourth (India is first) among the top ten recipients in 2007 (Yavuzer, 2008).

Anecdotal evidence suggests that migrants' financial transfers add to family incomes and help pay for education and health costs, thus improving human capital. Remittances likely offset the original investment on education, when the transfer of savings on income earned abroad outweighs the income that would have been earned at home (weighted by the probability of being employed in the country of origin).

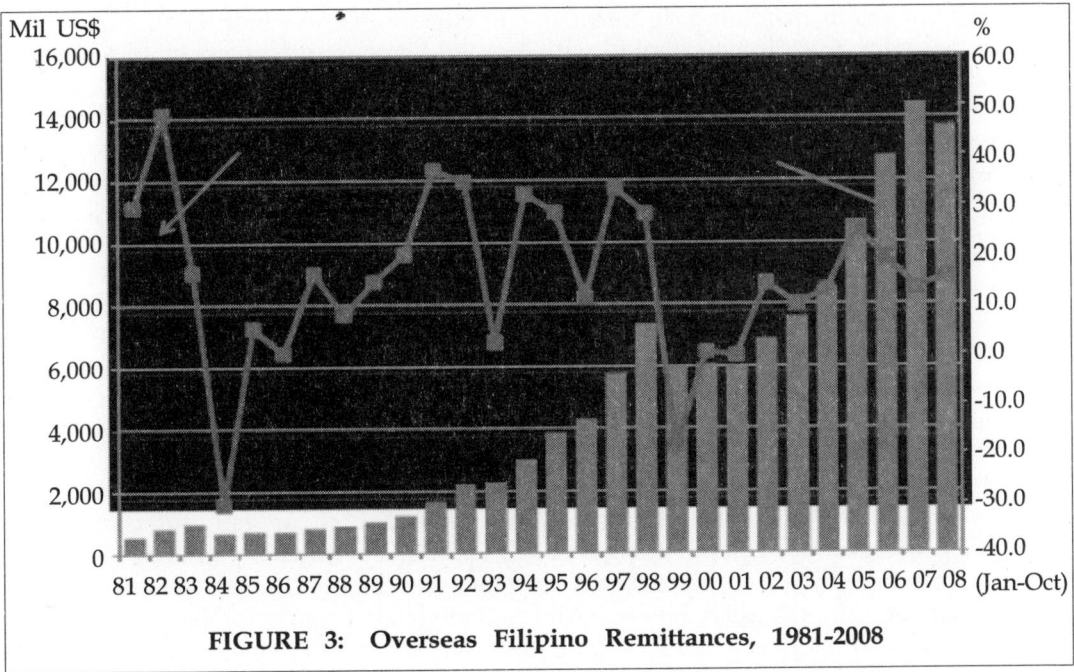

FIGURE 3: Overseas Filipino Remittances, 1981-2008

Asis (2003), cited in Yang 2009, finds that across the Philippines, children in migrant families are noticeably better off than non-migrant families along a number of socio-economic outcomes such as household income and schooling. Also, migrants' remittances have sent children to more expensive private schools (Asis, 2006) and provided emergency health needs (Aldaba and Opinionado, undated). Tullao, Cortez and See (2007), cited in Orbeta (2008), find larger responses on education expenditures to changes in income among remittance-receiving households. Panel data on 15 Philippine regions for the years 1994, 1997, 2000, and 2003 show that remittances add appreciably to regional development through increased spending for consumption, human capital and housing investments, and consequent multiplier effects. However, because the more advanced regions tend to get bigger shares of the total, remittances may contribute to regional disparities (Pernia, 2006). Tabuga (2007) cited in Orbeta (2008), shows similar results using the 2003 Family Income and Expenditure Survey: since richer households are known to spend more on education and health, remittances maybe adding to rising inequality on human capital expenditure across households.

Remittances received by households are potentially endogenous to human capital decisions and child labour supply. When faced with unexpected income shocks and liquidity constraints, at least in the short term, remittances serve as insurance mechanism (especially when fixed costs have to be paid in advance) in order to maintain school enrolment in response to these shocks (Calero, Bedi and Sparrow, 2008). Thus, migration may also be considered as household strategy to manage risk.

Yang and Martínez (2005), using a survey of Filipino households, exploit it successfully. They find that unanticipated exogenous increases in remittances caused by favourable exchange rate shocks raise non-consumption disbursements in several areas likely to be investment-related (in particular in educational expenditures), and lead to entrepreneurship in origin households, with less child labour and greater child schooling. Yang (2008) indicates that an improvement in the migrant's exchange rate of 25% against the Philippine peso leads to a 3.3 percentage point increase in the likelihood of girls attending school; at the same time, boys do experience a statistically significant reduction in mean hours worked per week. In other words, remittances increase the likelihood of being a student as the main activity and decrease the hours worked in the past week for children 10-17 years (Yang, 2009).

Prospect: Feedback effects on domestic education

There is a great deal of anecdotal evidence that greater competition for the "emigration slots" leads to increases in overall investments in human capital accumulation as individuals attempt to distinguish themselves from others vying for jobs abroad (Pozo, 2008); when this incentive effect dominates, the home country can gain (Rapoport, 2008; Kuhna and McAusland, 2009; Leipziger, 2008; Fan and Stark, 2007). That is, migration induces a mechanical increase in educational attainments even if migration propensities are constant across education levels. Alternatively, the number of people acquiring education who are unable to migrate gives the country a higher stock of human capital after emigration is netted out. This also suggests that an optimal level of emigration (greater than none but not too much) exists: at a sufficiently high volume of skilled emigration, the share of skilled workers in the source country can be regenerated (Lowell and Findlay, 2001).

In a cross section of some 120 developing countries, Beine, Defoort and Docquier (2006) made use of counterfactual experiments to evaluate the effect of skilled migration on the average level of schooling remaining in the origin country. Using a two-step regression procedure (first, test for the ex-ante effect—how many more invest in education; second, get the ex-post net effect—how many remain in the home country), they find (1) a positive effect of migration on gross (pre-migration) human capital formation, and (2) an overall absolute gain for developing countries in the number of skilled persons.

TABLE 1: Observed and steady state levels of human capital in some *origin* countries, 2000

	h(2000)	h(ss)	h'(2000)	h'(ss)
Malaysia	7.5%	7.3%	8.2%	8.0%
Thailand	11.3%	12.1%	11.1%	12.0%
Philippines	22.2%	21.9%	24.5%	24.0%
Vietnam	3.8%	4.0%	4.9%	5.2%
Indonesia	5.0%	6.1%	5.1%	6.3%
India	4.8%	4.7%	5.0%	4.8%

Observed and steady state levels of human capital in some *destination* countries, 2000

United States	51.3%	50.4%	51.3%	49.6%
UAE	12.5%	12.6%	12.6%	12.7%
Italy	8.7%	8.7%	9.1%	9.1%
Singapore	10.6%	12.3%	12.0%	14.3%
Saudi Arabia	12.5%	12.3%	12.6%	12.3%

Note: h(2000) = residents' proportion observed in 2000; h'(2000) = residents' proportion observed in 2000 with counterfactual emigration rates; h(ss) = steady state residents' proportion with observed skilled emigration rates; h'(ss) = steady state residents' proportion with counterfactual emigration rates.
Source: Beine, Defoort and Docquier, 2006

A selective country-by-country analysis yields Table 1, which shows that in low-income countries (Vietnam, Indonesia) and high-income countries (Italy, Malaysia), migration does not induce any incentive effect on human capital formation (the percentages are low). Hence, slowing skilled migration does not have an effect on natives' choice and cuts human capital losses. These countries would evidently gain from reducing the human capital flight. But in some other countries, like the Philippines and Thailand (both origin countries) as well as Saudi Arabia, Singapore and the US (all destination countries), the gains are quite significant, indicating that both sending and receiving countries benefit from skilled emigration.

Anecdotal evidence in the Philippines somewhat confirms the empirical findings: the choice of major fields of study (medicine, nursing, maritime training) among Filipino students responds to shift in international demand (Docquier, Faye & Pestieau, 2008). The expectation of emigrating may have increased the incentive to invest in specialised training such as nursing in the Philippines (Leipziger, 2008). Lucas (2004) also argues that the high, privately financed enrolment rates in these fields are certainly induced by the possibility of emigration.

Diaspora: Do migrant networks help?

Systems of linkages of highly skilled expatriates are referred to as expatriate knowledge networks. This diaspora option tries to set up backward linkages to the home country between developing economy insiders, with their risk-mitigating knowledge and connections, and outsiders in command of technical know-how and investment capital — paving the way for information and knowledge exchange and giving expatriates the chance to transfer their expertise and skills to the country of origin, without necessarily returning home permanently (Brown, 2000; Kuznetsov and Sabel, 2006).

More generally, diasporic networks are in a good position to act as intermediaries, and credibility-enhancing mechanisms enhancing information flows, lowering reputation barriers and enforcing contractual arrangements (Lucas, 2001). A classic instance is the Indian diaspora's success in Silicon Valley, which appears to be reflecting the reputational spillover effects of success in a leading sector in a leading country. Today, an "Indian" software programmer sends an ex-ante signal of quality (Desai, Kapur and McHale, 2001). Network diasporas, however, are not a self-generating, context-free answer to the recurrent problem of learning from abroad; they co-evolve with the political and economic circumstances within which they function (Kuznetsov and Sabel, 2006). Also, there is little authoritative appraisal of the cost effectiveness of these expatriate organisations, or whether there is "adverse selection" with the least skilled returning and the more skilled staying abroad (Leipziger, 2008).

In the Philippines, diaspora networks are few, but they profit from the absence of language and culture barriers, and more specifically, their ability to more effectively adapt, foreign approaches and technology to the homeland context. Diaspora members act as important liaison between the know-how and its originating context and the homeland recipients and culture (Brinkerhoff, 2006). Some examples, not widely known, include Filipino technicians in American laboratories, academics in US universities, animators hired by Pixar or Disney, and programmers employed in Silicon Valley.

Worldwide, Chinese, Jewish and Indian diasporas have had significant influence in their home countries (Lucas, 2001). There is far less mention of a Filipino diaspora (Lucas, 2001), and it appears the weakest effort to engage the diaspora is that of the Philippines. Asis (2006) attributes this to the almost exclusive attention towards promoting labour migration, which takes the wind out of the sails of attempts to organise expatriate professionals. Furthermore, the Philippine government has no clear and stated policy for diaspora participation (Siar, 2008). The country's early experiments of knowledge transfer in the 1980s and 1990s, consisting of government and UN-sponsored diaspora programs, have either been discontinued or have floundered. For instance, the Science and Technology Advisory Council, which sought to encourage overseas Filipino scientists to engage in knowledge exchange had worldwide chapters at one time. Today, only one active chapter remains, in Japan. UNDP's Transfer of Knowledge through Expatriate Nationals (TOKTEN) program (1988–1994), administered with the Department of Foreign Affairs, funded short-term knowledge transfer visits of skilled overseas Filipinos (Opiniano and Castro, 2007). The Department of Science and Technology's *Balik Scientist* program supported, from 1994 to 1999, short- and long-term assignments for 84 overseas Filipino scientists, who provided technical expertise to 27 major government programs including the space program, geothermal field development and hazardous waste management (Opiniano and Castro, 2007).

Perhaps the only active diaspora system is the Brain Gain Network, a multi-disciplinary network of professional engineers, scientists, and organisations with a special emphasis on high technology (see Figure 4). It has attracted over 800 overseas Filipinos in science and technology (Garchitorena, 2007).

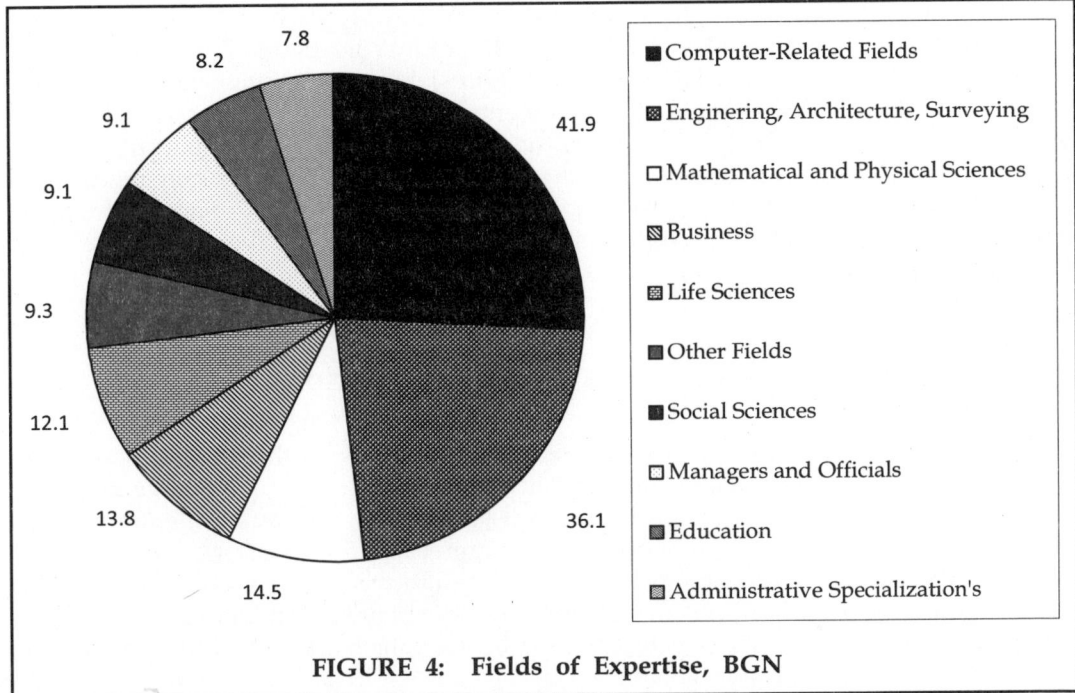

FIGURE 4: Fields of Expertise, BGN

Return: a question of domestic job opportunities

Brain drain may have other redemptive impacts: return migrants, especially those engaged in technical, scientific and management occupations are important for the development process because they embody the inflow of human capital through their newly acquired skills and knowledge from working overseas. The return option was first implemented in the 1970's through to the 1980's and 1990's. However, only a few newly industrialised countries like India, South Korea, Hong Kong and Taiwan have been able to implement this strategy effectively, since they have the economic and financial incentives to offer the expatriates they want to attract back (Brown, 2000).

Return migration in the Philippines illustrates, instead, adverse selection. Using little-used micro-data sets, Rodriguez and Horton (1995) came up with the following profile of Filipino return migrants: slightly older than migrants still away, have less education, and are more likely service or production workers. Controlling for demographic characteristics, they identified two factors which explain the probability of return. First, migrants coming from high unemployment areas delay their return. Second, time spent overseas is associated with an inverted-U pattern in the probability of return. In a similar vein, Ochi (2005) chronicles the paradox of highly-skilled Filipino women who abandoned their academic or professional career in the Philippines when they decided to engage in domestic work overseas, but which gave them little opportunity to acquire new skills that they could apply upon return.

Highly skilled or not, Filipino returnees can find solace in a Replacement and Monitoring Centre, established under the 1995 Migrant Workers and Overseas Filipinos Act. The Centre offers returnees job placement services, skills training, livelihood programs, and job opportunity assessments, and gives employers a database of skilled migrant workers (de Souza, 2006; O'Neil, 2004). But the government's poor data collection system makes the impact of this program hard to assess (Battistella, 2005). In general, despite some gains, Philippine authorities have not systematically identified re-entry problems, and there are hardly any initiatives to match returnees' skills with their home country's development priorities.

Critical governance constraints and policy options

The dilemma facing "soft states" (including the Philippines) is that skilled people are most likely to depart where institutional quality is worst. A soft state will have too much of disagreeable interventions (deficiencies in legislation, regulation and law enforcement), and by the same logic, will have too little of the agreeable interventions (as in the case of coordination failures) since the state does not take into account or internalise the effects of its own policies (Bardhan and Udry, 1999). The most talented individuals most likely to be active participants in the development process are the least likely to remain and the most likely to be globally marketable. Their departure may be compounded by the reduced demand for improved institutions, since it is precisely these productive individuals who have the strongest interest in seeing that the right institutions are established (Kapur and McHale, 2005). This triggers a vicious cycle of institutional deterioration. As McHale (2006) rightly argues, bad institutions can be left behind, but human capital travels with its owner. Once they reside in high quality institutional environments, expatriates are limited in what they can do to put better institutions in place in home countries.

In the end, the necessary conditions for migration to become a variable in human capital development may be social and economic, but the sufficient conditions are political and institutional. This demands solid policy measures with regard to the strengthening of diasporas, the facilitation of remittance flows, as well as the need to establish incentives for successful, highly-skilled migrants to return to their countries of origin (Steinweg, 2006). Following Kapur and McHale (2005), the policy options are divided in four broad categories: control, creation, connections and compensation.

Control related policies seek to hold back the flow of skilled immigrants or emigrants. Although there will be occasions when restraints are justified, in general it is not advisable to traverse this policy route. It is better to look for ways to make sure that everyone shares in the benefits when such openness is exercised (Kapur and McHale, 2005). It also makes no practical sense to adopt compensatory policies such as an exit tax on the individual migrant, since it is hard to gauge in exact measure the loss of human capital in monetary terms (Brown, 2000). Where control might yield some dividend is in ascertaining the balance between skilled migration and domestic education subsidies. In a context of beneficial brain drain, raising the proportion of skilled individuals who emigrate to a richer country lowers the rate of subsidy for education, until the socially desirable level of human capital without subsidies is reached (Docquier, Faye & Pestieau, 2008).

In *creation*, a good approach is to fashion incentives to return as opposed to prohibitions on staying Kapur and McHale (2005). Some policies that can encourage this to happen include portable social security entitlements, reducing transfer costs and helping receivers to handle migrant savings (Steinweg, 2006), and better use of official channels (such as the Development Bank of the Philippines) in sending remittances. Additionally, the government should ensure adequate compensation and job opportunities in the public sector for returnees and explore ways to invest in the infrastructure of the professional sectors from which the migrants originally came (de Souza, 2006). Encouraging the return of professionals may require strengthening public-private research linkages, and funding research through transparent, competitive processes (Leipziger, 2008). Altruistic sharing of expertise gained abroad with local communities, as well as consultancies for local government units can encourage staying. The key is to promote sustainable return, a situation where the migrant's additional skills, financial resources and social capital are wisely utilised.

Connections come from having a well-connected diaspora. The Philippines has done little to leverage its diaspora talent. The challenge, according to Kutnetsov, Nemirovsky, and Yoguel (2006), who studied Argentinean networks, involves intense changes in both productive and institutional systems, the development of demand-pull changes in the educational system, the development of mechanisms for disseminating knowledge among disparate actors in productive supply chains, and the creation of diverse forms of mediation to facilitate links between science, technology and production. There should be incentives for expatriates who invent products and processes that can be replicated at low marginal cost (such as a physician primarily engaged in research on new treatments and medicines) (Kuhna and McAusland, 2009). Some institutional support is necessary in reactivating initiatives such as the *Balik* Scientist Program. The Dual Nationality Act (Republic Act 9225) that enables Filipinos coming from abroad to regain Philippine nationality without giving up their foreign citizenship is a step in the right direction. At the regional level, consultative processes that focus on a multilateral regime (say in ASEAN) to secure human capital can place a great deal of emphasis on long-term goals such as increasing inter-country cooperation on information exchange and border enforcement.

Compensation requires encouraging developed countries to implement measures that would guarantee migrants' rights to decent work and social security (Steinweg, 2006). To secure the welfare of those remaining behind, the options include: tying development aid to human capital recruitment; and arranging for replacement of rich-country personnel. To be sure, all of these mechanisms face practical constraints and require the cooperation of developed countries (Kapur and McHale, 2005), but carefully designed policies can reconcile seemingly opposing interests of host and source countries.

Concluding remarks

This paper has taken into account the impact of the brain gain on the major source of externalities — human capital. It concludes that the redistributive outcomes of Filipino migration are mixed. Remittances are found to be a big factor in defraying the costs of basic education and health. There is counterfactual evidence, plus some anecdotal proof, on migration's feedback effects on education, thus enabling the country to maintain a fairly high level of skilled workers despite the outflow of highly educated individuals. But returns on the tiny diaspora network, and on brain circulation (return migration) are quite small, indicating the immense challenges that the Philippines faces in managing migrant flows and in putting in place more definitive policies regarding knowledge transfers.

References

Aldaba, Fernando T. & Jeremiah M. Opinionado. (Undated). Maximizing the Diasporic Dividend. Quezon City: Ateneo de Manila University.

Asis, Maruja M.B. (2006). International migration and development in the Philippines: Promising leads and missing links. Manila: Scalabrini Migration Centre.

Asis, Maruja. (2003). Hearts apart: Migration in the eyes of Filipino children. Manila: Scalabrini Migration Centre.

Bardhan, Pranab & Christopher Udry. (1999). *Development Microeconomics*. New York: Oxford University Press.

Battistella, G.raziano. (2005). Return migration in the Philippines: Issues and policies, *International Migration*, March, pp. 212-230.

Bayangos, Veronica and Karel Jansen. (2009). The macroeconomics of remittances in the Philippines. Working Paper No. 470. Institute of Social Studies. March.

Beine, Michel, Cecily Defoort & Frederic Docquier. (2006). Skilled migration, human capital inequality and convergence. Discussion Papers (ECON - Departement des Sciences Economiques).

Brinkerhoff, Jennifer M. (2006). Diaspora mobilization factors and policy options, in Asian Development Bank, *Converting Migration Drains into Gains: Harnessing the Resources of Overseas Professionals*. Manila: ADB.

Brown, Mercy. (2000). Using the intellectual diaspora to reverse the brain drain: Some useful examples. University of Cape Town, South Africa.

de Souza, Roger-Mark. (2006). Using return migration as a development tool: Are the right policies in place? Population Reference Bureau. September. http://www.prb.org/Articles/2006/UsingReturnMigrationAsaDevelopmentToolAretheRightPoliciesinPlace.aspx Accessed 15 October 2009.

Desai, Mihir A., Devesh Kapur & John McHale. (2000). Sharing the spoils: Taxing international human capital flows. Paper presented at the NBER-NCAER conference on India's Economic Reforms, December.

Docquier, Frédéric & Abdeslam Marfouk. (2006). International migration by education attainment, 1990–2000, in Çaglar Özden & Maurice Schiff, *International Migration, Remittances, and the Brain Drain* (eds.), A co publication of the World Bank and Palgrave Macmillan (Washington DC: World Bank).

Docquier, Frédéric, Ousmane Faye & Pierre Pestieau. (2008). Is migration a good substitute for education subsidies? Journal of Development Economics 86: 2 (June), 263-276.

Economic and Social Commission for Asia and the Pacific. (2005). Socially vulnerable groups: Tackling emerging issues in international migration. Committee on Emerging Social Issues, Second session, 1-3 November, Bangkok.

Fan, C. Simon & Oded Stark. (2007). International migration and "educated unemployment". *Journal of Development Economics* 83, 76 – 87. www.elsevier.com/locate/econbase. Accessed 10 October 2009.

Garchitorena, Victoria P. (2007). Migration and development: Philippine diaspora philanthropy. UN Institute for Training and Research. 7 March.

Kapur Devesh & John McHale. (2005). The global migration of talent: What does it mean for developing countries? A brief based on *Give Us Your Best and Brightest: The Global Hunt for Talent and Its Impact on the Developing World* (Washington, DC: Centre for Global Development, 2005). October.

Kuhna, Peter & Carol McAusland. (2009). Consumers and the brain drain: Product and process design and the gains from emigration. February.

Kutnetsov, Yevgeny, Adolfo Nemirovsky & Gabriel Yoguel. (2006). Argentina: Burgeoning networks of talent abroad, weak institutions at home, in Yevgeny Kuznetsov (ed.), *Diaspora Networks and the International Migration of Skills: How Countries Can Draw on Their Talent Abroad* (Washington DC: World Bank Institute).

Kuznetsov, Yevgeny & Charles Sabel. (2006). International migration of talent, diaspora networks, and development: Overview of main issues, in Yevgeny Kuznetsov (ed.), *Diaspora Networks and the International Migration of Skills: How Countries Can Draw on Their Talent Abroad* (Washington DC: World Bank Institute).

Leipziger, Danny M. (2008). "Brain drain" and the global mobility of high-skilled talent. PREM Notes No. 123, September. Washington DC: World Bank.

Lowell, B. Lindsay & Allan Findlay. (2001). Migration of highly skilled persons from developing countries: Impact and policy responses. International Migration Papers 44. International Labour Office, Geneva. December.

Lucas, Robert E.B. (2001). Diaspora and development: Highly skilled migrants from East Asia. Report prepared for the World Bank. November.

McHale, John. (2006). Skilled migration and institutional development. United Nations Symposium on International Migration and Development. Turin, June.

O'Neil, K. (2004). Labour export as government policy: The case of the Philippines. Migration Information Source. http://www.migrationinformation.org/Feature/display.cfm?ID=191 Accessed 1 October 2009.

Ochi, Masami Helen. (2005). Return migration of Filipina overseas workers - Some implications from "reintegration" programmes. Mobilités au féminin – Tanger, 15-19 Novembre.

Opiniano, Jeremiah M. and Tricia Anne Castro. (2007). Promoting knowledge transfer activities through diaspora networks: A pilot study on the Philippines. Ayala Foundation USA. Also in ADB, *Converting Migration Drains into Gains: harnessing the Resources of overseas Professionals* Manila: ADB, 2006.

Orbeta Jr, Aniceto C. (2008). Economic impact of international migration and remittances on Philippine households: What we thought we knew, what we need to know. PIDS Discussion Paper Series No. 2008-32. Makati City: Philippine Institute for Development Studies.

Pernia, Ernesto M. (2006). Diaspora, remittances, and poverty in RP's Regions. UPSE Discussion Papers No. 0602. Quezon City: University of the Philippines.

Pozo, Susan. (2008) International migration, remittances and economic development. Western Michigan University. August 12.

Rapoport, Hillel. (2008). Brain drain and development: An overview. Presented to the AFD workshop on Migration and human capital development, Paris, France, June 30.

Rodriguez, Edgard & Susan Horton. (1995). International return migration and remittances in the Philippines. Working Paper No. UT-ECIPA-Horton-95-01. Department of Economics, University of Toronto.

Siar, Sheila V. (2008). Bringing back what has been 'lost': Knowledge exchange through the diaspora. DevNet Conference on Peripheral Vision, Victoria University of Wellington, New Zealand.

Steinweg, Isabel. (2006). United Nations high-level dialogue on international migration and development. Friedrich Ebert Foundation New York. October.

Tabuga, A. (2007). International remittances and household expenditures. PIDS Discussion Paper Series 2007-18. Makati City: Philippine Institute for Development Studies.

Todaro, Michael P. & Stephen C. Smith. (2006). *An Introduction to Economic Development.* Singapore: Pearson.

Tullao, T., M. Cortez, & E. See. (2007). The economic impacts of international migration: A case study on the Philippines. Report to EADN.

Yang, Dean & C. Martinez. (2005). Remittances and poverty in migrants' home areas: Evidence from the Philippines, in Caglar Ozden and Maurice Schiff (eds.) *International Migration, Remittances, and the Brain Drain*, World Bank.

Yang, Dean. (2008). International migration, remittances, and household investment: Evidence from Philippine migrants' exchange rate shocks, *Economic Journal* 118 (528).

Yang, Dean. (2009). International migration and human development. Human Development Research Paper 2009/29. United Nations Development Programme, July.

Yavuzer, Özgür. (2008). Is the economic impact of international migration marginal in developing countries? *Uluslararasý Ekonomik Sorunlar*. May.

CHAPTER 8

AN EXAMINATION OF AUDIT FUNCTIONS IN INSTITUTIONS OF HIGHER LEARNING

Mohd Raime Ramlan, Mohamad Naimi Mohamad Noor and Raudah Danila

Abstract

The objective of this study is to examine the auditing function which serves the users of financial statements. The financial statements have been accepted as major sources of a company's financial position. In addition, the auditor is expected to enhance the quality of the financial report; its reliability, credibility and comparability through a proper and competent course of audit. This study has selected students of higher learning institutions in Malaysia. The researcher replicates a survey from Reynolds (1989) to examine how respondents actually view the audit functions in terms of their importance and effectiveness. The descriptive technique employed statistically indicated that all audit functions were perceived as important and effective. For perceived importance, the findings had indicated that the students expected auditors to enhance the reliability of financial statements and ensure that reports are prepared in accordance with Generally Accepted Accounting Principles (GAAP) and sufficiently carry out valuation of company liabilities. In terms of effectiveness, they agree that the auditors have effectively delivered audit functions such as performing an independent opinion of the financial report. The auditing profession is self regulated and auditors have ensured that the preparations of financial statements are according to GAAP. Finally, a comparison was made between results from the current and Reynolds' study to identify how different group of users actually perceive audit functions that are currently being performed by audit practitioners.

Introduction

Investors and other users of financial statements have long agreed on the usefulness or the leading role played by audit in financial reporting. Auditors usually present their view(s) or opinion in audit reports on the fairness of financial statements. The users of financial statements, on the other hand, share the view that auditing enhances the credibility and reliability of financial statements (Reynolds, 1989).

A number of surveys have demonstrated that many users of financial statements consider a 'clean' audit report as signifying that the auditor guarantees that the audited financial statements are accurate and/or the company is financially secure (e.g., Lee, 1970; Beck, 1973; Canadian Institute of Chartered Accountant [CICA], 1988). Previous studies, likewise, have indicated that some users of financial statements disagreed with the actual functions performed by the audit practitioners. The study carried out by Reynolds in 1989 revealed that there were significant disagreements between the auditor and the commercial bank loan officers concerning their perception of audit functions.

Previous studies have shown that most disagreements were found regarding the effectiveness of the audit function. And for quite sometime, the members of the accounting profession have expressed their concern on the accuracy of the user's perception on the message contained in audit reports. Obviously, different users perceive differently (American Accounting Association, [1971]; Peat Marwick, Michael & Co. [1976,p. 86]; AICPA[1978, chap.7]).

The existence of the expectation gap is primarily associated with the misconception regarding the auditor's responsibility and the nature of the audit work. To date, the scenario surrounding the misunderstanding of audit work and audit responsibility has been held responsible for the critical, litigious environment, which characterises auditing today (Porter, 1992). Those in the auditing profession assert that one of the major reasons contributing to the audit expectation gap is the public failure to appreciate the nature and the limitations of audit (Lowe, 1994). The public, in general, has come to view the auditor as a guarantor of the integrity of financial statements and as an insurance policy against fraud and illegal financial acts (AICPA, 1984). In understanding the nature of the audit work, the auditor generally cannot provide absolute assurance that the financial statements are free of misstatement. This is due to the nature and the limitation of audit itself. For example, during the planning of the audit work, the auditor sets a level of materiality, selects the size and, in most cases, he relies on his own judgement in carrying out the audit work.

In a nutshell, the auditing profession is facing problems with the audit expectation gap. So far, numerous studies have shown that proper measures have been taken by researches, academicians, regulatory bodies and accounting professional bodies to bridge the gap. Reynolds (1989) suggests that effective solutions to the problem in the auditing profession could be formulated if the factors underlying the problems are identified and that the possible areas of agreement or disagreement be specified. CPA firms are encouraged to improve the situation by changing the structure, personnel policies, recruitments and procedures, for instance, as an attempt to meet the public expectation. The main objective of this study is to measure how unit trust managers perceive audit functions. The specific objectives are to identify audit function(s) that are perceived as important and effectively performed by external auditor and to identify audit function(s) that are perceived as important but inefficiently performed by external auditor.

This study is exploratory in nature and seeks to examine the audit expectation gap in Malaysia. In view of the current scenario of unit trust industry in Malaysia, the objective of this study is to measure how unit trust managers who are directly involved in the investment decision-making perceive the audit function performed by the audit practitioners. Their perceptions are measured on the perceived importance and the effectiveness of the audit function. It is really hoped that the findings from this study (on the user's perception towards audit function) can contribute to the dissemination of knowledge among local educators, practitioners and members of the auditing profession.

Research Instruments

Twenty-nine audit functions were identified and used as variables for the questionnaire in this study. The variables were measured along two dimensions, i.e., the importance of the audit function in society and how effectively are they being delivered by auditors. Five point-Likert attitude scales were deployed to measure the respondents' perceptions on both variables. To measure "importance" the scale varied from "1" being "strongly disagreed" to "5" being "strongly agreed". Similarly for "effectiveness", the scales used varied from "1" being "strongly ineffective" to "5" being "strongly effective'. This study replicates the research instrument used by Reynolds (1989). The questionnaire was prepared to examine the perceived importance and the effectiveness of the audit function in society. In addition, the items found in the questionnaire stem from the functions discussed in the auditing literature. A list of functions as proposed by Reynolds (1989) is presented in Table 1.

TABLE 1: Audit Functions

Independent opinion on financial statements	Prevention of illegal and anti-social acts
Going concern assurance	Compliance with regulation
Statements are in accordance with GAAP	Report on unusual circumstance
Credibility	Report on material uncertainties
Reliability	Report on efficiency of operations
Internal control assurance	Report on efficiency of management
Detection of fraud	Assurance on appropriateness of allocations
Prevention of fraud	Mitigation of information risk
Stewardship	Underlying substance of transactions reported
Societal accountability	Presentation appropriate
Valuation	Consistency of reporting
Information for decision making	Mitigation of business risk
Accuracy of data	Detection of illegal and anti-social acts
Completeness of data	

The information on attitudes (perceived importance and effectiveness) was collected by using the 5 point-Likert attitude scale. The same audit function variables were used to measure the respondents' perception in terms of the functions' importance and effectiveness by using a columnar approach. As an exploratory study, this research focuses only on single constituency group; i.e., the unit trust managers who are directly involved in investment decision-making rather than the multiple constituency groups.

Data Analysis

The researcher uses SPSS to analyze the responses. A descriptive technique was employed to measure the respondents' perception with regards to the perceived importance and the effectiveness of the audit functions. Moreover, two hypotheses were tested in order to attest that some audit functions were perceived as important, and effectively performed by audit practitioners. Two hundred surveys were sent out to accounting students together with a letter that explained the objective of the study as well as the need for their participation. From the analysis, it was indicated that all audit functions were perceived as important and effectively performed by the external auditors. The researchers had identified ten most perceived importance and effectively performed audit functions and had ranked based on their total mean. Ten least important and effective audit functions were also discussed and presented in Table 7 and Table 8.

TABLE 2: Summary of Variables

Content	Importance	Effectiveness
Independent opinion	V1	V30
Going concern	V2	V31
Consistent with GAAP	V3	V32
Credibility of report	V4	V33
Reliability of statements	V5	V34
Internal control	V6	V35
Detect material fraud	V7	V36
Deter fraud	V8	V37
Management stewardship	V9	V38
Social control	V10	V39
Asset valuation	V11	V40
Information for decisions	V12	V41
Data accuracy, and completeness	V13	V42
Detect illegal acts	V14	V43
Detect to illegal acts	V15	V44
Deterrent to non-compliance	V16	V45

Unusual circumstances	V17	V46
Material uncertainties	V18	V47
Lack of reporting bias	V19	V48
Underlying substance	V20	V49
Comparability of reporting	V21	V50
Mitigates investment risk	V22	V51
Competent audit performance	V23	V52
Proper disclosure of fraud	V24	V53
Profession self-regulation	V25	V54
Dispersion of investment risk	V26	V55
Audit report signal	V27	V56
Valuation of liabilities	V28	V57
Efficiency of operations	V29	V58

Perceived Importance Measures

The first hypothesis to be tested is none of the audit functions would be perceived as important. The total mean for each variable were calculated and presented in Table 3. The perceived importance is scaled from "1" being "strongly disagree" to "5" being "strongly agree". Any score of 3 and above is classified as "agree", and scores of 4 and above are classified as "strongly agree" to the importance of the variables. The results in Table 3 show that all variables are perceived as important. Therefore, with regard to hypothesis one:

    Ho1. No audit function will be perceived as important.
    Ha1. Some audit functions will be perceived as important.

    The null hypothesis is rejected. No audit function has been perceived to be very important or not important. It is found that the respondents expect auditors to enhance the reliability of financial statements. The auditors are also expected to ensure that the statements were prepared according to the GAAP. The auditors are also expected to sufficiently conduct valuation on liabilities, to form independent opinion and most importantly to add credibility to the financial statements itself.

    However, since the number of the respondents is small (n=20), the results are only applicable to this study and do not represent the whole population. This study is exploratory in nature and is not conclusive.

TABLE 3: Audit Functions Perceived as Important

Variable	Type	Mean
V1	Independent opinion	4.250
V2	Going concern	4.100
V3	Consistent with GAAP	4.300

V4	Credibility of report	4.200
V5	Reliability of statements	4.350
V6	Internal control	4.100
V7	Detect material fraud	3.800
V8	Deter fraud	3.750
V9	Management stewardship	3.450
V10	Social control	3.400
V11	Asset valuation	4.050
V12	Information for decisions	3.950
V13	Data accuracy, and completeness	4.100
V14	Detect illegal acts	3.850
V15	Detect to illegal acts	3.800
V16	Deterrent to non-compliance	4.000
V17	Unusual circumstances	3.950
V18	Material uncertainties	3.750
V19	Lack of reporting bias	3.800
V20	Underlying substance	3.800
V21	Comparability of reporting	3.900
V22	Mitigates investment risk	3.550
V23	Competent audit performance	3.950
V24	Proper disclosure of fraud	4.150
V25	Profession self-regulation	4.050
V26	Dispersion of investment risk	3.550
V27	Audit report signal	3.900
V28	Valuation of liabilities	4.250
V29	Efficiency of operations	3.700

Perceived Effectiveness Measures

The results show that all variables are perceived as effectively performed. No variables are found either strongly ineffective, ineffective or strongly effective. The results in Table 4 indicate that the respondents agreed that the auditors had performed effectively on several functions such as in forming independent opinion, agreed that auditing profession is self-regulated and financial statements were prepared in accordance with GAAP. The auditor's work was viewed as enhancing the reliability of statements, and the auditor was seen to have sufficiently done evaluation of the company's assets. Again, because the number of respondent is small (n=20), the results are only applicable to this study and do not represent the whole population. This study is exploratory in nature and is not conclusive. The results can be seen in Table 4.

TABLE 4: Audit Functions Perceived Effectively Performed

Variable	Type	Mean
V30	Independent opinion	4.050
V31	Going concern	3.700
V32	Consistent with GAAP	4.000
V33	Credibility of report	3.750
V34	Reliability of statements	3.900
V35	Internal control	3.400
V36	Detect material fraud	3.050
V37	Deterrent to fraud	3.150
V38	Management stewardship	3.150
V39	Social control	3.250
V40	Assets valuation	3.900
V41	Decision-making	3.750
V42	Data accuracy, & completeness	3.700
V43	Detect illegal acts	3.300
V44	Deterrent to illegal acts	3.200
V45	Deterrent to non-compliance	3.700
V46	Unusual circumstances	3.850
V47	Material uncertainties	3.650
V48	Lack of reporting bias	3.550
V49	Underlying substance	3.400
V50	Comparability of reporting	3.650
V51	Mitigates investment risks	3.300
V52	Competent audit performance	3.800
V53	Proper disclosure of fraud	3.650
V54	Profession self-regulation	4.000
V55	Dispersion of investment risk	3.300
V56	Audit report signal	3.700
V57	Valuation of liabilities	3.700
V58	Efficiency of operations	3.200

Conclusion

Ten Most Important and Effective Audit Functions

Table 5 and 6 identify ten most important and effective audit functions as perceived by the respondents. Out of twenty-nine audit functions, it has been found that the respondents viewed the auditors mostly effective in ensuring the reliability of financial statements. Reynolds (1989) perceived investors, creditors, regulators, and labor as sophisticated users who used audited financial statements to make decisions. Therefore, they will rely only on those documents, reports, and material that are highly reliable to base their decisions. However, this audit function is only ranked fourth in terms of its effectiveness. Furthermore, the respondents also expressed the view that the auditors should put in more effort to ensure that the financial statements prepared is consistent with GAAP, sufficiently able to conduct valuation on liabilities and form independent opinion i.e., the auditors were not influenced by any interested parties in forming their opinion. However, the variable on valuation of liabilities has not been perceived as very effective compared to perceived importance. This variable only is ranked eleventh out of twenty-eight variables. Few other audit functions such as ensuring that the company has properly disclosed matters of fraud, good internal control and going concern were also perceived to be very important but they were not ranked among the very effective audit functions (ten most effective). In addition, the variable on professional self-regulation which was only perceived at tenth in terms of importance was ranked second with respect to its effectiveness.

Based on this finding, it can be summarised that some audit functions were found to be very important (in which the functions are listed as the ten most important) from the respondents' view but in fact were not very effectively performed by external auditors (not included in ten most effective). Only variables on reliability of statements, consistency with the GAAP, and independent opinions were ranked among the top four in terms of importance and effectiveness. Furthermore, some audit functions were found to be very important and very effectively performed. They were variables on the credibility of report, data accuracy and completeness, which can be found both in the ten most important and most effective of audit functions. In contrast, two audit functions, i.e., the asset valuation, and decision-making were found to be very effectively delivered even though the respondents did not perceive them to be very important.

TABLE 5: Ten Most Important Audit Functions

Variable	Minimum	Maximum	Mean
Reliability of statements	4.00	5.00	4.350
Consistent with GAAP	3.00	5.00	4.300
Valuation of liabilities	3.00	5.00	4.250
Independent opinion	4.00	5.00	4.250
Credibility of report	4.00	5.00	4.200
Proper disclosure of fraud	3.00	5.00	4.150
Data accuracy, & completeness	3.00	5.00	4.100
Internal control	2.00	5.00	4.100
Going concern	3.00	5.00	4.100
Professional self-regulation	3.00	5.00	4.050

TABLE 6: Ten Most Effective Audit Functions

Variable	Minimum	Maximum	Mean
Independent opinion	3.00	5.00	4.050
Professional self-regulation	3.00	5.00	4.000
Consistent with GAAP	3.00	5.00	4.000
Reliability of statements	3.00	5.00	3.900
Asset valuation	3.00	5.00	3.900
Unusual circumstances	2.00	5.00	3.850
Competent audit performance	3.00	5.00	3.800
Credibility of report	2.00	5.00	3.750
Decision-making	2.00	5.00	3.750

Ten Least Important and Effective Audit Functions

The respondents viewed the audit function on social control as the least important. As shown in Table 8, this social control function is ranked sixth. The results also indicate that the functions on management stewardship, mitigation and dispersion of investment risks are not considered as very important. Two audit functions: management stewardship, and the efficiency of operations have been identically ranked both in perceived importance and effectiveness, i.e., listed second and fifth subsequently. In terms of effectiveness, a variable on detecting material fraud was perceived to be the least effectively performed, followed by management stewardship and deterrence to fraud subsequently. Even though variables on detecting material fraud, management stewardship, and deterrence to fraud were not perceived as inefficient, their total mean indicate the tendencies to inefficiency.

TABLE 7: Ten Least Important Audit Functions

Variable	Minimum	Maximum	Mean
Social control	2.00	4.00	3.400
Management stewardship	1.00	5.00	3.450
Mitigates investment risks	3.00	4.00	3.550
Dispersion of investment risk	3.00	4.00	3.550
Efficiency of operation	2.00	5.00	3.700
Deterrent to fraud	2.00	5.00	3.750
Material uncertainties	3.00	5.00	3.750
Deterrent to illegal acts	2.00	5.00	3.800
Detect material fraud	2.00	5.00	3.800

TABLE 8: Ten Least Effective Audit Functions

Variable	Minimum	Maximum	Mean
Detect material fraud	2.00	5.00	3.050
Management stewardship	1.00	4.00	3.150
Deterrent to fraud	2.00	4.00	3.150
Deterrent to illegal acts	2.00	5.00	3.200
Efficiency of operation	1.00	5.00	3.200
Social control	2.00	4.00	3.250
Detect illegal acts	2.00	5.00	3.300
Mitigates investments risks	1.00	4.00	3.300
Dispersion of investment risk	2.00	4.00	3.300
Underlying substance	1.00	5.00	3.400

References

- Barkema, Harry G. (1995). Do top managers work harder when they are monitored? *Kyklos, 48(1)*, 19-42.
- Caplan, Dennid. (1999). Internal controls and detection of management fraud. *Journal of Accounting Research, 37(1)*, 1-9.
- Chenok, Philip B. (1994). Worth Repeating. *Journal of Accountancy, 177(1)*, 47-50.
- Commission on Auditors' Responsibilities. (1978). *Report, Conclusions and Recommendations.* AICPA.
- Epstein, Marc J.; Geiger, Marshal A. (1994). Investor views of audit assurance: recent evidence of the expectation gap. *Journal of Accountancy, 177(1)*, 60-65.
- Gill, Gurdarshan S.; Gosset, Graham W.P. (1996) 3rd ed. *Modern Auditing in Australia.* John Wiley : New York.
- Lowe, D. Jordon. (1994). The expectation gap in the legal system: Perception differences between auditors and judges. *Journal of Applied Business Research, 10(3)*, 39-44.
- Lowe, D. Jordon; Pany, Kurt. (1993). Expectations of the audit function. *CPA Journal, 63(8)*, 58-59.
- Ng.David S.; Stoeckenius. (1979). Auditing: Incentives and truthful reporting. *Journal of Accounting Research, 17*, 1-31.
- Penno, Mark. (1985). Informational issues in the financial reporting process, *Journal of Accounting Research, 23(1)*, 240-265.
- Reinstein, Alan; Coursen, Gregory A. (1999). Considering the risk of fraud: Understanding the auditor's new requirements. *The National Public Accountant, 44(2)*, 34-38.
- Reynolds, Mary Ann. (1989). An examination of the audit function in society. *Phd. Dissertation, The University of Utah.*

Section 2

HUMAN RESOURCE MANAGEMENT AND CAPACITY BUILDING

Chapter 9

ACADEMIC STANDARDS VERSUS POLITICAL LOYALTY IN HIGHER EDUCATIONAL INSTITUTIONS IN BANGLADESH:
The Case of Rajshahi University

Ishtiaq Jamil and Pranab Kumar Panday

Abstract

Higher educational institutions in Bangladesh are now more influenced by national level politics than characterised as seats of academic excellence. This paper analyzes how politics impedes academic standards and quality of education in Bangladesh. The 'impact' of bipolar politics has divided the academic world into two major political camps. This has bred nepotism, lobbying, and rallying under different political banners to achieve leadership positions, influence career advancement, and recruitment of new teachers. This has severely affected quality education and standards of scholarly work. Findings from the study of a public university – Rajshahi University - reveal that recruitment of fresh teachers as well as career advancement is an occasion where political loyalty of candidates plays an important role in the recruitment process. Candidates with strong affiliation to the political party in power have greater chances of recruitment than candidates with only excellent academic record. Political loyalty reigns supreme over academic qualifications. Almost all public universities are characterised by this trend. This has seriously affected knowledge production and dissemination.

Introduction

Higher education in Bangladesh[1] has undergone major changes since the country's independence in 1971. Many of these changes have however not helped to improve teaching and research; rather, they have compromised the quality of recruitment to academic positions (Siddiqui 1997:168). Faculty members are recruited and promoted according to politicised criteria (e.g., mere length of service), all of which have compromised principles of quality and achievement in public institutions of higher learning and research. No other public institutions in Bangladesh are as politicised and divided along political lines as the public universities.

During the 1960s, public universities in Bangladesh (then East Pakistan) were considered to be the intellectual centres of society and 'nurseries' for its future leaders. Society awarded special distinction to graduates and faculty members of such institutions. Today, however, due to political interference in every sphere, the universities have lost the degree of excellence for which they were commended during the 1960s.

Bangladesh's universities are now more characterised by political loyalty than by academic standards. Today when the government changes, the university leadership also does, sometimes it is elected by the (university) senate; at others the new government merely appoints loyal academics to administerial positions. These sort of manoeuvres have made the recruitment and promotion of university teachers more political. The major intention of this paper is to shed light on the process of recruiting university teachers in Bangladesh and to reveal the impact of political loyalty on the recruitment process. Our particular focus is on such processes and their impact on Rajshahi University (Bangladesh's second largest university). In this context, the 'impact' of political loyalty refers to an assessment of the outcome of politicised recruitment processes on the quality of education.

This paper is mainly based on secondary data. Two sources in particular have been explored and reviewed: first, published articles on higher education in Bangladesh; second, reports from different international organisations on higher education in developing countries. First-hand primary data collected from newspapers have also been used.

Conceptual discourse: Academic standard versus political loyalty

The concept of an 'academic standard' is highly contested. Scholars claim in fact that it cannot be universalised (Ehsan 2008:33; Williams 1997:64). In spite of the ongoing debate, however, the concept of 'quality' in academia usually refers to knowledge production and dissemination according to certain standards as delineated or conceptualised by a community of experts (usually senior faculty) of a particular academic discipline. Peer review is a common method of scrutinizing scholarly work, research engagement, and analytical skills of faculty during recruitment and promotion processes. Academic standards are also measured by the quality of graduates, their contribution to society and how society views their talents (Vries 1997:51). According to Williams (1997:65-66), one way of measuring academic standards is to understand them in relation to the 'chain' of academic inputs, processes and outputs, as shown in Table 1.

TABLE 1: Academic Standards in Teaching and Learning

Type of academic standard:	Which measure:	Using criteria defined by:
Inputs	- Students' entry qualifications - **Recruitment of teaching staff**	- Admission policies - **Selection procedure** - Adequate and available funding
Processes	- Students' learning experience and progress - Curriculum content and organisation - Teaching, learning and assessment strategies	- Program accreditation policies - **The quality of teaching staff;** learning resources; support services
Outputs	- Students' achievements in terms of a) knowledge, b) skills, and c) understanding	- Learning objectives - Assessment strategies

Maintaining and nurturing academic standards depend to a large extent on the linkage between the standard of inputs, processes and outputs. If there is any break in this chain, it jeopardises the whole system of academic standards.

What is the historical background for this 'chain' of standards and its present status in Bangladesh's academic culture? What is the relation between such standards and political loyalty? Universities in Bangladesh have a chequered history with respect to raising voices against the wrongdoings of governments. This was the case when the country was part of Pakistan but also after independence. Even under Pakistani rule there were protests against discrimination and neglect, and against policies that did not reflect citizens' interests and needs. During the Language Movement in 1952 and especially during the period leading up to independence (including the war period which ended in 1971), students and academics joined political parties and others in civil society to criticise the various Pakistani governments' politics of discrimination and centralisation of power. The nation still remembers the sacrifices of thousands of brave students and academics who were harassed, tortured and even killed during protests against the authoritarian establishment.

The role of universities in standing up for the oppressed and creating social and political awareness is significant. However, the trend of politics over the years has become polarised, now between the two major political camps: the Awami League (AL) and the Bangladesh Nationalist Party (BNP). The reason for this is that students and academics have now become 'extended hands' of the political parties. Narrow political interests permeate not only the selection of university leadership but also the selection of lower-level staff. This is because regimes who want to reign in peace rely on the loyalty and support of students and academics. Student agitation may force a government to resign, as was the case in 1990 when the authoritarian regime of General Ershad came to an end amidst massive protests spearheaded by students. This paved the way for the restoration of democracy in Bangladesh. Therefore, no matter which party wins an election and forms a government, it tries to consolidate its position in institutions of higher learning, the favourite institution being the University of Dhaka. The politicisation of students and academics as loyalists is thus a common phenomenon. Yet when academics are recruited based on the criteria of political loyalty, their academic merits and competencies are often ignored. It has often been referred that new faculty members are in fact 'voters' rather than teachers responsible for learning and disseminating knowledge to students.

The Politicisation of Administration

The politicisation of administration has become a common feature of Bangladeshi politics. On every bureaucratic level, every government has tried to offer undue privilege to loyal officials. Even so, this phenomenon is not unique to Bangladesh. It is also evident in many developed countries, especially the USA. It is argued that the politically-based recruitment of upper-level civil servants (although it should be done up to a moderate degree) may put a government in an advantageous position in implementing its policies (cited in Ali, 2004). For instance, ten percent of higher level posts in the US administration are political appointees. These officials are not career civil servants. In the UK, political or special advisers are recruited in order to advise ministers and help them better understand policies. Also in France, the ministerial cabinet is comprised of both political and administrative officials.

The politicisation of administration in these three countries is however practiced differently than it is in Bangladesh, where political loyalty is considered to be the *most* important appraisal criteria, more than professional skill or actual performance. Whereas in other countries, a political appointment may be made on the basis of high professional ability, in Bangladesh, a person can be given (awarded) a position merely for being a loyal supporter of the ruling party. In sum, political appointments are made in order to reward supporters of the ruling party. Supporters of the opposition are considered enemies and are often victimised for promotion or transfer, or when they are trying to obtain public services.

After the restoration of democracy in Bangladesh in 1991, politics has become more bipolar with the hegemony of two major political parties - the Awami League (AL) and the Bangladesh Nationalist Party (BNP) and their respective allies. Politics has now become more antagonistic with one accusing the other of corruption, misappropriation of public fund, and misusing public institutions for personal gain. The extent of polarisation has reached to such an extent that there is hardly any public organisation that is not affected by this politics. In this political blame game, influencing public policies depend on striking a favourable relationship with one of these parties and nurturing it so that once a particular party is in power, it may become easier to satisfy one's own or group preferences. From bureaucracy to academic institutions this trend is distinctly observed. This has bred lobbying (popularly called Tadbir) and corruption. In order to gain access to political favour in terms of influencing public procurement policies, business contracts, issuing of licenses, gaining access to lucrative posts, career advancement, recruitment and even influencing judicial decisions, political connections are vital. This practice has weakened institutional norms, values, and standard operating procedures. Lobbying has now become a routine rather than an exception. An alarming consequence of this is unpredictability of public organisations and uncertainty in the behaviour of public incumbents. This has enhanced citizens' distrust in public institutions. These days, most promotions and recruitment in public organisations are politically motivated. Those who have the "right" connections are bestowed with favour and those who fail to do so become a victim and feel the wrath of political victimisation. In this game, public institutions of higher learning are severely affected.

It is now taken for granted that with the change in government which took place in 2009; changes along narrow political interest are likely to be seen in the university administration as well. The Daily Star (a leading English daily) in its report published on 21/01/2009 stated that "Pro-Awami League (AL) teachers of different public universities are now lobbying hard with new government high-ups to get appointment as vice chancellor (VC), pro-vice chancellor (pro-VC) and other top leadership posts after the political change is over". Teachers from different universities try their best to lobby for getting appointment in the highest posts after a political regime change. This kind of situation is quite common when there is a change in the government.

Higher Education: A Brief Introduction

At the time of independence, Bangladesh inherited a rich heritage of six public universities: Dhaka University (established in 1921), Rajshahi University (established in 1953), Chittagong and Jahangir Nagor University (established in the late 1960s), Bangladesh University of Science and Technology (BUET) and Bangladesh Agriculture University (both founded in the early 1960s). Of these six schools, the first four are general universities and the last two are polytechnics. After independence, the government of Sheikh Mujibur Rahman passed the 1973 University Act, which granted enormous power to university teachers, students and other stakeholders (graduates, university non-teaching staff, parents, lay-public, politicians and so on).

Just as in many other countries in recent decades, the massification and commodification of higher education in Bangladesh has led to the creation of a number of new institutions, both public and private (Ferlie et al. 2009:4). At present there are 30 public and 56 private universities, one international university, 51 professional colleges (medical, dental, law, polytechnic, etc.), one university specializing in agriculture and one specializing in engineering and technology.

The Private University Act of 1992 enabled private universities to emerge in the '90s. These are located mainly in and around the Capital Dhaka and they do help meet the country's huge demand for higher education. The public universities nevertheless still bear the major 'burden', and access to higher level education in Bangladesh is still very limited. Competition for admission is stiff; only about 12 percent of those who finish secondary school (12 years) and who are eligible for higher education actually gain admission, and only one applicant out of 65 manages to get into a public university. There are now approximately 1,500 colleges under the umbrella of the National University – one of the world's largest such organisations in terms of enrolment. More than 80 percent of university-level students are enrolled in a National University affiliated college. The rest attend the public and private universities. In addition, the Open University offers long distance education programs and awards Honours, Masters and Research degrees. Parallel to all these, there is also a religion-based higher education system called Madrasah education (http://en.wikipedia.org/wiki/Universities_in_Bangladesh accessed on 18 December, 2009).

Although the number of private universities has increased in the last decade, the student population served by them has grown rather slowly (GOB, 2006). There are now around 1.3 million regular students studying at the various undergraduate to postgraduate levels (GOB, Statistical Pocket Book, 2006). Of these, more than 1 million students study under the National University system (UGC, 2006). Most often these students cannot pick the subject of their choice. The public universities' curricula are spread over basic science, humanities, engineering, agriculture and social sciences, and the medium of instruction is usually bilingual – Bangla and English. With respect to the cost of education, Bangladesh's public universities are heavily subsidised. Their entire development budget and approximately 90 percent of their recurring budget comes from the government exchequer. On average, recurring expenses in public universities are Taka 37,000 (US$ 550) per student per year, but the total amount of fees and charges an individual student pays per year is less than Taka 1000 (US$ 16) (UGC, 2006). But despite the government's allocation to the public universities, it is grossly inadequate. All public universities operate from their own campuses, which are built on land allocated by the government. Utilities are highly subsidised and salaries of teaching and non-teaching staff are relatively low. No taxes are levied on them and the salaries paid to all types of employees are tax free.

An Introduction to Rajshahi University

Rajshahi University, established on 6 July 1953, is the second largest university in Bangladesh and the highest seat of learning in the northern region. At its founding, a solemn promise was made to strive to achieve a high level of education and research. The university's main campus is close to the mighty river Padma and three miles east of Rajshahi City. Altogether there are seven faculties and 47 departments in the university, and in addition to hosting programs in the various faculties, it houses a number of institutes (Retrieved from http://www.ru.ac.bd/ibs/ibshome.htm, on 10/11/2009).

The university is run according to the Rajshahi University Act of 1973. This act allows the school considerably more autonomy than most other peer institutions. The president of Bangladesh (Md. Zillur Rahman), whose role is mainly ceremonial, is the de-facto chancellor. The next highest official is the vice-chancellor, selected, in theory, by the university senate every four years. The real world situation is however different from the provisions of the Act. For the last ten years or so, there have been no elected vice chancellors in Rajshahi University. All vice chancellors since 1999 have been selected by the chancellor. Other important officers of the university include the pro-vice chancellor, the registrar, the controller of examinations and the proctor. The proctor is directly in charge of student activities and has more first-hand contact with students than the other officers. The university's most important statutory bodies are the senate, the academic council and the syndicate. As a public institution, most of Rajshahi University's funding comes from the government. (The University Grants Commission (UGC) is the body responsible for allocating funds to all public universities.)

A prerequisite for prospective students is that they must pass the Higher Secondary Exam (HSC exam). They then take entrance examinations, a separate one for each department. Admission tests are held at the individual department level. As a public institution, Rajshahi University's tuition fees are relatively low; nevertheless, a hike in admission fees during the 2006-07 school years drew criticism from many students. As of 2007, the university awarded a total of 340 scholarships; the annual value of this is around 1.1 million Taka (US$ 1,600). In addition, there are merit awards given by residential halls, departments and the university itself. Students also compete for the prime minister's "Gold Medal" award. All colleges of the northern and southern regions of the country used to be affiliated with Rajshahi University. Since 1992, however, college administrations across the country have been taken over by the National University system.

The Procedure for Recruiting Teachers

In Bangladesh's universities, teachers are recruited at the following levels: lecturer, assistant professor, associate professor and professor. All recruits can be 'fresh', nevertheless, the position of lecturer is considered to be the entry level. In most cases the other three types of recruitments are promotions based on merit, or seniority or a combination of both, but there are also exceptions such as direct appointments. Apart from these four categories, there are provisions for appointing emeritus and supernumerary professor. Only a few teachers have been appointment as emeritus professors at Rajshahi University. There is no supernumerary professor at the university. Since lecturer posts are considered entry level teaching position, we, therefore, concentrate mainly on the terms and conditions for appointing lecturers.

To be eligible for the post of a lecturer, candidates must have a Master's degree with at least one first class, either at the Honours or at the Post Graduate level. A candidate with a third class in any of the degrees may be eligible for appointment as a lecturer if he or she has a PhD. If no suitable candidates are found, the required qualifications may be relaxed (Rajshahi University Calendar, 2006, Vol. 2, p. 60). The following is an overview of the various steps involved in the recruitment process.

First, the departmental planning committee sends a letter to the office of the registrar with a request to recruit teachers. In the letter the committee usually states the number and nature of posts to be filled. **Second**, the office of the registrar advertises those posts and invites prospective teachers to send in applications. **Third**, after the application deadline has passed, the office of the registrar sends all the applications to the department in question. **Fourth**, the departmental planning committee, after scrutinizing the applications, makes recommendations for calling qualified applicants in for a personal interview (*viva-voce*, it is like an oral exam). **Fifth**, the office of the registrar, upon receiving the recommendations from the departmental planning committee, sends all the selected applications to the expert member of the selection board for his/her recommendations. **Sixth**, upon receiving the letter of recommendation from the expert, the registrar calls all the qualified applicants and invites them to come for a *viva-voce* interview. It is important to note that recruitment is based solely on the personal interview between the applicant and the selection board of the department. The selection board is answerable to the chairmanship of the vice-chancellor. Of the selection board's members, two are also syndicate members, one is an expert member, and the chairperson of the concerned department. If, however, the chairperson is an assistant professor, he/she cannot sit on the interview board. Only associate professors and above are permitted to do so. **Seventh**, the selection board, after conducting an oral examination of all candidates, makes a list of the candidates and recommends for the final selection process. The list must be approved by the syndicate. The following table shows the steps involved in the recruitment of lecturers in Rajshahi University.

TABLE-2[2]: Steps Involved in the Recruitment of a Lecturer

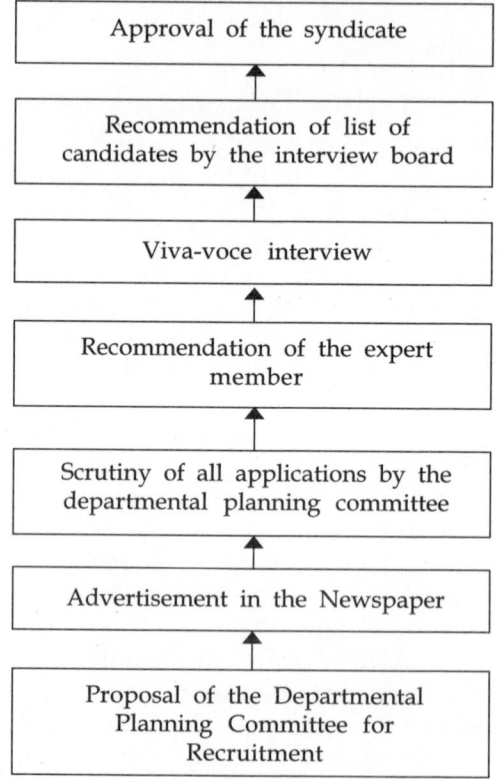

Who Gets Recruited: The Impact of Political Loyalty

The account we have just given describes the formal steps involved in recruiting lecturers. It is however idealised and far removed from reality. In almost all Bangladesh's universities there have been wide-ranging allegations regarding how university teachers are recruited. The whole system has been politicised. The process of politicisation starts with making changes in the top positions in accordance with the changes in government. It is important to mention here that along with change in the central government, changes in the administration of public universities have become routine. Yet even though it is a part of our political culture, the practice has become more frequent after the 1990s. For instance, changes were made in university administration during the army-backed caretaker government (2007-2008). Its intentions were to select administrators who looked relatively clean. Nevertheless, there were complaints that many of the new administrators were indeed involved in party politics. Once a politically loyal teacher is made the vice chancellor of the university, that person will strive to serve the interest of the party in power.

The teaching community is also politically divided. One group of teachers have affiliated themselves with the more liberal Awami League party which also played an active role in the liberation struggle against the Pakistani regime. This group is popularly called the 'blue' group who claims to be in favour of the War of Independence. Another group of teachers is loyal to the Bangladesh Nationalist Party (BNP). These teachers and the Jamat-e Islami (a fundamentalist Islamic religious party) prefer to see themselves as 'white' group members. Since vice chancellors are usually elected from one or the other of these groups (for the last 19 years either the AL or the BNP has ruled the country, with the exception of two years, from January 2007 to December 2008, when the country was ruled by the army-backed caretaker government), they try to remain faithful to their respective political parties, even to the extent of giving undue privileges to its supporters.

It is also important to mention here that the syndicate and senate, which are the highest policy making bodies in the universities, are composed of the elected and nominated members. Since there are provisions for electing teachers' representatives to these bodies, every administration tries to recruit teachers who will be loyal to them, with the expectation that they will cast their votes in favour of the candidates nominated from the group to which they are most loyal. In the process of recruiting voters instead of teachers, sometimes a candidate's political identity plays a more important role than his or her professional skill. Sometimes applicants with excellent academic achievement- and performance records are bypassed on account of their political neutrality. Since this happens frequently, it disrupts the chain of inputs, processes and outputs (described in Table 1) which the university needs to establish and maintain academic standard. The bypassing of highly qualified applicants impedes the dissemination of knowledge and the building of competence among students. Since the selection procedure and all documents produced in connection with it are classified and therefore beyond public scrutiny, it is difficult to unveil cases of foul play. The following example substantiates how the recruitment process is politicised and how applicants with political power can supersede those with greater academic merit.

> In mid 2005, the Departmental Planning Committee recommended that three lecturers be recruited to the Department of Public Administration. Eight candidates applied for the three posts of lecturer. Among them, two candidates had four first classes and the remaining six had three first classes.[3] The selection committee recruited six lecturers and ignored the Departmental Planning Committee's recommendation to recruit only three lecturers. But what was striking was that one candidate who had four first classes was not selected. Five candidates who had only three first classes were recruited as lecturers. Some informal sources said that the candidate with the four first classes was excluded because her father was active in the Awami League and the recruitment took place while the Bangladesh Nationalist Party was in power (Panday, 2009a).

This example is not unique; it describes the usual way in which teachers are recruited. In the case of promotions, the impact of politicisation is also immense. Sometimes appointments are made based on wrong motives, other times they may be based on a lack of clarity in how to interpret the University Act, but whatever is the case, the university authorities do give undue privileges to teachers who are politically loyal to them. One such example is the exemption of service experience requirements when a 'politically correct' teacher is being reviewed for promotion.

> The Act allows any university teacher to obtain an exemption of one year's experience at any level for purposes of promotion (in order to be qualified to become an associate professor or professor) if he/she has five publications which are of international standard. The provision suggests that in order to receive an exemption, one must have published in international or refereed journals. However, this provision has not been applied in letter or spirit. Since journal names are not specified, no one knows what 'international standard' should mean. Is the phrase used only to remind the readers that there is an international standard which measures the quality of a journal? For instance, there is the Social Science Citation Index (SSCI) for social sciences and the Science Citation Index (SCI) for [life] sciences. These lists include a large number of journals that have achieved world-wide recognition. When a teacher, for the sake of promotion, receives a one-year service exemption only on merits of publication, the quality of his/her publications should be judged properly. No administration had put effort into ensuring the quality of the publications. Instead, every administration has promoted teachers loyal to it along political lines and grossly ignored the quality of their publications. Numbers of article have gained paramount importance without considering their quality. Such manipulation is a serious offence. The clause could have been amended by simply including a few names of journals listed in SSCI or SCI or any other [qualitative citation index] (Panday, 2009b).

It is important to stress here that every application for an exemption from the required length of service is assessed on the merit of the applicant's political identity. Supporters belonging to the ruling party found that their applications got processed quickly while applications of those who support the opposition party suffer from being not processed and given due attention. However, there have been some exceptions, but these are infrequent. We can cite another politically motivated case:

> The provision of transforming temporary posts into permanent posts automatically was introduced by the immediate past administration of Rajshahi University. The University Act stipulates that any teaching staff serving in a temporary post must apply for an advertised post for the purpose of making his/her job permanent. However, the immediate past administration passed an act in the syndicate which allows any teacher serving in a temporary post to be eligible for a permanent position if he/she completes two years of service and if his/her application is recommended by the departmental planning committee. This provision is contrary to the 1973 Rajshahi University Act (Panday, 2009b).

It is obvious here that the Act in question was politically motivated. When we sought to discover the background why this particular Act was introduced, we found that almost forty teachers who held temporary posts were made permanent at the end of the BNP-Jamat regime's tenure (at the end of 2008 when the university administration was still loyal to BNP-Jamat coaltion). Moreover, there was at that time an injunction from the University Grants Commission to stop recruiting more teachers. Under such circumstance, the administration feared that if it could not retain power, the people working in temporary posts might lose their jobs. Thus, by applying the new criterion, the administration rendered the temporary employees permanent on 30 December, 2008 (just after the day of the 9th Parliamentary election, which the Awami League overwhelmingly won).

Appointments to posts such as registrar, proctor, student advisor, hall provost and house tutor are also made on the basis of political connections. Intra-group political power plays the most significant role in these appointments. Party members who are politically active and remain close to the party nucleus and the vice-chancellor are usually appointed to these positions, regardless of their level of academic excellence. Thus universities, once considered as centres of excellence, have become centres of politics.

The allegation of politicisation in the recruitment process seems to have a strong ground when we found that the University Grants Commission (UGC) formed a three member committee in 2008 to investigate into alleged irregularities and corruption in recruitment at Rajshahi University (RU) between 2005 and 2008 (The Daily Star, 03/08/2008). The probe committee, which found gross irregularities in recruitment of 700 teachers and employees at Rajshahi University (RU) since 2004, has asked the RU authorities not to recruit any manpower till 2010. The UGC probe body also found that most of the recruitments were made on political consideration. Qualified candidates giving better academic records were left out while less meritorious candidates were recruited in the process (The Daily Star, 01/08/2008).

Such claims find stronger ground when we find that the authority of Rajshahi University has formed a four member enquiry committee based on the recommendation of the Ministry of Education to investigate charges of corruption and irregularities in recruitment, implementation of educational programmes and projects of planning, development and engineering departments involving about Tk. 23.22 crore during the period from 2001 and 2008. Report of the investigation committee was unanimously accepted by the Rajshahi University Syndicate in its meeting held on 18th of July, 2010. The investigation committee has found proof of corruption and irregularities and have suggested punitive action against persons responsible for dishonest acts (The Daily Star, 21/07/2010).[4]

Politicisation in the recruitment process threatens to destroy the quality of education in Bangladesh. Due to political influence, less qualified applicants are sometimes recruited as teachers. These teachers lack a sufficient knowledge base, one which would enable them to provide high quality teaching. They are unable to help build the competence of graduate and post graduate level students. Significant gaps in the teachers' knowledge deprives students not only of good understanding of social realities and existing problems, but cannot be used to generate new ideas. The purpose of higher education is to develop inquisitive minds and to be innovative in knowledge production and dissemination. These objectives are seriously impeded. Knowledge remains largely stagnant and is seldom upgraded.

It is important to mention here that teachers' recruitment process is politicised not only in the Rajshahi University but also in the other public universities in Bangladesh. Mannan (2010) in his writing in *the Daily Star* (published on 25/02/2010) mentioned an example of mediocrity in the selection process in the following way:

> Mediocrity has replaced merit in most of the public universities and recently there was a report that in a leading university of the country, the Chairperson of the teacher selection committee, who also happens to be the Pro-Vice-chancellor of the same university decided to recruit his wife as a lecturer in the Department of Mathematics

though her position in the merit list of candidates was 27th out of 27 candidates. In some universities such practice became a regular phenomenon since 2001 and still continues to plague some of them.

Another important issue deserving special mention is the university teachers' decreasing quality of productivity in terms of conducting research, publishing quality papers, attending seminars and being part of the international network of researchers. Since promotion is mainly determined by political power and connections, there is almost no differentiation between real academics and politicians parading under an academic guise. Naturally, if scholars never receive recognition for their hard work, they will lose motivation at some point in time. For instance, if a scholar has managed to publish a substantial body of work in internationally recognised journals but receives no credit for it in terms of promotion (the law determining promotion requires only two published papers in any journal), it is more likely that the scholar will either lose motivation or will leave his or her job in search of better employment opportunities elsewhere. This problem has already created a large vacuum of serious academics in the university.

The consequences of compromising standards by recruiting political loyalists as faculty members poses a serious threat to knowledge building, knowledge dissemination and skill development. The major sufferers are students, for they fail to contribute fruitfully to building the society and the nation. Students who enter higher education, especially those enrolled in public universities, are the brightest and the best – because only a limited percentage of secondary school graduates manage to surmount the steep competition and get admission into these institutions. The nation is deprived of their talents because those academics whose job is to upgrade and build competence are insufficiently motivated or ill-equipped to disseminate knowledge.

Conclusion and Recommendations

The overall quality of higher education depends to a large extent on the recruitment of academics who would delve seriously in the production and dissemination of knowledge. Most of the higher educational institutions in most developing countries suffer from corruption, favouritism and patronage in the teacher selection process. Bangladesh is no exception. Thus, there is an urgent need to make the process of recruitment of teachers open, fair, and competitive. However, it is a matter of great concern that the recruitment process of teachers in public universities in Bangladesh is often plagued by nepotism, political preferences, and racial discrimination. In politicised educational institutions, quality education is more of a dream than a reality. The universities become political hubs rather than centres for excellence in teaching and research. In order to overcome this problem, the government should take the following steps:

First, the government should reduce the extent of its influence on university administration. The vice chancellor should be elected through the university senate and should not be appointed by the government. As previous experiences testify, a government appointed vice-chancellor will always try to uphold the interests of his or her political party, even at the expense of educational quality.

Second, the process of recruiting teachers should be streamlined and made more transparent, because recruitment based only on *viva-voce* interviews allows the interview board to manipulate the process. In recent times, the process of faculty recruitment has been politicised. Thus, quality is over shadowed by the Political affiliation of those recruited. In order to ensure quality of teaching, some private universities have introduced a system where a job seeker has to give a presentation or trial lecture before the selection board. Unfortunately this system is not in practice in any of the public universities in Bangladesh. If this system could be introduced, there is a possibility that qualified candidates would get recruited.

Third, there is no denying the fact that teachers of public universities enjoy more autonomy than teachers of private universities. In most cases public university teachers are not accountable for their deeds. Thus it is very often observed that a teacher cancels his scheduled class without any prior notice. Also, some teachers remain absent for days without giving any valid reason. These practices would be very difficult to stop until teachers are made accountable. In this regard, public universities may follow the culture of evaluation of teachers by students. There should be a system of reward and sanction mechanism for the teachers which would be based on the evaluation of the students. Only then public university teachers may become more accountable of their activities which would ultimately help improve the quality of higher education in Bangladesh.

Finally, there is an urgent need to review the University Act of 1973, which has given enormous powers to all concerned. An act comprises different rules, regulations and standard operating procedures about how one should act, perform, and behave. In this regard, another appropriate act needs to be formulated to discipline, reward as well as make academics committed to knowledge production and dissemination in order to promote quality education and research.

References

- Ali, A.M.M. Shawkat (2004) *Bangladesh Civil Service: A Political - Administrative Perspective*, Dhaka: The University Press Limited.
- Ehsan, Mohammad (2008) 'Higher Education Governance in Bangladesh: The Public Private Dilemma', Dhaka: AH Development Publishing House.
- Ferlie, Ewan, Christine Muselin, and Gianluca Andresani (2009) 'The Governance of Higher Education Systems: A Public Management Perspective' in Catherine Paradeise, Emanuela Reale, Ivar Bleiklie, and Ewan Ferlie (eds) *University Governance: Western European Comparative Perspectives*, Springer.
- GOB (2007) *Statistical Pocket Book*, Bangladesh Bureau of Statistics, Planning Division, Ministry of Planning.
- Mannan, Abdul (2009) *Higher Education in the 21st Century Bangladesh*, Available online at: http://www.articlesbase.com/education-articles/higher-education-in-the-21st-century-bangladesh-1017170.html, accessed 22 September 2009.
- .... (2010) Higher education Deficits in a Drift, The Daily Star, 25.02.2010), Retrieved from http://www.thedailystar.net/suppliments/2010/02/ds19/segment3/drift.html, on 01/08/2010.
- Panday, Pranab Kumar (2009a) 'Revitalising Rajshahi University', *The Daily Star*, (widely circulated English daily from Dhaka), 01 July 2009.
- .... (2009b) 'Manipulation of the University Act', *The Daily Star*, (widely circulated English daily from Dhaka), 19 September 2009.
- Rajshahi University Calendar, Modified up to 2006, Vol. II, p. 60.
- Siddiqui, Zillur Rahman (1997) *Visions and Revisions: Higher Education in Bangladesh 1947-1992*, Dhaka: University Press Limited.

- The Daily Star (A widely circulated English daily) 01/08/2008, 03/08/2008, 21/077/2010.
- UGC (2006) Annual Report of the UGC 2006, Dhaka: Bangladesh University Grants Commission.
- UNESCO (2000) World Education Report: The Right to Education towards Education For All Throughout Life. United Nations Educational Scientific And Cultural Organization, Paris: UNESCO Publishing.
- Vries, Peter de (1997) 'Academic Standard and the Quality Management Debate in British Higher Education', in John Radfor, Kjell Raaheim, Peter de Vried, and Ruth Williams (eds) *Quantity and Quality in Higher Education*, London: Jesica Kingsley Publishers.
- Williams, Ruth (1997) 'Factors Impacting on Academic Standards' in John Radfor, Kjell Raaheim, Peter de Vried, and Ruth Williams (eds) *Quantity and Quality in Higher Education*, London: Jesica Kingsley Publishers.
- World Bank (2000) *Higher Education in Developing Countries: Peril and Promise*, Washington DC: World Bank.

End notes

1. An earlier version of this paper entitled 'Impact of Politicization on the Recruitment of University Teachers in Bangladesh: The Case of the University of Rajshahi' was submitted at the NAPSIPAG conference, held in Malaysia on 11-13 December 2009.
2. The figure is drawn by the authors and based on the Rajshahi University Calendar.
3. 'Four first classes' means the scholar attained the highest level of grades in secondary school certificate exams, (i.e., after 10 years of education), higher secondary certificate exams (i.e., after 12 years of education). The scholar also received a first class in her honours and master degrees.
4. For more detail about the findings of the investigation committee please visit http://www.thedailystar.net/story.php?nid=147662

Chapter 10

BUILDING SELF EFFICACY AND RESILIENCE IN CREATING POSITIVE GOVERNANCE

Lipi Mukhopadhyay

Abstract

Human capabilities may be enhanced systematically by positive emotion and resilience. One's sense of self-efficacy is determined by an array of personal, social, and environmental factors. From the social-cognitive perspective, these factors can be changed not only to influence one's level of self-efficacy, but also subsequent performance on significant tasks. The key to staying successful in the role, despite the challenges is finding ways to bounce back. Resilient people need to be able to solve problem with a calm, confident sense of being able to overcome adversity. They need to approach challenges with learning agility: the ability to learn from each experience, positive or negative. These characteristics could be identified and utilised in creating a positive atmosphere for development of good governance.

Introduction

Human development is a continuous and complex process. It is influenced by personal, environmental and situational characteristics. Scientific understanding of that relationship helps to identify such factors that shape positive and negative influences on human behaviour. Many of the problems that arise later in life have their origins in the first years of the child's life. This means that parents are the main contributors to the child's genetic, psychological, emotional and intellectual resources. At the same time they are also the primary mediators of society's norms and demands which act as a filter for the effects of society on the child. All children are more than the sum of their parent's psychological and physiological characteristics. In addition to the genetic inheritance of their parents' physical emotional and overall psychological traits, they also inherit to a lesser extent the traits of a wider collective environmental influences including the child's own environmental influences. The development of human behaviour is a complex yet an interesting subject to study.

Human beings consist of positive and negative resources. Positive resources contribute greatly to the overall adjustment. These positive resources are satisfactions they derive from work, love and play, (Powell, 1982) and how they cope with negative influences. *Self efficacy* beliefs provide the foundation for motivation, well-being and personal accomplishment in all areas of life (Pajares 2005). Research studies have made noteworthy contribution to the understanding of self-efficacy and its relation to motivation and achievement. This paper examines the influences of personal and environmental characteristics in adjustment to diverse situation, individual difference in coping pattern, positive adaptation and determinants of good governance from the research findings.

Defining Self-efficacy and Resilience:

Human capabilities may be enhanced systematically by positive emotion and resilience. Human conduct is viewed to be the product of personal, behvioural and environmental influences. Research studies show that self-efficacy holds significant power for predicting and explaining academic performance in various domains (Lent, Brown and Larkin, 1986; Marsh, Walker and Debus, 1991; Zimmermen, Bandura, and Martinez-pons, 1992). Self-Efficacy means one's self-judgement of personal capabilities to initiate and successfully perform specified tasks at designated levels, expend greater effort, and preserve in the face of adversity (Bandura, 1986). This perspective enables researchers to gain a deeper understanding of the interactive relationship between self-efficacy and performance.

One's behaviour is constantly under reciprocal influence from cognitive and other personal factors, such as motivation and environmental influences. The growth and reduction of self-efficacy is influenced over time by social comparison with peers and is more pronounced as one grows older.

Social Cognitive Theory Provides a framework for explaining how personalisation and modeling are used to enhance the capabilities of human learning. Self-efficacy is a major construct of this theory. People's judgements of their capabilities to organise and execute courses of action required to attain designated types of performances. It is not concerned with the strategies one has but with judgements of what one can do with whatever strategies one possesses. Studies indicate that self-efficacious when they are able to picture themselves succeeding in challenging situations, which in turn determines their level of effort toward the task (Paris & Byrnes, 1989).

Resilience

Resilience is bouncing back from challenging situations or in the face of adverse situation finding oneself overcome adversity. They respond to challenges with learning agility, the ability to learn from each experience, positive or negative. Strength in the face of adversity is one of human being's most desirable characteristics. Challenges and disappointments are an inevitable part of life. People encounter adversity in the form of relationship problems, health issues, financial stresses, work, grief, etc.

Resilience is one of the keys to satisfaction in life. It maximises performance, improves physical health, prevents depression and enhances relationship. Resilience is not a quality that someone possesses or does not possess. It is a way of behaving, acting and thinking that anyone can learn or develop. (Janey Hool, 2008).

Sources of Self-efficacy and Resilience

People make judgements about their capabilities based on enactive experience, observation, persuasory information, and physiological states. In school, children gain knowledge and experiences through experiential activities. They also gain information based on seeing how peers they judge to be similar to themselves perform at various levels under given circumstances. They also are told by teachers, peers, family and others about their expected capabilities. These sources of efficacy information are not mutually exclusive, but interact in the overall process of self-evaluation. Social cognitive theory postulates that the aforementioned sources of self efficacy information are the most influential determinants of performance.

Enhancing Personal Capabilities

Within the model of triadic reciprocality, the ability to influence various personal determinants is accorded to five basic human capabilities: symbolizing, forethought, vicarious, self-regulatory, and self-reflective.

Symbolizing

People are generally gifted with the capability of symbolizing. In an academic context, this allows learners to process abstract experiences into models that guide their learning and performance.

Forethought

Forethought, the cognitive representation of future events, is also a powerful causal influence on one's learning.

Vicarious

Vicarious capability occurs by observing others and vicariously experiencing what they do.

Self-regulatory

Students typically self-regulate by determining what capabilities they have with regard to a given task and in effect compare those capabilities against a set of standards they maintain for themselves.

Self-reflective

Self reflection is an important factor in self improvement. Without the capability to self-reflect, human beings would be reactive without the capacity for self-improvement. It is found that purposeful and proactive self-reflection has powerful adaptive qualities (Pajares, 2005).

School Environment

School climate has been found to be associated with maladjustment. School that emphasise competition, testing and tracking and have low expectations have a higher number of school failures and dropouts than do schools that have high expectations, encourage cooperation and have teachers who are supportive (Powell-Cope & Eggert, 1994).

Sex Difference

Boys and girls mature at different ages. It is found that boys mature later than girls. It is found that females are less likely to be involved in behaviour problems in school (Barnes and Farrel, 1994). Gender difference in thought process and emotion was found (Gurian, 2004). It was found that boys reported lower levels of knowledge and different sources of stress than girls. Negative attitudes were more common among boys than girls. (Mukhopadhyay, 2008). The interacting perceptual influences of confidence and gender stereotyping are influential sources of self-efficacy information, but not determinants of beliefs about capabilities with regard to specific tasks.

Positive Adaptation

Positive adaptation is the key to development. It has been defined in several ways, including absence of psychopathology, behavioral and cognitive competence (Kim-Cohen, Moffitt, Caspi, & Taylor, 2004), and mastery of appropriate developmental tasks. The importance of both external adaptation to the environment and internal sense of well being as part of a comprehensive assessment of resilience is emphasised. Moreover, resilience is better characterised as a dynamic process, because individuals can be resilient to specific environmental hazards or resilient at one time period but not another (Rutter, 2006). Despite conceptual inconsistencies, research has reliably reported a number of characteristics associated with resilience like positive and supportive care, family relationship, competent parenting, child's temperament and higher cognitive ability (Masten et al., 1999; Wyman et al., 1999). Parental warmth, positive expectations, support and low derogation predict children's behavioral and emotional adaptation under a wide variety of adverse circumstances (Katz & Gottman, 1997; Kim-Cohen et al., 2004). Thus children whose mothers are available and supportive will be able to develop self-regulation abilities within the context of effective mother-child interactions (Wyman et al., 1999).

Developing Efficacy and Resilience

An important assumption of Social Cognitive Theory is that personal determinants, such as forethought and self-reflection, do not have to reside unconsciously within individuals. People can consciously change and develop their cognitive functioning. This is important to the proposition that self-efficacy too can be changed, or enhanced. From this perspective, people are capable of influencing their own motivation and performance according to a model of triadic reciprocality in which personal determinants (such as self-efficacy), environmental conditions are mutually interactive influences. Improving performance, therefore, depends on changing some of these influences ,Pajares, 2005 (see figure 1.1).

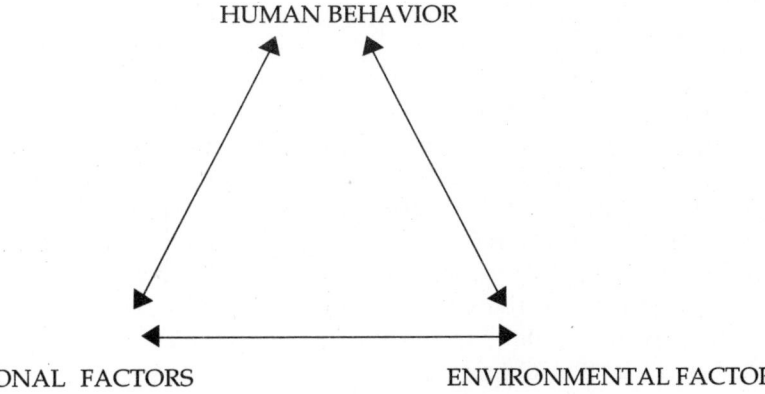

FIGURE: 1.1: Model illustrating relations between determinants in triadic reciprocal causation.

Flexibility is essential to developing and enriching resilience. It means keeping emotions from hijacking good reason. In short, the greater the resilience, the greater the chances of overcoming them and even getting rewarded by them. Recent evidence has shown that the brain goes through a remodeling process during adolescence. It is possible that neural plasticity facilitates the development of social cognitive skills required during the period of adolescence.

Development of self-esteem

Self-esteem is a sense of competence, achievement and self-respect. Maslow felt that the most stable source of self-esteem is genuine accomplishment rather than public acclaim or praise. Poor self-esteem and aspirations are linked with maladjustment. Adolescents who perform poorly in school and who possess low educational aspirations are more likely to become involved in alcohol and substance use/abuse (Dryfoos, 1990). People compare their performance with that of their peers in various contexts. The accuracy of their assessments determines whether they overestimate or underestimate their capabilities. Consequently, accurate self-reflection is critical to the development of self-efficacy.

Positive emotions are learnt in early lives through socialisation and strong cultural work ethic. This was supported in studies conducted on children, athletes and musicians. Those who resisted temptation at four years of age were able to cope with the frustrations of life in adolescence. Deficits in social skills and social competence play a significant role in the development and maintenance of many emotional and behavioural disorders of childhood and adolescence. Social skills training (SST) to increase the ability to perform key social behaviours that are important in achieving success in social situations (Spence, 2009).

Good Governance

Good governance has eight major characteristics. It is participatory, consensus oriented, accountable, transparent, responsive, effective and efficient, equitable and inclusive and follows the rule of law (OECD, 2001). Thus good governance may include excellence in public administration, capacity building for good governance, and partnerships among stakeholders in society. There is a need for educating public officials in two vital values: the ownership of responsibility and respect for human dignity. Capacity building for good governance involves an *investment in human capital*, which is a holistic process requiring the State to develop its own capacities, those of civil society, the private sector and other constituents. "Regardless of age, people must live with the escalating pace of change, and learning must allow them to embrace all kinds of changes in all settings throughout their lives ", stated Secretary-General Manalo.

According to UNESCO Director-General " Education emerges as the most crucial and basic factor in establishing good governance which in turn has the ultimate goal of achieving sustainable human development and respect for human dignity. ".
From the above discussion it is evident that self-efficacy and resilience are positively

related. With more self efficacious and resilient people in society there will be continuous improvement in the thoughts and skills that need to be developed for improved performance and good governance. The characteristics mentioned about *good governance* are linked with self-efficacy and resilience. All those characteristics emphasised for developing self-efficacy and resilience are important factors for good governance.

Conclusion

It is evident from the above discussion that self-efficacy and resilience are positively correlated. If an effort is made consciously to construct positive characteristics among the young children then they are able to adjust better in the society later as adults. With the knowledge of self-efficacy one can develop resilience in the face of adverse situation. Positive emotions play a crucial role in human being from mental disorder specially anxiety and heath problems.

A governance that can take note of these human capital resources may play a significant role in developing self-efficacy and resilience among the community for sustainable positive society free from health disorder and violence. This is an optimistic capacity building task that all educationists, administrators and civil society own a shared responsibility and accountability.

References

Bandura, A. (1986). *Defines Self- Efficacy.* www.psychologyinspain.com/content/reprints/1997/14.pdf
Barnes and Farrel, (1994). *Handbook of Psychology, Development Psychology,* books.google.co.in/books?isbn=0471384054.
Dryfoos, J. (1990). *Adolescents at Risk Prevalence and Prevention,*
Gurian, Michael. *What could he be thinking? How a man's mind really works.* Reported in Times of India September, 2, 2004.
Janey Hool (2008), Paws and reflect.
    laughing1wolf.blogspot.com/2008_10_01_archive.html
Katz & Gottam J.M. (1997). Buffering Children from marital conflict and dissolution. Journal of clinical Child Psychology, 26, 157-171.
Kim-Cohen, J., Moffitt, T.E., Caspi, A. & Taylor, A. (2004). Genetic and environmental processes in young children's resilience and risk to socio economic deprivation. Child Development, 75, 651-668.
Lent, Brown & Larkin, (1986). CPP/Efficacy/Self Efficacy, www.positivepractices.com/Efficacy/SelfEfficacy.html
Mukhopadhyay, Lipi (2008). *Character Strengths of School Children*; Research Report under publication.
Masten, A.S. & Coatsworth, J.D. (1999). The development of competence in favorable and unfavourable enviornments: Lessons from research on successful children, *American Psychologist,* 53, 205-220.
OECD (2001) *Citizens as Partners- Information, Consultation and Public Participation in Policy-Making,* UNESCO.
Paris & Byrnes, (1989) Self regulation. www.mindmatters.edu.au/...and.../self-regulation.html.
Pajaras, F.& Urdan.T.(eds.) (2005). *Self-efficacy and Adolescence.* Greenwich, CT: Information Age.
Powell-cope & Eggert, (1994). *Handbook of Psychology.* books.google.co.in/books?isbn=0471176699..

Powell, D.H. *Understanding Human Adjustment* (1982).

Rutter, M. (2006) Implications of resilience concepts for scientific understanding. Annals of the New York Academy of Sciences, 1094, 1-12.

Spence, Susan H.(2009) Longitudinal examination of the associations between emotional dysregulation, coping responses to peer provocation, and victimization in children.

http: espace.librart.uq.edu.au

Wyman, P.A., Cowen, E.L., Work, W.C., Hoyt-Meyers, L., Magnus, K.B. & Fagen, D.B. (1999). Caregiving and developmental factors differentiating young at-risk urban children showing resilient versus stress-affected outcomes: A replication and extension. *Child Development*, 70, 645-659.

Zimmermen, Bandura, and Martinez-pons, (1992). *Self Efficacy linkinghub.elsevier.com/retrieve/pii/ S0361476X99910160.*

CHAPTER 11

EMPOWERMENT OF WOMEN THROUGH EDUCATION:
Innovative Policy Interventions in Rajasthan

SHEILA RAI

Abstract

If transition towards knowledge based development and well being is to be the aim and objective of the Millennium Development Goals, then education of women is definitely a non-negotiable. In a globalizing economy, it is increasingly important to consider what must be done to help women and girls not simply to get by, but to emerge empowered and thrive. It's high time the international development community and developing country governments began investing in girls' education to achieve gender equality and women's empowerment. Based on Rajasthan, this paper attempts to assess the interventionist role of the state and its resultant impact on the actual status of women's education in this largest state of India.

Introduction

Persistent inequality between men and women has been found to be the most crucial disparity in India. Prevalence of disadvantage to girls in comparison with boys is more pronounced in the field of education, which is illustrative of the broader phenomena of gender based inequality. As a matter of fact, and grave concern, women in general tend to fare quite badly in comparison to men, even within the same families, in matters such as nutrition, health, survival and opportunity to develop capacities. In addition, because social institutions are organised around gender inequality, the system also patterns one's life chances and directs men and women's social, economic, and political experiences.

(Joshi, S.C. 2005:138). Nonetheless, adequate investment in education and most importantly appropriate government policies could prove effective in mitigating the perpetuation of inequalities.

Biological explanations of inequality have frequently appeared during historical periods of rapid social change in traditional societal arrangements. In the post Civil War period, women's exclusion from educational institutions was explained as necessary to protect their reproductive organs. It was assumed that women's wombs dominated their mental life and that studying hard would damage their reproductive systems. Young girls were even warned not to study at all during menstruation for fear of draining their reproductive power! These historical examples indicate that biological explanation of sex and race differences have been used to justify existing social arrangements. (Joshi, S.C. 2005:145)

However, the last quarter of the past century has been a period of intense activity the world over to secure for women the status due to them. India has also made its presence felt in this context, especially with its constitutional assurances of "Justice, social, economic and political" and equality of status and opportunity, for all its citizens. The benefits of educating women have come to stay, specifically as a catalyst for promoting gender equality and empowering women.

Historical Perspective

At the time of India's independence, less than a fifth of the population was literate. The elitist orientation of the colonial educational policy was reflected in the neglect of mass education. Colonisation in the sphere of education meant the replacement of indigenous institutions of learning, including village schools, by a new structure of state supported institutions. The devaluation of the traditional system and teacher weakened and snapped communicating support and linkages. The societal aspiration of entering the modern stream through formal schools needed resources and extensive paraphernalia, more than what the colonial state was willing to expend. As a result, only a minority could be educated. Other than that such a system left most, more so the women, out and unattended. (RamChandran, Vimla, Sethi, Harsh and Kaul, Rekha. 2001).

However, with the establishment of a free nation, and enshrining of the goals of democracy, socialism and secularism in the Constitution, the post colonial state became an instrument of social transformation. Appropriate interventions to deal with certain target groups viz. women, were identified with the realisation that they were handicapped by social customs and values and, therefore, special endeavours for their rehabilitation were emphasised upon. Ironically, while all agreed that women were entitled to education, there seemed to be ambivalence not only about the proper role for women in India but also about the kind of education appropriate for them.

A comprehensive review of the entire education system was undertaken only two decades after independence. Previous reviews had been, at best, sectoral. The University Education Commission or Radhakrishnan Commission was the first review body, which submitted its report in 1949. The Secondary Education (Mudaliar) Commission (1952-53) was followed by the National Committee (Durgabai Deshmukh) on women's Education in 1958-59. The recommendations of the Hansa Mehta Committee on differentiation in curricula for Boys and Girls in 1964 were endorsed by the Indian Education Commission (1966), better known as the Kothari Commission, which was followed by the National Policy on Education in 1968. The next National Policy on Education came up with a Plan of Action only in 1986. Both documents were revised further in 1992.

The ambivalence regarding role of women was more than pronounced in the first all male commission headed by Dr. Radhakrishnan which, while discussing various dimensions of University education, devoted only one chapter to women's education with unjustified emphasis on the 'wife-mother' role of women. But ever since the first 5-year plan, this wavering between the specific 'wife – mother' role on the one hand and the need to equip her for wider participation on the other has been witnessed, with a perceptible tilt towards the latter (Desai and Thakkar. 2001 : 48).

It was the Durgabai Deshmukh Committee (1958-59) which made a significant contribution to the issues of women's education. The hindrances and difficulties in the progress of girls' education were identified and suggestions to bring about parity with boys' education were examined and adequately recommended. The Hansa Committee (1962) unequivocally took a stand against differentiation between education curriculum on gender basis and attributed the attitudinal behaviour of policy makers in particular and those of people at large to the 'biological deterministic' approach. Recommending co-education at the primary and secondary stages, the commission also advised provision of home science and vocational courses for both boys and girls (Desai & Thakkar. 2001:50).

The Kothari Commission (1964-66), although endorsing the views of the Hansa Mehta and Durgabai Deshmukh Committees, did not devote adequate attention to higher education of women. The committee dwelt on the gender issue by suggesting provision of financial assistance and hostels to girls who wished to pursue careers in higher education.

In a nutshell, it may be mentioned that all such committees in post-independence India failed to articulate the relationship between women's equality, their participation in national development and the pattern and thrust of education itself. No thought was given to the adverse impact of the educational process on social values, the construction of gender, and how women's equality as a value could affect the educational process.

Changing Domestic & International Scenario

Perhaps the attempts made by the government up to the late sixties for eradication of illiteracy and promotion of women's education did not achieve the desired success as the nation was then largely preoccupied with problems of food scarcity, unemployment and lack of self-reliance. The burgeoning population also added to the army of illiterates. Lack of a coherent, well worked out plan of action which could unite the centre, states and voluntary organisations in a cumulative all embracing national effort in the educating mission was also conspicuously absent.

The United Nations General Assembly, meanwhile, adopted a Resolution on "Declaration of Elimination of Discrimination against women" in 1967 and requested all member states to prepare reports on the 'status of women' in their countries. But this call was heeded in India only after a reminder was sent from the UN in 1975. The declaration of 1975-85 as International Women's Decade by the UN further turned the entire debate into a global phenomenon.

The Government of India, in the background of the above, geared itself into action and constituted a commission of enquiry to study the status of women in the country. The report entitled 'Towards Equality', which was prepared by a team of academics, social workers, non-governmental personnel and members of Parliament, has been an eye opener to the stark inequalities between men and women. The chilling statistics of subordination of women in almost every realm of social, political and economic life was significant enough to propel and affect government politics towards promoting women's welfare and empowerment. The culmination of all ensuing government efforts was the declaration of a National Policy on Education which was adopted in 1986, followed by the formulation of a 'Programme of Action'. The significance of the policy vis-a-vis women was that besides setting targets for universalisation of elementary education for children of 6-14 years age group by AD 2000 and stepping up of the outlay on education (exceeding 6% of the national income), it specifically mentioned that education would be used as an agent to bring about diametric change in the hitherto pathetic status of women. It was proposed that the National Education System would play a positive interventionist role in the empowerment of women and that accumulated distortions of the past would sought to be neutralised by a well conceived edge in favour of women. Removal of women's illiteracy and initiating their access to, and retention in, elementary education was prioritised in the said policy, mentioning therein the provision of special support services, setting of time bound targets and effective monitoring to achieve the proclaimed objectives. A highlight of the policy was the proposed adoption of non-discrimination to eliminate stereotyping in vocational and professional courses and promotion of women's participation in non-traditional occupations, as well as in existing and emerging technologies.

Impact of Recent Education Policies

The adoption of the National Policy amply testifies the long distance covered from the initially hesitant, reluctant and limited approach to women's education and also signifies the forward leap towards accepting establishment of gender equality in access, objectives and commitment of the government to the goals enshrined in the Constitution. A plethora of governmental programmes and schemes were consecutively initiated and operated to achieve the targets pronounced in the document. The 1990's saw fresh initiatives like the District Primary Education Programme (DPEP), Lok Jumbish[1] and the recent Sarva Shiksha Abhiyan[2] to name but a few. Since then, there has undoubtedly been an overall fillip in female education in the country.

The Constitution of India originally placed the primary responsibility for elementary education on the State Governments resulting in a decline in share of central funding from about 18.66% (1950-51) to zero (1970-01) (RamChandran, Vimla, Sethi, Harsh and Kaul, Rekha. 2001). It was only in 1976 with the 42nd Amendment that education became a concurrent subject and the Central Government started taking a serious interest in basic education. After becoming a concurrent subject, central funding was increased even in primary education. After the 73rd and 74th Amendments which ushered the third tier of government, schooling has become the domain to be jointly worked by all three levels.

There are regional variations which ominously relate to social, cultural, demographic and other variants. As a welfare state with development as one of its primary goals, the state had initially taken the responsibility of providing free education to girls in some states even upto college level. But with the onset of new economic policies and liberalisation of the economy in the name of structural adjustments there has been a decline in public expenditure in various sectors, including education – which is more marked in higher education. Nonetheless, one witnesses a vibrant atmosphere in some states where education has been adopted as an emancipatory tool and agency for social transformation. It is not possible to draw a coherent picture of its impact on the states in totality but a representative micro-study would facilitate a better understanding of the situation on the ground. Selecting for the purpose the state of Rajasthan would be justifiable on two counts:

- It is the largest state in the country with a hitherto infamous record of rampant illiteracy
- In recent years it has traversed in an exemplary manner from ignominy to valuable eminence and has been rewarded internationally for outstanding achievements in the field of education.

Rajasthan: Bridging the gap between Policy and Ground Reality

Rajasthan is the largest state in India comprising 32 districts spread over 3.4 lakh square kms, geographically it is the most disadvantaged state with 11 of its districts being complete deserts and five semi-deserts. Frequent droughts and unfavourable climatic conditions for successive years result in failure of crops and inadequate agricultural produce. Mother nature's unkindness has not been the only challenge facing Rajasthan, it has borne the stigma of comprising the highest rate of illiteracy in the country till almost half a decade ago[3]. Due to its rich cultural heritage and ancient architecture, Rajasthan is arguably one of the most popular tourist destinations in the country. It is also a state of striking gender disparities and rigid patriarchal traditions.

With the state recording one of the highest rates of population growth – it has a total population of 5.65 crores. The declining sex ratio (922/1000) in the state has also been a cause of grave concern. For consecutive decades post independence, the entire government machinery and even the voluntary sector had been making noises about the need of improving the level of education in general and women in particular. A plethora of policies and programmes were sporadically and half-heartedly planned and implemented for the purpose. Yet there persisted several deterrents to women's education in the state, some of which were universal, some locale specific and some empirical and functional e.g. child marriages, purdah, sibling care, household chores, helping parents in their occupation etc. Traditionally among thousands who got enrolled in schools only a fourth of them ever completed primary education and a miniscule fraction reached the college or university level.

Several programmes such as DPEP[4], Sarva Shiksha Abhiyan were effectively implemented by the Bhartiya Janata Party government, led by the first ever woman Chief Minister of the state Mrs. Vasundhara Raje, which transformed this hitherto lumbering 'elephantine state' into a 'running tigress' in the field of education in general and female education in particular. Rajasthan which earlier ranked as low as 23rd in the context of literacy amongst the States and Union Territories of the country somersaulted to the 7th position, thus carving an enviable niche for itself both at the national and the international level. The crowning glory was the felicitation of its educational endeavors by being rewarded the Confucius Award by UNESCO on 23rd Sept. 2006. With this remarkable international recognition for its exemplary achievements; Rajasthan has indeed created history by being the only state so far to have received an award which had been instituted to be rewarded to a country rather than any specific state.

It has generally been observed that policy statements languish on paper as they fail to correspond to the ground realities. Indisputably, it is political will which can actually help translate policies into achievements. A glimpse of the initiatives undertaken by the State government would amply testify the major preoccupation of both the government and civil society in this context.

Initiatives & Instrumentalities

In a gendered society, in which the education of a girl has always been a low priority, a significant shift has manifested in the allocation of expenditure on education in Rajasthan. The earlier budget of 400 crores was increased to 1400 crores for the purpose. Acknowledging the fact that access to education does not rely solely on political will but more on the availability of educational institutions, the government of the state augmented a phenomenal increase in the number of education institutions in Rajasthan. In the 59 years of independence the total number of schools was 45000 to which 39,000 more were added and upgraded in a very short span. (GOR.2006). Besides granting recognition to 15,000 private schools in the region, the government further enhanced accessibility to education by tirelessly and persistently fulfilling the commitment of ensuring at least one school within the radius of every one kilometer in the state. This definitely made access easier for the girls and their parents who were earlier deterred due to long distances, more so in the rural areas. The corresponding creation of one high school for every two primary schools and at least one middle school in every Panchayat Samiti are other remarkable accomplishments, definitely worthy of emulation and replication by other states in the country, if the agenda of social transformation through education is to be accomplished.

Maximizing the organisational structure by recruiting almost 2.80 lakh teachers which comprised 28% female teachers for the primary and upper primary government schools the government did not stop at that but further recruited 74,888 female teachers in the upper primary schools at Panchayat Headquarters (GOR 2006). Approximately 2000 community teachers were recruited from the relevant communities thus providing unprecedented opportunities of employment to the hitherto unemployed. Numerous orientation, training and capacity building programmes were implemented for the enhancement of teaching skills.

To ensure requisite quality control policy changes were initiated for realisation and achievement of goals. Voluntary teachers, alternative schools, residential schools to fulfill faculty requirements and counter teacher absenteeism were adopted. Bridge courses and residential schools catered as forward linkages to under privileged girls who were dropouts. In the year 2006-07, 1326 camps under Bridge Course Programmes were organised in which 60,659 boys and girls were enrolled out of them 34919 were helped in joining mainstream education (CRC 2004-05, 2006-07). The National programme of Nutritional Support for Primary Education (commonly known as Mid-day Meal scheme) launched in 1995 has contributed towards enhancing school enrolment and attendance. Various surveys have revealed that Rajasthan has out-performed many states in terms of increase in enrolment and retention of students under this programme (CUTS. 2006).

Skillfully engineered awareness campaigns were conducted to spur community participation – both in the gender and geographic connotations. Parent teacher interactions were promoted, so that parents develop interest in their child's progress. Flexible timings and free of cost conveyance facilities to facilitate regular attendance of students have been provided.

Incentives and Aids

Almost 30% girl schools were upgraded annually and 2300 new sections added for them at Secondary / Senior Secondary level. More than 31 girls' hostels were created at divisional and district levels and 170 girls secondary schools have been equipped with computer labs. Over and above free education for girls upto class XII and Gargi Scholarships, in districts where female literacy was found to be below 40%, scholarships to students securing highest marks in class 3, 4 and 5 was provided by the District Education Officer. Physically disabled children were provided tricycles, calipers, wheel chairs, crutches, hearing aids etc., as per their requirement. Incentives such as textbooks, stationery, uniform, bus passes, health and accident insurance etc., were provided to several categories to ensure their entry and retention in schools. The government thus reinforced its aim to reach out to those remaining at the bottom rung, thereby addressing the need of female education in the state.

Laudable Innovations

To overcome traditional and cultural barriers, gender sensitivity training was provided to project personnel, teachers and educational administrators. Under DPEP 648 girl child motivators from 11 districts were recruited in 2003-04 who reached out to 31,037 girls (IDS 2007: 27).

Some very innovative schemes and programmes were initiated and implemented in the state, which deserve specific mention viz. 'Kasturba Gandhi Residential Schools' (56 Residential schools were provided for 3748 girls from backward and deprived classes and minority community) (GOR 2006). 'Life Skill Education' (women were trained to use tractors and initiated to usage of modern technological equipment), 'Aapki Beti Scheme' (girls from BPL families whose either parent or both have died were provided 1500/- per year to continue their studies upto 10th class, there have been 5,76,500 beneficiaries in 2004-05 and 81,75,600 in 2005-06 (CRC)). Similarly under the 'Gargi Scheme' scholarships of Rs. 1000/- were provided to girls who secured highest marks in class VIIIth at the Panchayat Samiti & District Head Quarter level and desired to further continue their studies. 10804 girls were given this scholarship in 2005-06 (CRC), girls residing in rural areas and travelling beyond 5 kms to attend secondary or senior secondary school were paid Rs. 5 (per day) for commuting purposes), 'Scheme of Vehicles' was expedited by distributing bicycles to girls of rural areas who lived within 2-5 km. from school and pursued studies after IXth class. To facilitate continuation of studies of tribal girls who passed 10th class with 65% marks Scootys were distributed by the government. Under a special scheme MMSSB Programme initiated by the Chief Minister 12256 cycles were distributed free of cost to tribal girls studying in 9th to 12th class in the TAD area (CRC). Besides training women to use tractors and initiating them to usage of modern technological equipment, 20% seats have also been reserved for them in B.Ed. courses. 'Jhola Pushtakalay' (Bag library) was another noteworthy innovative scheme aimed at including within the ambit of education shepherds and cattle-grazers who due to their nature of work could not attend school. Reading material was provided to them in bags so that they could read them while their cattle grazed (GOR 2006). 'Mobile Educational Centres' were created with books loaded on to camel carts in the areas of Barmer and Jaisalmer where hamlets were far flung and schools inaccessible. The 'mobile schools' moved to various destinations in the desert area and thereby facilitated access to education to even those who would otherwise have remained uneducated.

Towards Higher Learning

As part of the educational effort the government expanded the realm of higher education as well. 428 new colleges (government and private) were created. Rajasthan can boast of having one college for every 63000 (population) in comparison to one for every 77000 at the national level (GOR 2006). With 12 Universities, 8 deemed universities, 5 research institutes, 751 colleges for general education, 50 engineering and architecture colleges and 34 medical colleges the state definitely augurs well for the cause of higher education. The financial assistance to girls for higher and technical education from economically poor backgrounds is provided through Balika Shiksha Foundation. Based on the PPP model more than 10 MOUs have been signed with organisations like Microsoft, Intel, Azim Premji Foundation, America India Foundation etc., for promotion of female education (IDS 2007).

Nevertheless, one cannot ignore the paradox of women's' educational statistics which reveals a very insidious pyramid at the national level . There are 6,64,041 recognised primary schools, 2,19,626 upper primary schools and 1,33,492 high schools in India. As we go higher there are only 8737 colleges for general education, 2409 professional institutions and 272 institutions of national importance (GOI Department of Education MHRD Web site). This essentially reveals a very disturbing picture wherein there is only one upper primary school for three primary schools and one high school for approximately 5 upper primary schools. This obviously implies the competition to enroll at higher levels is tougher, children from poor quality government formal and alternative schools are the ones who would be left out almost as if by design. (Ramachandran, Vimala. 2004). The prognosis is quite clear. Ordinary middle and high school education is not adequate. Given the changing scenario in the country there is a marked decline in public expenditure in higher education and noticeable expansion of privatisation. The obvious fallout is increase in fees and imposition of capitation fees in professional courses. Serious planning and investment in higher education and professional training opportunities is of significant import if women's education is to be promoted.

Concluding Observations

Nonetheless, it could be rightly said that the various experiments, methodologies and schemes initiated in Rajasthan were extremely innovative. What is interesting is that the programmes pursued planned interventions for the promotion of girls education, by rightly first identifying issues and subsequently organizing area intensive approaches to reach out to girls.

The enormity of the task can be truly appreciated taking into account the impediments[5] and challenges[6] which have often outnumbered the facilitative aspects. Notwithstanding, progressive changes have actually been witnessed in:

- Attitude of, and towards, women's education
- Significant improvement in key developmental indices like infant mortality rate, use of contraceptives, child immunisation, AIDS awareness etc., (GOI, Ministry of Health and Welfare. 2007-2008)
- Level of cleanliness and hygiene
- Transformation of caste dynamics[7]
- Gradual shedding of Purdah (veil) and significant reduction in instances of child marriage
- Acceleration of community mobilisation
- Incremental expansion of repertoire of skills and abilities of women

However, the marked buoyancy in the state is not bereft of the areas of despair. The infrastructural facilities are yet far from adequate viz. class rooms, toilets, drinking water and sports facilities etc. There has been definitely a marked enlargement of choice of courses in the areas of higher education but the contingent areas of concern can not be over looked. The structural adjustments in the wake of globalisation is witnessing a withdrawal of state from vital areas of health, environment, social services and even education, which are nothing short of alarm signals. This is substantially and adversely affecting the cause of higher education in general and women's education in particular in the state of Rajasthan in India.

Opening the field of education to the private sector, market forces and other nations have resulted in the escalation of fees which makes education inaccessible for those from the economically weaker strata, especially women. The strategy of lowering the cost of girls' education needs to be given serious thought if they are to be empowered and protected from gender discrimination. The fact remains that the path to empowerment through education is long and full of challenges but nonetheless the journey should continue. Linking education to empowerment, survival, awareness of social, political and economic rights as citizens can yield handsome results for a country like India that is experiencing unprecedented social and economic transformation.

References

- Consumer Unity & Trust Society (CUTS). (2006). *Aage Badhno Hossi (Women Marching Ahead)*.
- Department of Education, Government of Rajasthan. (2006). Report on Education: 3 Years of Development.

- Department of Women & Child Development, government of Rajasthan, in Association with UNICEF (2004-05 to 2006-07). Convention on the Rights of the Child (CRC), Rajasthan State Report.
- Desai Neera and Thakkar Usha. (2001). Women in Indian Society. National Book Trust, New Delhi.
- Directorate of Economic & Statistics, Yojna Bhawan, Rajasthan, Jaipur. (2006). Statistical Abstract.
- Government of India, Ministry of Health and Family Welfare. (2007-2008). District Level Household and Facility survey. *Fact Sheet Rajasthan.*
- Government of India: New Delhi (1950). Report of the University Education Commission.
- Hansa Mehta Commission. (1964). Report on Differentiation in Curriculum for Boys and Girls. New Delhi.
- IDS, Government of Rajasthan. (2008). Human Development Report. *Strengthening state plans for human development: an Update.*
- Joshi, SC (2001). Social Problems Genesis, Causes and Magnitude. Akanksha Publishing House, New Delhi.
- Kothari Commission. (1965). Report on Education in India.
- National Commission (1958-1959). Report on Women's Education.
- Ramchandran, Vimla. (1999). Visible but unreached. *Seminar,* No: 474 February.
- .... (2004) The best of times the worst of times, *Seminar,* No. 536 April.
- Ramchandran, Vimla, Sethi Harsh and Kaul, Rekha. (2001). Basic education in India. *Advocacy Research Paper Commissioned by CARE, India Educational Resource Unit, Jaipur and Delhi.*

End notes

1. Education for All - a movement started in 1989 aimed at ensuring education for all in the state of Rajasthan through mobilisation of the community.
2. Is a tool for universalisation of education and it focuses on girls, children belonging to SC/ST community, urban slum dwellers, low female literacy blocks, disabled children and children in difficult circumstances.
3. Overall literacy in the state was a dismal 60.40% which was lower than the national literacy rate 64.80, Census 2001
4. District Primary Education Programme initiated in India in 1994 in 18 states and 272 districts.
5. Contextual factors like community setups, accessibility of rural habitations in desert areas.
6. The challenge of preparing young adolescent girls with no previous exposure to education to acquire proficiency through alternative schooling and clear formal examinations apart from socializing them to lead more aware and enlightened lives.
7. Noticeable change in attitudes amongst castes, more harmony and intermingling among the lower and upper caste groups, reduction of caste divides.

CHAPTER 12

PREPARING HUMAN RESOURCE FOR E-GOVERNMENT:
Some Evidence from Bangladesh Civil Service

SHAH MOHAMMAD SANAUL HOQUE,
AND
FATEMA-TU-ZOHRA BINTE ZAMAN

Abstract

Human resources are the driving force of any organisation. The public workforce, as main driver, is a critical element on the 'supply side' of e-government applications. It is also key to planning, designing and implementing any e-government initiative. Therefore, necessarily the workforce must be equipped with the right aptitude (skill) perception (understanding), attitude (desire) and to move with changes. This paper investigates the preparedness of the Bangladesh Civil Service (BCS) for e-government. In particular it deals with the groups of entry level, mid level and senior level public officials working in the BCS. It provides a general insight into their levels of aptitude, awareness and attitudes towards e-government.

The study notes that regarding preparedness, members of the BCS show considerable strengths for e-government in respect of their interest and adaptability to new technologies. However, despite their levels of awareness and positive attitudes towards e-government they have low levels of ICT aptitude. Further, the ICT facilities for civil servants are often locked up with word processing and other elementary applications. Robust training and motivational programs are needed to provide a brilliant supply side for e-government service delivery in Bangladesh.

1. Introduction

E-government offers a new platform of social contract which binds three parties: the public at large, government and business (UN 2003). To translate this new social contract into public value, one of the important requirements is the readiness of public managers, who contribute as the driving force of e-government applications. Therefore, transformation from traditional government to e-government is only possible if the public management system is prepared and people are enabled to undertake the control, transmittal and proper use of information and resources.

E-government systems require adequate access to modern technology and the ability to reconstitute governance mechanisms. To ensure proper implementation of e-government and to avoid the risks of resistance, the motivation and effective participation of public officials are critical prerequisites. This paper investigates the supply side's preparedness. Particularly it deals with the groups of entry level, mid level and senior level public officials working in Bangladesh Civil Service. It provides a general insight into their levels of aptitude, awareness and attitudes towards e-government.

1.2 Background

E-government is the use of technology to enhance the access to and delivery of government services to benefit citizens, business partners and employees (Silcock 2001). It presents the prospects of better and cost effective service delivery and greater citizen empowerment (UN 2003 in Smith and Teicher 2006). An important goal of e-government in the public sector is the promotion of engagement of people and other stakeholders in public policy making and implementation. (Clark 2003). Another important feature of e-government is that it works as a means to cost saving on service delivery, whilst making the government more accountable and transparent by creating higher awareness of and accessibility to government activities.

Transformation from traditional governance to e-governance is not a linear process. Success in the area of e-governance requires more than just deployment of technology and building connectivity. It requires much broader and far-reaching readiness in terms of policy initiatives, infrastructure building and skill development, most of which are not technical in nature (UN 2004). Developing countries are lagging behind because of many reasons, including dearth of the preparedness of government officials, who are supposed to act as the supply side of e-governance. In the same way, the subsequent reports (UN 2005 & 2008) demonstrate deficiencies of e-readiness among the developing countries. A quick view on the e-governance readiness index of some selected countries is presented below:

TABLE 1: E-Governance Readiness Index: 2008

Rank	Country	e-Governance readiness Index
1	Sweden	0.9157
4	USA	0.8644
6	Republic of Korea	0.8317
8	Australia	0.8108
10	UK	0.7872

95	Maldives	0.4491
101	Sri Lanka	0.4244
113	India	0.3814
122	Pakistan	0.3042
142	Bangladesh	0.2936
World average		0.4514
Southern Asia region average		0.3395

Source: Computed from UN E-Government Survey 2008: From E-Government to Connected Governance.

Structural and human capital related changes are needed at a government level to introduce effective e-government practices (I-Ways 2003). There is a need to increase the supply side e-readiness through training and development supported by operational plans to execute policies. Lodge (2003) articulates that e-government is a powerful device, which is devoid of political meaning; it is an information server to the community. But the public managers as the suppliers of cost effective and quality services should have the required e-readiness. E-government systems require an adequate access to modern technology and the ability to reconstitute the governance mechanism. Adequate human resource capability is needed to coordinate the internal and external services factors so as to be able to handle a demand for services (Wimmer 2002).

1.3 Statement of the Problem

Human resources are the driving force of any organisation. The public workforce, as the main driver, is the 'supply side' of e-government It is the key to planning, designing and implementing any e-governance initiative. Therefore, necessarily civil servants need to be equipped with right aptitude (skill) perception (understanding), attitude (desire) and to move with changes.

Amongst public officials, globally, a generic lack of e-governance leadership and commitment is observed because of lack of awareness, knowledge, skills and confidence. This lack leads to such e-governance initiatives that are basically planned and driven by vendors, donors or by consultants. As a result, inappropriate systems from other sectors or countries that do not fit specific realities are often being forced in. This is partly because of the human capacity and regulatory constraints within government (Heeks 2001).

In Bangladesh, e-governance has become an agenda for public sector reform and good governance. Some preparatory initiatives have been taken to implement e-government practices at various levels of public management system. However, initiatives for introducing e-governance in Bangladesh need well prepared public sector managers as the driving force. For successful implementation, e-governance initiatives, *inter alia*, depend on answers to the following questions:
- What portion of the BCS officers does have ICT skills?
- What portion of them has access to ICT
- What type of ICT skills currently they posses?

- What is their competency level?
- What are the levels of awareness and attitude towards e-governance?

1.4 Objectives

The broad objective of the research is to study the supply side preparedness especially in different levels (entry level, mid level and senior level) of public managers to provide insights on their status in terms of ICT aptitude, awareness and attitude towards e-government in Bangladesh. Specific objectives are to-
(a) determine the ratio of trained and non-trained officials and their level of ICT skill;
(b) assess their levels of aptitude, awareness and attitude towards e-government.

1.5 Methodology

This study is an exploratory one and uses qualitative and quantitative data collected from primary and secondary sources. A survey among 222 members of the Bangladesh Civil Service working in ministries, departments and in various agencies throughout the country has been conducted. Purposive sampling techniques have been adopted to select the respondents. The actual number and ratio of the respondents of different levels are as follow:

TABLE 2: Distribution of Respondents by Levels

Levels	Number	Percentage (%)
Junior level (entry level officers)	122	54.95
Mid level (Deputy Secretary & equivalent)	50	22.52
Senior level (Joint Secretary/equivalent or above)	50	22.52
Total	222	100.00

A questionnaire survey was conducted to collect primary data in respect of IT training and IT operational skill of the respondents, availability of ICT around them, use of ICT, their awareness, perception and attitude towards e-governance, etc.

Descriptive analysis, based on simple and cross tabulation, arithmetic average, frequency distribution, mean, range, and standard deviation. Has been used to provide outputs of different points of investigation. Categorical scales were adopted to assess the levels of aptitude, awareness and attitude. Specific levels of awareness and attitude have been categorised as follow:

Low level:	< Mean - Standard Deviation
Moderate level:	< Mean ± Standard Deviation
High level:	> Mean +Standard Deviation

2. E-READINESS OF THE BANGLADESH CIVIL SERVICE

2.1 ICT Training among BCS Officers

The survey observes that out of 222 respondent officers of the Bangladesh Civil Service, about 56% have received formal training on ICT. In respect of ICT training, significant difference is not prevalent among the three levels of officers. Almost all of the training courses, received by the officers, are concentrated around basic literacy In most of the cases, government has provided the training for officers; nevertheless, 23.4% of the ICT trained personnel have received training from self-initiative.

TABLE 3: ICT Training among Sample Population

Levels of Officers	Formal Training on ICT Yes	No	Total
Junior Level Officers	73 (59.8%)	49 (40.2%)	122 (100.0%)
Mid Level Officers	24 (48.0%)	26 (52.0%)	50 (100.0%)
Senior Level Officers	27 (54.0%)	23 (46.0%)	50 (100.0%)
All	124 (55.9%)	98 (44.1%)	222 (100.0%)

(n = 124)

Distribution of ICT Training by Sex (%)	Male 79.8	Female 20.2
Officers' ICT Training by Course Type (%)	Basic ICT Literacy 92.7	Diploma & Above 7.3
Distribution of ICT Training by Home & Abroad (%)	Home 93.5	Abroad 6.5
ICT Training by Sponsorship (%)	Government Sponsored 76.6	Self Sponsored 23.4

2.2 ICT Operational Skill

Among all respondents, 57.2% officers have ICT operational skill. When compared by the levels, junior level officers stand ahead in respect of ICT skill; on the other hand, mid level officers lag behind. It is observed that 68.8% of junior level officers, 40% of mid level officers, and 46% of senior level officers can operate a computer.

2.3 Adaptability to ICT

As indicated by the respondents 57.2% of the officers can operate a computer, which is 1.3% higher than the percentage of IT trained personnel. It represents a growth through adaptability or informal training. The growth is not significant when compared between aggregates of the officers who are trained on ICT and who can operate computer. However,

TABLE 4: Distribution of ICT Operational Skill by Levels of Officers

	ICT Operational Skill		Total
	Yes	No	
Junior Level Officers	84 (68.8%)	38 (31.2%)	122 (100.0%)
Mid Level Officers	20 (40.0%)	30 (60.0%)	50 (100.0%)
Senior Level Officers	23 (46.0%)	27 (54.0%)	50 (100.0%)
All	127 (57.2%)	95 (42.8%)	222 (100.0%)

when considered by the levels of officers, an 8% decline can be observed among mid and higher levels of officers. In contrast, among the junior level officers, a 9% increase is observed. This observation demonstrates an existing adaptability among junior level officers towards change and innovation that might be considered as an added strength for movement towards e-governance in the country.

2.4 Level and Type of IT Proficiency

The following table projects the level and type of IT proficiency among IT literate respondents. When they were offered a five point categorical scale to evaluate their own proficiency level in eight specific types of software, as well as an open type ("others"), 20.5% of them informed that they were not able to work with any other software except word processing. They further tend to show a concentration of their skill within four types of application, namely: word processing, spreadsheet analysis, presentational and Internet. The table, however, indicates general limitations as to handling other important computer applications and shows that most of the respondents virtually have no aptitude in statistical work, database management or in any other advance use of ICT.

TABLE 5: Level and Type of IT Proficiency among IT Literate Civil Servants

(n = 127)

Skill Type	Skill Level				
	Excellent	Good	Working	Little	No
Word Processing	14.2	23.6	50.3	11.8	0
Spread Sheet Analysis	4.7	15.0	35.4	24.4	20.5
Statistical Package/Software	0	5.5	8.7	10.2	75.6
Database Management	0	8.7	12.6	25.2	53.5
Project Management	0	0	0	5.5	94.5
Graphical Presentation	7.1	15.7	32.3	19.7	25.2
Internet	7.9	18.9	34.6	14.2	24.4
Programming	0	2.3	6.3	7.9	83.5
Others	0	0	0	6.3	93.7

In most cases officers limit their activities to word processing, browsing the Internet and preparing presentational work, with a high concentration on the first activity. However, in respect of skill, almost 52% of the IT literate respondents inform that they do not find their own skill sufficient to perform daily work, 38.6% notify that their skill is sufficient for performing daily work, and 9.4% evaluate that their skill remain underused.

FIGURE 1: Respondents' Views about Own ICT Skill

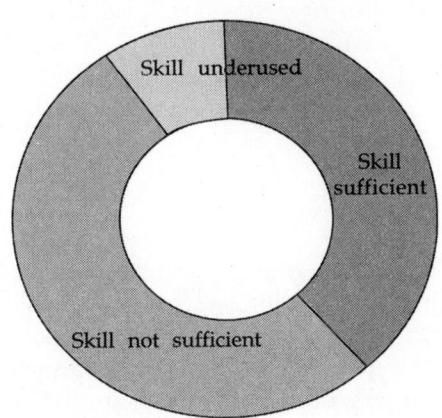

2.5 Officers' Aptitude Level

Based on the individual data on IT proficiency, general level of IT aptitude is evaluated through calculating respondents' scores. Individual scores in classes and corresponding levels of aptitude are shown in the following table.

TABLE 6: Frequency Distribution by Individual Scores and Aptitude Level

Score	f	%	Level of Aptitude
1-5	60	47.2	Low
6-10	30	23.6	Moderate
11-15	18	14.2	Moderate
16-20	12	9.5	High
21-26	7	5.5	High
Total	127	100.0	-

Distributions of individual scores show that 47.2% of the IT literate officers have the 'Low Level of Aptitude'. This group has a score of maximum five only. Meaning that they are not able to manage three types of applications at a working proficiency level and pose a low level of IT aptitude. Further effort, in particular, supplementary training is necessary for this group to improve their aptitude level. About 38% of IT literate officers

(21.6% of total respondents) show a 'Moderate Level of Aptitude', members of this group hold an equivalent ability of managing at least three types of computer applications, and for each type, they have no less than a 'working' level of proficiency. These officers are expected to be able to inflate their present level of competence by themselves as well as gradually adapt with further technological applications and changes in their official activities. In that regard they are presently ready for e-governance applications. Fifteen percent of the 'IT Literate' (8.6% of total respondents) personnel possess a 'High Level of Aptitude'. Officers, within this group, have an equivalent ability of handling minimum 4-5 types of applications, and having 'excellent' level of proficiency for each type.

2.6 AVAILABILITY AND USE OF ICTS AMONG OFFICERS

2.6.1 Availability

As to availability, 27.5% of total respondents inform that they have individual PC(s) in their own offices. An additional 15.3% has access to computers that are under else's jurisdiction or located elsewhere in their respective offices, and can get their important tasks done over there. These figures show that in the Bangladesh Civil Service 42.8% of officers have access to computers, either directly or indirectly.

Only 15.3% of respondents say that a LAN exists in their respective offices. On the other hand, 66.7% indicated that their offices are connected to the Internet. However, only 26.6% respondents' own PCs are connected with Internet.

FIGURE 2: Availability of and Accessibility to ICT

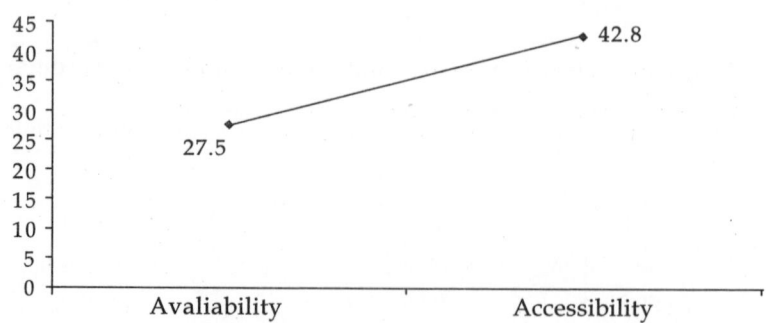

2.6.2 PC User in Civil Service

Among the IT literates, 22.8% officers do not use computers because of absence of or limited access to technology or because of they can get work done by their supporting staff; another 9.4% do not use it because of lack of confidence or they do not feel that it is convenient to use a computer. PC user officers in the civil service can be calculated as 67.7% among the IT literates and 38.7% among the total respondents.

FIGURE 3: PC User in Civil Service

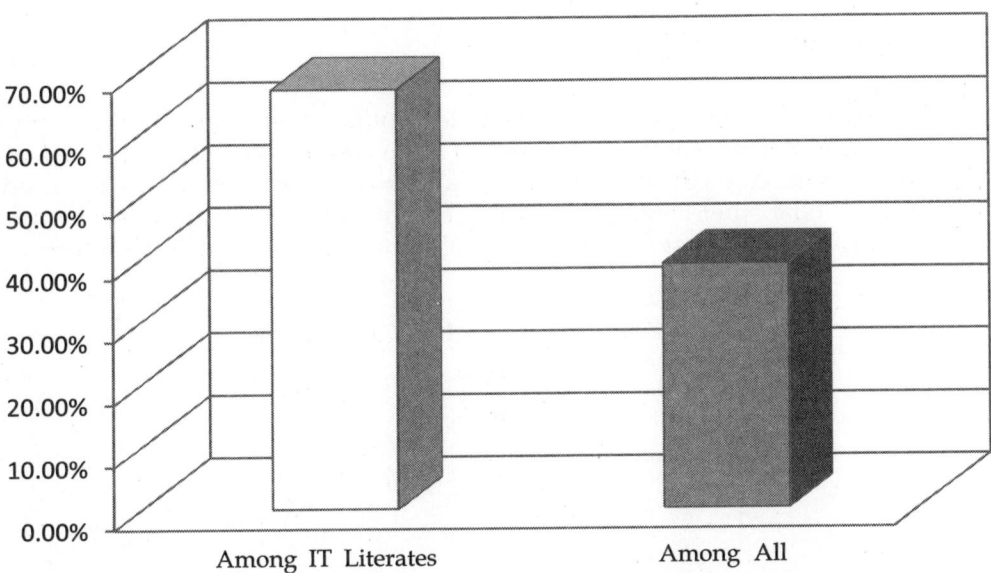

With the statistics, mentioned above, a 15.3% rise in terms of accessibility can be recorded if compared to the availability of ICT in Bangladesh Civil Service. At the same time, a 4% decline is noticeable if the statistics of accessibility of ICT are compared to the statistics of PC users in the civil service. However, an encouraging escalation (11.2%) still can be observed if the statistics of availability of ICT and user of ICT are compared together. It indicates a positive trend of interest and mind-set towards adaptation of ICT by the members of the BCS.

FIGURE 4: PC Users Compared to Availability and Accessibility

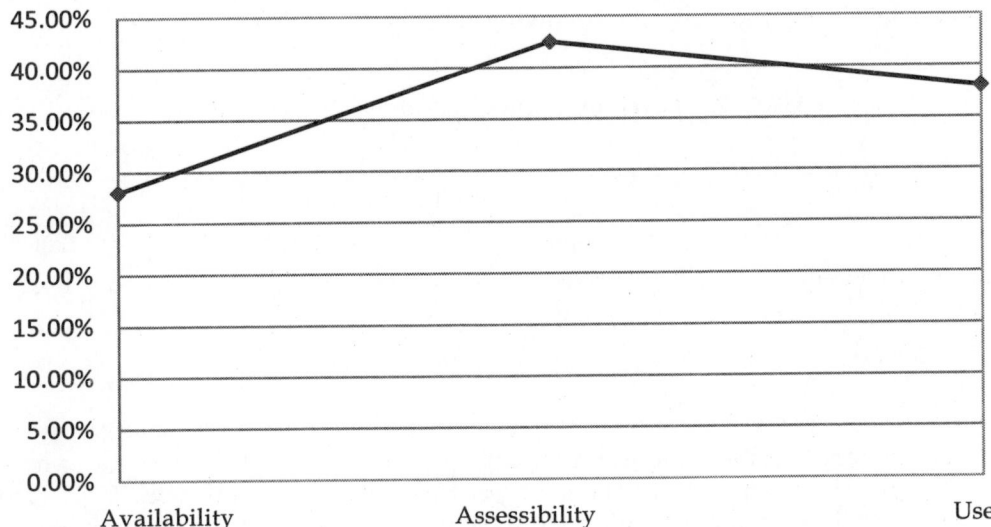

2.7 READINESS FOR E-GOVERNANCE

2.7.1 Aptitude

The study shows that about 30.2% of the sample population presently have an aptitude level of managing technological applications of e-governance. Among them 8.6% of the total respondents have an advanced level of IT aptitude who can contribute to introduce e-governance. On the other hand, almost 70% of the members of the civil service are not currently in a position to manage technological applications in public administration.

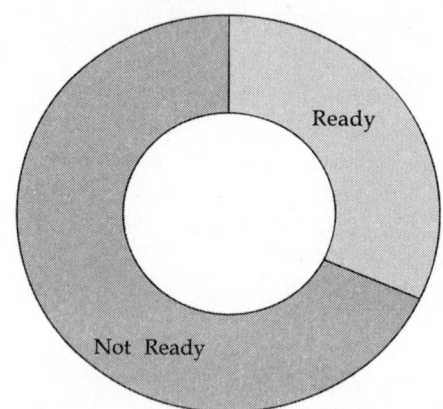

FIGURE 5: Readiness by ICT Aptitude

2.7.2 Awareness

To evaluate awareness level, individual responses were coded into five point values, and then individual scores were calculated. Based on the calculated scores, respondents' awareness levels are shown in the following table:

TABLE 7: Level of Awareness about E-Governance

(n=222)

Officers	Level of Awareness		
	High	Moderate	Low
Junior Level Officers	23.8	59.8	16.4
Mid Level Officers	28.0	58.0	14.0
Senior Level Officers	32.0	62.0	6.0
All	26.6	59.9	13.5

It is evident that the sample respondents possess significant level of awareness as to the concept of e-governance i.e., about happenings of its relevant premises. In particular, about 86.5% of the respondents belong to the clusters of 'moderate' and 'high' levels of awareness. Basically, the 'low level of awareness' cluster comprises the junior and mid levels of officers. Compared to the senior level civil servants, the junior level officers show a lower level of awareness. Appropriate training plan including awareness-building programme can contribute to further their awareness level.

2.7.3 Attitude

Based on responses given by the sample population, levels of attitude of the respondents have been assessed adopting the same way that is mentioned in the case of measuring awareness levels. Respondents' attitudinal states are clustered under three categories as provided in the following table:

TABLE 8: Officers' Attitude towards E-Governance

(n=222)

Officers	Level of Awareness		
	High	Moderate	Low
Junior Level Officers	20.5	59.8	19.7
Mid Level Officers	32.0	54.0	14.0
Senior Level Officers	34.0	56.0	10.0
All	26.1	57.7	16.2

The table shows that high-ranking officers show higher levels of attitude towards e-governance compared to the junior officials. Out of the total respondents, 26% has a high level of attitude, 57.7% has moderate level of attitude and 16.2% officers hold unfavourable or low level of attitude. If moderate and high levels of attitudes are combined together, it can be shown that more than 80% officers can be assembled under a cluster of favourable attitude towards e-governance.

FIGURE 6: Readiness of BCS by the Levels of Attitude

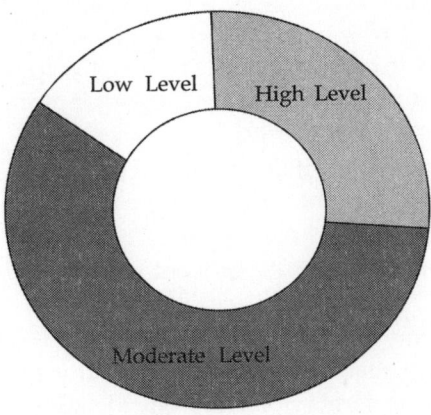

Study of the aptitude, awareness and attitudinal factors exhibits a mixed status of readiness of the officers towards e-governance. They show lower levels of readiness in terms of technological skill (aptitude) compared to their levels of awareness and attitude. From an overall context, it can be mentioned that a considerable portion of the civil servants is currently able to adapt with the e-governance take off, to some extent. But with the observation of a lower level of technological skill among officers, smooth implementation of e-governance applications requires a comprehensive training program for civil servants that would effectively deal with awareness issues, mindset, motivational and cultural aspects that are consistent with e-governance goals and focus, in general. On the hand, that would also be able to foster a wide range of perception about use of ICT in public administration, provide necessary skill and build attitudes towards change and reforms in particular.

3. FINDINGS AND CONCLUSION

3.1 Findings

a. About 56% of the respondent officers have received formal training in ICT mostly (76.6%) from, government training institutes.
b. In general, 57.2% officers have ICT operational skills.
c. Officers are found to limit their ICT activities mainly to word processing, browsing the Internet and preparing presentational work with a high concentration on the first activity.
d. Almost 52% of the IT literate respondents stated that they do not find their own skills sufficient to perform daily work.
e. About 30.2% of the sample population presently have adequate level of skills to manage technological applications of e-governance.
f. About 27.5% of respondents have individual official PCs, 42.8% have access to official computers, and 38.7% use ICT in their official activities. The rise in the number of PC user officers compared to the number of PC owners further confirms a positive trend of interest and mind-set towards adaptation of ICT by officers.
g. More than 82% indicated their needs for training on ICT; although 56% of them already received formal training. This situation points toward a 26% overlapping respondents who need further training. It partially speaks about ineffectiveness or inadequacies of ICT training received by the overlapping respondents and partially about respondents' further interest on IT.
h. Members of the Bangladesh Civil Service possess significant level of awareness as to the concept of e-governance; when 86.5% of the respondents belong to the clusters of 'moderate' and 'high' levels of awareness.
i. On the other hand, more than 80% officers show favourable attitudes towards e-governance.
j. Comparative scrutiny on the levels of aptitude, awareness and attitudinal factors exhibit a mixed status of readiness of the officers towards e-governance. They show lower level of readiness in terms of technological skill (aptitude) compared to higher levels of awareness and attitude.

3.2 Conclusion

As an emerging concept, e-governance has become popular since the mid 1990s around the world, with various governments integrating information and communication technologies into public sector management and in delivering services for citizens. However, the growth and status of e-governance varies from country to country regarding degrees of preparedness that relate to availability, accessibility and the nature and level of use of e-governance tools by civil servants in respect of providing services directed at the convenience of citizens. This study notes that regarding preparedness, members of the Bangladesh Civil Service show considerable strengths for e-governance in respect of their interest and adaptability to new technologies. This is the case also in respect of their levels of awareness and attitude towards e-governance. However they have lower levels of ICT aptitude. Besides, use of ICT by civil servants is often locked up with word processing and other elementary applications. A robust training and motivational program is needed to erect a brilliant supply side for e-governance service delivery in Bangladesh.

References

Basu, S. (2004). E-Government and Developing Countries: An Overview. *International Review of Law Computers and Technology*. Vol. 18, No.1.

Bhatnagar, S. (2004). E-Government: From Vision to Implementation. Sage Publications.

Clark, E. (2003). Managing the Transformation to E- government: An Australian Perspective. *Thunderbird International Business Review*. Vol. 45, No. 4.

Heeks, Richard (2001). "Understanding e-Governance for Development". IDPM, University of Manchester, UK.

Heeks, Richard (2006). *Implementing and Managing eGovernment: An International Text*. Vistaar Publications.

Lal, Bhavya (1999). "Information and Communication Technologies for Improved Governance", Cambridge : Abt Associates Inc., Available at: www.abtassoc.com/reports/ict.pdf.

Lee- Kelley, L. and James, T. (2003). E-government and Social Exclusion: An Empirical Study. *Journal of Electronic Commerce in Organisations*. Vol. 1, No. 4. Lodge, J. (2003). Towards an E-commonwealth? A Tool for Peace and Democracy? The Round Table.

Millard, Jeremy (2004), "Reorganising the Back-office and Changing the Public Administration", Paper presented in the e-GovIndia International Workshop, Chandigarh, India.

Sharma, S.K. (2003). Building Blocks of E-government – A Framework. *Journal of Electronic Commerce in Organisations*. Vol. 1, No. 4.

Silcock, R. (2001). What is E-government? *Journal of Parliamentary Affairs*. Vol. 54.

Smith, R.F.I. and Teicher, J. (2004). Improving Governance and Services: Can E-government Help? Chinese Public Administration Review, 3(3/4) 2006.

Teicher, J. and Dow, N. (2002). E-government in Australia: Promise and Progress. *Information Polity*. Vol. 7.

Thomas B. Riley. (2003). "Information Management and e-Government", p. 7. Available at: http://www.rileyis.com/ publications/research_papers/tracking03/IntlTrackRptMar03no1.pdf

UN. (2004). Global E-Government Readiness Report 2004 : Towards Access for Opportunity.

UN. (2008). UN E-Government Survey 2008: From E-Government to Connected Governance.

Wimmer, M.A. (2002). Integrated Service Modelling for Online One-stop Government. *Electronic Markets*. Vol. 12, No. 3.

CHAPTER 13

VOCATIONAL EDUCATION AND PARTICIPATORY DEVELOPMENT IN THE NORTH EASTERN REGION OF INDIA

SYLVIA YAMBEM

Abstract

The North East of India, comprising of the eight states of Arunachal Pradesh, Assam, Manipur, Mizoram, Nagaland, Sikkim and Tripura constitutes about 25,5000 sq. kms or 7.9% of the country's total geographical area. Home to about 3.9% of the total population of India, the region boasts of a literacy level higher than the all India average, at 68.5%. The state of Mizoram with 88.49% has the second highest literacy rate in the country, after Kerala. However, this high literacy level does not translate to higher productivity or higher employability. To counter this dilemma, the North Eastern Region Vision 2020 proposed the adoption of vocational skill building and training based education within the framework of participatory development with comparative advantage for ushering growth and development in the region, as one such strategy. The paper looks at two issues: the prevailing state of education, the participatory development based vocational education and technical programme framework advocated in the North Eastern Region of India.

Introduction

The development discourse in the North Eastern Region[1] (henceforth NER) of India has witnessed a paradigm shift from a top-down public policy centric approach to a bottom-up participatory approach to development. The North Eastern Region Vision 2020 (henceforth Vision document) writes that in order to achieve inclusive development, planners must adopt a strategy of participatory development articulated through grass-root planning to develop sectors and sub-sectors with comparative advantage. Such an approach would help "evolve a development strategy based on the resources, needs and aspirations of the people" [North Eastern Region Vision 2020, 2008: 3], raise productivity and empower the youth with employable skills.

The Vision document asserts that despite the region's higher literacy level of 68.5% and female literacy of 61.5%, as compared to the All India average of 64.8% and female literacy at 53.7%, higher literacy does not translate to higher productivity or employability.

State wise profile   Table 1

STATE	AREA (sq. km)	POPULATION (in lakhs)	LITERACY RATE (%)
Arunachal Pradesh	83,743	10.98	54.74
Assam	78,438	266.55	64.28
Manipur	22,327	22.94	68.87
Meghalaya	22,429	23.19	63.31
Mizoram	22,081	8.88	88.49
Nagaland	16,579	19.9	67.11
Sikkim	7,089	5.41	69.68
Tripura	10,486	31.99	73.66

To arrest this negative developmental trend, participatory development, through vocational education and technical programmes build employable skills to correct the mismatch in labour supply and demand. Participatory development as conceived by the Vision document has five interlinked components:
1. People-centric grass-root planning
2. Harnessing the regions' natural resources
3. Market driven education and skill development for building the capacities of the people and institutions
4. Development of sectors and sub-sectors with comparative advantage
5. Enabling good governance

Implementing Participatory Development

Participatory based development policies were to be centred upon the abilities and potential of the region and investments designed with the objective of harnessing the natural resources. Consequently, planning and implementation would be located at the smallest units of administration, i.e. the Panchayati Raj Institutions (PRIs), Urban Local Bodies (ULBs) and District Planning Committees (DPCs). This involvement by the people and community would usher "efficiency", "accountability", "greater responsiveness", "corruption-free administration" and "social accountability", thereby transforming governance.

However given the similarity in productivity levels amongst the eight states, selected items based upon a principle of comparative advantage- in terms of areas, activities, sectors, productivity, market networks etc., was to be given priority. For example, in the primary agricultural sector crop specialisation based upon either the Regional Specialisation Index (RSI)[2] or the National Specialisation Index (NSI)[3], establishment of agro-processing units for manufacturing services and development of hospitality and tourism services would get priority. Specific production based on the respective states' potential would help move the NER from the prevailing phase of self-sufficiency to one of specialisation, expansion of trading markets both within and outside the region, increasing employment opportunities and improving the region's productivity.

Therefore capacity development through vocational education and technical programmes was to be initiated. This would build employable skills, impart job based vocational training courses to, "prepare students for occupations in agriculture, artisan trades, crafts, small and medium enterprises, the latter geared at those planning to set up their own businesses, which would include entrepreneurship development and some ICT training to enable them to undertake all the functions of their enterprise" [Peace, Progress and Prosperity in the North Eastern Region Vision 2020, 2007: 52] and harness the regions' natural resources and indigenous raw material. This would develop employable skills, generate productivity and employability not only in the traditional sector but also in emerging market driven areas like "agro-processing, IT sector, paramedical, biotech, aviation, entertainment and hospitality industries" [Peace, Progress and Prosperity in the North Eastern Region Vision 2020, 2007: 29]. Based upon the principle of comparative advantage, training should be based upon the NSI or RSI indices. For example, the NSI notes specificities of the NER states as:

NSI Index for the North Eastern States   Table 2

STATE	PRODUCT
Arunachal Pradesh	Ginger, bananas, small millet
Assam	Tea, bananas, turmeric
Manipur	Pineapples, ginger, chillies
Meghalaya	Pineapples, ginger, potatoes
Mizoram	Ginger, pineapple, sesame
Nagaland	Pineapples, small millet, turmeric
Sikkim	Ginger, potatoes, maize
Tripura	Natural rubber, pineapples, banana

Source: North Eastern Region Vision 2020, Volume 2- Annexure pp 43.

Keeping these core specialisations in mind, priority would be given to introducing such vocational/technical courses that would fuel the opening of sectors that utilise the region's resources- raw material and human skills. Such as, in the state of Assam focus could be placed upon professionally developing turmeric plantation, natural rubber in Tripura, small millet in Nagaland and so on. Further, since the core item overlaps like small millet in Arunachal Pradesh and Nagaland or pineapples and ginger in Manipur and Meghalaya professional exchanges between the technical institutes was to be encouraged. Market linkages for both external and internal consumption are to be developed within the region so that in case of crop failure in one state, the demand could be met from the other states. With this consideration focus was to be placed upon:

- Courses in horticulture[4], floriculture, bamboo and silk, agro-based sciences like biotechnology, patent awareness, organic farming, water conservation, veterinary sciences, seismology, agro-based industries like medicinal plants, food processing and preservation, tourism, hospitality sector and teacher training.
- ITIs and polytechnics were to be upgraded to incorporate market driven trainings.
- Upgrade existing educational infrastructure to provide advanced scientific grade laboratories, computers and Internet networks for online materials and other research sites and connectivity between the students of NER and other states.
- Government schemes/programmes were to incorporate vocational or skill development strategies.[5]
- Public-private partnership (PPP) model with institutions specializing in silk making, handicrafts, bamboo and cane works, fashion designing, product designing etc., to either develop such institutes in the NER or facilitate student exchanges between participating institutes.
- Industrial associations benefiting VET programmes were to be encouraged to develop the market for employment, generate local revenue, encourage private sector growth and create employment and entrepreneurship opportunities.[6]

Speaking on the prospect of education and employment the Nagaland State Human Development Report [2004: 137] states:

> Most students at the higher education levels are well versed in English. This comparative strength, along with technical know-how in computers, can open employment opportunities in the services sector. Even within the State, there is wide scope for employment opportunities in medical and nursing sector, higher education, management, computer science, electronics, biotech, engineering, law, teaching, technology-based service sector, tourism and engineering-based industries.

Therefore such strategies would bridge the mismatch between available labour skills and market demands, build professional skills and expertise and help generate entrepreneurial abilities.

Background

For the NER, the new paradigm shift is both a challenge and an opportunity. The region's major difficulty is the inability to translate education into employment or productivity. This is because of the sectoral inequalities of the economy leading to the predominance of the public sector, limited private sector- both in terms of investment and absence of a conducive environment- and, fairly restrictive educational curricula with limited emphasis on skill building and vocational technical education.

Modes of production in the region have failed to make a successful transition from the agrarian production system. Even after independence, the primary agro-based sector enjoys majority share while the manufacturing and service sectors have limited presence.

In some states like Manipur, the services sector is still at a nascent stage. However even within the primary sector, there exists huge deficits and all of the eight states have to resort to imports. For example, even despite the region's non-vegetarian diet, the region "imports about 50% of the milk consumption and over 87% of the consumption of egg" [North Eastern Region Vision 2020, 2009: 26].

Inevitably the sectoral inequalities have led to the emergence of the public sector or the government as the primary source of employment. This lopsided development of the public sector versus the private sector has huge consequences for growth and productivity. One area of disastrous impact is seen in the struggle for employment. This is true for all of the NER states, even in the case of Assam, where private sector employment is only a small percent higher than public sector- at 5.38% and 5.26% [in lakhs] respectively [Employment Review, Directorate General of Employment and Training 1981-2002]. The state of Mizoram, at 0.01 [in lakhs] has the least private sector employment, followed by Nagaland and Manipur at 0.03 [in lakhs] each, Meghalaya at 0.09 [in lakhs] and Tripura at 0.13 [in lakhs]. The total number of people in the private sector and public sector employment in the NER stands at 5.67 and 9.03 [in lakhs]. Thus the high literacy level does not translate to higher productivity or higher employability. Rather unemployment is endemic in the region:

Unemployment in the NER   Table 3

STATE	1993-1994			1999-2000		
	MALE	FEMALE	PERSONS	MALE	FEMALE	PERSONS
Arunachal Pradesh	1.3	0.5	1	1	0.9	0.9
Assam	4.6	9.5	5.6	3.7	8	4.6
Manipur	2.2	1	1.8	3.7	3.1	3.5
Meghalaya	0.5	0.3	0.5	0.9	0.9	0.9
Mizoram	0.9	0.5	0.8	2.5	1.3	2
Nagaland	3.2	0.6	2.4	4	2.9	3.5
Sikkim	0.7	1.9	1	3.6	2.7	3.4
Tripura	2.2	8.4	3.4	1.6	4.5	1.9
India	2.1	1.7	2	2.5	1.8	2.3

Source: National Human Development Report, 2001, Planning Commission, Govt. of India.

Higher Education in the North Eastern Region

Writing in the context of higher education, the Vision document [2008: 28] notes that "there are few higher educational institutions, and the focus of those that exist has been to prepare the youth for routine government jobs." While this statement may be partly true, the argument reveals the dilemmas and complexities inherent in the region's development.

Firstly, the region's educational policy has not kept pace with global developments, seen in the very late entry of professional studies, outdated infrastructure, low quality education, limited training programmes and the continued dominance of the arts and social sciences curricula. In Nagaland, 33 colleges offer arts, 8 colleges offer commerce while science, law and B Ed. are available only in 3 colleges [Nagaland State Human Development Report, 2004: 132]. The issue is not of lack of demand of professional institutions, rather the majority of the youth migrate to other Indian states and overseas for higher professional courses, diplomas and training.[7] It is estimated that of the 24,000 students pursuing higher education, nearly 10,000 students were studying outside Nagaland [Directorate of Higher and Technical Education 2001]. The state of Mizoram also maintains- 2 boys and 1 women hostel at Shillong to provide accommodation to students. The North East Hostel for Delhi University Post-Graduate Students was established to accommodate students from this region.

The limited presence or in some NER states the non-existence of technical skill centres is also a problem. While Assam has 5 Central Universities- Assam University, Assam Agricultural University, Gauhati University, Tezpur University, Dibrugarh University, Manipur has 2- Manipur University and Central Agricultural University Imphal. The remaining states have one each; Rajiv Gandhi University, Arunachal Pradesh, North Eastern Hill University (NEHU), Meghalaya, Mizoram University; Nagaland University, Tripura University and Sikkim University. Until the establishment of Nagaland University, the NEHU-Nagaland Campus served as an educational centre for Nagaland. Under the central university, the affiliated colleges within the state offer studies in subjects like social sciences, life sciences, business and commerce, language etc.

Secondly, professional centres like medical, management, science and technology, engineering institutes are largely conspicuous by their absence. The irony is that for the NER, there exist single centres for medical study, agricultural study, management and science and technology. Assam has four government engineering colleges- Assam Engineering College, Indian Institute of Technology, Regional Engineering College and Jorhat Engineering College; three medical colleges- Assam Medical College, Guwahati Medical College and Hospital and Silchar Medical College and Hospital, and one hospitality college- Indian Institute for Hotel Management. Manipur has a Central Agricultural University, Institute of Bio-diversity, Performing Arts Academy (Jawaharlal Nehru Manipur Dance Academy), medical college (Regional Institute of Medical Sciences); in Arunachal Pradesh- North Eastern Regional Institute of Science and Technology (NERIST) and in Meghalaya, the Rajiv Gandhi Indian Institute of Management (RGIIM) is placed on par with the IIMs[8].

Higher Learning Institutions   Table 4

STATE	MEDICAL COLLEGE	ENGINEERING COLLEGE	CENTRAL UNIVERSITY	PROFESSIONAL CENTRES
Arunachal Pradesh	-	1	1	-
Assam	3	4	5	2
Manipur	1	1	2	2
Meghalaya	1	1	1	1
Mizoram	-	1	1	-
Nagaland	-	-	1	-
Sikkim	1	1	1	-
Tripura	-	1	1	-
TOTAL	6	10	13	5

These institutes through a provision of reservation cater to limited number of students in the NER. In total the educational sector is visibly marked by the absence of such institutions that will directly equip the youth with employable and marketable skills. This inequality is reflected in the stream wise enrolment:

Stream wise College Enrolment   Table 5

STATE	ARTS	SCIENCE	COMMERCE	EDUCATION	OTHERS
Arunachal Pradesh	68.0	8.0	5.0	2.0	0.0
Assam	74.0	12.0	6.0	1.0	0.2
Manipur	52.0	35.0	5.0	1.0	0.4
Meghalaya	71.0	14.0	6.0	8.0	0.2
Mizoram	86.0	4.0	2.0	1.0	0.0
Nagaland	77.0	9.0	7.0	2.0	0.0
Sikkim	49.0	16.0	6.0	2.0	0.0
Tripura	70.0	14.0	11.0	0.6	0.8
India	**46.0**	**20.0**	**18.0**	**1.0**	**0.9**

Source: University Development in India, 1995-96 to 2000-01, University Grants Commission, Information and Statistics Bureau, New Delhi (Cited in North Eastern Region Vision 2020 Annexure pp 120)

In terms of vocational education, Vocational Education Programme[9] (VEP) and Vocational Education and Training (VET) have been designed. Under the "Vocationalisation of Secondary Education", VEPs delivers higher secondary (grade 11 and 12) students with courses in agriculture, business and commerce, humanities, engineering and technology, home science, social sciences and health and para-medical skills. VET imparted by the respective State Councils for Vocational Training (SCVT), through ITIs (Industrial Training Institutes), ITCs (Industry Training Centre)[10], target youth within the age of 14-40 years. They provide basic skills and expertise in 32 engineering trades and 22 non-engineering trades with course duration running up to 3/4 years for engineering and six months for others. The distribution of ITIs and ITCS are as:

VET Distribution   Table 6

STATE	ITIs		ITCs		TOTAL CAPACITY	TOTAL NUMBER OF ITIs and ITCs
	NUMBER	CAPACITY	NUMBER	CAPACITY		
Arunachal Pradesh	5	512	0	0	512	5
Assam	28	5696	3	80	5776	31
Manipur	7	540	0	0	540	7
Meghalaya	5	622	2	320	942	7
Mizoram	1	294	0	0	294	1
Nagaland	8	944	0	0	944	8
Sikkim	2	516	0	0	516	2
Tripura	8	944	0	0	944	8
NER TOTAL	**64**	**10068**	**5**	**400**	**10468**	**69**

Source: Directorate General of Employment and Training

Polytechnic education also offers three year diploma courses for civil, electrical and mechanical engineering, electronics and computer science, medical lab technology and hospital engineering, etc., and diploma programmes in leather technology, sugar technology, etc. Women polytechnics (exclusively for women), offer courses in tourism, home science, mass communication, fashion designing, jewellery designing, interior decoration, garment technology, textile designing and beauty etc. In all of the NER there are 19 government polytechnics.

Thus the educational scenario in the NER is beset with challenges. This skewed educational-development policy has adverse consequences beyond the educational sector:

- The high number of youth migration has repercussions on the local revenue, and on the buoyancy of the state economy, as a major chunk of the income is sent to other states or overseas.
- Further, after the completion of their education most of the youth continue to stay away from the region on grounds of employment. It is estimated that only 5% of youth return after completing their education, thus, depriving the region of able bodied youth.
- In this vicious cycle, educated unemployment is a reality. The NER has a high percentage of youth qualifying college but without a robust private sector, avenues of employment are restricted.

The Vision document however needs to enquire about the credibility of vocational education training and skill building. The merit of VET has been challenged foremost on the ground that the significance of VET is overstated. The 2008 World Bank Report writes that ITIs/ITCs graduates did not suit employers' needs. The lack of skill was reflected in the use of computers, practical use of machines, communications and team work, practical knowledge and on-the-job training to bring their skill levels to match the industry needs [2008: iii-iv]. Moreover, VET is primarily aimed at providing general trade skills for the informal sector, while majority of the youth are already armed with skills surpassing the demands of the informal sector.

The Participatory Approach

Participatory development has two integral components: "placing local realities at the heart of development interventions" and to "transform agents of development from being directive 'experts' to 'facilitators' of local knowledge and capabilities [Chambers 1983 cited in Hickey & Mohan, 2005: 241]. Through the, "involvement of 'local' people's perspectives, knowledge, priorities and skills" [Cooke & Kothari, 2001: 5], participation is aimed towards the empowerment and transformation of the community. However, participatory development as envisioned for the NER though firmly rooted in its theoretical underpinnings fails to take into account local realities and therefore suffers in praxis. For the NER, without manoeuvreing the fragmented civil society and contested state, the aims of participatory development will not be achieved.

Participatory development is based on the principles of trust, empowerment, engaging with the issues of power and politics and not treating civil society as a homogenous entity. Critics of this approach range from definitional differences to the means-end dilemma, the inability to engage with local power, politics and community, the appropriateness of participatory techniques (Participatory Rural Development, Beneficiary Assessment, Participatory Rural Appraisal, Social Analysis etc.), tokenistic use of participation, manipulating participation for accessing local resources particularly natural resource management, the role of structure and agency, mapping local knowledge to fit developmental agendas, the myth of the homogenous community and others [Hickey & Mohan, 2005, Cooke & Kothari, 2001]. The Vision document fails to analyse these local realities. In the NER along with increasing democratic deficit associated with the emergence of a state within a state, civil society is highly fragmented and divided by group identities of ethnicity, clan, tribe, language, religion, politics and power. This contestation, according to Hassan is historical in nature and has shaped the process of state formation. Writing in the context of Manipur and Mizoram, Hassan [2008: 27] says that, in Manipur the presence of multiple identities "sparked off a scramble for state-making by the elite representing different social groups". This consequently led to the emergence of a weak state, while in contrast in Mizoram, state making centred on the Mizo identity "facilitated state-wide mobilisation of inclusive identities" leading to the establishment of a strong state. A fragmented civil society and the contested state is however not exclusive to either Manipur or Mizoram.

Local governance units are also not void of contestation. The panchayats act as public spaces in the interface between the state funded development and implementation of programmes. Pai's [2004: 26] research amongst the dalit community in Uttar Pradesh shows that panchayats often become an arena of conflict and contestation "over scarce resources, social status and political arena". Jayal [2004: 27] in the context of forest conservation in the Tehri Garhwal district in Uttaranchal says that with the introduction of panchayats the pre-existing social capital gets mobilised into smaller affiliations and subsequently introduces elements of disparities, differences and divisions within the community.

In the NER, local governance is restricted not only by partial decentralisation but also a fragmented civil society. Local governance administered under the 73rd-74th Constitutional Amendment (PRIs, ULBs and DPCs) and the Sixth Schedule (ADCs) for the tribal areas in the state of Meghalaya and parts of Assam, Mizoram and Tripura, have not been constituted and empowered satisfactorily. DPCs have not been constituted in the states of Arunachal Pradesh, Assam, Tripura and in two districts of Manipur. In local governance, the PRIs, ULBs and DPCs are interlinked tiers while the PRIs and ULBs are entrusted with economic and welfare development, the DPCs act both as a monitoring and facilitating body whose task is to integrate the PRIs and ULBs plans. Therefore without DPCs, an efficiently co-ordinated welfare and economic development of the rural and urban areas is only effectively partial. Partial devolution of administrative functions and financial powers is also the norm, rather than exception:

Table 7

STATE*	No. of Departments/Subjects Transferred			No. of Departments/Subjects yet to be transferred		
	FUNDS	FUNCTIONS	FUNCTIONARIES	FUNDS	FUNCTIONS	FUNCTIONARIES
Arunachal Pradesh	5	13	2	24	16	27
Assam	-	-	-	29	29	29
Manipur	-	22	4	29	7	25
Sikkim	29	29	29	-	-	-
Tripura	-	12	-	29	17	19

Source: The State of the Panchayats, A Mid-Term Review and Appraisal, 22 November 2006, Vol.II., p.102, Ministry of Panchayati Raj (Cited in North Eastern Region Vision 2020, pp 9)
*Does not apply to Meghalaya, Mizoram and Nagaland

Without administrative, financial, and political decentralisation empowering the local bodies to raise taxes, perform administrative functions and enjoy political powers to carry out their functions, local governance has failed to transform into "vibrant democratic institutions" [Brara 2001]. Except for the state of Sikkim, PRIs, ULBs and DPCs of the remaining NER states are not equipped to act as agents of participatory development.

In Arunachal Pradesh and Mizoram ULBs have not been constituted. The case of the Imphal Municipal Council exposes the contestation over administrative, financial and political power between the state and the ULB. The Council is mired in factional dispute, corruption, financial abuse, administrative mismanagement to the extent that the Council has been suspended for six months, beginning August 2010. Urban governance in Manipur is in a state of ineffective institutional establishment, marked by poor infrastructure and limited transfer of functions and powers.[11]

The Vision document also does not engage with power relationships prevailing in the NER. Civil society cannot be construed without politics of representation and power capture. Fukuyama's [1995] argument that the "rights revolution" which promoted "individualism and self-seeking behaviour and weaken group solidarity"[12] is a given reality. In the NER the explosion of the "rights revolution" implied the emergence of multiple "people's groups" based upon language, religion, ethnicity, tribe, territorial affiliation etc. The Institute of Conflict Management [2010] lists 39 such groups for Manipur, the highest in the region, followed by 36 for Assam, Meghalaya 4, Nagaland 3, Tripura 30, and 2 in Mizoram. Such identity based affiliations operate within the same state and civil society arena. These group identities work on the basis of social capital or what Putnam defines as "feature of social relations that contributes to the ability of society to work together and accomplish certain goals". The NER traditionally has a rich social capital, built by the dense associational networks of clan, tribes, community, market exchanges and others. However the region's social capital has been generously eroded by the invasion of group identities, clan politics, demand for autonomy or separate state and competition over limited opportunities and resources.

Politics of power and representation is also visible in the construction of gender relationships. Researching the matrilineal Khasi community in Meghalaya, Nongbri [2008] says that as compared to the mother, males in their position as father and mother's brother enjoys "jural and uxorilocal marriage and economic authority", respectively. This assertion of rights is perpetuated by the cultural symbols associated with male and female. At the naming ritual while the male child is associated with the symbols of bow and three arrows, a conical basket and strap and or a winnowing tray is placed for the girl child. Nongbri argues that these are further reinforced by the gendered language which expresses that women are both physiologically and intellectually inferior, almost equivalent to a child. Similarly, enforced through myths and folklore, Aier [2008: 92] writes that "the fundamental premise of gender relations have remained traditionally inspired" in Nagaland. Women's participation in the political arena therefore remains nil, to the extent that women candidates were not allowed to even file their nomination papers for the 33% reserved seats in the Municipal Council.[13] This unwillingness against women participation in the political space is however not confined to Nagaland alone. In Manipur, Irina [2008: 94] writes that though the women play an important role in state formation, their role is restricted to the "power to resist" and not "power to share" equal space with their male counterparts. Thus the respect and status enjoyed by the NER women does not necessarily translate to empowerment and participation.

Towards an Empowered Participation

Participation is a contested category. However, the fact cannot be ignored that a system of institutionalised decentralised governance facilitates the inclusion of previously excluded communities and groups. Research on participatory governance in West Bengal and Kerala asserts that, "decentralisation has been credited with ensuring the participation of subordinate groups- such as women, landless groups, sharecroppers and small peasants- and being directly linked to redistributive policies that have had pro-poor outcomes" [Harris, 2000: 15, Heller, 2001: 142, Cited in Hickey & Mohan, 2005: 243]. Therefore Parfitt states that even though problematic, participation has, "the potential to deliver real benefits to those who have hitherto been incorporated in the project of development as objects of the manipulations of developmental agencies" [2004: 538].

Likewise the participatory approach to development as envisaged for the NER, is innovative yet not without contestation. To maintain the inclusive character of participation, implementation must be along double lines: to strengthen the mechanisms of local governance and incorporate the visible fractures within state institutions and civil society. Skimming over the contestation and multiple group identities prevalent in the region will only adversely strengthen the notion of participatory development as a top-down approach.

References

- Aier, Anungla. (2008). Folklore, Folk Ideas and Gender among the Nagas. *Eastern Quarterly: Gender Studies in the Northeast.* Vol.5. Issue II & III, July-December 2008, pp.87-93.
- Chandhoke, Neera. (2003). *The Conceits of Civil Society.* New Delhi: Oxford University Press.
- Chaudhury, Dipanjan Roy, Manipur Seeks Development to Defeat Insurgency. *Dialogue*, Volume-7, No. 4., pp 170-178.
- Cooke, Bill & Uma Kothari. (2001). (Eds.) *Participation: the New Tyranny?* Zed Books.
- D. Bhattacharyya., G. N. Jayal, B. Mohapatra, & S. Pai., (Eds.) (2004). *Interrogating Social Capital: The Indian Experience.* New Delhi: Sage Publications
- Hassan, Sajjad M., 2008. *Building Legitimacy: Exploring State-Society Relations in Northeast India.* New Delhi: Oxford University Press
- Hickey, Sam and Giles Mohan. (2005). Relocating Participation within a Radical Politics of Development. *Development and Change* 36(2): 237-265.
- Irina, Ningthoujam. (2008). Solidarity as Social Capital: Gender, Roles and Potential. *Eastern Quarterly: Gender Studies in the Northeast.* Vol.5. Issue II & III, July-December 2008, pp.94-103.
- Jayal, Niraja Gopal., 2004. Democracy and Social Capital in the Central Himalaya: A Tale of Two Villages. In D. Bhattacharyya., G. N. Jayal, B. Mohapatra, & S. Pai., (Eds.) *Interrogating Social Capital: The Indian Experience* (pp. 72-95). New Delhi: Sage Publications
- Ministry of Development of North Eastern Region and North Eastern Council, Government of India. (2008). *North Eastern Region Vision 2020.*
- Nagaland State Human Development Report 2004, Department of Planning & Coordination, Government of Nagaland
- National Institute of Public Finance and Policy. (2007). *Peace, Progress and Prosperity in the North Eastern Region Vision 2020.* New Delhi.
- Nongbri, Tiplut. (2008). Deconstructing Masculinity: Fatherhood, Matriliny and Social Change. *Eastern Quarterly: Gender Studies in the Northeast.* Vol.5. Issue II & III, July-December 2008, pp.75-86.

- Parfitt, Trevor. (2004). The Ambiguity of Participation: A Qualified Defence of Participatory Development. *Third World Quarterly*, Vol. 25. No. 3, pp. 537-556.
- Phanjoubam, Pradip. (2001). Insurgency and its impact on the Development of Manipur. In, In C. Joshua Thomas, R. Gopalakrishnan & R.K. Ranjan Singh, (Eds.) *Constraints in Development of Manipur* (pp 19-28). New Delhi: Regency Publications.
- Singh, M. Amarjeet. (2001). Problem of Unemployment among the Educated Youth in Manipur. In C. Joshua Thomas, R. Gopalakrishnan & R.K. Ranjan Singh, (Eds.) *Constraints in Development of Manipur* (pp 57-65). New Delhi: Regency Publications.
- Sinha, C. A. Political Culture and Development in North East India, *Dialogue*, Volume- 7. No 4., pp 120-134.
- *Skill Development in India: The Vocational Education and Training System*. (2008). Human Development Unit South Asia Region. The World Bank.
- *World Bank Participation Sourcebook*. (1996). Environmentally Sustainable Development. The World Bank: Washington DC

End notes

1. The use of the term North Eastern Region of India, apply to the geographical location of the eight states in the Indian sub continent- stretching from the foothills of the Himalayas in the eastern range and sharing international boundaries with countries of Bhutan, China, Nepal, Myanmar and Bangladesh.
2. The RSI calculation is based upon the share of net sown area of a particular crop compared to the average for the region. A value greater than 1 indicates that the particular state has a comparative advantage in that crop vis-à-vis other NER states. Under the RSI calculation the following crops considered are: rice, maize, small millet, wheat, total cereals, total pulses, total food grains, sesamum, rapeseed and mustard, total oilseeds, tea, coffee, natural rubber, bananas, sugarcane, potatoes, chillies, ginger, coconut, turmeric, and pineapple. See, North Eastern Region Vision 2020, pp 43.
3. NSI is calculated on the basis of the share of net sown area in the state devoted to the production of a particular crop as compared to the national average. A value greater than 1 indicates the production advantage of producing that particular crop in comparison to their production in other parts of the country. Ibid.
4. The Centre of Excellence, funded by the Central Government's Horticulture Mission act as an interface between Zopar Exports Private Limited, Bangalore and the farmers producing flowers, fruits and vegetables. The first shipment of 1,000 cut flowers from Mizoram and Meghalaya was exported to Al Lokrit, Dubai, within 24 hours via Air Emirates from Kolkata. A similar Centre has been established in Sikkim. See, North Eastern Region Vision 2020, pp 55-59.
5. Nagaland government's Providing Urban Amenities in a Rural Areas (PURA) scheme in collaboration with the Nagaland University aims to create vocational training institutions for developing the service and manufacturing sector. Ibid, pp 227
6. In Mizoram, the Entrepreneurs Training Centre and Prometric Testing Centre was established in 2005 through a partnership between the IT Cell of the Mizoram government and New Horizons India [a US based company]. The Centre provides employment-related training and skills to the young educated unemployed in software development and business communication. Further, New Horizons will establish a prometric testing centre to enable the students apply for certification from IT giants like Microsoft, Cisco and Oracle to equip the youth with such skills that will help them venture out nationally or internationally. Ibid, pp 226
7. At the secondary level, majority of students leave home to pursue course in Engineering, Medical, Administration, Finance, IT, Hotel Management, Mass communication etc., and educational institutions providing better employment prospects. See, Student Out-flux from North East India, http://www.assamchronicle.com/node/240

8. On 4th July 2008, the seventh Indian Institute of Management called Rajiv Gandhi Indian Institute of Management (RGIIM) was opened at Shillong.
9. The All India Council for Vocational Education under the Ministry of Human Resource Development is responsible for VEP in India.
10. ITIs and ITCs entrusted with imparting the Craftsmen Training Scheme (CTS) is affiliated with the National Council for Vocational Training (NCVT), Ministry of Labour. However while ITIs are public institutions ITCs are private in nature.
11. The Municipal Council performs only the following services: Registration of Births and Death, Public Health, Sanitation, Conservancy and Solid Waste Management, Maintenance of Cattle, Ponds, Parking lots, Roads (leikai) and Bridges (co-shared with PWD). The remaining functions are performed by the respective Departments- Town Planning, Public Health and Engineering, Fire Services, Forests, Planning and Development Authority, Power, Social Welfare, Art and Culture, Education etc.
12. See Neera Chandhoke, The Conceits of Civil Society, pp 59
13. Since the introduction of democracy, no Naga woman has been elected to the State Assembly nor are there any prominent women in the political arena. The introduction of women's reservation in the ULB's also evoked protests from the Ao tribe. See, Aier, pp 92.

Section 3

ISSUES IN HIGHER EDUCATION AND POLICY REFORMS

Chapter 14

CIVIL SERVICE RECRUITMENT POLICY IN BANGLADESH:
An Agenda for Reform

M. Abdul Wahhab

Abstract

The present paper deals with the civil service recruitment policy of Bangladesh. It reveals that a sound and appropriate civil service recruitment policy does not exist in Bangladesh. Executive orders govern the recruitment policy in civil service. Instead of merit, the existing recruitment policy gives emphasis on quotas and reserves the majority of posts of civil service for preferred groups. Likewise, ad hoc appointments also dominate civil service recruitment policy. Through quota and ad hoc appointment, the government politicises the civil service. The paper recommends the principle of merit in civil service recruitment. It proposes the abolishment of all types of quotas except for the tribal people. It also proposes the need to avoid ad hoc appointments. Since a single Public Service Commission is unable to hold competitive examinations regularly and timely, the paper suggests the establishment of two Public Service Commissions. It also proposes the reform competitive examinations to avoid lengthy selection processes; and to minimise political pressures and corruption.

Introduction

Civil service of a country includes all permanent functionaries of government employed in civil administration excluding judicial and defence service and are usually recruited on the basis of merit. The functions of civil service in modern states are many and varied including the routine functions of day to day administration as well as providing advice to the minister on all matters of policy. But their main function is the implementation of policy taken by the ministry/cabinet. Since the ministers are busy with political affairs they are dependent on the civil servants for running ministries. According to a writer as quoted in Ahmad (2003) "in Britain, in ninety nine cases out of one hundred, the ministers simply accept the views of civil servants, and sign their names on dotted line (P.455). A country may run without ministers, but it cannot run a day without civil servants. Hence, the question of recruitment of best talents to civil service occupies an important place in the study of public policy in a country.

The present study deals with the civil service recruitment policy of Bangladesh government especially the policy for direct recruitment. It also deals with the reforms needed in this regard. The data of the study were collected from secondary source materials.

Bangladesh and its Civil Service

Bangladesh is a unitary country having parliamentary form of government. It was a province of united Pakistan from 1947 to 1971 and became independent in December 1971 following a nine-month war of liberation. Bangladesh is a country of Bengali speaking people consisting of more than 99 percent of total population. Linguistic minorities include as many as 13 tribes totalling about 1 million. Like linguistic homogeneity, there is also religious homogeneity. Muslims constitute 89 percent of the population and the Hindus, the largest religious minority constitute 9.2 percent. The rest are Buddhists, Christians and Pagans. Male female ratio is 105:100 and literacy is 63 percent. Labour force is very poor consisting of 31.5 percent.

Broadly the civil service of Bangladesh consists of all government employees who vertically belong to four categories viz. Class I Officers, Class II Officers, Class III employees and Class IV employees. The officers are also classified as gazetted and non-gazetted officers. The officers whose recruitment, posting, transfer, promotion and the similar are notified in government gazettes, are known as gazetted officers. All Class I officers and some of the Class II officers are treated as gazetted officers. Class I officers are also divided into cadre and non-cadre services. Cadre Service basically refers to the organisation of civil servants into well-defined groups, services or cadres. On the other hand, non-cadre service is mostly based on positions with no definite structure of mobility either horizontally or vertically. Bangladesh Civil Service, more popularly known by its acronym BCS belongs to cadre service. BCS is the elite service in the country and includes about 70 percent of total class I services.

Recruitment Policy: Predominance of Quota

Bangladesh Constitution was introduced in the country on 16th December 1972 and eight months before it, an interim recruitment policy known as the Interim Recruitment Rules 1972 was issued on May 9, 1972 by a Presidential Order. It came into operation on the 5th of September 1972 when the Establishment Ministry through an office memorandum spelled out that only in class I posts of the civil service 20 percent would be recruited on merit and 80 percent would be recruited from the preferred groups on the basis of quota (Table 1).

TABLE 1: Showing Quota and Merit in Recruitment Policy of Class I Services
(Figures in percentages)

Distribution of quota and merit	1972	1976	1985 (I & II)*
Merit (national)	20	40	45
Freedom fighters (national)	30	30	
War affected women (national)	10	10	
District quota on merit	40	20	
District quota (55%) for preferred groups below:			
a. Freedom fighters or if freedom fighters are not available then their children since 1997			30
b. Women			10
c. Tribal			05
d. District merit			10
Total	100	100	100

Source: Interim Recruitment Rules 1972 and Establishment Division Memorandum 1972, 1976 and 1997
*Note: Class 11 services were included in the recruitment policy of Class 1 services in 1985

It emanates from Table 1 that out of the total vacancies in civil service during 1972-1976, only 20 percent posts were recruited on merit and 80 percent posts were recruited form three preferred groups viz. (i) freedom fighters who joined liberation war of 1971 to free Bangladesh (30%), (ii) women affected by liberation war (10%) and (iii) district quota (40%).

The 20 percent merit and 80 percent quotas for provinces were maintained in the former Pakistan for the recruitment to central civil service. This was necessary for federal Pakistan. Bangladesh is a homogeneous nation and unitary in character. It has no such necessity and problems. However, East Pakistan now Bangladesh had a separate quota policy according to which 80 percent civil servants were recruited on merit and only 20 percent posts were reserved for preferred groups based on religion. It was expected that the government of the post liberation period would follow the quota policy of East Pakistan. But without considering the realities, the discussion of which follows in the next sections, the government introduced 80 percent quota for preferred groups including 30 percent for freedom fighters and 10 percent for war affected women. However, merit was increased to 40 percent in 1976 by decreasing district quota from 40 percent to 20 percent. Again merit was increased to 45 percent in 1985 and quota was reduced to 55 percent and all preferred groups were brought under the district quota.

It is surprising to note that women and tribes were not given quota in 1972. Women were given a quota of 10 percent in 1985 by replacing war affected women because of their non availability and tribes were given 5 percent quota in the same year by reducing district quota from 60 percent to 55 percent. It can, therefore, be said that the move towards promoting merit and also female and tribal quotas happened during two martial law regimes, not during the civilian governments.

Policy Implementation: Recruitment Process

Bangladesh Public Service Commission, popularly known by its acronym PSC, is a constitutional body (Articles 137-141 of Bangladesh Constitution) which is assigned the task of selecting suitable persons for appointment to the services of the Republic through competitive examinations. The Establishment Ministry is the final authority for appointing the persons in civil service selected by PSC. The chairman and members of PSC are appointed by the President with advice from the Prime Minister.

Competitive examinations, came to be held in Bangladesh since 1982 according to the BCS Recruitment Rules introduced in 1981. Before 1982, the civil servants were recruited either only by interview or through a short written examination and interview. From 1982 to 2006, PSC conducted 27 BCS examinations of which 14 were general for all cadres and the rest were special for technical cadres. The competitive examinations for BCS consist of three tests viz. (i) Preliminary examination; (ii) Written examination and (iii) Viva voce examination. The Preliminary examination is a Multiple Choice Question (MCQ) based test to screen out less qualified candidates. The candidates who qualified in MCQ preliminary examination are invited to sit for a written examination on selected subjects. The candidates obtaining 50 percent marks in written examination are qualified for viva. Minimum qualifying marks for viva is 40 percent. The final list is prepared on the basis of written and viva marks. After completing the merit list, the candidates are selected for different types of quota. PSC sends the final list of selected candidates to Establishment Ministry for appointment to the vacancies.

Policy Evaluation and Recommendations

a. Legality and Impact of Quota

Merit system is a general principle for civil service recruitment to ensure equal employment opportunity for all citizens. Bangladesh Constitution provides principle of merit for ensuring equal employment opportunities for all citizens without any discrimination (Article 29 [1, 2]). The constitution also provides exceptional appointment for the advancement of backward sections in the country (Article 29 [a, b, and c]). The exceptional appointment i.e. quota is an exceptional principle that can not be larger than the general principle of merit. Hence larger quota is inconsistent with the general principle of equal opportunity of employment for all without any discrimination as guaranteed in the constitution. Also Article 27 (All citizens are equal before law) of the constitution provides no scope for the division of divide society into freedom fighters and non-freedom fighters and Article 28 does not protect such division.

Quota is an interim measure. It should have time limit, but no time limit is fixed for employment quotas in Bangladesh. Quota may be misused and to avoid this, there should be formal institution(s) to monitor its implementation but there is no such formal institution(s) in the country. It is also surprising to note that the appointments under different quotas have never been made public either by PSC or by Establishment Ministry in official document/gazette. PSC annual reports do not provide adequate information on it. In short, quota has always been implemented in country without transparency.

It indicates from the above discussion that executive orders govern the civil service recruitment policy in Bangladesh. The policy is dominated by quotas which have no constitutional sanction. Since quotas (especially the quota of freedom fighters/their children) is a sensitive and emotional issue it has not been challenged in the courts. However, long term quota is bound to create adverse impact on the efficiency of administration because less qualified officers are recruited.

b. Abolishing Quota and Restoring Merit

Although government has consistently upheld the quota system, there have been some effort and movement to reduce/abolish quota from civil service recruitment policy. The Pay and Service Commission 1977 opposed district quotas and raised the question about the necessity of female quota. The Public Administration Reform Commission 2000 recommended the gradual abolition of quota. In 2005 the Parliamentary Standing Committee on Establishment Ministry discussed the quota issue and proposed its reduction but no measure was taken to implement it. In early 2008 there was a movement among the students against the quota, but it was discontinued after the present government came to power.

Sponsored by PSC and funded by World Bank, a working paper was prepared in 2008, which suggested that recruitment on merit should be a minimum of 50 percent and a maximum of 70 percent. One year before, Transparency International Bangladesh (TIB 2007) suggested that at least 75 percent of posts in civil service in Bangladesh should be on purely merit basis, while the remaining may be distributed on the basis of gender, ethnic and religious identity. TIB also suggests that the existing quota for freedom fighters/ their children and district quotas are no longer logical and hence should be abolished (P. 11). We agree with TIB regarding the abolition of district quota and quota for freedom fighters/their children but disagree with the advocacy of religious and gender quotas.

With regard to religious quotas, the proposal of TIB conflicts with another finding. The TIB (2007) studied 19 BCS examinations and observed that non-Muslim appointments include 8.46 percent in BCS general cadre and 11.27 percent in professional/technical cadre. In Bangladesh the largest religious minority, the Hindus consist of 9.2 percent of the population. The other religious minorities include Buddhists, Christians and a few pagans; and almost all of them belong to tribal groups. Although tribal quota is fixed at 5 percent, in reality they get according to Khan and Ahmad (2008) less than one percent due to the absence of qualified candidates (P.50). So, non-Muslim appointments are in fact the appointments of the Hindus. This invariably proves that the Hindus are equally competent with the Muslims to join the civil service. Hence we find no justification of religious quotas in civil service recruitment as advocated by TIB.

As for gender/female quota, it may be said that female quota played an important role in encouraging the women to join civil service and yield good result (Wahhab 2008, Pp.11-12). But female quota is no longer essential, because civil servants are mainly recruited from the graduates of universities. There is no female quota for admission to the universities. Every year a large number of female students are enrolled in the universities. Their performance in university education is in no way inferior to that of male students. Similarly there is no female quota in appointing university teachers. According to the report of Ahmed (2008), female students in the Dhaka University, the oldest and largest university in the country, comprise about 50 percent; and as of June 2007, women teachers constituted 26.2 percent of the total teachers. Five years back, female teachers comprised about 16 percent. So like religious quota, we find no justification of female quota in civil service recruitment.

Similarly, 10 percent district quotas, is not a proper solution; rather government should take measures to improve the schools and colleges so that the students of the less developed districts come out with capability to compete with the students from developed districts.

With regard to the quota of freedom fighters, it may be said that 30 percent quota for them was given by the government as sympathy for their role in the war of liberation. It has no constitutional sanction unless they are proved to be disadvantageous. It is difficult to prove this, because no data on the socio-economic background of freedom fighter recruits are available. The issue was further made complicated in 1997 when the children of freedom fighters became eligible for the same privilege of 30 percent quota. It is also very difficult to justify 30 percent posts of civil service for freedom fighters/their children who constitute less than one percent of the total population in the country. According to the Ministry of Liberation War Affairs, the total number of freedom fighters is 146,790. Assuming that an average 5 person per family, total population eligible for the facility of 30 percent posts is about 0.006 percent only (calculated in Khan and Ahmad 2008, P. 18). Thus 30 percent quota is larger than the size of its beneficiaries that can produce only 2.2 to 10.8 percent qualified candidates (Calculated from the records of PSC). As a result, most of the vacancies under the quota of freedom fighters/their children remain unfilled.

Freedom fighters are the best sons of the nation. The people of Bangladesh have strong commitment to the issue of improving the socio-economic conditions of freedom fighters. If government really wants to help the children of freedom fighters, their better education should be ensured by providing special stipend as the government did for female education which has yielded good results. Now the enrolment of girls in secondary and higher secondary schools is almost equal to that of boys (Wahhab 2008a, P.387).

Against the backdrop of the realities mentioned above, we propose the introduction of the principle of merit for the recruitment to civil services and suggest the abolishment of all types of quota except for tribal people who are backward sections in the country. However, the tribal quota should not exceed more than 1 percent as they enjoined before liberation in 1971, because the tribes constitute about one million people only.

c. Stopping Ad Hoc Appointment

Like the quota system, ad hoc appointments also dominate the recruitment policy of civil service in Bangladesh. Ad hoc appointments may not be stopped totally, but it should be minimised as far as possible. Immediately after the liberation, ad hoc appointments were necessary and hence a lot of ad hoc appointments were made. From 1972 to 2000, a total of 24,230 persons were appointed on ad hoc basis (TIB 2007, P. 24) against 36,161 persons who were appointed through competitive examinations (Ali, 2000, Pp. 298-300). This means out of the total appointments, 40.12 percent were made on ad hoc basis. In 1991 the government took a decision to stop ad hoc appointments to revenue budget posts. It checked the open-door policy for ad hoc appointments to a great extent. But again open-door policy for ad hoc appointments got a lease of new life when the present government on 13 July, 2009 took a decision for ad hoc appointments to the vacant posts of public services including 4,000 physicians under the Health Ministry (Cabinet decision July 13, 2008). The plea was that the lengthy process of PSC recruitment will hamper the activities of ministries/divisions due to the shortage of man power. By this time, how many ad hoc appointments were made in all services we do not know, but the Prime Minister in a public meeting said that ad hoc appointments of 3000 physicians were completed and 500 are in the process (The Daily Star, 5th August 2010).

Since ad hoc appointments are politically made to provide the party men with employment, it results in inefficiency in administration. We think ad hoc appointments should be avoided as far as possible to increase the efficiency in administration.

d. Stopping Politicisation of Civil Service

It has been mentioned above that many posts reserved for preferred groups including freedom fighters/their children remain unfilled due to non availability of qualified candidates. In 2002 the government took a decision for transferring such unfilled posts to special merit category. But the present government decided not to fill up the unfilled posts of quota by special category and brought the quota from district to national level (Cabinet decision on April 3, 2010). However, quota again got a fresh life.

Why is the government unwilling to abolish quota and avoid ad hoc appointments? The answer is very simple. Since PSC is constituted on political considerations, the government can easily arrange to appoint its own people to unfilled posts of quota. For this reason, we find no transparency in quota implementation. Similarly ad hoc appointment means the provision of party men with employment. Thus politicisation of civil service is made by the government through quota policy and ad hoc appointment practices. Politicisation of civil service not only enhances inefficiency in administration, but also it seriously hampers the neutrality of civil service. However, politicisation of civil service may be minimised by reorganizing PSC and reforming competitive examinations.

e. Reorganising PSC

According to the study of TIB (2007), average time spent for a general BCS examination was 24.75 months and for special 14 months (P. 73). This indicates that a single PSC is unable to hold regular BCS examinations in a timely fashion The delay paves the plea for government to recruit officials on ad hoc basis. For regular and timely recruitment to civil service we propose the establishment of two PSCs viz. PSC (First) and PSC (Second). The PSC (First) will recruit all Class 1 officers including BCS and other officers; and PSC (Second), would recruit Class II officers. There is no constitutional bar, because constitution provides for one or more PSCs.

Since the inception of PSC, with a few exceptions, the chairmen and members were appointed on political consideration. As a result there have been allegations of recruiting candidates aligned to the ruling party. In a democratic country like Bangladesh, political considerations cannot be avoided totally, but the appointment of chairman and members of an institution like PSC must be from among the persons of high integrity, strong moral courage; and sufficient knowledge and experience on administration.

f. Reforming Competitive Examinations

One of the causes for the lengthy process of BCS examination is a separate preliminary examination to screen out the less qualified applicants. Screening out of less qualified candidates is essential because of a large number of applicants. For example, in the 29th BCS examination there were 1, 23,745 applicants for 1,581 posts (The *Shamokal*, a daily Bengali newspaper, August 14, 2009). It is difficult for a single PSC, to conduct the written examination of such a huge number of applicants all over the country. However, preliminary examination takes a considerable time. So we propose to abolish preliminary examinations and instead, the marks secured by applicants in the public certificate examinations necessary for competitive examinations may be considered to screen out the less qualified applicants.

The list of selected candidates for viva is prepared on the basis of marks of written examination only. We propose giving equal weight of marks secured by the candidates in public certificate examinations with the marks of written examination to prepare the list for viva. The consideration of public certificate marks in both preliminary and written examinations not only will provide justice and encourage the students to make good academic record but also it will minimise corruption including bribery for leakage of question papers as is often alleged against BCS examination.

Another cause of delay of BCS examination is the long list of candidates for viva. Viva of a BCS examination takes 4-5 months. The long list of viva creates wider scope for political pressure and bribery. We think for each post, 4-5 candidates may be selected for viva. The lesser candidates for viva not only minimises lengthy process, but also minimise the scope of political pressure and corruption.

We also propose one competitive examination for both BCS cadre services and other non-cadre services. After completing the appointments to the vacancies of BCS cadre posts, vacancies of non-cadre posts will be filled up from the rest qualified candidates of the list. This will save time and money.

Conclusion

Bangladesh is a developing country. It has many problems and challenges to address for its all-round development. This gigantic task can only be performed by meritorious, efficient and honest civil servants. To recruit such civil servants, an appropriate, effective and updated recruitment policy based on merit system is essential, but such a policy is yet to be formulated in Bangladesh. The executive orders still govern recruitment policy.

The study has identified some major limitations for this policy. These are: emphasis on quota system; unbridled ad hoc appointments; lack of capacity of a single PSC for holding BCS examinations regularly and timely; appointment of chairman and members on political considerations; lengthy process of BCS examinations; and politicisation of civil services.

The study recommends the introduction of the principle of merit for civil service recruitment and proposes to abolish all types of quotas except 1 percent quota for tribal people. It also proposes to halt unbridled ad hoc appointments. This will minimise politicisation of the civil services. Since a single PSC is unable to hold BCS examinations regularly and timely, two PSCs may be created. In order to avoid partisan recruitment and corruption, the appointment of chairman and members to the PSCs must be from among the persons of high integrity, strong moral courage, sufficient knowledge and experience in administration.

The study proposes the abolition of preliminary examination and suggests that the marks secured by the applicants in their public certificate examinations should be declared to screen out less qualified applicants. It also proposes giving equal weightage to the marks of public certificate examinations with the marks of written examination to select candidates for viva. Besides, the list of candidates for viva should be reduced to 4-5 for one post. There should be one competitive examination for Class I services including BCS cadre services and other non-cadre services. After completing appointments to the vacancies of cadre posts from merit list, the appointments for non-cadre posts should be made from the rest of the list.

A high powered committee may be instituted to suggest the methods of implementation of the recommendations. If the recommendations are implemented, it is expected to build an efficient and impartial civil service for better governance in the country and also to make Bangladesh competitive in the world. This, however, largely depends on the political will. Both government and opposition should be united on the issue. The present government may not agree with the abolition of quotas, especially the quota of freedom fighters/their children, because the issue is very emotional and sensitive. The teachers, journalists, women activists, bureaucrats, ethnic minorities and students may play an important role to create pressures on government. Let us be more pragmatic, rational and less emotional in order to promote our national interests.

References

- Ahmad, Emajuddin (2000). *The Tale of Political Science* (in Bengali) 25th edition, Dhaka: A F. M. khalilur Rahman, Bangladesh Book Corporation Ltd.
- Ahmed, Kamal Uddin (2008). "Quota system for civil service", *The Daily Star*, 07-18.
- Ali, A. M. M. Shawkat (2002). *The Lore of the Mandarins: Towards a Non-Partisan Public Service in Bangladesh*, Dhaka: The University Press Limited.
- Flippo, Edwin B. (1984). *Personnel Management*, sixth edition, Singapore: Mc Graw Hill.
- Government of Bangladesh, Ministry of Establishment (1972) *Interim Recruitment Rules, 1972*, Dhaka: Bangladesh Government Press
- Government of Bangladesh, Ministry of Establishment (1981). *Bangladesh Civil Service Rules, 1981*, Dhaka: Bangladesh Government Press
- .... Ministry of Law and Parliamentary Affairs (2008). *The Constitution of the People's Republic of Bangladesh* as printed with latest amendment.
- .... Ministry of Liberation War Affairs (2005). *Annual Report* 2003-2004, Dhaka: Bangladesh Government Press.
- Khan, Akbar Ali and Ahmad, Kazi Rakibuddin (2008). "Quota System for Civil Service Recruitment in Bangladesh: An Exploratory Analysis". Retrieved from http:// www.bpsc,gov.bd/documents
- Stahl, O. Glenn (1962). *Public Personnel Administration*, New York: Harper & Row Publishers, Fifth edition.
- Transparency International Bangladesh (2007). "Public Service Commission: A Diagnostic Study" (Draft). Retrieved from http://www.ti-bangladesh.org

- Wahhab, M A. (2008). "Women in Bangladesh Civil Service", *Ebong Authopor......*, (Annual Journal of Public Administration [Students]), University of Chittagong, PP. 10-14.
- .... (2008a). "Education and Women's Empowerment: Challenges and Commitment" in Sharif as Saber and Singh, Amita (eds.) (2009). *Strengthening Governance in Asia-Pacific: Myth, Realities and Methods,* New Delhi: Macmillan Publishers India Ltd. Pp. 385-397.

CHAPTER 15

HIGHER EDUCATION:
Recent Reform Initiatives In India

SUMAN SHARMA

Abstract

Education is of critical importance for development. It has intrinsic and instrumental value and is considered a human right in the modern parlance with potential of empowering the underprivileged. India with its ancient heritage of imparting education through the Gurukul system (students staying at Guru's or teacher's home to complete education) created institutions of higher learning which were of international repute. In recent times, the Indian Supreme Court raised the bar high when in a landmark judgement in 1993 it construed the right to education as inherent in the right to life enshrined in the Indian Constitution. There is, however, a serious and a deep crisis that afflicts the education sector in India today. India which is emerging as an important member of the 21st century global order, has realised the magnitude and the seriousness of this crisis. It has taken the first steps in articulating the issues and the problems in education, including higher education, by setting up a National Knowledge Commission to initiate reforms for the expansion in higher education consistent with the standards of excellence and inclusive of the vast deprived sections of its population. This paper is an attempt to evaluate India's efforts at reforming the higher education sector including the controversy on the future shape of the regulatory authority for the higher education.

Introduction

India of the twenty first century, after six decades of freedom from colonialism, is on the move and in ferment. While it has an ancient rich heritage to fall back on, it is confronted with a myriad of complex problems due to mass deprivation and poverty. The recent sustained economic growth has brought focus on its policies and aspiration to play a larger role in global sweepstakes. In this context, the debate on education per-se and on higher education in particular, is evolving at a fierce pace and has shaken policy establishment in the country out of slumber.

There is a growing realisation that the economic march to progress can be meaningful and democracy sustainable only if it is inclusive in character. This realisation also informs the debate and policy formulation on higher education. At the same time it is well recognised that the quality of education needs to match the complexity of the growing economy and the nation. The three pillars of policy regime on higher education, therefore, are 'Expansion', 'Inclusion' and 'Excellence' with inclusion being the essence of the national vision.

While policy planning establishment is pro-actively pursuing the national objectives on education, the judiciary in an enlightened mode catapulted the education to a right inherent in the right to life enshrined in the constitution of the country. The stage is thus set for higher education in India to carry on the march of democracy, peace and progress in the sub-continent of South Asia.

Ancient Indian Initiatives

Education is the fulcrum of life, for peace, progress and development. It provides seedlings for the culture and the civilisation. It is a passport for freedom and liberty and a higher calling in life. The South Asian sub-continent is the inheritor of an ancient, rich civilisation and also a victim of western imperialism which ravaged the sub-continent in the not so distant past. South Asian or more specifically Indian perspectives on education are, therefore, richly endowed with the possibility of complete human development.

The achievements of Indian education in ancient times were fascinating. Sages and scholars orally imparted education in the Gurukul system (students staying at Guru's or teacher's home to complete education). While the original Vedic education was confined to the upper strata of society in a complicated stratified social order, the later spread of Buddhism and Jainism enriched education and was available to everyone in society. The problems of lack of inclusiveness though, in some measure, persist to the present day.

The famous institutions at Nalanda, Vikramshila and Takshashila were celebrated symbols of the educational and cultural achievements of India. Nalanda University, during the fifth to thirteenth centuries AD was known for its educational excellence. The university was a convergence point for international scholars. The contribution of India in the field of education during the ancient and medieval times was thus very significant.

Critical Importance of Education

In the post-colonial era, development economists, focussing on the individual, perceived the independent value of education. Education develops faculties and enlarges opportunities to participate in the life and culture of the nation and the world. They also attributed instrumental value to results of education which produces knowledge, skills and changed attitudes. The practical, utilitarian view was also underlined since education provides the chance for individuals to increase their incomes and raise their level of living. Education along with health, which are central to the contemporary debate on the human development indicators, were thus recognised as a 'human right'.[1] The *South Asian countries must strive for a much speedier dissemination of the attitudes, knowledge, and skills favourable to development, inasmuch as they have vast handicaps to overcome in their planning for development, including an unprecedented high rate of population increase.*[2]

Further, the modern economists who are imbued with the spirit of liberal democracy and sensitive to the deprived millions in an iniquitous social order expanded the scope to emphasise the empowerment and the redistributive role of education. They collected evidence to prove that greater literacy and educational achievements of the disadvantaged groups can increase their ability to resist oppression. They can also politically organise themselves for a fairer deal. Underlining the great strategic importance of health and education in the process of economic development, they wondered at India's lack of policy in matters of health and education:

> India's failure to have an adequate public policy in educational and health matters can be , thus , of profound significance in assessing the limited success of Indian development efforts over the last half a century.[3]

The Indian Supreme Court made a historic construction of the right to life enshrined in the Indian constitution (Article 21) to include right to education to take this debate at a higher pedestal.

> The citizens of this country have a fundamental right to education. The said right flows from Article 21.[4]

Policy Initiatives in India: National Knowledge Commission

As if taking a cue from the on-going debate on education, the Indian policy establishment formulated a suitable legislation and after prolonged debate, the Constitution of India has been amended by an Act of Parliament to insert an Article 21-A in the Constitution to provide for Free and Compulsory Education to children up to the age of 14 years. The policy establishment also did not lose sight of building the edifice of a knowledge society on a strong foundation of primary and secondary education. A National Knowledge Commission (NKC) was accordingly set up to prepare a blue print to tap in to the enormous reservoir of knowledge base to confidently face the challenges of 21st century. The terms of reference of National Knowledge Commission were wide ranging, incorporating issues like access to knowledge, knowledge concepts, creation of knowledge, knowledge applications and delivery of services etc. The Commission addressed these wide range of issues including a comprehensive reform of higher education.

National Knowledge Commission on Higher Education

The recommendations of the Knowledge Commission on higher education focussed on expansion, excellence and inclusion. While acknowledging the islands of excellence like Indian Institutes of Technology (IITs) and Indian Institutes of Management (IIMs) and higher education in general making significant contribution to economic development, social progress and political democracy in India, the Commission nevertheless underlined the deep crisis in higher education in India in the following words:

> There is, in fact, a quiet crisis in higher education in India that runs deep. It is not yet discernible simply because there are pockets of excellence, an enormous reservoir of talented young people and an intense competition in the admissions process. And, in some important spheres, we continue to reap the benefits of what was sown in higher education 50 years ago by the founding fathers of the Republic. The reality is that we have miles to go. The proportion of our population, in the age group 18-24, that enters the world of higher education is around 7 per cent, which is only one-half the average for Asia. The opportunities for higher education, in terms of the number of places in universities, are simply not enough in relation to our needs. What is more, the quality of higher education in most of our universities requires substantial improvement.[5]

The crisis is not merely in terms of the restricted access but also of the quality and equality of the educational opportunities. The statistics are revealing in comparison to advanced industrialised countries. In OECD countries one-quarter (26%) of population have achieved tertiary level of education.[6] In the age group of 20-25 the enrolment in higher education is only 9% to 11% in India as compared to 45% to 85% in developed countries.[7] Further, only a small proportion of Indian population graduate from upper secondary level, drop out rates between the secondary and the upper secondary is extremely large and expenditure on the higher education in India is extremely inadequate. According to Government of India's National Sample Survey Organisation (61st Round on Employment and Unemployment, 2004-05) only 5.9 per cent of population in the age group of 15-60 years attain educational levels of Graduate and above.[8] The average for OECD countries in respect of attaining tertiary education among population between 25 to 64 years, on the other hand, is 26 per cent.[9] National Knowledge Commission in India recognised the imperative need for a meaningful reform of the higher education and noted the following about the Universities in India:

> There is, however, a serious cause for concern about universities in India. The number of places for students at universities is simply inadequate. The quality of education at most universities leaves much to be desired. The gap between our universities and those in the outside world has widened. And none of our universities rank among the best, say top fifty, in the world.[10]

Reform Measures

Expansion of Higher Education

The National Knowledge Commission underlining the imperative need for a long term perspective while undertaking meaningful reforms in higher education made very specific recommendations on expansion of the system, maintaining excellence and at the same time making it inclusive for every segment of population in the country.

National Knowledge Commission has recommended a massive expansion by suggesting creation of 1500 universities nationwide with an objective to achieve gross enrolment ratio of 15 per cent by the year 2015. This target has to be evaluated in the light of the fact that the country at present has approximately 378 universities[11]. The Commission perhaps realising the ambitious nature of its recommendation on creation of large number of universities also advised that clusters of colleges selected on the basis of similar standards or geographical proximity could be considered for granting autonomy and groomed for later upgrading as universities.

Some other important recommendations of National Knowledge Commission on expansion include change in the system of regulation for higher education, increase in public spending and diversifying sources of financing and establishment of 50 national universities. The Commission envisaged an important leadership role for proposed national universities:

> ...National Universities ... can provide education of the highest standard. As exemplars for the rest of the nation, these universities would train students in a variety of disciplines, including humanities, social sciences, basic sciences, commerce and professional subjects, at both the undergraduate and post graduate levels. The number 50 is a long term objective. In the short run, it is important to begin with at least 10 such universities in the next three years.[12]

One serious impediment in realising the goals of much needed expansion of educational facilities is scarcity of resources. It is indeed a tragic irony that South Asian countries spend huge resources on defence rather than on education. Human Development Report on South Asia in 1998 with its focus on Education noted that only $12 billion were spent during 1990-96 on education as compared to $70 billion on defence by South Asian countries.[13] India has been making and reiterating its national pledge of investing at least 6 per cent of its GDP on education for quite some time now but the target seems difficult to be achieved in view of adverse security situation in South Asia and lack of will power among a corrupt political elite. India Vision 2020 document published by India's national Planning Commission in December 2002 notes the following on resource allocation:

> *Full development of India's enormous human potential will require a shift in national priorities, to commit a greater portion of the country's financial resources to the education sector. India currently invests 3.2-4.4 per cent of GNP on education. This compares unfavourably with the UMI reference level of 4.9 per cent, especially with countries such as South Africa, which invests 7.9 per cent of GNP on education. A near doubling of investments in education is the soundest policy for quadrupling the country's GDP per capita.[14]*

[UMI: Upper Middle Income countries]

The National Knowledge Commission while recommending diversifying sources of financing, maintained that the enhanced level of funding must come from both public and private sources but Government financing should remain the cornerstone of resource allocation and, therefore, expected that at least 1.5 per cent of GDP out of total 6 per cent GDP bench mark for education, would be spent on higher education.

Excellence in Higher Education

The ambition and necessity of expansion of the system obviously raises the issues of excellence. The Knowledge Commission advocates an intense reforms of existing universities by revising or restructuring curricula at least once in three years, supplementing the annual examinations with continuous internal assessment, transition to a course credit system where degrees are granted on the basis of completing a requisite number of credits, monitoring and upgrading the infrastructure like libraries, laboratories and connectivity on a regular basis, preservation of autonomy and promotion of accountability in governance of universities etc. The Commission makes a fervent plea to make the universities the hub of research and to attract and retain talented faculty members through better working conditions.

Inclusion, the Core of Reforms

While the expansion and excellence have rightly been emphasised in the discourse on higher education in India, it is perhaps the third pillar of the National Knowledge Commission's report, i.e., inclusion which would be the sine-qua-non of any reforms process in India. The critical need for the inclusive model of reforms in education is not only a necessity to fulfill the aspirations of deprived population but also an imperative need if India is to achieve its future potential and live up to its ancient heritage. The divide between haves and have-nots in education in India has been succinctly captured in the country's Eleventh Plan (2007-2012) document in the following words:

> Our GER (Gross Enrolment Ratio) of around 11% is very low compared to the world average of 23.2%, 36.5% for countries in transition, 54.6% for developed countries, and 22% for Asian countries. Further, with high disparities (Table 1.3.2), inclusive education has been an elusive target. 370 districts with GER less than the national average need enrolment drives and rapid expansion of higher education institutions.

TABLE 1.3.2: Disparities in GER, 2004-05[15]

Disparities	GER
Area:	
Rural	6.70
Urban	19.90
Gender:	
Male	12.40
Female	9.10
Social:	
SCs	6.57
STs	6.52
OBCs	8.77
Others	17.22
ALL	*11.00*

SCs: Schedule Castes, STs: Scheduled Tribes,
OBCs: Other Backward Castes

A just and fair knowledge society can not be established without adequately addressing the serious issues raised by the disparity indicated above. The delivery of expansion and equity has to be married with excellence as well. The task for Indian policy establishment is, therefore, very daunting and challenging. The Government of India has declared a policy of reservation of seats in the institutions of higher learning for SCs, STs and OBCs to promote this objective. The Chairman of the Oversight Committee on Implementation of this reservation policy in the higher education and an important member of ruling establishment in India, Sh. Veerappa Moily in his final report provides the philosophical justification to this policy in the following words:

> A society is just when all its components are in a state of harmony. A society which keeps a large section of its people in a state of denial or deprivation or where all its citizens do not enjoy equality of opportunity to develop themselves can never be in a state of stable equilibrium. Pythagoras has said "Justice as a square number is in perfect harmony since it was composed of equal parts and the number of its parts is equal to the value of each part. A number is square, so long as the equality of its parts remains. When this equality is breached the State must intervene....".

> Providing assured access to higher education is the best way to empower the excluded sections of society and is the most painless way to redress their historic wrongs. In the words of Plato, Education enables us to "prepare a citizen, by the light of knowledge and not by rule of custom, to perform the duties of his station," and further that Education "seeks to tune in the feelings and imagination of youth, as one would tune a lyre with many vibrating strings." Education enables us to bring the individual "to resonate in unison with society".[16]

The National Knowledge Commission put forth a very specific and a significant concept of a *needs-blind admissions* policy meaning thereby that it should be made unlawful for the educational institutions to take into account any financial factor while deciding on admission of the students. This is proposed to be backed up by a well funded and an extensive National Scholarship Scheme targeting economically underprivileged and historically/socially disadvantaged student. While the pitfalls of transferring the burden of the financial provision to the students need to be avoided in India, the international experience in this regard is noteworthy as summarised in OECD Report of 2007:

> So far, the Nordic countries have achieved expansion by viewing massive public spending on higher education, including both support of institutions and support of students and households, as an investment that pays high dividends to individuals and society. Australia, Japan, Korea, New Zealand; and the United Kingdom have expanded participation in tertiary education by shifting some of the burden of financial provision to students. In Australia, for example, a risk-free loan programme that suppressed liquidity constraints for poorer students was introduced; this has not, however, had a negative effect on the equity of access for students from low socio-economic backgrounds. In contrast, many European countries are not increasing public investment in their universities nor are universities allowed to charge tuition fees, with the result that the European average for spending per tertiary student is now well below half the level of spending in the United States.[17]

The affirmative action in India in respect of deprived sections of society has universal support and an article of faith for the political class. Public funding of higher education and on its expansion, therefore, would continue to be an important policy measure in India.

Regulatory Mechanism and Governance: Area of Conflict

While 'inclusion' is the core of the affirmative action in India, it is the regulatory mechanism and the governance of the higher education which is the most conflict prone issue area. The regulatory regime obviously needs an overhaul in the context of expansion and emerging paradigm of an evolving knowledge society. At the heart of this matter are the vested interests who control the higher education in an archaic fashion, crass commercialisation by private investment and system of political patronage which bedevils the higher education in India today. National Knowledge Commission has underlined the over-regulation but under-governed nature of regulatory regime at present in India. The present system is presided over by a University Grants Commission-UGC (which is very tightly controlled by the Government) and a plethora of distinct segregated bodies like All India Council of Technical Education (AICTE), Medical Council of India (MCI) etc. National Knowledge Commission perceiving confusion and overlap in mandates of multiplicity of regulatory agencies has recommended establishment of an Independent Regulatory Authority for Higher Education (IRAHE) which should be at an arm's length from all stake holders including Government of India. Independent Regulatory Authority for Higher Education conceptualised by National Knowledge Commission is to be set up by an Act of Parliament and would be the only agency authorised to accord degree granting powers. National Knowledge Commission explaining the rationale and philosophy of regulation of higher education suggests segregation of functions and a very limited role for existing University Grants Commission:

> In higher education, regulators perform five functions: (1) Entry: licence to grant degree. (2) Accreditation: quality bench marking. (3) Disbursement of public funds. (4) Access: fees or affirmative action. (5) Licence: to practice profession.
>
> India is perhaps the only country in the world where regulation in 4 out of 5 functions is carried out by one entity, that is, the UGC. The purpose of creating an IRAHE is to separate these functions. The proposed IRAHE shall be responsible for setting the criteria and deciding on entry. It would, in addition, licence agencies to take care of accreditation. The role of the UGC will be limited to disbursing public funds. Issues of access will be governed by state legislation on reservations and other forms of affirmative action. And, professional associations may, in some institutions set requirements to determine eligibility for conducting a profession.[18]

The Ministry of Human Resource Development, Government of India set up another Committee, post- National Knowledge Commission, under the chairmanship of eminent physicist and a former Chairman of UGC, Prof. Yashpal, to guide the efforts at reforms process[19]. This Committee known as the Committee to Advise on Renovation and Rejuvenation of Higher Education submitted its report very recently (June 2009) and advised a different structure and role for the regulatory authority than the one suggested by National Knowledge Commission. Prof Yashpal Committee maintained that a holistic view of knowledge requires a regulatory system which treats the entire range of educational institutions in a holistic manner. The Committee recommended a single, all encompassing higher education authority since it considered all higher education including engineering, medicine, agriculture, law and distant education as an integrated whole. This Committee noted that there were 13 professional Councils created under various Acts of Parliament to promote and regulate specialised areas of education and underlined the need to bring them under a national apex body for bringing greater coordination and integration in the planning and development of higher education system including research as already envisaged in the National Policy of Education (1986) and the Plan of Action (1992). The Committee accordingly proposed to create an apex body to subsume academic functions of all professional bodies to be called The National Commission for Higher Education and Research (NCHER).[20]

The differing perceptions and prescriptions of National Knowledge Commission and Yashpal Committee on regulation and governance of higher education in India should not provide an opportunity to the status quo vested interests who would like to perpetuate their power on higher education. The need and necessity of urgent and wide ranging reforms has been well established. The protagonists who articulated the road map for reforms in National Knowledge Commission Report and Yashpal Committee Report are very eminent, well meaning experts. There is an apprehension that the clever segments in the bureaucracy and society at large may use the differing perceptions of the two Reports to defeat the higher goal of recovering the idea of a university which has been eloquently captured by Yashpal Committee in the following words:

> A university is a place where new ideas germinate, strike roots and grow tall and sturdy. It is a place where creative minds converge, interact with each other and construct visions of new realities. Established notions of truth are challenged in the pursuit of knowledge.[21]

Independent Regulatory Authority for Higher Education of National Knowledge Commission or National Commission for Higher Education and Research of Yashpal Committee must be decided through a healthy and democratic debate among all stakeholders including society at large. The idea of university must be recovered and the larger picture of creation of a just and an equitable knowledge society must not be made captive to the power games of lobbies canvassing for capturing the regulatory governance mechanism of higher education in the country.

Conclusion

In conclusion, it would be appropriate to remind all stake holders that India is moving[22] and in ferment. It has the grain of a rich ancient heritage to achieve the highest standards in education and research and to contribute to the onward march of mankind to peace and progress. The reforms in higher education in India would be propelled not only by the compulsions of a fast growing national economy and the national priority for inclusive growth but also due to a critical awareness among policy planners of the value of education and necessity of reforms to survive in a competing global environment. There could be some pockets of resistance since a small segment of the elite and middle class, perceiving a threat to their established status, is not reconciled to the necessity for 'inclusion' by affirmative action citing the merit and dilution of excellence in its support. But the consensus on affirmative action and the 'mantra of inclusion' would provide the necessary political will since it would, as a by product, ensure popularity of the ruling dispensation and perhaps a better chance of perpetuation in power.

References

Aggarwal. P., Feb. 17-23, 2007 'From Kothari Commission to Pitroda Commission', Economic and Political Weekly, Vol. XLII, No.7: 554-557
– 2009 : Indian Higher Education : Envisioning the Future, New Delhi : Sage.
Anandkrishnan, M. Feb 17-23, 2007, 'Critique of Knowledge Commission', Economic and Political Weekly, Vol. XLII No.7 : 557-560.
Altbach, Philip G., June 6-12, 2009, 'The Giants Awake : Higher Education Systems in India and China, 'Economic and Political Weekly, Vol. XLIV No. 23 : 39-52.
Altbach, P.G. and J. Balan, ed. 2007: World Class Worldwide : Transforming Research Universities in Asia and Latin America, Baltimore : Johns Hopkins University Press.
Bastu, A 1974 : The Growth of Education and Political Development in India, 1898-1920, Delhi : Oxford University Press.
Bhushan, Sudhanshu 2008: 'Financial Requirements in Higher Education during XI Plan Period' in Sukhadeo, Thorat (ed.), Higher Education in India: Issues Related to Expansion, Inclusiveness, Quality and Finance, New Delhi: University Grants Commission, 215-76.
Chattopadhyay, Saumen, July 18-24, 2009, 'Market in Higher Education', Economic & Political Weekly ,Vol. XLIV, No. 29 : 53-62.
Gupta, A, D.C. Levy and K.B. Powar, (ed.) 2008 , Private Higher Education : Global Trends and Indian Perspectives, Delhi: Shipra.
Hatchkar, Neeraj, April 23, 2010, 'NCHER and State Universities: An Exercise in Redundancy', Economic and Political Weekly, Vol. XLV No. 16, 15-17.
Jayaram, N 2003 : 'The Fall of the Guru : The Decline of the Academic Profession in India' in P.G. Altbach (ed.), The Decline of the Guru : The Academic Profession in Development and Middle-Income Countries, New York : Palgrave-Macmillan, : 199-230.
Jha, A 2009: 'Abysmal Global Ranking of India's Best University' Education World, February, : 64-72.
Kaul, J.N. 1974: Higher Education in India, 1951-1971 : Two Decades of Planned Drift, Simla: Indian Institute of Advanced Study.
Mahajan, N. , 2007, 'The Cream of India's Colleges Turns Sour', Far Eastern Economic Review, January-February, : 62-65.
Ministry of Human Resource Development, India 2009: India: UNESCO Country Report, New Delhi: Ministry of Human Resource Development.
OECD 2007 : Cross-border Tertiary Education: A Way towards Capacity Development, Paris: Organisation for Economic Cooperation and Development.
Rajendran, M. Jan. 15-31, 2010, 'Curriculum-cum-Quality Assurance : A Major Ingredient for Assessment and Accreditation in Higher Education', University News Vol. 48, No. 04 : 4-9.
Sachidanand Sinha, 2007, Redefining Educationally Backward Regions, Study sponsored by UGC.
Sarswati Raju, 2006, Gender Differentials in Access to Higher Education, Study sponsored by UGC.
Shah, Beena, July 12-18, 2010 'Indian Higher Education: New Horizons and Plausible Challenges', University News, Vol. 48, No. 28: 64-75.
Shanthi, K. July 12-18, 2010, 'Issues and Challenges in Higher Education', University News, Vol. 48, No. 28 : 76-80.
Singh, Karnjeet, Aug 9-15, 2010, 'Policy Dilemma in Indian Higher Education', University News, Vol. 48, No. 32 : 1-7

Srivastava, Ravi, March 10-16, 2007, 'National Knowledge Commission : Meeting Social Goals or Neo Liberal Reforms?', Economic and Political Weekly, Vol. XLII, No. 10: 812-15

Sudhansu Bhusan, 2007, University and Colleges for 15% Enrolment Target during 11th Plan – An Estimate, Study sponsored by UGC.

Shivkumar. V., Nov 16-22, 2009, 'What ails our Higher Education System' University News, Vol. 47, No. 46: 11-12.

Tapas, Majumdar, 1983, Investments in Education and Social Choice, Cambridge: Cambridge University Press.

Tilak, J.B.G. Sept. 10-16, 2005, 'Higher Education in Trishanbu : Hanging between State and Market, Economic and Political Weekly, Vol. XV, No. 37 : 4029-37.

Throat, Sukhadeo, Sept 14-20, 2009, 'Higher Education – Approach, Strategy and Action Plan in the 11th Plan' University News, Vol. 47:   30-43.

Tilak, B.G.J., May 8-14, 2010,'The Foreign Educational Institutional Bill : A Critique', Economic and Political Weekly, Vo. XLV, No. 19: 12-15.

End notes

[1] Mrydal, Gunnar. 1985 reprint, Asian Drama: An Inquiry Into the Poverty of Nations, New Delhi- Kalyani Publishers , Volume III, Chapter 29, p.1537. Gunnar Myrdal maintained that access to education and enjoyment of health acquired recognition as a human right.

[2] Ibid, Chapter 31, p 1621.

[3] Dreze Jean and Sen Amartya,1995, India: Economic Development and Social Opportunity, New Delhi, Oxford University Press, pp.15-16. Amartya Sen expanded the significance of education to emphasise its empowerment and redistributive dimensions – he maintained that greater literacy and educational achievements of disadvantaged groups can increase their ability to resist oppression, to organise politically and to get a fairer deal. Further, the redistributive effects can be important not only between different social groups and households but also within the family, since there was evidence that better education(particularly female education) contributes to the reduction of gender based inequalities.

[4] Unnikrishnan, J.P. and Ors. Vs. State of Andhra Pradesh and Ors., Date of Judgment 04/02/1993, Citation:1993 AIR 2178   1993; SCR   (1) 594 1993; SCC   (1) 645   JT 1993 (1)474 1993 SCALE (1)290. The Supreme Court of India held that the Article 21(Right to Life) of the Constitution of India is the heart of Fundamental Rights and it includes education as the right to education flows from the right to life.

[5] National Knowledge Commission , 2007, Report to the Nation 2006. New Delhi: Government of India, p- 21.

[6] Organisation for Economic Cooperation and Development, 2007, Education at a Glance 2007: OECD Indicators, p.26.

[7] Final Report of The Oversight Committee on the Implementation of The New reservation Policy in Higher Education in India, 2006, New Delhi ,Government of India, September, 2006.

[8] Source: India Labour Report 2007 – The Youth Unemployability Crisis By Team Lease Services, Table A8, p.95

[9] Organisation for Economic Cooperation and Development, 2007, Education at a Glance 2007: OECD Indicators. Table A1.1a. p.36.

[10] National Knowledge Commission , 2007, Report to the Nation 2006, New Delhi : Government of India, p-2.

[11] Planning Commission of India, Eleventh Five Year Plan Document, New Delhi, Government of India, Volume I p. 22.

[12] National Knowledge Commission, 2007, Report to the Nation 2006, New Delhi- Government of India, p-3.

[13] Huq, Mahbu bul, Huq Khalida 1998, Human Development Report on South Asia: The Education Challenge, Karachi, Human Development Centre, Oxford University Press, p.6. Also see Mahbu bal huq Human Development Centre, 2007, Human Development in South Asia- A ten year review, Karchi, Oxford University Press, pp. 199-140.

[14] Planning Commission of India, 2002, Report of the Committee on India Vision 2020, New Delhi, Government of India, p.47.

[15] Planning Commission of India, Eleventh Five Year Plan Document, New Delhi, Government of India, Volume I p. 22.

[16] Moily, M. Veerappa, 2006, Final Report of The Oversight Committee on The Implementation of The New Reservation Policy in Higher Education, New Delhi, Government of India, p-7.

[17] Ischinger,Barbara, 2007, Education at a Glance 2007: OECD Indicators, Organisation for Economic Cooperation and Development, pp.11-12.

[18] National Knowledge Commission, 2007, Report to the Nation 2006, New Delhi- Government of India, p.54.

[19] A 22 member committee was set-up under the Chairmanship of Professor Yash Pal in February 2008 by the Ministry of Human Resource Development with the limited original mandate, which was to review the functioning of University Grants Commission (UGC) and All India Council for Technical Education (AICTE), the two main statutory bodies regulating Higher Education in the country. In September 2008, its scope was widened to make recommendations for the rejuvenation of entire Higher Education sector. For details see the interview of Professor Yash Pal, Ramachandan. R., July 17, 2009 'Renovation and Rejuvenation of Indian Higher Education', Frontline, 22-24.

[20] Yash Pal Committee gave due importance to the role of the States in the field of Higher Education. It recommended that it would be necessary to create Higher Education Councils (HECs) in the States which would be in constant dialogue with National Commission for Higher Education and Research (NCHER).

[21] Yash Pal Committee 2009, Report of Committee to Advise on Renovation and Rejuvenation of Higher Education, New Delhi : Ministry of Human Resource Development, Government of India, p.9.

[22] Five legislative bills are being formulated by the Ministry of Human Resource Development which are at the various stages of preparation. Four of these bills were introduced in Parliament on 3rd May, 2010. The five bills are – a bill for setting up the National Educational Tribunal, a bill for setting up a National Accreditation Authority, a bill for checking malpractices in Higher Education, a bill for setting up National Commission for Higher Education & Research and a bill for Foreign Educational Institutions.

CHAPTER 16

REVAMPING HIGHER EDUCATION IN THE CONTEXT OF KNOWLEDGE ECONOMY:
Perception of Academia

BAIJU K.C., FACULTY AND ASHA J.V

Abstract

The education and learning paradigm around the world is under increasing pressure to better itself to meet the demands of the new knowledge and information-intensive global economy. A developing country like India is facing challenges in managing its vast human resource in constructive ways. For realizing the concept of inclusive society that can provide the foundations for a knowledge society, an exhaustive and systematic overhaul in education, especially in higher education is imperative. Against this backdrop, this paper focuses on the perceptions of the academia on the key aspects of education, which helps in building human capital instilling skill, knowledge and competence leading to human resource development and economic growth. The data were collected from 80 college teachers selected from two representative districts of Kerala, India through a questionnaire focusing on strategies for fostering independent learning, need based specialisation and market driven skill generation, enhancing quality and competence of teachers, reasons for supply- demand mismatch and suggestions to meet these challenges. The major challenges identified include challenge to guarantee quality, to preserve national culture and identity, to ensure that the government sets national policy objectives for higher education and to assure equity of access to higher education. The suggestions emphasise the need to strengthen strategies to develop independent learning and knowledge management and to throw open the portals of higher education. This would contribute to the on going process of revamping in higher education in Kerala, India in consonance with the 'new mantra' of 'expansion, excellence and inclusion' of National Knowledge Commission (NKC) as accepted in the Eleventh Five Year Plan.

Introduction

Human capital is the end product of human resource development. Education is an important instrument in building human capital instilling skill, knowledge and competence leading to human resource development and economic growth. The educational and health processes result in the formation of human capabilities which are inputs into these processes themselves as well as into other processes of production. If education is a process of generation, transfer and utilisation, health and nutrition are means of strengthening both acquisitive process and the flow of services over time. "Education is a human right with immense power to transform. On its foundation rest the cornerstones of freedom, democracy and sustainable human development." (Kofi Annan, 2005) The major single source of human capital has always been formal and informal education. (Alex, 1983) Accumulation of knowledge and skills through training, apprenticeship and adult education programmes comes under non-formal education. Learning in the workplace, through collaborations (that sometimes span the global and at other times involve tightly knit local communities) with similar interests, include the informal knowledge gathering ways. The complex and dynamic growth process needs to be planned meticulously and executed with great sensitivity for the development of a knowledge society.

In the third millennium, with the change in human conditions, brought about by the industrial as well as technological revolution and Toffler's *third wave* of information, relationship between individual and the universe has taken more material, focused and central place than ever before. Globalisation, which is affecting the economy, culture, information, internationalisation of relations and increasing mobility of individuals, has effected a complete revolution in the automation of daily life and the world of work thereby bringing a multi-dimensional impact on the system of education. It has underlined the need for reforms in the educational system with particular reference to the wider utilisation of information technology, giving productivity dimension to education and emphasis on its research and development activities. With the emergence of a new development model, particularly in the highly industrialised economies, knowledge and information take on increasing importance.

The National Knowledge Commission, India (2007) observed that Higher Education has made a significant contribution to economic development, social progress and political democracy in independent India. However, the proportion of our population, in the relevant age group, that enters the world of higher education is about 7%. The opportunities for higher education in terms of intake of universities are not simply adequate in relation to our needs. What is more, the quality of higher education in most of our universities leaves much to be desired. It is widely accepted that higher education needs an exhaustive overhaul. This becomes quite significant as the transformation of economy and society in the 21st century would depend, in significant proportions, on the spread and the quality of education among our people, particularly in the sphere of higher education. And it is only an inclusive society that can provide the foundations for a knowledge society. The 'National Knowledge commission' commission stressed that the objectives of reform and change in the higher education system, must be expansion, excellence and inclusion.

Perceptions of Academia

The perceptions of teachers play a crucial role in the realisation of the objectives in the new paradigm envisaging reforms in the higher education system. As persons directly involved in the preparation of youth, 'much will be expected and much demanded of teachers. Teachers have a crucial role to play in preparing young people not only to face the future with confidence, but also to build it with purpose and responsibility' (The International Commission on Education for the 21st Century, 1996). In this context, this study examined the perceptions of teaching faculty of the University of Kerala and its affiliated colleges, particularly from two representative districts of Kerala, India. The opinion of teachers were collected on the different aspects related to 'expansion, excellence and inclusion' in higher education such as: strategies for fostering independent learning, need based specialisation and market driven skill generation, enhancing quality and competence of teachers, reasons for supply- demand mismatch and suggestions to meet the challenges. The respondents were 80 college teachers, of which 42 belonging to arts and science colleges (Male:11&Female:31) and 38 from colleges of teacher education (Male:8 &Female: 30) of Trivandrum and Kollam districts selected at random. Percentage analysis of the responses were done as discussed below.

a) Strategies for Fostering Independent Learning

Peer tutoring was suggested by 82 percent of the total sample as an effective strategy for providing inclusive education and for handling heterogeneous groups. Seventy eight percent of the teachers suggested that independent learning can be made possible only when the student community has acquired 'how to learn'. Instead of transmitting information stored by the teacher to the store house (lecture notes) of students, they should be empowered in the process of 'learning to learn'. Many of them (62%) suggested skills of referencing, skills in presentation, participating in group discussions and tutoring small groups, if made part of the curriculum, will help revamping the quality of courses. Teachers need to possess the above mentioned skills as a pre requisite to develop similar skills in their students. Moreover, such practices in the classrooms will develop confidence in the students as the group performance as well as individualised learning, are simultaneously taken care of. For this, the role of teachers is to be changed to that of a facilitator rather than a mere lecturer. Innovations in teaching/learning are to be encouraged at institutional/university level. A think tank at institutional level which in turn be developed at cluster level which will contribute greatly to help the distance/virtual learners. The teachers (84%) also suggested that networking the colleges, making web-logs, portals etc., will help pooling resources at university/state/national levels. A portal on higher education and research would increase interaction and accessibility. A knowledge network would connect all Universities and colleges for online open resources. These strategies will also be contributory to the suggestion of NKC to transform India to a knowledge society by ensuring access for all at deserving standards.

b) Need-based Courses and Institution-Industry Affiliations

As regards expansion, 64% teachers have the opinion that need-based courses and institution-industry affiliations should be taken care of rather than encouraging mushrooming of institutions. In order to ensure relevance, need-based specialisation and market driven skill generation the post-graduate and doctoral programmes/research and extension activities should be oriented towards applied fields. Setting up of knowledge repositories, exchange programmes, open universities and arranging virtual learning options are some of the sure ways to reach inclusion in the realm of higher education.

c) *Quality and Competence of Teachers*

The majority of the respondents agreed the fact that there is a dearth of competent as well as dedicated teachers. The views, needs and beliefs of practising educators are not always given serious attention while academics generate educational theories and prepare curricula. Efforts are often inadequate to bridge the gaps in curriculum through refresher or orientation programmes offered. Another reason cited for the shortage of teachers is the growing demand for professional degrees, like IT and management studies where the degrees are highly lucrative. Hence lesser talented students come to universities and colleges to pursue teaching as a profession. This also leads to the degradation of the quality of teachers. However, 'some totally dedicated and committed people may still come to the academic profession, but they constitute the exception rather than the rule'. (Patnaik, 2007)

d) *Supply-Demand Mismatch*

In response to an open ended question about the causes of the severe mismatch between supply and demand of education as a merit good, respondents made a myriad of suggestions. The state sponsored education afflicted with poor governance, dearth of teachers, lack adequate infrastructure and shortage of funds at least at the state level. In spite of massive development, there exist regional imbalances in infrastructure and academic climate, gender divide, marginalisation of vulnerable lot etc. Expansion without vision often has to compromise on quality. To support these observations some researches (Kumar, 2004; Hashim, 2008; Balakrishnan, 2007) also exist. The delivery systems in the realm of higher education are very poor. The academic community seems to be demoralised which has lead to the decline in the commitment of the faculty. Spread of rampant commercialisation has diluted the quality of education. Barring a few institutions, the quality of education in the majority of private institutes is questionable. There is often exchange of many in higher education which renders the institutions as shops offering degrees for sale. Some sort of lethargy is visible among the academic fraternity to make new ventures in regular updating of the course material. In terms of international rating only one university and two professional institutions are in the ranking as per the London Higher Education Supplement a year ago. Low morale and poor functioning plagued by corruption all contribute to the delivery of substandard education.

e) *Issues and Challenges*

Quality improvement warrants fundamental changes in the academic environment which cannot be improved by increase in funding alone opined the teachers. Hence, the means of overcoming the crisis of higher education must include increased not reduced involvement by the State or scrupulous social regulation of the private sector in terms of better emoluments to faculty and maintaining quality norms. The states and governments should maintain their role in defining policies of higher education, assuring its quality and ensuring that it performs all its missions and functions in society, not solely economic development. Their suggestions to overcome these difficulties included:

- Establishment of new institutions having all the infrastructural facilities and qualified teachers to teach them.
- Converting state sponsored colleges and institutions into knowledge, research and extension centres (centres of excellence) which can provide high level of teaching, well equipped libraries, labs and a good academic ambience.
- The higher education system must provide for accountability to society and accountability within.
- ICT infrastructure, web sites and web based sources should be strengthened. A portal on higher education and research would increase interaction and accessibility. The explosion of IT based knowledge out sourcing and the inability of our system of education to break the cocoon of straight jacketed curriculum frame are also posing problems in responding to the emerging needs of the student community.

Relying upon the recommendations of NKC, expansion, excellence and inclusion budgetary allocation for higher education is set to witness manifold rise during Eleventh Five Year Plan. Ensure expansion with excellence and inclusion, universities will be set up in regions with Gross Enrolment Ratio (GER) less than the national average. The most important challenge on this context as per the opinion of the teachers (68%) is, that the new institutions established may take time to gain credibility and become centres of excellence as time proves to be the touch stone of quality in case of universities.

f) Policy Questions

In the domain of higher education, government of India faces a multitude of challenges. Since 1991, the Government has been pursuing neo-liberal policies in higher education as in the case of other sectors. However, the government continues to grope in choosing the right path and striking a balance between the conflicting interests. The NKC itself meaningfully recognises the role of private providers, both domestic and foreign players in higher education. As India is getting integrated into the world economy, and education being considered a part of GATS, the role of market and private providers in particular, the foreign players assume greater importance in higher education. In this regard, the teachers (86%) criticised the political parties, which instead of taking decisions with vision, contradicting their opponents and often 'drain the baby with bathe water'.

g) Public Private Partnership

Privatisation of education, opined most of the teachers (88%) turns it into a commodity where the buyer's preference must necessarily enter to determine the nature of the commodity produced. There is a basic difference between education that satisfies the preference of the buyer and education that is undertaken in the interests of the people. And if education is to be undertaken in the interests of the people, to defend their interests, then it must be publicly financed. If it ceases to be publicly financed, then the education that increasingly gets to be produced is one that is intrinsically incapable of serving the interests of the people. (Prabhat Patnaik, 2007) The advent of globalisation helps the commoditisation of services, education in particular, traditionally considered to be in the stature of public good. The extent of public and private provisioning depends crucially on the degree of commercialisation of higher education. To the question: 'Can education be treated at par with any other commodity\service?" 72% argued that as the state sponsored institutions are failing to deliver quality education and reduced to mere degree awarding institutions, students look forward to those private institutions which deliver market initiated course or products.

Kapoor and Mehta (2004) argue that the higher education suffers from 'Circle of statism' when they state that privatisation process is caught between half baked capitalism and socialism. Leaving everything to the market need not solve the problem as even under the best of the conditions, there is indeed a role of the regulatory authority. Again the quality aspects of education should be examined from the actual delivery system. The profit maximizing measures of a company cannot be applied in the service sector of education. The philosophy of treating education at par with any other commodity poses so many unpleasant questions and promotes sharp dualities within the education system. However, it would be better to share the view of Barack Obama: "We have an obligation and a responsibility to be investing in our students and our schools. We must make sure that people who have the grades, the desire and the will, but not the money, can still get the best education possible." As identified by UNESCO, the most important challenges which arise from the globalisation of higher education lie in the challenge to guarantee quality, to preserve national culture and identity, to ensure that governments set national policy objectives for higher education, and to assure equity of access to higher education.

Conclusions

The perceptions of the academic staff reported in this paper highlight the following aspects relevant to the revamping of the higher education sector:

a) *Independent Learning and Knowledge Management*: Human resources, particularly with large young population, are unique core strength of a nation. Skilled, unskilled and creative man power can be transformed into wealth generators in all fields of economic activity. Knowledge explosion is considered as the most striking feature of the present era because new knowledge domains are mushrooming up at a tremendous speed, so it is high time to think about a management process to reduce the complexities due to knowledge explosion. Increasing competitiveness, re-engineering of production and social processes require continuous up-gradation of skills for personal growth and innovative technologies. Knowledge has been termed as power, not only in terms of strength, but also in terms of decisive factor controlling economic and productive sectors. Currently there has been a close association between the economic performance and applicability of ideas gathered through education. Hence knowledge management gained the significance in the field of technology and education.

'Knowledge management is the explicit and systematic management of vital knowledge-and its associated processes of creation, organisation, diffusion, use and exploitation.' (Reddy, 2007) By managing knowledge effectively, an innovative teacher can enhance the cognitive skills, technical skills and different behavioural skills. Both the popular and professional literature use the phrases: "Critical thinking skills," "problem solving" and "decision making" in reporting on skills that must be provided to equip students for the 21st century. All three of these phrases refer to cognitive skills that are necessary to create new knowledge and to learn how to learn. Recognition of learning how to learn is fundamental to economic and personal success in the present information age. (SCANS, 2000 reports & Doyle, 1994). This idea of empowering students in 'learning to learn' makes it necessary to develop the skill of independent learning. Independent Learning focuses on creation of the opportunities and experiences necessary for students to become capable, self-reliant, self-motivated and life-long learners. For this, the students should value learning as an empowering activity of great personal and social worth. Students will be motivated to learn if the learning activity is meaningful; the knowledge generated is useful and managed for achieving a desired goal. Such learning activities provide a stimulus to reflective inquiry and continuous intellectual development. In contrast, learning activities in which the student has no interest lead to increasing dependence on external motivation and extrinsic rewards. However the present approach to teaching has the effect of diminishing student initiative, rather than encouraging student participation in learning for its own sake.

Knowledge has become the product churned out of the ideas in the minds of people with their interactions or interrelations in the society. An individual in the present knowledge society has to construct new knowledge and at times, reconstruct existing knowledge through their own perception and action. This process requires time, energy and personal skills. The teacher has a prominent role to play in this realm and it is rather deviant from the conventional role. The new dimensions of teachers can be described as: knowledge engineer/editor/broker/analyst/shepherd/gatekeeper/ navigator /asset manager and so on. The teachers are to mould their students in the varied skills and strategies for managing information, constructing knowledge out of it and retrieving/ reusing/reconstructing independently for delivery in a suitable format. In many cases this is leading towards the alignment of vision and mission, goals and policies of organisations and institutions. The Flagship programme like SSA (*A time bound Govt. of India mission launched in 2001 aimed at universalisation of elementary education and bridging of gender and social gaps by 2010.*) is making inroads in spreading universalisation of elementary education across the country. In the state of Kerala, the coordinated efforts of IT@school (*one of the major schemes imparting computer education to high school students for the qualitative improvement in the conventional learning systems and also to equip teachers to use computers as an educational tool*) and SCERT (*State Council of Educational Research and Training (SCERT) is the state level agency for revision and monitoring of school curriculum, giving inservice training to teachers and to implement research oriented educational reforms in school education*) are laudable as they try to bring in the constructivist paradigm upto higher secondary level. The new pedagogical method and integration of ICT are to be integrated in the higher education in consonance with the 'new mantra' of 'expansion , excellence inclusion' of NKC as accepted in the Eleventh Five Year Plan.

b) *Portals of Higher Education in Kerala:* Kerala, the small strip of land lies to the south-western tip of India, has successfully tackled the first generation problems of illiteracy and inadequate school enrolment. School education has become equitable between the sexes and among social groups and regions in the state, unlike in many other states in India. However, Kerala had remained a relatively underdeveloped region among the states of India in respect of higher education, till about the beginning of the 1990s. The progress made by the state during the past decade and a half was phenomenal, a period during which the portals of higher education were thrown wide open to private commercial agencies. At the same time, a perceptible decline in the quality of education was observed in recent years. The job prospects of the highly educated persons have also been decreasing in the state. There is a mismatch between the institutions of higher learning and the world of work and industry in Kerala. (GOI, 2008) One could see a severe mismatch of supply and demand of education as a merit good. This is quite paradoxical to a region that is highly integrated with the global economy, which in turn heading towards knowledge-based development and well being.

Education includes all the influences which act upon an individual during his passage from cradle to grave. In other words, "Education is life and life is education." It is not the giving of facts and details alone, but it is a man making process. Cognitive and behavioural skills are needed to equip students for the 21st century. Recognition of learning how to learn is fundamental to economic and personal success in the information age. The purpose of higher education is to produce "global human capital" of the people. Hence initiatives should be taken to attract quality intake of the faculties in higher education institutions in order to interact with students to make the people non-parasitic thinkers and turn our society into a cradle of innovative thoughts and knowledge .

References

Aggarwal, J.C (2008) **Educational Reforms in India for the 21st century**. New Delhi: Shipra Publications.
Alex, Alexander V.(1983): **Human Capital Approach to Economic Development**. New Delhi: Metropolitan Book Company (P.Ltd).
Altbach, PhilipG (2001): Higher Education and WHO cited in **University News** Vol 39 No.37 Sept 10-16
Balakrishnan, P (2007) Higher Education in India: Will Six Percent Do It? **Economic and Political Weekly**, September,29
Hashim, S.R. (2008) State of Higher Education in India in India. **Development Report, 2008** edited by R.Radhakrishna, IGIDR. New Delhi: Oxford University Press.
Kapur, D. and Mehta, B. (2004) Indian Higher Education Reform: From Half-Baked Socialism to Half-Baked Capitalism, Harvard University: **Working Paper**.
Kumar, A (2004) **Challenges Facing Indian Universities**. New Delhi: JNUTA.
Ministry of Education, **Report of the University Education Commission** (1948-49) GoI, New Delhi.
Ministry of Education, **Report of the Secondary Education Commission** (1952-53).GoI, New Delhi.
Ministry of Education, **Report of the Education Commission** (1964-66), GoI, New Delhi.
MHRD, **National Policy on Education** (1986) GoI, New Delhi.
Mukherji, S. N. (1966) *History of Education in India*. cited in www.education.nic.in as on 28-04-2009.
NKC Blue Print for Reform (2007) **National Knowledge Commission**, GoI, New Delhi.
Patnaik, Prabhat (2007) Alternative Perspectives on Higher Education. **Social Scientist**, *Vol35*/Nos11-12 Nov-Dec pp3-14.

Quotes About 'education' cited in Google © 2005 **Quoteopia**

Reddy, rathan B. (2007) Knowledge **Management –Tool for Business Development**. New Delhi: Himalaya Publishing House

Report to UNESCO of the International Commission on Education for the 21st Century. President of the Commission, Jaques Dealors (1996).

Schultz, T.W.(1961) Investment in Human Capital **American Economic Review**, Vol.60 No.1

World Bank (2002): **Constructing Knowledge Societies; New Challenges for Tertiary Education**, Washington D.C.

Critical Thinking: What It Is and Why It Counts in www.criticalthinking.org.

http://www.thenation.com/doc/20070611/hayes

http://www.unesco.org/education/higher_education/quality_innovation

CHAPTER 17

IS HIGHER EDUCATION A PUBLIC GOOD?
Policy Dilemmas in a Democratic State

Rumki Basu

Abstract

The post globalized era has seen a fairly consistent worldwide reform agenda for the management of institutions of higher education. The universe of tertiary education is undergoing enormous change in terms of expansion, diversification, accountability and relevance. Though home to the world's largest youth population, India faces an enormous shortage of employable talent and skills in diverse sectors of the economy. The biggest challenge the country faces is to impart marketable skills and competencies to the young so that they can meet the needs of a rapidly expanding economy. Today India is at the crossroads with regard to its Education Policy. Judgmentally clouded in its policy gestures by conflicting pulls and pressures India avoids any hard policy on issues such as 'equality' vs. 'quality', or the 'merit criteria' vs. issues of 'social justice'.

Introduction

The decade of the 90's and beyond has seen a fairly consistent global reform agenda for the management of institutions of higher education. The universe of tertiary education is undergoing enormous change which can be seen in the context of five developments.
- expansion in the enrolment of students and diversification of courses.
- a felt need to substitute public funding with non-governmental revenues.
- the demand for greater accountability on the part of institutions and faculty on behalf of students, employers and those who pay.
- the need to enhance the standards and relevance of higher education by establishing more linkages with the market.

Higher education meets many of the conditions identified as characteristics of a private good, amenable to the forces of the market. It displays conditions of rivalness (limited supply), excludability (often available at a price) and rejection (not demanded by all), all of which reflect some important conditions of a private good. A greater reliance on market signals shifts the decision making power from government to the consumer or client, i.e. the student and to the institution. With taxes increasingly getting difficult to collect and with competing public needs, (e.g. basic education, public health, public infrastructure) an increasing reliance on tuition fees, and the entrepreneurship of the faculty maybe the only alternatives to cope with the fiscal pressure in public universities – as measured in low and declining per student expenditures and as witnessed in overcrowded buildings, low paid faculty and lack of academic equipments/ libraries.

Home to the world's youngest population, India faces an enormous shortage of employable talent and skills. Our hospitals do not have adequate number of medical and paramedical personnel, there are not enough engineers to build our bridges and roads, nor teachers in our schools and colleges. Our rapidly growing IT enabled service sector, manufacturing sector and financial services are not able to hire as many people as they would need. Yet we have a huge number of people in the working age group (both skilled and unskilled) who do not have any regular means of livelihood as they do not possess the competencies that our diversified economy needs.

In case the GER (Gross Enrolment Ratio) in higher education is to increase to 15% by 2015, (stated as a goal of our Education Policy) either the capacity of existing institutions or the number of institutions would have to be doubled. A paradigm shift would be needed to focus on use of new technologies, better utilization of existing capacity, as also increased enrolment in distance learning and in vocational education. Ways and means will also have to be found to provide increased funding for higher education, including innovative models of public private partnership to seek private participation in higher education, without compromising on equity and excellence.

Higher Education in India: Problems and Challenges

Eighteen percent of the world population is young, (ages 15-24) of which 550 million live in India[1]. These young Indians face unprecedented challenges in accessing higher education and related skills which would enhance their employability in the post globalized world labour market. Moreover, it is disturbing to note that while the accessibility of school education has improved for most of the developing countries in the last two decades and the post '91 liberalization of the Indian economy has led to a burgeoning young middle class population, this has not readily enhanced the employment opportunities or self reliance strategies for today's youth in India. Why this has not happened would require a detailed examination of the complex interrelation between the impact of educational policies and teaching methodologies in India with the requirements of global or domestic job markets. The gross enrolment percentage of youth in higher education in India is 13% as compared to 92% in the US, 52% in the UK, 45% in Japan, 11.1% in all Asia, even 10.3% in all developing countries[2]. In India, the educated youth seek employment mostly in the organized sector which creates only 5% jobs for the total workforce. Almost 95% of newly created jobs are still in the unorganized sectors. Clearly, the aspirations of half a billion youth for a better living standard and higher income jobs cannot be engineered by the agricultural sector which accounts for 61.6% of the labour market, 17.2% jobs being in industry and 21.2% in the service sector[3]. Keeping pace with the demand of a globalized economy with shifting focus on knowledge workers and skilled manpower driven employment structure, India's youth needs to be endowed with a balanced value based education and necessary employment skills. India's growth (in GDP terms and in labour participation terms) has followed a non conventional route of shifting the engine of growth directly from agriculture to services almost bypassing the industrial or manufacturing sector. The critical issue is, however the low ratio of skilled to unskilled labour in India (0.15) as compared to USA (0.54) Japan (0.22) UK (0.39) or Russia (0.39) which prohibits the growth of new skill intensive and skill specific job markets in the expanding knowledge based economy. However on the positive side, due to the formidable size of the labour force in India, even this low ratio can translate to a dominating force in the economy if education and manpower planning policies are initiated and implemented with the right approach and vision catering to the specific demand of training our young labour force. Given the low gross enrolment ratio and the capacity limitation of the higher education system, the informal sector will continue to be the employment base for the largest share of our labour force. Therefore India's education policy should not only focus on the high end skill development of the formally educated youth, but also address the responsibilities of providing informal and vocational education to the vast sections of youth with less formal education to help them achieve self reliance and financial freedom.

Privatization of higher education: Issues and Dilemmas

The present regulatory and control structure in higher education is complex. From 1976-77 education has been in the concurrent list of the constitution. Although the Ministry of Human Resource Development is involved directly or indirectly in the ultimate resort, there are multiple layers of control[4]. Traditionally in India, public financing has been the major support of educational institutions of higher education with state governments bearing almost 80-90% financial burden and the central government accounting for the rest. However a radical transformation in the financing of higher education started after the nineteen eighties. Numerous private players ventured into the educational sector responding to the demands of the market. They offered flexible and adaptive curricula, job market responsiveness, focused training in highly sought after specializations and vocational streams, and offered development opportunity in 'soft skills' such as personal communication, presentation and team work. Huge expansion of information technology enabled services fueled further growth of private institutions (more than a lakh) for training the required pool of skilled workers. More recently private institutes catering to the need of other rapidly expanding and promising non-IT sectors (for example, hospitality, fashion design, pharmacy, dentistry and creative arts) are coming up in large numbers. These are vocational courses which the private sector can help to tap the vast talents of the youth in the unskilled labour force to make them marketable. Polytechnics have mushroomed in India catering to the needs of the vast sections of our student population who cannot access on merit the prized technical institutions of higher education in India.

There are nearly 10 million such students in 6500 privately run institutions in different parts of India.

Court Interventions

In matters of policy, the government of India's ambiguity in matters of privatization has led courts to often step in, interpreting the law as it stands today. If one reviews the major Supreme Court judgments on the issue in the past decade, one notices a gradual transition and shift in its philosophy and attitude towards the issue. Beginning with an undisguised hostility towards the emergence of private players in the business of education to a grudging acceptance of their reality and de facto presence, the Supreme Court perhaps has under a self imposed ethical compulsion attempted to reconcile contradictory principles.

Shortly after the introduction of New Economic Policies in 1992, in two landmark judgments[5] the court endorsed public intervention in the admission policy and fee structure of private professional institutions asserting that education is a 'public good' and therefore could not be the object of 'profit seeking activity'. In the Unni Krishnan case, the judgment argued that all colleges offering professional courses would have to reserve 50 percent of all seats on 'merit' and the college would be entitled to charge only the level of fees prescribed for government institutions. 25 percent of seats would be reserved for admission with merit, but the college would have discretion over the fees, while over the remaining 25 percent, the college would have jurisdiction with respect to both admission criteria and fees.

In absolute contrast to the Unni Krishnan verdict, the TMA Pai Foundation Vs. State of Karnataka judgment had an extended discussion extolling private enterprise in education as 'one of the most dynamic and fastest growing segments of post secondary education for which a combination of circumstances and the inability or unwillingness of government to provide the necessary support are responsible. This became the Court justification for restraining state interference in the running of private institutions. The verdict referred to 'the logic of economics and the ideology of privatization' as having contributed to the resurgence of private higher education. This verdict was a non-judgmental acceptance of the de facto reality of privatization in higher education in India.

Off and on the courts have been drawn into defining and redefining the rules for the allotment of seats in professional colleges and setting the fee structure for different categories of candidates. Subsequently in August 2005, the Supreme Court, in P.A. Inamdar & Ors. Vs. State of Maharashtra & Ors. ruled that private colleges, or those that do not receive government aid, (minority or non-minority institutions) are not required to meet reservation quotas, and further maintained that these institutions can have full autonomy in their admission policy. This was definitively the strongest judgment given by the court in favour of granting full autonomy to private educational institutions. Institutions were also given independence in the fee structure with the caveat that such tuition fees could be regulated to prevent 'unreasonable profits'. Apart from restoring greater autonomy, the court had tried through this judgment to narrow the gap between the liberties enjoyed by minority institutions and the freedoms enjoyed by non-minority unaided institutions.

However fundamental issues regarding matters of policy still remain. In the absence of greater conceptual clarity on 'the issue of non-profiteering' a good deal of regulatory ambiguity is likely to remain. Besides what could be a 'legitimate' fee structure is also difficult to define. There is a definite clash between the judiciary which is taking into account the constitutional provision with regard to education and the legislature (along with the executive) which wants to appropriate the private non-aided education sector without putting in budgetary funds.

The Inamdar ruling was catalytic in enforcing an amendment to the constitution, allowing Parliament to enact legislation mandating reservations in private higher educational institutions. This amendment led to the subsequent passage of the Central Educational Institutions (Reservation in Admission) Act, 2006 providing for 49.5% of seats in higher educational institutions to be reserved for SCs, STs and OBCs in aggregate. (Applicable to all but sixth schedule institutions, institutions of excellence, and minority institutions)[6].

Admission policies, fee structures, entrance examination criteria etc. are continuously being challenged in federal and state courts. Minority status of institutions can also be a bone of contention[7]. Looking at the judgments in the last 2 decades, certain conclusions can be drawn : a) the courts have been reluctant to sanction fee hikes in central or state universities b) the courts have allowed some freedom to private institutions in matters of admission policies and fee structure though they are still upholding the policy of reservation of some seats for SCs/ STs/OBCs on the basis of social justice c) interventions are more on grounds of procedural equality in admission process /fee structure than on issues of standards or quality of education.

Role of Higher Education: Specific recommendations

In 2005, the World Bank published a report on India and the knowledge economy[8]. The thrust of the World Bank Report was on education's role as a fundamental enabler of the knowledge economy and its requirement of a special set of skills and competencies. Simply put, a country's per capita national income is nothing but a measure of the average productivity of its citizens[9]. With ageing populations in developed countries, there has been talk of India's demographic dividend[10]. However, there is no automaticity about a demographic dividend leading to sustained high growth rates. One should not forget that relatively higher growth in population will happen in backward states of India like Assam, Bihar, Madhya Pradesh, Rajasthan and Uttar Pradesh[11] in the next decade where education systems have been rated as extremely backward and regressive.

In 2001 the Montek Singh Ahluwalia Task Force[12] had stated 'Only five percent of the Indian labour force in this age category (20-24 years) has vocational skills whereas the percentage in industrial countries is much higher, varying between 60% to 80%'. The National Knowledge Commission's recommendations on higher education is extremely important as a consultative document on matters of policy by the Central government. Some of its recommendations reiterate what had been said earlier about educational reform. They are a) it is necessary to overhaul the entire regulatory structure governing higher education b) every possible source of financing investment in higher education needs to be explored c) it is important to think about pro-active strategies for enhancement of quality in higher education. There are recommendations about the number and size of universities, curriculum, examinations, research, faculty, finances, infrastructure, access and governance. The National Knowledge Commission (NKC) constituted in June 2005 was entrusted with the task of preparing a blueprint for reform of our knowledge related institutions and infrastructure. The Commission has submitted over 200 recommendations on 24 focus areas[13]. 3 key areas in which NKC recommendations can be used most effectively will be – Demography, Disparity and Development. India's demographic profile, with 550 million below the age of 25, has the potential to constitute one fourth of the global workforce by 2020. We need a focused agenda for higher education with vocational development as an additional concern. In the post globalised era, access to knowledge is the source and manifestation of disparity. NKC's focus on expansion in educational opportunities in backward areas and the disadvantages, specifically seek to create an inclusive society. Finally efforts have to be made to develop the Human Capital requirements of a growing economy and the efficient delivery of public services to enhance citizen-government interface.

Roadmap for Reform – Indian policy makers stand at the crossroads today. We have the third largest university system in the world[14]. There are huge problems of quality and standards which need to be addressed. As the 11th Five Year Plan (2007-12)[15] document states: there is need for expansion and greater access (our gross enrolment ratio is abysmally low), besides enhancing standards to meet the requirements of the emerging knowledge economy. The government's top priority was to universalize elementary education which is recognized as a 'public good' and by making elementary education a fundamental right, the government has rightly prioritized in matters of education policy. If 6% of GDP is to be spent on education, not more than 3% is to be expected to fall in the higher education kitty. Professional education in the tertiary sector – (engineering, management and medicine) has already been privatized to a great extent – largely due to the state's fiscal incapacity to expand further. State regulation of these institutions is still a matter of debate, with the government not really able to give the requisite autonomy to these institutions in matters of admission policies or determining fee structures. There is no interference however in matters of course structure and standards of education. Courts also have not been very creative in interpreting the law. Many questions have been raised in courts: quality vs. access, reservations vs. merit, profiteering vs. social justice, autonomy versus state control – all very knotty issues in which judicial interpretations have also tended to change over the years. The courts have been very suspicious of privatization of institutions of higher education for a long time and are still reluctant to give them full autonomy in matters of admission policy or determining fee structures.

In 1997, the Government of India in its proposals for subsidies accorded higher education the status of a 'non merit good' for the first time while elementary education remained a 'merit good'. The Ministry of Finance later reclassified higher education into a 'merit 2 good' implying thereby that it need not be subsidized by the state at the same level as a merit good.

India's higher education policy of the 50's, which envisaged schools of excellence, specially in technology and sciences, did finally pay off rich dividends. The creation of IITs, IIMs, Schools of Sciences, Schools of Law, Schools of Medicine have now been well and widely accepted. With so much of admiration and brand equity for Indian technology and knowledge, it is time to cash in on its advantage. **We have the largest pool of scientific and knowledge workers in the world.** We have had great success in entering the Services Sector through new communications technology for not only low-end backroom service work, but also top end Research & Development (R&D). Our unique selling point is the pool of skilled manpower, which we need to continue to grow to maintain our competitive edge.

The professional education streams are plagued by the problems similar to the higher education system. NKC has recommended that the present regime of regulation in all professional education streams including medical, legal, management and engineering education, be replaced by subgroups on different streams under a proposed Independent Regulator. Other measures for improving professional education include: allowing greater autonomy to institutions reforming the current examination system, developing contemporary curricula and encouraging research. It has been further analyzed that in order to make education demand driven we need to allow private sector to enter higher education by relaxing bureaucratic hurdles and putting an accreditation system in place for private providers of both higher education and vocational training. This will also in involve university and industry participation, which is currently lacking.

Higher education provisioning is a fairly capital intensive process. It is generally accepted that higher education contributes more to individual career enhancement than wider 'public good'. We have to remember that the largest number of illiterates belong to India. So the urgent demand on public resources is for school education. **Therefore full public funding of a highly diversified scheme of higher education in India (general + technical + vocational) is virtually impossible.** The fact is privatization of higher technical and vocational education has happened by default of public investment in these areas rather than as a matter of policy.

Finally we come to the issue of Regulation. There are basically 2 agencies in India regulating Higher Education:– University Grants Commission (UGC) and All India Council for Technical Education (AICTE). In higher education, regulation performs five functions a) Entry: Licence to grant degrees b) Accreditation: quality benchmarking c) Disbursement of public funds d) Access: fees or affirmative action and e) Licence: to practice profession. Four of the five functions mentioned here are performed by UGC. The Human Resource Department (HRD) Ministry will introduce in the Indian Parliament 3 major bills, including one for setting up an overarching body replacing the existing regulatory authorities. The ministry has circulated a draft cabinet note for creation of National Commission for Higher Education and Research (NCHER). The proposed NCHER will replace UGC, AICTE and act as an apex body for higher education & research. The ministry has prepared another bill for entry of foreign education providers into the country. The bill seeks to allow entry of foreign universities and ensure that these institutions offer quality education to students in India. For checking malpractices in higher education, the HRD Ministry has prepared a separate bill. Besides, the ministry has prepared a few other bills providing for educational tribunals for redressal of disputes and setting up of an accreditation body for higher education.

Concluding Observations

India is at the crossroads with regard to its Education Policy. **This may well lead to a paradigm shift in higher education.** For years the government and even the courts were gripped by a collective paranoia and suspicion of private enterprise. They were torn between the idea of education as 'social service/philanthropy' and education as 'business'. Today 'edu-business' in school and tertiary education is a de facto reality[16] which the legislature, the executive and the judiciary have come to realize. There is a need to institutionalize this trend in reality by making relevant changes in law and public policy. Significant educational innovations and experiments are taking place in educational institutions in course content and pedagogical methodologies. The private institutions have been more responsive to the demands of the economy and industry and the changing employment scenario.

Globally, tertiary education is undergoing enormous reforms and this reform agenda can usefully be viewed in the context of five themes:

a) Expansion and Diversification – of enrolment, participation rates and number and types of institutions.
b) Fiscal pressure – impacts of low public funding on the university system in terms of low paid faculty, declining per student expenditures, lack of infrastructure in classrooms and laboratories.
c) Markets – the search for private and non public sources of revenue.
d) The demand for greater accountability – on the part of institutions and faculty, students and employers.
e) The demand for greater quality, relevance and excellence in standards.

Indian public policy makers will also have to include all these concerns in their policy documents in the future. Though publicly arguing for reforms, all stakeholders in the educational system (Students, parents, teachers, employers and governments), also understand that restructuring upsets the sectional interest of some stakeholders in India. The State in India is generally averse to any reduction in its power of control and patronage, therefore giving more autonomy to educational institutions is often resisted by the state itself. The private colleges owned and managed by sections of minorities, castes, religious or business groups have also emerged as powerful interest groups often with political clout and powers. The 'soft state' in India is often judgmentally clouded in its policy gestures by such conflicting pulls and pressures. The state avoids hard policies or taking a clear stand on such crucial issues:- **How do we advance equality without sacrificing quality? Should edu-business like any other business – thrive on profit or should it be based on a philanthropic mindset? Should the merit criteria by pass claims of social justice? How far should seats be reserved for any group in the education sector?** However, the answer does not lie in handing over higher education to the private or voluntary sectors. Hard policy decisions (e.g. privatization of higher education) are not without social costs. In a polity such as India with deep structured inequalities, privatization is sure to reinforce and perhaps foster inegaliterian tendencies. **Even with limited privatization, how do we control the private sector without curbing its creativity and initiative?** These are some of the policy challenges for the 21st century policymakers of higher education in the largest democracy in the world, i.e. India.

References

Agarwal, Pawan, (2007), "Higher Education in India: Growth, Concerns and the Change Agenda", *Higher Education Quarterly*, 61 (2): 197-207.

Dam, Shubhankar, (2006), "Unburdening the Constitution: What has the Indian Constitution got to do with Private Universities, Modernity and Nation-States", *Singapore Journal of Legal Studies*, pp. 108-147. Available at SSRN http://ssrn.com/abstract=952211

Rani, Geetha. P., (2002) "Financing Higher Education in India during the Post Reform Period: Focus on Access and Equity", *NIEPA Occasional Paper*, No.31, NIEPA, New Delhi, September, 2002.

Rani, Geetha. P., (2003), "Financing Education in India in the Economic Return Period: Focus on Intra-sectoral Allocation of Resources to Education", in *Globalisation and Challenges of Education*, (ed), NIEPA, 2003.

Salmi, J., (1992), "Perspectives on the Financing of Higher Education", *Higher Education Policy*, Vol.5, No.2, pp.13-19.

Srivastava, D.K. and Tapas, K. Sen, (1997), *Government Subsidies in India*, National Institute of Public Finance and Policy, New Delhi.

Srivastava, Ravi, (2007), "National Knowledge Commission: Meeting Social Goals or Neoliberal Reform", *Economic and Political Weekly* March 10, pp. 812-815.

Stewart, F., (1996), "Globalisation and Education", *International Journal of Educational Development*, Vol.16, No.2, pp. 327-333.

Tilak, J.B.G., (1983), Voluntary Contributions to Education in India, *Punjab School of Economics and Business*, Vol.4, No.2.

.... (1997), "Lessons from Cost Recovery in Education", in: *Marketising Education and Health in Developing Countries: Miracle or Mirage?* (ed.: C. Colclough). Oxford: Clarendon Press, pp. 63-89.

.... (1997), "The Dilemma of Reforms in Financing Higher Education in India", *Higher Education Policy* 10 (1): 7-21.

.... (2000), "Higher Education in Developing Countries:," *Minerva*. Vol.38, pp.233-240.

.... (2001), "Education and Globalisation: The Changing Concerns in Economics of Indian Education, Editorial", *Perspective in Education*, Vol.17, Special Issue, pp. 5-8.

.... (2003), "Public Expenditure on Education in India," in *Financing Education in India* (New Delhi: NIEPA: Ravi Books).

World Bank, (1994), *Higher Education: The Lessons of Experience*. Washington, DC: The World Bank.

.... (2002), *Constructing Knowledge Societies: New Challenges for Tertiary Education*, Washington, D.C.

Ziderman, A. and D. Albrecht, (1995), *Financing Universities in Developing Countries. The Stanford Series on Education and Public Policy*, The Falmer Press, Washington, D.C.

Reports

- Government of India Report on Tax Exemptions (Kelkar Committee Report).
- Government of India, (2007), Selected Educational Statistics 2004-2005.
- Kumarmangalm Birla Report on Higher Education, Prime Minister's Task Force.
- National Knowledge Commission Report, GOI, October 2008.
- NIEPA Report on Consultative Meeting for Funding Higher Education.
- UGC Annual Reports, 2001-2009.
- UGC Committee Reports (Punayya, Pylee, Anand Krishnan, Rehman).

End notes

1. Projection of the UN Population Division as quoted in the World Youth Report 2003.
2. Though the Gross Enrolment Ratio is low, higher education has seen a stunning 100 fold enrolment growth in India – from 1.7 lakh students in 1951 to over 13 million currently. Projected GER: 15% by 2015 in India. The world average of GER is 26.7%, the average of the developed countries is 57.7% and that of the developing countries is 13%.
3. There is a mismatch between the relative contribution of these 3 sectors to the Indian economy and their capacity for employment generation. Contribution of agriculture to GDP is 21%, the industrial sector's is 27% and the contribution of the services sector has zoomed to 52% in 2008.
4. If an item is in the Concurrent List of the Constitution, both the Central and the State Legislatures are empowered to pass Laws on that item. There are 40 central universities, 130 deemed universities under the University Grants Commission (UGC) which is the apex regulatory body with regard to the control of higher education in India. There are 243 state universities with the coordination function supposed to be shared by the UGC and the Central Advisory Board of Education. Several forms of professional education are regulated by statutory councils like All India Council for Technical Education (AICTE).
5. St. Stephens Vs. University of Delhi 1992 and Unni Krishnan Vs. Andhra Pradesh 1993.
6. In March 2007 a 2 member bench of the Supreme Court stayed in particular the provision for 27% reservations for Other Backward Castes (OBC's) in elite higher education institutions such as the Indian Institutes of Technology and Management on the ground that the government could not implement OBC reservation without accurate data and the old 1931 census (the benchmark census) could not be the basis for numerically identifying OBCs.
7. This referral of May 2007 will address the following issues: the power of the government to impose and amend 'reservation' policies in light of possible conflicts with fundamental rights, whether 'minority' institutions can be included from implementing the quota policy, whether measures to prevent the 'creamy layer' from benefiting disproportionately are mandatory, and the constitutionality of the 93rd constitution amendment itself.
8. Dahlman, Carl and Anuja Utz, 2005, India and the Knowledge Economy, Leveraging strengths and opportunities, World Bank, Washington.
9. National income divided by the working age population is a measure of the average level of labour productivity.
10. Debroy, Bibek, 16th May 2008, 'Higher education in India – Ducking the Answers. ISAS Insights No.31. He states that between 2001 and 2026, India's total population in estimated to increase by 371 million (as per technical projections) and 83% of the increase will occur in the age group of 15-59 years. The quality of the labour input can increase and this is reflected in what economists call total factor productivity (TFP) growth, measured after netting out the contribution of increased labour and capital inputs. Demographic dividend is a result of the bulge in the working age population, lower dependency ratio and surge in the population share of the youth. If the demographic dividend is to be utilized, it has to be ensured that the growing population of the youth not only makes it to the workforce but they are better educated and skilled so that what they deliver is of high quality.
11. Of India's 600 districts, 100 are truly backward by any criterion.
12. Report of the Task Force on Employment Opportunities, Planning Commission July 2007.
13. National Knowledge Commission Report NKC, GOI, October 2008. These recommendations are likely to be the foundation of any policy document on higher education by the government of India.
14. Some relevant statistics related to the university system in India are:

Total Universities	– 504
State Universities	– 243
Central Universities	– 40
Deemed Universities	– 130
Private Sector Universities	– 53

Institutions established under
state legislation — 5

Institutions of national importance
established by Central Legislation — 33

Total Colleges — 25,951

Total students in colleges and
in universities — 136.42 lakhs

In June 2007 the Central Government announced plans to set up and fund 30 new Central Universities in 19 states of India which do not have one. In addition, the Central government announced that it would work with the states to support the expansion of colleges to the 340 districts that have extremely low college enrolments. It also announced its plans to set one high quality school in every block of the 6000 blocks in the country.

15. Towards faster and more inclusive growth, An Approach to the 11th Five Year Plan, Planning Commission Govt. of India, December 2006.
16. Examples of Privatization of professional education may be cited below:

Type of College	Percentage (Privatized)
Engineering	84%
Medical	40%
Business	90%

CHAPTER 18

THE HUMAN RIGHTS BASED APPROACH AND GOVERNANCE PRINCIPLES –
A Higher Education Perspective

Maria Clarisa R. Sia

Abstract

In a true democracy, there exists a perpetual struggle for an environment of enhanced freedom, where public officials and leaders of institutions are held accountable for their actions. With this in mind, effective governance and improvement have become the core strategies in developing countries and development agencies since the 1990's. One of them is the mainstreaming and application of a human-rights based approach to governance and to the development process. This paper aims to define good governance and its importance in managing government affairs both at the national and the local/community levels, and to illustrate interventions for capability-building through courses and activities in public administration and social development specifically in the University of the Philippines. The end view is to build greater trust and confidence in political and administrative leaders, have a responsive, effective and efficient governmental service delivery system for democratic stability and progressive economic growth.

Introduction

The issue of governance came to the fore as one of the priorities in international development frameworks and policy packages due to the failure of structural adjustment programmes and neo-classical economic reforms. It was recognised that the role of the state has to be given more emphasis for a transparent, responsive and participatory voice to emerge i.e. accountability and governance in a legal and regulatory framework.

This paradigm shift led to the development of new opportunities in the early 1990s for the enhancement of the capacity of stakeholders for managing government mechanisms. One of the reasons for this was that the basic rights of the people were not being fully realised e.g. participation in public affairs and free access to information in a framework of accountability. In response to this need, the decision was taken for the integration of the concepts of good governance and the human rights-based approach in higher level teaching and capability-building exercises in order to develop morally integrated leaders and supervisors upon whom political and social responsibilities could be placed. Likewise, there was a realisation that a holistic approach to development had to be imbibed in higher education discussions to offer effective structures, processes and mechanisms in different spheres of governance (political, socio-economic and administrative).

Governance as Defined and Assessed

In the study of governance at the University of the Philippines particularly at the National College of Public Administration and Governance (NCPAG), the framework and models that are explicated are focused on the process of decision-making. What is studied is the manner the decisions are implemented or not implemented by the stakeholders, whether formal or informal and at what level i.e. international, national and local together with the civil society. The World Bank book (1992) defined governance as "the manner in which power is exercised in the management of a country's economic and social resources for development (Noor, 2008). As also defined by Noor from lens of the International Institute on Governance (1990), 'governance comprises the traditions, institutions and processes that determine how power is exercised, how citizens are given a voice and how decisions are made on issues of public concern.'

Particularly, three dimensions are focused on in teaching and capability-building for good governance i.e. (1) sense of service and performance resulting in presence of equality and fairness in treatment of clients/citizen; (2) work accountability and management, i.e. service to clients and to the public in general; and, (3) prevention of the establishment of an environment where conflict of interests may prevail.

During the study of the didactics of governance, students and participants assessed governance from three dimensional perspectives: (1) political and administrative processes by which leaders are selected, held accountable, monitored and replaced or reinstated; (2) capacity of governments to formulate, implement and enforce sound policies, laws and regulations as well as the methodology for planning managing and monitoring resources efficiently and effectively; and, (3) mechanism of citizens' participation in national and local affairs. These dimensions are also assessed by researchers according to Aminuzzaman (2007). Additionally, continuing discussions are held to evaluate policy reforms on financing developmental projects considering particularly, the difficulties and the propriety of mechanisms in mobilizing domestic resources and debt servicing for effective governance.

Characteristics of Good Governance

As indicated by UNESCAP, good governance has eight major characteristics. These characteristics are the same principles adhered to in the human rights-based approach to development and governance (Figure 1). Guided by, but not necessarily adhering to the definition of UNESCAP, the following characteristics are integrated and emphasised in the discussions of the public administration and social development disciplines.

Participation

The essence of good governance is the active participation of the citizen – both men and women – at all levels, either directly or through legitimate representation.

FIGURE 1: Characteristics of good governance

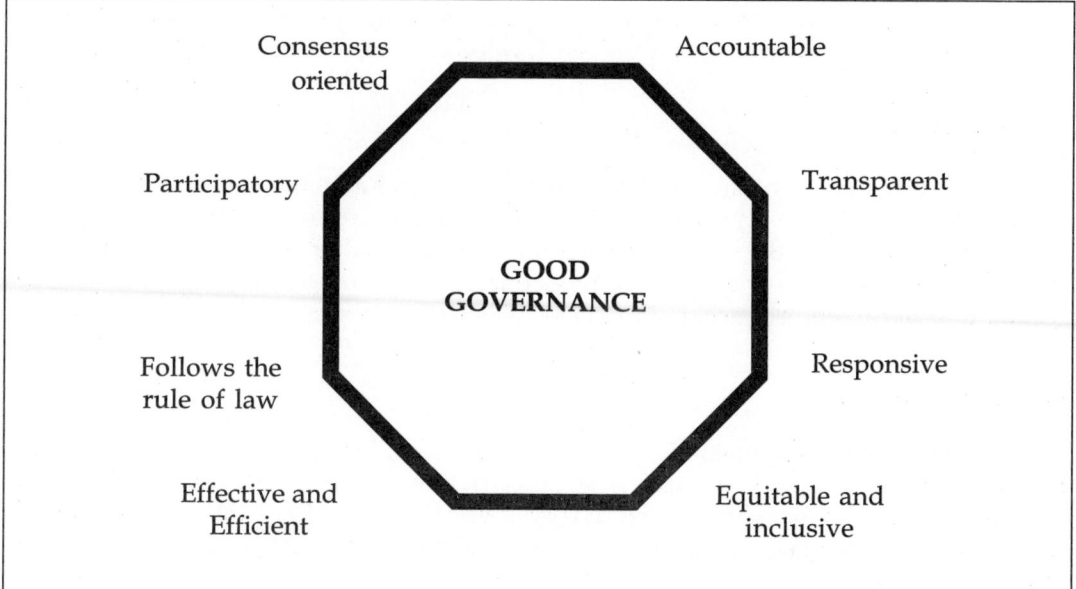

Source: United Nations Economic and Social Commission for Asia and the Pacific (UNESCAP).

According to Chattopadhyay (2008), there are two ways for people to participate in order to make institutions responsive to citizens' desires and to provide more effective service delivery, i.e.:

- representative participation through voting in elections (political) i.e. citizens can try to influence and critique government actions and decisions and to establish a check on making the representatives accountable to the people; and,
- direct participation either at the community or project level - institutions providing citizens equal opportunity for actively taking part in the decision-making process by subjecting all decisions to discussion and approval by the complete membership of the relevant community. Thus, an environment of accountability is built up on the (political and administrative) decision makers to respond to the needs and preferences of the citizens.

The second point is taking into consideration the decision-making concerns of the most vulnerable and excluded segments of society. In the public administration discipline, discussions are clearly focused on decentralised power in local decision-making since implementation schemes affect livelihood and quality of life of the people. In short, participation makes the government, civil society, academe and the wider public well-informed and organised to express, monitor and evaluate their plans and programs.

Consensus oriented

Good governance has two requirements for consensus-building irrespective of the diverse perspectives of stakeholders, i.e.: 1) mediation of interests and divergent groups for reaching a broad consensus on what is in the best interest of the whole community, together with identifying the mode to achieving it; and 2) broad and long-term perspectives on what is needed and the required interventions for development of human capital.

Accountability

This is a key requirement and a vital indicator of good governance. To whom one is accountable depends on (1) whether decisions or actions are internal or external to an organisation; 2) level of the structure (international, national or local) and 3) who will be affected by the decisions or actions. Transparency and rule of law are two characteristics needed in order to enforce accountability.

Transparency

Decisions and their enforcement is said to be transparent when the process follows rules and regulations (rule of law), and when information is freely available and directly accessible to those who will be affected by these decisions (right to information). In addition to this, adequate information is provided that is easily understandable in forms and media.

Responsiveness

As an evaluation indicator, responsiveness measures whether the institutions and processes serve all stakeholders within a reasonable timeframe. Historical, cultural and social contexts of a given society or community are important dimensions to be considered in gauging responsiveness.

Equity and inclusiveness

This indicator ensures that a society's members feel that they have a stake in development efforts which affect them and that they do not feel excluded from the mainstream. This characteristic needs to be particularly addressed for the most vulnerable, so that they have every opportunity to improve or maintain their own well being.

Effectiveness and efficiency

This management indicator of service delivery is focused on the processes and institutions it produces. It measures whether decisions taken by policy makers and development efforts meet the needs of society while making the best use of resources at the disposal of a community. Moreover, the concept of efficiency also covers the sustainable use of natural resources and the protection of the environment.

Rule of law

The government must ensure that fair legal frameworks are enforced impartially by an independent judiciary and incorruptible police force for full protection of human rights, particularly those of minorities and the marginalised.

Governance Need and Approaches as Perceived by the Poor

In social and community development spheres, the concept of good governance is illustrated as a system where everyone has gets a fair share (equal) of public resources that would create more opportunities for human development. The poor also expect honesty and integrity of leadership especially from the local elected officials and leaders. Likewise, leaders have to remain accessible in times of need and the scope of participation of the poor in governmental affairs should be well defined and enhanced.

According to Aminuzzaman (2007), there are some conceptual distortions and missing ingredients in understanding and analyzing the concept of governance. One of them is sharp income inequalities and intense distributional conflicts affecting the democratic process and governance. This outcome, according to him is a result of the concentration of power in the hands of the political elites that leads to political instability and the creation of room for abuse of power, and the violation of the rights of the poor. Secondly, it is the absence of internal democracy in political parties that creates a platform for individuals to become more important than the policies. In this situation, the result is the erosion of public confidence in the political system and, with prevailing ignorance and pervasive poverty, democracy often locks the poor into a patron-client relationship with their political representatives.

To Aminuzzaman, good governance should be: (1) seen as the people's own interest (ownership) and perspectives in relation to advancement of human capital; (2) conducive to building a society in which none feel humiliated (decency and dignity); (3) embodied in structures which ensures law and order and safety (safety and security); (4) focused on development of support systems for better livelihoods and employment opportunities through continued provision and extension of services (better life); (5) designed around a system and process that is governed by honest and dedicated leaders not tainted by corruption and malpractices (accountability), not only in the sphere of elected government but also the civil society and other institutions; and, (6) a system that ensures elimination of all forms of discrimination against women and other disadvantaged and marginalised groups (accessibility).

In short, good governance for the poor should adopt reform approaches to improve the planning and management of services especially in order to ensure participation, transparency and accountability. Likewise, it is necessary to formulate legislative and policy reforms directed towards the poor and the disadvantaged i.e. broad-based and pro-poor growth (see Figure 2).

FIGURE 2: Pro-poor governance routes to address poverty

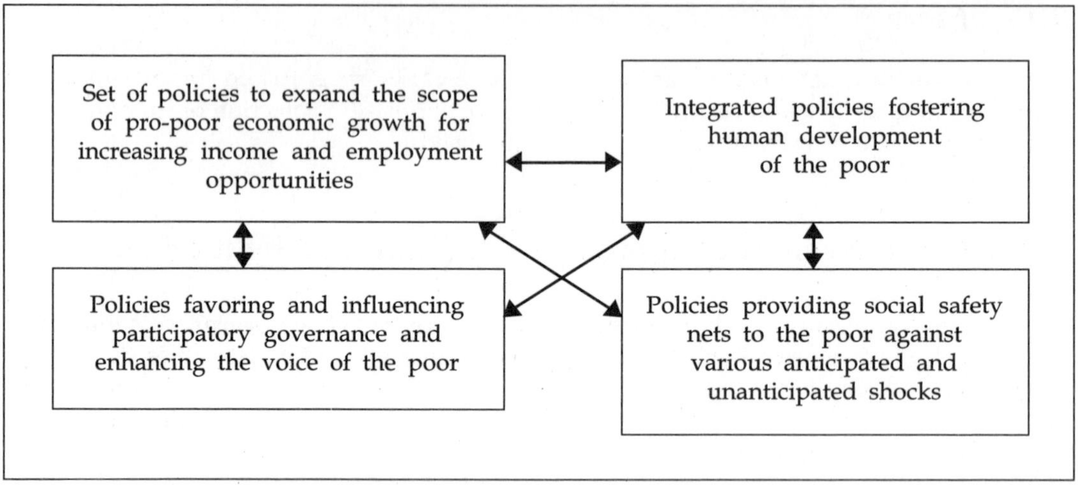

```
┌─────────────────────────────┐         ┌─────────────────────────────┐
│ Set of policies to expand   │         │ Integrated policies         │
│ the scope of pro-poor       │ ◄─────► │ fostering human development │
│ economic growth for         │         │ of the poor                 │
│ increasing income and       │         │                             │
│ employment opportunities    │         │                             │
└─────────────────────────────┘         └─────────────────────────────┘
         ▲            ╲          ╱              ▲
         │             ╲        ╱               │
         ▼              ╳                       ▼
┌─────────────────────────────┐         ┌─────────────────────────────┐
│ Policies favoring and       │         │ Policies providing social   │
│ influencing participatory   │ ◄─────► │ safety nets to the poor     │
│ governance and enhancing    │         │ against various anticipated │
│ the voice of the poor       │         │ and unanticipated shocks    │
└─────────────────────────────┘         └─────────────────────────────┘
```

Source: Aminuzzaman, 2007.

Need for Key Performance Indicators (KPIs)

The academic institutions give great importance to developing key performance indicators (KPIs) in all governance areas for measuring the achievement of human development. According to different stakeholders who have undergone higher education and training, the development-driven thrusts and areas are as follows: (1) level of improvement in the quality of life especially in health, education and livelihood; (2) effective mechanisms for sustainable development and (3) equal opportunities given to women. These indicators are aimed at ensuring the improvement in the social well-being of individuals resulting in a situation where people are empowered and free to express their needs and interests. The reformulation of indicators takes into consideration the changing environment and the various international requirements and indicators.

There are governance performance criteria and indicative checklists developed by the NCPAG. These aim to measure effectiveness and efficiency in the delivery of public services and to serve as measurements for clients' evaluation of government programs and projects. The criteria specifically indicated in the UNDP-Users' Guide (2006) are as follows (Figure 3):

FIGURE 3: Governance Performance Criteria and Indicators

Criterion	Indicators
Participation	Conducting of public consultations, functioning local development councils, presence of performance monitoring and evaluation committees with private sector/NGO/civil society participation and involvement of beneficiaries in programs/processes
Account-ability	Presence of performance measurement and appraisal system, performance/financial audit reports, local ombudsman or grievance based committees, laws on public accountability publicised, assets and liabilities adequately accounted for
Transparency	Presence of a management information system, use of IT that includes socio-economic profiling as presented in community data boards and spot maps, updated accomplishment reports clearly posted and measured against targets, participation of media
Effective and responsive basic service	Devolved services adequately funded, and equitable and rational distribution of basic services amongst beneficiaries illustrated further, in the budget
Rule of Law	Ordinances periodically reviewed and updated, existence of a legislative tracking mechanism, establishment of work flow permanently posted for guidance of all, legal and cultural laws effectively implemented, and availability of information and statistics, e.g. crime arrests and convictions, no cases filed in court for traffic violation, etc.
Leadership	Presence of a clear and consistent vision articulated by government executives, participation in activities at all levels, ability to network nationally and with donor institutions, attainment of planned targets and, ability to harness civil society and the business sector for support to government initiatives
Organisation/Management	Presence of a clear organisational structure, a master development plan with quantifiable and measurable targets, clear delineation of responsibilities between the executive and the legislative, performance evaluation periodically conducted, staff meetings/department meetings conducted regularly.
Program Sustainability	Continuing efforts to augment resources through short term and long term grants and loans, continuous consultation with local constituents, programs and projects subject to regular evaluation and continuous enrichment and development plan updated regularly
Preference for the Poor	Use of Poverty Mapping conducted and updated regularly and MBN surveys in designing local programs and projects, provision of livelihood programs, funds set aside for poverty alleviation projects, and presence of poverty alleviation programs, heath insurance of indigents, senior citizens, etc.

Source: United Nations Development Programme, 2006.

Governance as Practiced in Higher Education and Efforts at Capability-Building

In 2005, the Commission on Higher Education (CHED) conducted a review and evaluation of graduate programs in the Philippines in education, public administration and business. In the field of public administration, the NCPAG rated its program as 'excellent' using the following criteria as applied to good governance:

Factors	Criteria
Curriculum and Instruction	• The program of studies is (1) consistent with global, national and institutional goals, and the specific objectives of the course offerings; (2) systematically arranged learning experiences that are interdisciplinary and multidisciplinary; and (3) provision of professional and technical preparation needed by graduate students
	• Well-defined curriculum, (1) providing for the professional and technical preparation needed by graduate students; (2) requiring students to undertake research (term paper, project paper, practicum paper)
	• Periodic evaluation keeps curricular offerings abreast with the times and considers flexibility of offerings in major fields
	• Faculty members and students participate in evaluation and revision of the curriculum
Instructional Materials, Procedures & Techniques	• An approved syllabus is required for each subject which is updated periodically and indicates the opportunity for independent study and training in research methodology
	• Instructional materials are relevant and adequate
	• Course requirements lead to the attainment of course objectives, ensure development of desirable attitudes towards life-long learning and strategies contribute to the infusion of desirable values
	• The level of teaching in graduate programs is advanced and based on state of the art findings, which are according to prevailing paradigms; level of class discussion manifests critical thinking and analysis
Student Learning	• Faculty members use appropriate techniques to evaluate performance in a participatory framework with students
	• The grading policy is fair, well-defined and made known to the students
	• Comprehensive examinations measure student competence/performance

Source: Commission on Higher Education, 2005.

Conclusion

Good governance is vital for attaining the objectives of public administration and social development particularly in enhancing human capital. Governance is not only linked to the working of the formal government but it also involves the various development actors at all levels (from the village to the international level) i.e. the civil society, non-governmental groups, community organisations, academe, the private sector and international donors. It concerns itself with how these collectivities manage resources, their relationships and their internal organisational affairs. Three factors are necessary to measure the state of governance i.e. the quality of leadership, service delivery to the governed, and the structures, strategies and processes which are adopted for efficient, responsive and effective service. These three factors entail the building of capacity of the citizen through well-planned and organised higher education and capability-enhancing activities.

If institutions provide for the meaningful participation of citizens in the conceptualisation, implementation and evaluation of policies and programs, then the people with the necessary capacities would be able to affect and manage change. There is an emerging international consensus on the core characteristics of good governance in a democratic society i.e. participation, accountability and transparency guided by the rule of law and equality, among others.

Thus, truly enlightened institutions of governance - those that are devoid of corruption which do not engender public trust - would emerge only with collective decision-making and concerted actions guided by principles of inclusiveness.

References

Aminuzzaman, S. (2007). Poverty and governance-A quest for alternative focus: Bangladesh test case. *Journal of Administration and Governance, 2 (1)*, 11-20.

Ahmad, R. (2008). Governance, social accountability and the civil society. *Journal of Administration and Governance, 3* (1), 10-21.

Carino, L. (1991). Accountability, corruption and democracy: A clarification of concepts. *Asian Review of Public Administration, 3* (2), 1-9.

Chattopadhyay, S. (2008). *Decentralized urban governance: Participation and accountability in West Bengal's municipalities.* Unpublished manuscript.

Commission on Higher Education (2005). *Review and evaluation of graduate program in the Philippines-Indicators of quality graduate programs.* Unpublished manuscript

Dimzon, C. (2003). An evaluation of the pre-departure orientation seminar program for women overseas household workers: Implications for good governance. (Doctoral dissertation, University of the Philippines).

Noor, A. (2008). Ethics, religion and good governance. *Journal of Administration and Governance, 3* (2), 62-77.

Rai, S. (2008). *Transparency and accountability in governance and right to information in India.* Unpublished manuscript.

Sia, M. C. (2009). Necessary conditions to development and corrupt-free society: A governance approach. (Doctoral paper requirement in Social Development 301- History and Perspective in Social Development, University of the Philippines).

United Nations Development Programme.(2006). Governance indicators in the Philippines: A users guide. Retrieved from http://www.undp.org/oslocentre/docs07/gip_philippines-users_guide.pdf

_____(2006). Rights-Based Approach Orientation Training Manual: Towards Mainstreaming Human Rights in the Development and Governance Processes

United Nations Economic and Social Commission for Asia and the Pacific UNESCAP) . What is Good Governance. Retrieved from http://www.unescap.org/pdd/prs/Project Activities/Ongoing/gg/governance.asp

CHAPTER 19

STUDENT MOBILITY IN ASIA:
An Appraisal

A.K. MALIK

Abstract

Some scholars describe the twenty-first century as the century of "educational mobility" and global schooling (Lee 2001). In the earlier era there was increased student mobility from developing world to developed world. However, in the recent times intra-regional student mobility is increasing. Student mobility, as discussed in this paper, is the movement of higher level students from one country to another in quest of knowledge and cross-cultural experiences. This is being discussed in relation to countries within Asia. Student mobility is more from Asian countries to developed countries. There is also considerable mobility between South East Asian countries. In East Asia and Pacific, increased numbers of students are remaining in their own region. Foreign students are admitted for both educational and economic considerations. Keeping this in view, this paper explains the effects of home and host countries on institutions of higher education and of mobility of students. This is highlighted independently, describing factors determinant of mobility, objectives and reasons for studying abroad and benefits of student exchange, changing strategies of student mobility in Asian countries. Finally, the paper discusses strategies to stimulate, maintain and widen intra-Asian educational interaction as a central feature of university level cooperation.

Introduction

Since ancient times students have been going abroad to pursue higher education. The numbers involved were less and the destinations few. The number of students going to other developed countries began to increase substantially with the end of World War II and took a quantum jump in the 1970s. The student mobility was more from developing countries to developed countries. However, there was some student mobility from developed world to developing countries mainly for gaining experience in other countries and their cultures. There was also student mobility within the developing countries. Egypt, India, Saudi Arabia were common destinations as they had a more-developed and wider network of higher education institutions than the countries from where students came.

Student mobility, as discussed in this paper, is the movement of higher level students from one country to another in quest of knowledge and cross-cultural experiences. This is being discussed in relation to countries within Asia. The paper explains the recent trends of student mobility to and from Asia, mobility determinants, benefits of student exchange, changing strategies of student mobility in Asian countries and finally suggests strategies to have a balanced student mobility in the Asian region.

Student Mobility: Recent Trends

Over the years, the number of students seeking higher education in foreign countries has been consistently increasing. It increased from 0.60 million worldwide in 1975 to 2.90 million in 2006, a more than four-fold increase. Growth in the internationalisation of tertiary education has accelerated during the past eleven years, mirroring the growing globalisation of economies and societies (OECD 2008). This consistent growth indicates an increasing demand for cross-border education and efforts by many countries to attract more international students in higher education.

Data about number of mobile students vary due to various reasons like unavailability of exact data from certain countries or estimates on the basis of partial data or traditionally treating foreign students on the basis of criterion of citizenship. This gets reflected from the data in Global Education Digest 2005 according to which mobile student population has been rising with three notable surges in growth. The first occurred between 1975 and 1980 when the total number of mobile students grew by 30% from 800,000 to just over one million. The next wave took place between 1989 and 1994 with a rise of 34%. The third and biggest surge of 41% is also the most recent observed between 1999 and 2004. This data is somewhat at variance with OECD (2008).

The student mobility used to be more from developing to developed countries. Although this continues to be the trend but it is changing. This shows the emergence of new players on the international education market. The United States continue to receive the most foreign students worldwide in absolute terms (20%), followed by United Kingdom (11.3%), Germany (8.9%) and France (8.5%). Total for these four countries account for 48.7% of all tertiary students pursuing their studies abroad.

Over a six-year period, the share of the United States as a preferred destination dropped from 25% to 20%, for UK from 12.6 to 11.3% and for Germany from 10% to 8.9%. However, the market shares of Australia and Japan expanded by around 1 percentage point. France and New Zealand with the growth of 1.2% and 1.9% respectively places them among the big players in the international education market.

Inter-country student flow 2005 (Table 1), as per IIE (2007), indicates that these eleven countries together account for nearly 70 per cent of the cross-border student flow. Most of the developed countries are host countries. Most of the developing countries (Algeria, China, India, Korea, Malaysia and Morocco) send a large number of students abroad, notably to Australia, France, Germany, UK and USA (Varghese, 2008).

More than 70 per cent of all Asian students study in three English speaking countries, namely, Australia, the UK and the USA. This trend is changing. Between 1995 and 2004, the share of Chinese students going to the USA more than halved (from 59.6 per cent to 25.6 per cent) and from India it declined by 14 per cent (from 78.5 per cent to 64.5 per cent). Australia, however, gained as it received increased number of students from China (an increase of 20 percentage points) and India (12 percentage points) (Varghese, 2008). One of the reasons for this is attributed to low cost of cross-border education in Australia when compared with that of the UK and the USA.

TABLE 1: Inter-country student flow 2005 (%)

Host /Sending	USA	UK	Germany	France	Australia	Japan	Korea	China	NZ
India	13.5	4.9	..	..	14.2	..	..	2.3	3.6
China	11.1	15.4	10.5	4.8	27.0	63.0	51.3		59.0
Korea	10.4	1.0	2.2	..	2.3	13.5	..	38.3	2.9
Japan	6.9	1.9	..	..	1.9	..	12.0	13.4	2.3
Canada	5.0	1.1	..	1.1	1.8	..	..	..	..
USA		6.2	1.4	..	2.0	1.5	5.2	7.3	5.6
France	2.0	4.6	2.1		..	..	..	2.2	..
Ireland		4.8	..	..	..	..	..	..	..
Morocco	0.3		3.4	13.8	..	1.8	..	..	..
Algeria	..	..	..	9.4	..	..	..	..	..
Malaysia	1.1	3.4			8.8	1.5	..	..	2.2
Total (000s)	568.0	344.0	246.0	238.0	168.0	118.0	23.0	141.0	37.0

Notes: 1. Only those countries which appear in the top 10 sending countries are indicated in the above Table
2. Denotes negligible (less than 1 per cent) or the same country.
Source: IIE (2007) quoted by Varghese (2008), p.20

International Student Mobility to and from Asia

British Council's Report on review of student data (2008) shows that throughout the major part of the first half of this decade most East Asian markets experienced growth to varying extents in student numbers from their East Asian neighbours. The data demonstrates increased student mobility in the Region. In China, Japan and South Korea between half to three quarters of foreign students come from the other two neighbouring countries. According to the above report, approximately 40 per cent of the respondents projected either modest or significant growth in student enrolments from the Region over the next five years. In line with many of their Major English Speaking Destination Countries (MESDC), China was most commonly rated the number one source of East Asian students for institutions participating in this research. South Korea was most commonly ranked their number two source of East Asian students

In the Asian region there has also been increased flow of students from within the Asian continent (Table 2). According to the 2009 edition of the Unesco's Global Digest, in East Asia and the Pacific, 42 per cent of students who left home remained in their

TABLE 2: Foreign Students in Tertiary Education by Hosting Country and Continent of Origin – ASIA

Regions Hosting country or territory	Number of foreign students		Foreign students as % of tertiary enroll-ment	Continent of origin						
	MF	%F		Africa	America, North	America, South	Asia	Europe	Oceania	Unspecified
ASIA										
Armenia	3,035	...	4	2	22	2	2,328	681	-	-
Azerbaijan	1,864	27	2	6	1	-	1,695	162	-	-
Bahrain	1,331	33	7	90	8	-	1,227	6	-	-
Cyprus	5,282	23	29	83	13	5	4,262	852	6	61
Hong Kong (China), SAR	2,355	44	2	7	43	3	2,131	71	24	76
India (p)	7,738	...	-	1.893	343	10	4,452	138	40	862
Iran, Islamic Republic of	1,450	40	-	62	4	2	1,346	36	-	-
Iraq (n)	8,280	15	3	...	...	...	...	...	...	8,280
Japan (p)	74,892	47	2	778	1,596	810	69,034	2,208	458	8
Jordan (p) (i)	15,816	...	8	640	248	23	14,671	218	7	9
Kazakhstan	6,523	...	1	4	4	-	4,803	1,701	-	11
Kyrgyzstan	13,440	47	7	-	-	-	12,868	572	-	-
Lebanon	12,210	50	8	...	...	...	...	...	...	12,210
Macao, China	17,541	26	67	8	2	3	17,453	74	1	-
Malaysia (p)	27,731	...	4	2,417	65	7	24,112	523	42	565
Philippines (p)	4,744	...	-	158	797	6	3,615	108	58	2
Qatar	1,633	60	21	180	5	-	1,431	17	-	-
Republic of Korea (p)	4,956	45	-	65	255	35	4,392	181	27	1
Saudi Arabia	11,046	28	2	2,668	172	31	7,238	561	12	364
Tajikistan	2,208	18	2	1	1	-	1,601	605	-	-
Thailand (q) (p) (i)	4,092	...	-	16	154	2	3,054	133	13	720
Turkey (p)	12,729	38	1	384	25	8	7,106	5,177	29	-

Global Education Digest 2005-Comparative Education Statistics Across the World, UNESCO Institute for Statistics, Montreal, 2005, P. 106

Symbols and footnotes:

(n) Data for the School year 1999/00
(p) Data for 2002 or later years are provisional
(q) Data cover only 80% of total number of students
... No data available
- Magnitude nil or negligible

region in 2007 compared with 36 per cent in 1999. This has been attributed in part to the growing local availability of higher education. Singapore, Malaysia and Hong Kong all want to attract thousands more international students. Malaysia wants 100,000 foreign school and university students by next year, compared with 71,000 enrolled in the current academic year. Singapore plans to attract 150,000 by 2015, up from 97,000 in 2008. Hong Kong has recently doubted its quota for non-local students in its public universities. These three countries are attempting to capitalise on their offering university education in English and being less expensive than Western nations. (Liz Gooch 2009). However, there is not much flow of students in the Asian region from other continents of the world.

The above discussion indicates that there is change of international student mobility in Asian countries. Some flow of international students has emerged within Asia and to Asia from outside. The important thing is that the international student mobility is caused by the political and economical strategies of the countries, but at the same time. People's demand for more attractive transnational programs has also accelerated the mobility, and its process can be explained as the transition of Asian Higher Education Network (Sugimura, 2008)

Mobility Determinants

The objectives of the receiving and sending countries of students include not only the real benefits of international education in general but also the specific benefits of increasing or decreasing flows of students between particular regions or countries. General benefits are usually couched in such rather vague terms as the enhancement of international understanding or of peace and cooperation among countries. More limited benefits include the promotion of diplomatic relationships and the increase of trade between particular countries or the discharge of obligations by the rich countries of the West towards their former colonies or the transfer of technology from the more to the less developed countries (Encyclopedia of Higher Education, 1992). Cummings explains student flow from Asian and other countries. He sees oversees study as an extension of domestic study and not a substitute. He shows that "the nations with the largest higher educational systems also send the largest numbers of students overseas; and in most cases, as the domestic systems have expanded the volume going overseas also increased". Small countries, he finds, reach a limit to their capacity to export students, while the capacity of large countries is difficult to exhaust. "If we consider Asia as a whole", he says, "we can appreciate that the expansion of the Asian student flow builds on two fundamental characteristics of the Asian region, large populations and stable economic growth" (Encyclopedia of Higher Education, 1992). This gets reflected from the figures indicated above about the number of students going abroad from the China and India which have large population.

Benefits of Student Exchange

The broad rationale for encouraging foreign student flow is four-fold (Commonwealth Secretariat, 1992):

1. It is a means of promoting international understanding, regional cooperation and national development.
2. It is a means of promoting greater international exchange of knowledge and intellectual stimulation, which are fundamental to the mission of higher education.
3. It is essential to modern human resource development, since it facilitates global, multi-cultural competence in both sets of students (incoming and outgoing) and, in view of the international integration of labour markets, it can meet the demand for persons who can function effectively in different socio-economic and cultural environments (the demands, for example, of commercial diplomacy).
4. It is an essential factor in institutional strengthening for universities; polytechnics and research and training agencies of all kinds.

In addition to above, another very important benefit of student exchange is economic consideration.

Changing Strategies of Student Mobility in Asian countries

Asian universities are among the few fully modern institutions in their societies. They are peripheral in the international sense and depend on foreign institutions in many respects while at the same time they are quite central to the local society.

The role of universities in Asian countries is complicated and diverse. Generalisations are difficult to draw because of variations in colonial development, current economic and political realities and different conceptions about the role of higher education in the modernisation of society. Different colonial traditions have had a continuing impact on the nature of higher education. The most obvious colonial impact is that of language. Colonial authorities without exception established higher education in their colonies through the use of European languages. The impact on the use of Western languages was immense. European languages continue to occupy a key place in higher education despite considerable effort in Indonesia and some attempts in India, Pakistan and a few other countries. Further, the colonial powers had quite different educational policies. The British in India were relatively permissive in the establishment of educational institutions while in Africa they were more reluctant to invest funds or permit local initiative. The French had their own values on the role of education while the Dutch, Belgians and Portuguese did their best to restrict the growth of a full-scale educational system and were particularly opposed to the emergence of universities in their colonies (Altbach, 1980).

In Asian countries substantial contemporary differences exist. Countries like India and the Philippines have large and diverse University systems covering a significant urban population. Other Systems remain highly elitist, within the reach of a tiny portion of the urban upper classes. There are important differences among Universities in Asian countries in terms of size, infrastructure facilities language of instruction. Several universities function as mediators between the international universities in the industrialised nations and majority of peripheral institutions in Asia. The University of Delhi, Jawaharlal Nehru University, University of Cairo and some other universities have trained large number of students from other countries in their region (Malik, 1998).

Although many Asian and African countries had highly developed indigenous educational systems, the institutional models followed in the creation of modern schools were uniformly Western. No third world nation, regardless of political ideology or orientation, has basically altered a Western university model (Altbach, 1980).

Two important strategies being adopted by Asian countries for increased student mobility (Sugimura, 2008) are as follows:

1. Political Strategy: There has been increased flow of students from Asian countries to developed countries. At the same time, a trend which has been observed indicates that there is increased flow of students in Asian region. Investment in academic institutions and in research infrastructure is taking place in many Asian countries, and higher education will inevitably become more central as Asian economies become more technology based, more heavily dependent on informatics and more service based (Altbach 2004). Many Asian countries have begun to compete in attracting international students. For example, Malaysia has tied up transnational programs with several higher institutions of some Western countries like USA, UK, Canada, Australia and New Zealand. Malaysian education promotion offices abroad have been set up not only in South East Asian countries but also in Africa, the Middle East and East Asia etc.

Other Asian countries (Singapore, Thailand and China) have also been adopting strategies to attract more and more international students. Singapore is aiming to become an "Educational Hub" among Asian countries. Singapore's educational strategy focuses on not only higher education but also primary and secondary education. It is estimated that about 66,000 international students are studying from South Korea, China, Vietnam, Thailand, Indonesia, Malaysia, etc. They have been attracting young minds to study in Singapore. Benefits like waiver of tuition fees, fellowship to meet living expenses etc. are being given. One of the riders is that after receiving education they will have to work in Singapore for a minimum period of two years. It implies increasing international human resources for Singapore's future development. Singapore aims to get 150,000 international students by 2012 (Sugimura, 2008).

2. Economic Strategy: Higher education is increasingly seen as an engine of economic development. Higher education institutions of some countries are strongly interested in generating income through fees paid by foreign students. Some experts consider this the most successful strategy of increasing mobility: "Academic mobility (students, programmes, providers) is considered by many as a huge commercial business and is expected to increase exponentially" (Knight, 2007:2). Others argue: "But there is a danger...if the perception builds overseas that international students are subsiding Australian higher education and getting little in return, it will eventually reduce enrolments: (Meek 2007). In contrast, other countries stimulate student mobility by other means and pursue a broader mix of educational, cultural and economic objectives including assisting the developmental objectives of the sending countries (Meek et al 2009).

The enrolment of foreign students represents an "invisible export in the form of the associated income flow. All expenditures made by international students in the receiving countries are considered as export revenue from the students' home country for the receiving country." Similarly, the tuition fees of a student enrolled in a branch campus of a foreign university operating in his or her country are considered as returns on foreign direct investment (Stella and Gnanam, 2005).

Encouraging more and more international students to come for education is also beneficial to the host country. For example, international students contributed more than $ 15.5 billion to the US economy in 2007 with 67 per cent of all international students' primary funding coming from sources outside of the USA. (Shin-who 2008). In Australia and New Zealand educational services rank third and fourth respectively, in terms of services exports and fourteenth and fifteenth respectively in terms of exports as a whole. In 1998, the international market for student mobility alone amounted to around US $ 30 billion in exports or 3% of global services exports (Larsen et al 2002).

Other strategies:

Establishment of University Mobility in Asia and the Pacific (UMAP) conceived in 1991 and founded in 1993. It is a voluntary association of government and non-government organisations which administer student mobility from 34 eligible member and more than 364 participating universities. Its mission is to "facilitate the mobility of university students and staff in the Asia Pacific region with the established aim of achieving better cultural, economic and social understanding within the region". The current goal and objectives are: to identify and overcome impediments to university mobility; to move beyond bilateral to multilateral and consortium arrangements; and to develop and maintain a system for granting and recognizing academic credits.

Establishment of Association of Southeast Asian Institutions of Higher Learning (ASAIHL) in 1956. Important objectives, amongst others, include assisting member institutions to strengthen themselves through mutual cooperation in order to achieve international distinction in teaching, research and public service and promoting the exchange of professors and students.

Establishment of The Academic Consortium 21 (AC 21) in 2002. AC 21 consists of educational research and industrial organisations throughout the world. The consortium has been established to encourage the further advancement of global cooperation to the benefit of higher education and to contribute to world and regional society. Important activities include exchange of students, faculty members and administrative staff; development of cooperative educational programs; and shared access to information on research interests and academic activities.

Introducing Courses in English Language:

In South East Asia, the national universities of Hong Kong and Singapore have long been considered good alternatives to US and UK institutions due to their intensive use of English, but several non-English speaking countries in the region, including China, Japan, South Korea and Malaysia have also recently introduced programmes taught in English.

Models of Good Practices: Different types of established models of good practice exist and many more new ones are developing. With a supportive environment, organised initiatives for favourable increase of student flows can be worked out.

The Branch Campuses Set Up by Foreign Universities

Under Branch Campus, provider in country 'A' establishes a satellite campus in country 'B' to deliver courses and programs to students in Country B (may also include Country 'A' students taking a semester/courses abroad). The qualification awarded is from provider in country 'A'. 81 offshore campuses have been identified in 36 different countries with the US accounting for 42 wholly owned and operated campuses overseas, Australia (10), UK (4) and Canada (3)) (OBHE 2006). Asia accounts for 19 international campuses while Western Europe accounts for 10 such campuses.

Other strategies for student mobility are: Exchange Student Program, Dual-Degree Program, Joint-Degree Program, Online Education/Distance Education, Award Schemes, Link Schemes, Split Site Courses and Direct Student Exchange.

Strategies to Strengthen Student Mobility

The following strategies are suggested to have balanced student mobility in the Asian region.

1. Academically, universities may like to emphasise their readiness to receive students in departments and subjects in which they have a comparative advantage. They may also like to have exchanges at undergraduate or postgraduate level.
2. Asian Universities may consider having a built-in policy with the international aspects of universities in their Charters or Statutes. For example, one of the objectives of the Jawaharlal Nehru University is "to provide facilities for the students and teachers from other countries to participate in the academic programmes of the university."
3. Recognition of qualifications, part or full modules of curricula semester accreditation can be further crystallised by sharing teaching or exchange of teachers. Reservation of seats for foreign students or a waiver of local entry test, like in India (JNU being one of them) clears an initial academic hurdle.
4. Subjects which could be of necessity for both receiving and sending countries need to be identified. This could be fostered through specific award schemes. Examples are Australia's National Asian Languages Scholarship Schemes and its Awards for Research in Asia.
5. Within the Asian region, students from less developing countries and also who can't afford the full fees prescribed for foreign students, but have good academic records, be considered for partial or full fee waiver (in JNU this policy is in vogue).
6. There is need for increased teacher's mobility within the Asian region, especially to less developed countries. They can teach a particular course for a semester or so. The students who can't afford to move to other countries will have the benefit of knowledge and teaching of a particular subject in their home country.
7. Prestigious universities within the Asian region may consider having branch campus in other countries. This trend is already catching up.
8. There is wide variance in terms of academic standing, objectives, delivery methods of the countries receiving higher number of mobile students. In some cases economic considerations have overriding effect on the quality of education being provided by the

cross-border service providers and academic considerations are less important. Therefore, the following issues require consideration:
- Status of institutions (recognition, registration, academic standing) providing cross-border education
- Quality of cross-border education providers program – Chine initiated "Enhancing Higher Education Quality" program in 2003 to overcome with quality problems in Chinese higher education. Recognition of qualifications in the home countries and other countries
- Regulatory system of cross border education in home country – national quality assurance system – China has also a rule on cooperation and linkage of Chinese universities and foreign institutions for promotion of transnational programs of Chinese universities with foreign institutions (Min, 2004).

Conclusion

The pattern of educational exchange as discussed above indicates that student mobility is largely into the USA, UK, Germany, France. This trend is changing. Australia, Japan and New Zealand have recently been receiving more foreign students. Asia Pacific is the main importer of higher education. There remains a concentration of main sending countries, China, India and Malaysia. The population in this region do not have infrastructure and facilities of international standards and a large number of young population who could receive higher education is deprived of the same. The number of students from the poorer African countries and Asian subcontinent have gradually reduced in the United Kingdom. Mobility among the Asian countries is increasing but still very limited; countries like India draw students from about one hundred countries but in a few disciplines only.

The changing economic development in the world will necessarily affect Asian educational scene and highlights the need for intense student mobility so as to bring about a greater awareness, particularly at the higher education level about the cultures of the world. Political and economic strategies play an important role in cross-border education. Countries within Asia have a tremendous scope to open their institutions to foreign students. A new trend of students exchange within Asia (China, Korea, Japan) is emerging. While the number of Asian students studying in Western countries continue to increase there is also increased student mobility within Asia. This trend will not only expose its students to diverse cultures but would also improve the financial position of educational institutions within the region and in the world. This will also usher a new era in socio-political and economic cooperation specifically between Asian Countries. However, issues of quality of education service providers in the region, cultural and demographic concerns also need to be considered while increasing student mobility not only in Asia but in other parts of the world. There is scope for increased academic cooperation within the Asian countries. Since increasing number of students from developing countries have been moving to developed countries, in particular to USA, these countries also need to encourage their students to be mobile and move to developing countries to understand their culture, traditions, political and economic position. This will ultimately help them to have increased academic and social collaboration.

Bibliography

Altbach, Philip G. (2004), The Past and Future of Asian Universities, Twenty-First Century Challenges in Altbach, Philip G & Toru Umakoshi (2004), Asian Universities: Historical Perspectives and Contemporary Challenges, The John Hopkins University Press, Baltimore and London, pp.13-32.

Altbach, P.G. (1980). University reform: An international perspective. AAHE-ERIC/Higher Education Research Report No. 10. Washington, DC: ERIC Clearinghouse on Higher Education.

British Council East Asian Student Mobility Project Report (2008), International Student Mobility in East Asia: Executive Summary, prepared by JWT Education, pp.6-8.

Chandler, A (1989), Obligation or Opportunity: Foreign Study Policy in Six major Receiving Countries, Institute of International Education, New York.

Commonwealth Secretariat (1992), Student Mobility in the Context of International Cooperative Programme in Study Mobility, Commonwealth Report of a Workshop in National University of Singapore, 7-10 April, Commonwealth Secretariat, p.12.

Cummings (1992), Encyclopedia of Higher Education, Clark, Burton R and Guy R Neate (ed), Vol.2, Pergamon Press, UK.

Encyclopedia of Higher Education (1992), Clark, Burton R and Guy R Neate (ed), Vol.2, Pergamon Press, UK.

Global Education Digest 2005-Comparative Education Statistics Across the World, UNESCO Institute for Statistics, Montreal, 2005, p. 106

Goodwin, C., Nach, M. (1988), Student Mobility, Encyclopedia of Higher Education (1992)

Kazuo Kuroda (2007), International Student Mobility for the Formation of an East Asian Community, Graduate School of Asia Pacific Studies, Waseda University, January, p.3

Knight, J (2007), Implications of Cross-border Education and GATS for the Knowledge Enterprise" submitted to UNESCO Forum on Higher Education, Research and Knowledge

Kuroda, Kazuo (2007), International Student Mobility for the Formation of an East Asian Community, Waseda University, January, p.3.

Larsen, K., Martin, J. and Morris, R (2002), Trade in educational services: trends and issues, The World Economy, 25(6), pp.849-868.

Lee Hyun-Chong (2001), Universities Going with the 21st Century", Seoul, Mineum Publisher

Liz Gooch (2009), More Asian Universities Cast a Net for Foreign Students, The New York Times http://www.nytimes.com/2009/09/19/world/asia/19iht-study.html?_r=1&ref=asia &pagewa accessed on 10.9.2009.

Malik, A.K. (1998), Student Mobility between Europe and Asia in Chopra, H.S. (ed), India and the European Union into the 21st Century, Indian Council of World Affairs, New Delhi.

Meek, Lynn V. (2007), Internationalisation of Higher Education and the Australian Higher Education Research, in: Meek, Lynn V., Teichler, Ulrich, Kearney, Mary-Louise (ed.)(2009), Higher Education, Research and Innovation: Changing Dynamics, Report on the UNESCO Forum on Higher Education, Research and Knowledge 2001-2009, International Centre for Higher Education Research Kassel, 2009, Chapter 4, Changing Challenges of Academic Work: Concepts and Observations by Ulrich Teichler and Yasemin Yagci, p.89.

Meek, Lynn V., Teichler, Ulrich, Kearney, Mary-Louise (ed.)(2009), Higher Education, Research and Innovation: Changing Dynamics, Report on the UNESCO Forum on Higher Education, Research and Knowledge 2001-2009, International Centre for Higher Education Research Kassel, 2009, p.89.

Melisa Bank et. al. (2007) Global Student Mobility : An Australian Perspective.

Min, Weifang (2004) Chinese Higher Education: The Legacy of the Past and the Context of the Future quoted by Sugimura, Miki (2008) op. cit.

Observatory on Borderless Higher Education (2006), Branch Campus Update available www.obhe.ac.uk.

Observatory on Borderless Higher Education (OBHE) , March 2007, p.1.

OECD (2006), Education at a glance, Paris: OECD

OECD (2008), Education at Glance, Chapter C: Access to Education, Participation and Progression, p.352.

Selvaratnam, V (1986), Higher Education Overseas: Growing External and Internal Constraints on Commonwealth South Sending Countries; New Directions for Commonwealth Student Mobility – A Pan-Commonwealth Experts Meeting, New Delhi, 27-31 January, Commonwealth Secretariat.

Shin-who, Kang (2008), Koreans Studying in US Continue to Rise, 19.11.2008 (http:www.koreatimes.co.kr/www/news/include/print.asp?newsIdx=34685 accessed on 14.7.2009.

Stella, Antony and Gnanam, A (2005), Cross-border Higher Education in India: False understandings and true overestimates, Quality in Higher Education, 11:3, 227-337 pp.231-232.

Sugimura, Miki (2008), International Student Mobility and Asian Higher Education Framework for Global Network, Paper for Asia-Pacific Sub-regional Preparatory Conference for the 2009 World Conference on Higher Education, 24-26 September, 2008, Macau, PR China.

Varghese, N.V. (2008), Globalisation of Higher Education and Cross-Border Student Mobility, International Institute for Educational Planning, pp.20-21.

CHAPTER 20

REVISITING THE BANYAN TREE CLASSROOM
A Prognosis for Future

AMITA SINGH

Introduction: Governance a Plea for Exploring Human Capabilities

There is no denying the fact that governance is more about human ability to explore original solutions rather than hierarchical controls and imitative therapies. Then, good governance would be more an enterprise of those who dare to undertake risks for innovating processes in place of bland and repetitive search for best practices and quick solutions. Yet, this quality of human capital which contains the spark of originality is rarely encouraged in government as a result innovations remain trapped and locked within a placid or authoritative administration. Weak capacities thereafter, becomes the most sustaining factor for authoritative bureaucracy.

Human capital is largely locked because despite the apt use of 'governance' as a metaphor to replace 'administrative incapacities' concealed within the claustrophobic deliberativeness of bureaucracy, most decisions affecting human lives are generated in situ. The framework of hierarchy neglects originality and expertise hence governance is likely to be achieved only through the blunting of the hierarchical pyramid. This slippage from the original intent behind the idea of governance is effectively maintained through an educational system dipped into rote learning and memorisation of best practices. The tendency to remain clustered within the hierarchical pyramid is also sustained through inability of the administrator to process the barrage of asymmetrical information into required solutions. A simplistic understanding to success in government has been the administrator's ability to bring more cash through effective marketing of programmes before international donors. During this past decade Asia-Pacific has been xenophobic about its accumulated wealth and least bothered for the lack of imagination, creative solutions and sustainable initiatives. Large scale digitalisation, e-strategies and Internet applications have opened up global knowledge gates but reduced relevant individual experience. There is a clear lack of innovative enterprise or the capacity to create it and very few regions have actually achieved transforming solutions. Ironically, global interaction has brought immense opportunities for ordinary people but for the lack of administrative capacity are being lost.

This paper is a plea for the need of originality in making governance sustainable rather than continuing it as an experiment of technology and accounting from developed nations. The capacity building efforts have quite substantially generated heightened interest in technology, engineering and management . One can see the stampede of private investors for undertaking programmes for infrastructural modernisation in these specific areas. Sadly enough, Social Sciences have taken a backseat as being completely out of focus in solving problems of the under-privileged and livelihood generation challenges. Economics has emerged as the new anchor of governance. It is rarely asked if the long theorems and graphical presentations are asserting to re-establish a neo-sanskritisation of the old economic order which helped the elites to rule the world of ordinary people. In the last two decades there has been sufficient emphasis upon improving education at every level starting from pre-school to the universities. Many inexpensive reforms have alerted the lethargic, apathetic and the ignorant in education yet the delivery of quality teaching continues to plague this sector as much as in the past. The disjunction of classroom teaching to the real world problems existing outside the classroom continues till today even though the challenge today is all about creative partnerships for sustainable well being.

As a plea for re-introducing the principles of equity and fairness in the governance of human capital the process begins with 'Unlocking Human Capital'[1]. The most powerful phenomenon which obstructs the liberation of human capacities is the practice of dividing society on grounds of class, caste, creed, race and gender. It may help yield power to some elites for a short while but in the long run it does irreparable harm to the whole society by preventing human psyche from raising meaningful partnerships, work as a team and strengthen the competitive edge of society. The ghost of equity and fairness has haunted the oriental society from time immemorial. The two leading flag-marchers of high growth rate in Asia Pacific, India and China may continue to boast about their civilisations being more than 5000 years old, they cannot have much to share on bridging gulf with the poor and non-elites in their governance which respects the two basic principles. Very meagre amount of grassroot research goes into problem solving and remains confined to the collection of secondary information obtained from the NGOs and local government agencies. Consequently, even in some of the top most research universities students are found struggling to transcend condescending academic bureaucracy and set free the wings of learning. Wherever, discrimination remains unresolved quick short term solutions continue to ruin long term national performance. Very few academicians are able to see the world beyond the doctrines of meritocracy.

Bringing reforms through 'unlocking human capital' does not need high investment but may deliver in many quality ways to strengthen society and its advancement. Thus one may be tempted to call it a banyan tree classroom, where the banyan tree represents a tree of knowledge which in ancient scriptures were used by the knowledgeable teachers for imparting true learning through a union of mind, body and soul in full consonance with its modest and pro-poor ethos and environment. This paper aspires to make a strong argument in support of relevant education which builds up human capacity to find innovative solutions to problems of governance.

Relevant Learning and the Banyan Tree Classroom:

Ancient Oriental literature is replete with traditional education passed from the master sages to pupils and downwards into generations following them. A banyan tree demonstrates a tradition of learning which is an interaction of life experience , open deliberation as it has no boundaries, equitable as one's place under the tree is not demarcated on eligibility but the desire to learn. Thus banyan tree classroom supposedly inculcates courage in expressing one's opinion and respect for diverse views. Teaching is transparent and content is not imported from those unrelated to problems. The banyan tree classroom may not be the most appropriate arrangement for resolving complexities of global and trans-boundary complexities of governance but it remains the foundation of the unadulterated strategies of learning. Recently, a veteran educationist from USA Samuel W. Micklus who is President of 'Creative Competitions' and the Executive Director of the 'Odyssey of the Mind' conducted workshops in 27 countries across the world on 'revisiting learning and classroom lessons'. He admitted that the existing examination system does not have the ability to evaluate knowledge since much of the learning is based upon rote system and learning by memorisation rather than learning through ground based problem solving training. (Source: IANS, 2010 on visit to the Ryan International School in Delhi)

Many scholars like Alfred Marshall who have a substantial influence upon the theory of governance have suggested de-sanskritisation of knowledge for the welfare of ordinary people. He clearly suggested, 'the study of the causes of poverty is the study of the causes of the degradation of a large part of mankind.'[2] Like the use of Sanskrit in ancient Indian learning which kept a large majority of ordinary people uneducated, Mathematics in Economic theory kept relevant solutions outside the understanding of laymen. Marshall[3] has conveyed some relevant learning material to contemporary economists. In his letter to A.C.Pigou he suggested ways to make learning relevant and problem solving;

(1) Use mathematics as shorthand language, rather than as an engine of inquiry.
(2) Keep to them till you have done.
(3) Translate into English.
(4) Then illustrate by examples that are important in real life.
(5) Burn the mathematics.
(6) If you can't succeed in 4, burn 3. This I do often. (Buchholz 1990, 151).

The problem of effective governance is the problem of unlocking human knowledge from the cudgels of elite literature and making it relevant towards transformation of ordinary lives.

Strengthening Equity and Fairness in the Learning Curriculums;

Divisions have only been deepening as Asia-Pacific societies become affluent in contemporary times. China declared in 2007 that only ten percent of the population remains poor yet data on inequality and social unrest indicates that Chinese society has become more iniquitous after economic reforms to reduce poverty[4]. Dennis Tao Yang

(May,1999:pp.306-310) found that since 1978, economic reforms have deepened inequality in China. Its Gini coefficient increased from 28.2 in 1981 to 38.8 in 1995[5]. Another study by Azizur Khan and Carl Riskin (1998) suggest a much higher Gini ratio of 45.2 in 1995 which far surpasses the whole of Asia Pacific in deepening divides within an affluent society. Recent meeting of the China's National People's Congress Premier Wen Jiabao's greatest concern is widening inequality. In view of more than 100,000 demonstrations every year he warned that more efforts are needed to overcome it. (The Japan Times, March 27,2010, China's Leaders Walk a Fine Line, Tokyo). Growing affluence has weakened the concern for inequality in governance and as analyzed by Galbraith, "The concern for inequality and deprivation had vitality so long as the many suffered while the few had much". (Galbraith, 1998: p.239). Galbraith further found that inequality declines as an issue in a society where most people have much even though some have much more than any of them.

Beyond economic determinants of the causes of inequality, 'caste' exists in India as a historical fact of Hindu society. India has a very powerful caste system, unique in many ways from the rest of the region but an additional armoury in the hands of the affluent to control knowledge and wealth. While caste (discriminated castes are referred to as Scheduled Caste or SC, Scheduled Tribes or ST and Other Backward Classes or OBC) is prohibited by law and the Constitution it is practiced in subtle ways. So deep is its impact that it pervades some of the apex institutions of governance such as the Supreme Court. In 1998 the President of India, K.R. Narayanan, made an extraordinary comment on one file relating to appointments of judges to the Supreme Court: "While recommending the appointment of Supreme Court Judges, it would be consonant with constitutional principles and the nation's social objectives if persons belonging to weaker sections of society like SCs and STs, who comprise 25 per cent of the population, and women are given due consideration." (*Kutty*, 1999). In sixty years of independence and Constitutional remedies to discrimination, Justice Ratnavel Pandian in the famous Advocates on Record Case (1993) lamented about the prejudice occurring against women, Other Backward Classes, Scheduled Castes, and Scheduled Tribes in the appointment of judges to the Supreme Court. A study of the recruitment process under Article 16(4) which enabled the State to make provisions for the reservation of judges from the backward classes in the Supreme Court indicates discrimination in the appointment of judges. Even the former Chief Justice K.G. Balakrishnan, who belongs to the Scheduled Castes category, had been initially rejected for elevation to the Supreme Court. He was finally elevated to the Supreme Court in 2002. (Singh, 2010)

Human Capital remains lodged in a divisive and discriminatory society.

Capacity, Skills and Efficiency

The final section of this paper is about capacities, skills and training which have become the lighthouses of income generation. A conventional understanding about these three challenges is referred to as a process of empowerment. As the meaning of empowerment expands to an ability to resolve disputes, legal literacy and leadership qualities so does the conventional parameters of capacity, skills and training changes. 'Capacity' refers to 'managing change' , 'skills' indicate special training to address a particular problem and 'efficiency' is more than the number of pieces produced in a particular time span. The substantive change which has influenced understanding about the three terms moves in the direction of a rights based approach , which look at them as indispensable requirements of human needs fulfilment or well being. These are partnership ability, team building and The Hot Spots Movement led by the Human Capital Leadership Institute at Singapore selects four critical capabilities as basic requirements of improving human capital;

- Developing a leadership cadre and talent pool adept at collaboration and high value networking
- Building and supporting valuable networks, communities and ecosystems
- Supporting teams and collaborative working in an increasingly virtual context
- Helping critical organisational functions understand future needs and build essential competencies for the future

(http://www.singaporehcsummit.com/)

Capability approach explains how human abilities remain locked when individuals do not get access to their entitlements. While goods can bring enhanced comfort in human lives they cannot be treated as a boost to capacities. Like inequalities, deprivation of required goods such as education, health and livelihood suppresses human capital from taking flight. Sen (1981) and Dreze and Sen (1989) distinguish between production and exchange entitlements. While the former refers to the fruits of one's labour such as farm produce or wages of a labourer, the latter is the right to trade through one's production entitlements and control other commodities in the market. In 1990, Sen moves still further to say that institutional as well as economic factors influence entitlements. This brings in a wide array of factors such as traditions, customary arrangements, rules, laws, programmes and welfare measures into the parameter of entitlements. This widening of approach enabled Sen to zero down on one basic capability of 'equality of opportunity' and capabilities become a matter of choice for every individual enabling higher level of activity and multi-functionality. Programmes such as National Rural Employment Guarantee Scheme in India indicates a change in the traditional model of understanding capacities as it has been able to balance entitlements with human choices in the wide array of legal and welfare measures. This enables the poor to exchange the wages for education (Sarva Shiksha Abhiyaan or Education for All) and health (National Rural Health Mission). The objective of NAREGA moves beyond wages and payments to create a general well being of the poor. Sen however, did not develop a normative argument for social justice hence Martha Nussbaum (2000: 78-80 and 2003:40-43) adds to it the strong case in favour of Constitutional guarantees as an assurance for social justice. (See Srinivasan) In the wide ranging discourse on capabilities the Basic Needs Approach of Streetan (1979, 1981) which confines development to the fulfilment of basic needs is better equipped with a clear-cut and simplistic formula for the bureaucracy to follow. Why, the formula fails to perform is an explanation which grasps Sen as well as Nussbaum on their elaboration of capabilities which generate and unlock human capital.

Conclusion

Can diverse people having different backgrounds come together to learn? A Banyan Tree Classroom is a hypothetical design of the most equitable and open platform to learn and build capacities as it relates teaching to the real world problems. Human capital remains locked in poverty, lack of skills and in divided societies of Asia. An estimated 1.4 billion people were still living in extreme poverty in 2005. This , when added to the globally turbulent and unstable economy of present times, poverty becomes entrenched into national psyche. For lack of policies in the management of human capital it is human entrepreneurial contribution to society which is most likely to generate sustainable wealth for the nation.

To make human capital soar the sky without obstructions and inhibitions, education need to be treated as emancipating and transformatory. However, education remains the first step towards unlocking human capital. It is important to guarantee entitlements, build capacities and provide access and guarantee of Constitutional rights to citizens. The Banyan tree should be revived to ensure true learning in a particular direction.

References

"Unlocking Human Capital: Entitlements and Governance, A Case Study". Second Administrative Reforms Commission, Second Report July 2006, Government of India, Delhi. http://arc.gov.in
Galbraith, John Kenneth, 1998, The Affluent Society,Mariner Books, USA.
Hot Spots Movement , Singapore (http://www.singaporehcsummit.com/)
Advocates on Record Association v. Union of India Case 1993(5) SC 479.
Khan, Azizur and Carl Riskin,1998, 'Income and Inequality in China: Composition,Distribution and Growth of Household Income,1988 to 1995' *China Quarterly,* June 1998.
Nussbaum, Martha., 2000, Women and Human Development: The Capabilities Approach (Cambridge: Cambridge University Press).
Nussbaum, Martha., 2003, "Capabilities as Fundamental Entitlements: Sen and Social Justice" in Feminist Economics vol 9 (2 – 3), 33 – 59.
Sen, A.K.., 1981, Poverty and Famines: An Essay on Entitlement and Deprivation, (London:Oxford Clarendon Press)
Sen, A.K., 1989, Women's Survival as a Development Problem, *Bulletin of the American Academy of Arts and Sciences,* Vol 43,pp14-29.
Singh,Amita 2010, Hinduism: Contemporary Expressions, Palmer,M. (ed.)Blackwell Publishers, USA(in publication)
Marshall, A. 1927, *Principles of Economics,* 8th edition, Macmillian, London, p.2.
Buchholz, Todd G. 1990. *New Ideas from Dead Economists.* Plume Books, London.p.151
Zhou,Xueguang 2000, 'Economic Transformation and Income Inequality of Urban China, Evidence from Panel Data' *The American Journal of Sociology,*Vol. 105,No. 4,Jan. pp.113.
Yang, Dennis Tao, 1999, 'Urban Biased Policies and Rising Income Inequality in China', *The American Economic Review,*Vol.89, No.2, pp.306-310, May.
Streetan 1979, 'Basic Needs, Premises and Promises', *Journal of Policy Modelling*
Streetan 1981,*First Things First*, OUP, New York.
Kutty,V. K. Madhavan, Behind the Leak, *Frontline* 16 (3), 30 Jan. - 12 Feb. 1999. Retrieved 24 February 2006.
*The Japan Times,*March 27,2010,China's Leaders Walk a Fine Line,Tokyo

About the Contributors

Norsiah Abdul Hamid is currently a Senior Lecturer at Media Technology Program, Universiti Utara Malaysia, Malaysia. She received her Bachelor of IT (Hons) from Universiti Utara Malaysia (1998) and MSc in Communications Studies from University of Leeds, United Kingdom (2001). She is currently undertaking her doctoral degree at Universiti Kebangsaan Malaysia focusing on the Knowledge Society. Her research interest is in social media and computing, knowledge society, women studies, and impact of ICT to society.

Halimah Badioze Zaman is currently a Professor in Multimedia Technology, Universiti Kebangsaan Malaysia, Malaysia. She is the Head of ICT cluster in Malaysian National Professors' Council. She received her PhD degree in Information Science from Loughborough University, United Kingdom in 1983. Her research interest covers 3D multimedia, multimedia for special learners, voice recognition for visual impaired learners, augmented reality, virtual reality and virtual learning environments. She is a member of IEEE.

Chamila Jayashantha is a development consultant in Sri Lanka. He is also a visiting scholar of University of Colombo and University of Kelaniya. Development Communication and Rural Development are among his top research interests. He has contributed more than ten national and international publications with his academic writing. Presently Mr. Chamila is pursuing his doctoral studies in affiliation with University of Hyderabad, India.

Eleanor E. Nicolas is University Extension Specialist IV at the Center for Leadership, Citizenship and Democracy of the National College of Public Administration and Governance, University of the Philippines. She is presently pursuing her doctorate in social development at the College of Social Work and Community Development of the University of the Philippines. Her research interests are in the areas of leadership, civic and citizenship education, social development policies, social protection and people's empowerment.

Aristeo C. Salapa, is a graduate professor, Master of Public Administration and Local and Regional Governance, Department of Governance Studies, College of Governance, Business and Economics, University of Southeastern Philippines, Davao City. His interest includes development planning, organisational analysis and development, community organizing and development topics for youth, women, indigenous peoples and governance. He is a member of Philippine Society for Public Administrators. He has presented a research paper for EROPA conference in 2008 as well as receiving the Raul P. De Guzman award.

Tek Nath Dhakal is Professor at Central Department of Public Administration, Tribhuvan University in Nepal. He conducted researches on the role of NGOs, governance, institutional analysis, and community development. He has published 3 Books and 3 Edited Volumes both from Nepal and abroad. In addition, he has also contributed 14 Journal Articles, 10 Edited Volume articles, 20 other articles published both from Nepal and abroad. Besides he also served as an editor of Nepalese Journal of Public Policy and Governance, and also presents papers in different national and international forums and conferences.

Faraha Nawaz is a lecturer in the department of Public Administration, Rajshahi University, Bangladesh. She has conducted various independent researches and published different scholarly articles in national and international journals.

Eduardo T. Gonzalez, is Professor, Asian Center, University of the Philippines. He is Senior Editor, Asian Politics & Policy, a peer-reviewed international journal published quarterly by Wiley-Blackwell, Senior Fellow, Development Academy of the Philippines and Honorary Fellow, Asian Productivity Organization. His areas of research interests include public policy, public administration and governance, institutional economics, political economy, urban and regional development. He has 3 international journal publications, 6 national journal publications and authored about 20 books.

Raudah Danila is senior lecturer, College of Business of Universiti Utara Malaysia located in Kedah, Malaysia. Her research interest includes accounting information systems, audit and management accounting. She has published a paper in Asian Review of Accounting Journal. She has also co-authored two undergraduate text book on Accounting Information Systems and Management Accounting published by Prentice Hall and Thomson Learning. She is also a member of National Institute of Accountants of Australia.

Ishtiaq Jamil is Associate Professor, Department of Administration and Organization Theory, University of Bergen, Norway. His research interests include administrative culture, public policy, governance, and trust in public and political institutions. He is currently leading two projects on public policy and governance in South Asia. He publishes widely in the *International Political Science Review, Asian Survey, Journal of Commonwealth and Comparative Politics, International Review of Sociology, Journal of Contemporary South Asia,* and *Journal of Middle Eastern and South Asian Studies.*

Pranab Kumar Panday is Associate Professor and Chair, Department of Public Administration, University of Rajshahi, Bangladesh. His main research interests include Public Policy and Governance (both Urban and Local Governance), Public Sector Reforms, and Gender and Governance in South Asia. He publishes widely in the *Asian Survey, International Political Science Review, Local Government Studies, Journal of Commonwealth and Comparative Politics, the Public Organization Review, the Asia- Pacific Journal of Social Work and Development, the Asian and Pacific Migration Journal,* and *Asia- Pacific Journal of Public Administration.*

Lipi Mukhopadhyay, Associate Professor at the Indian Institute of Public Administration, New Delhi, India. Her area of research interests include Community Psychology ,gender issues in development, tribal development, disaster prevention and others .She has about fifty academic publication in national/international journals/books and a book on 'Tribal Women in Development'. She was awarded the special prize for writing critical comments on disaster mitigation by Cranfield University, U.K. and is accredited trainer on ToT, University of Slough, U.K.

Sheila Rai is an Assistant Professor in the Department of Political Science, University of Rajasthan, Jaipur (India). *'Political Thought- Indian and Western', 'Indian Government and Politics'* are the special areas of her interest. Besides having authored five books she has more than twenty research papers published in national and international publications on subjects related to Gandhian philosophy, public administration, gender and other contemporary issues. Amongst eminent positions held by her in national and international associations, she is presently the *Vice Principal of Rajasthan College* and *Editor of 'Rajyashti'* the quarterly journal of Rajasthan Political Science Association.

Shah Mohammad Sanaul Hoque, presently working in the Bangladesh Public Administration Training Centre, belongs to the Administration Service of the Bangladesh Civil Service. He is the author of many academic articles, published both in national and international levels.

Fatema-Tu-Zohra Binte Zaman is currently working as full time permanent lecturer of Psychology at the Department of Psychology, Jagannath University, Dhaka, Bangladesh. During her studies and profession she had completed few research papers and published articles.

Sylvia Yambem, is research scholar, Centre for the Study of Law and Governance, Jawaharlal Nehru University, New Delhi. Her area of interest includes public policy and governance. She is also the Associate Editor of Development North East and is presently the Executive Research Coordinator, NAPSIPAG.

M. Abdul Wahhab, Ph D is Professor, Department of Public Administration, University of Chittagong, Bangladesh. Professor Wahhab joined Chittagong University in 1981 and became Professor in 1985. He chaired the Department of Public Administration for three years from 1985-1988. He has three books and 34 publications to his credit including the present one. He is a NAPSIPAG member and regular paper contributor to its annual conference. He is also a member of ASAA. His current research interests are globalization, governance, local government, constitutional law and women.

Suman Sharma is Associate Professor, Department of Political Science, Motilal Nehru College, University of Delhi. She has a PhD in South Asian Studies from Jawaharlal Nehru University. She has written research papers and articles on South Asian Politics and Regional Co-operation in South Asia. She has also authored the book India and SAARC.

Baiju K.C is Associate Professor, Development Economics, Institute of Management in Government (IMG), Govt. of Kerala. His area of interest includes Development economics and the Kerala economy. He has 17 academic publications in his name.

Rumki Basu is Professor of Public Administration, Jamia Millia University, India Her area of interest includes public policy and administration, political economy of development in India. She has 7 books, 25 articles, in her name. She was honoured with the ICSSR Teacher Fellowship award.

Maria Clarisa R. Sia is University Researcher IV at the NCPAG, University of the Philippines. Her field of interests are policy development and advocacy, program planning and management and corruption prevention. Her two latest published works funded by UNDP are on human rights based approach in development (HRBAD) and governance on public enterprise and an orientation manual on mainstreaming the HRBAD in the development processes. At present, she is a Technical Working Group Member of the Center for Asian Integrity, Board Member of the College Foundation and a doctoral student in Social Development Program, NCPAG.

Achal Kumar Malik is currently working as Registrar, Ambedkar University, Delhi. He has his Ph.D. from Jawaharlal Nehru University, and holds master's degree in Public Administration, MBA, PG Diploma in Journalism. He attended a six month Course of Specialisation in the Programme for Development Administration (Rome) and Advanced Training European Community Institutions (Brussels). His areas of interest are e-governance, educational administration, educational finance, international collaboration. He has a variety of published work to his credit.

Amita Singh, Professor and Chairperson, Centre for the Study of Law and Governance, Jawaharlal Nehru University, New Delhi, India and Secretary General NAPSIPAG. Working in the area of New Public Management led reforms and pro-poor governance she has authored four books, edited three and published more than a dozen research papers in peer reviewed Journals.

About NAPSIPAG

Network of Asia Pacific Schools and Institutes of Public Administration and Governance which is commonly known as NAPSIPAG was launched in 2004 as the first non-west platform for governance research in the Asia-Pacific. During the Miami Conference of the American Society for Public Administration the Asian scholars realised the disconnect and the distancing of the larger discipline of public administration with the realities of the Asia Pacific governance. Time had arrived for Public Administration to break through the cage of American exceptionalism and take up more serious comparative research within the Asia Pacific region.

Asian Development Bank (Manila) under the leadership of their Director (Education) Dr. Jak Jabes and after him Mr. Raza Ahmad supported NAPSIPAG for the first three years and held its first conference at Kuala Lumpur hosted by INTAN of the Government of Malaysia. As ADB support waned in the third year, NAPSIPAG had already consolidated itself as a group of more than hundred plus institutional members across the region. In 2005 Beijing (China National School of Administration), 2006 Sydney (University of Sydney), 2007 Manila (National College of Public Administration and Governance, University of the Philippines), 2008 New Delhi (Jawaharlal Nehru University) and 2009 Malaysia (Universiti Utara Malaysia), NAPSIPAG marched forward with the support of public sector management and research institutions and universities. The current year with the historic annual meeting to be held at Trivandrum, Kerala, in partnership with the Institute of Management in Government NAPSIPAG is closer to its desired objective of working closely with administrative departments towards the Millennium Development Goals. Hence the appropriate theme, "Reaching Out to People: Achieving MDGs through Innovative Public Service Delivery". In the last seven years NAPSIPAG has undertaken several concerns of governance in the region and published 7 volumes of research papers by the Asia Pacific scholars.

In 2009, the Secretariat moved out of INTAN to Jawaharlal Nehru University (JNU) and since then the NAPSIPAG experts are also invited to provide advisory and consultative services to fellow developing countries. The South Asia Chapter of NAPSIPAG held its first meeting at JNU in 2006 and produced two volumes, Governance and the Cage of Best Practices (PHI-PUBLISHERS) Governance and Access to Justice (same publ.). The next meeting was held at BPTAC and BUP (Dhaka) in March 2010 on the concerns of e-governance and 'Digital Bangladesh Programme'.

The core of NAPSIPAG research are the public sector programmes for the people of Asia Pacific. The process of formulation is disjunctive and disconnected with the realities of implementation but governments fail to undertake required feedback and evaluation due to the low priority for democratization in the Asia Pacific region. This remains a pressing concern for NAPSIPAG.

The present Chairperson of NAPSIPAG is Dr. Sharif As-Saber from the Monash University, Melbourne, Australia and Secretary General Prof. Amita Singh, currently Chairperson of the Centre for the Study of Law and Governance, Jawaharlal Nehru University. It works through a five nation Steering Committee and three international research advisors. The Technical Head is Mr. Chetan Sharma of Datamation Foundation, Delhi and the Executive Research Coordinator is Ms. Sylvia Yambem from JNU. NAPSIPAG events can be reached at:
http://www.napsipag-research.com/events.asp.Email:< jnu.napsipag2008@gmail.com >.

During the LMI process, a laser beam with a diameter of 3 mm irradiated the Al substrate's surface, the W particles were injected into the tail of the laser molten pool, and argon with a flow rate of 4 L/min was used as the delivering and shielding gas. As the laser head scanned, the W particles were captured by the molten pool, and a W/Al composite layer was finally formed, with an overlapping ratio of 50%. In order to investigate the effect of powder feeding rate on laser melt injection, the powder feeding rate was set to 7 g/min, 10 g/min, 13 g/min, or 16 g/min, and the laser power was 3000 W, while the laser scan speed was 700 mm/min. The specimens were machined using an electric spark CNC machine (DK7750, Taizhou Zhongxing CNC Machine Tool Plant, Taizhou, China), and transverse sections of the samples were ground, polished, and then etched with Keller's reagent for 2–3 s at room temperature. The microstructure of the W/Al composite layer was characterized by scanning electron microscopy (SEM, JSM7600F, Shanghai Baihe instrument Technology Co., Ltd., Shanghai, China) and energy-dispersive spectroscopy (EDS, IncaXMax50, Oxford instruments co., Ltd., Oxford, UK). The chemical composition and elemental distribution of the W/Al composite layer were analyzed with an electronic probe microanalyzer (EPMA, EPMA-8050G, Shimadzu Corporation of Japan, Shimadzu, Japan) equipped with a wavelength-dispersion spectrum (WDS). The phases in the W/Al composite layer were identified with an X-ray diffraction meter (XRD). The hardness of W/Al composite layer was tested using a microhardness tester (HXD-1000TM, Shanghai changfang optical instrument co., ltd., Shanghai, China) with a t load of 2.94 N and holding time of 20 s. The hardness distribution was measured along its depth direction. Room-temperature sliding wear was tested using an abrasion tester (UMT TriboLab, Brooke Technology Co., Ltd., Billerica, MA, USA), as shown in Figure 3, where a Si_3N_4 ball with a diameter of 6.3 mm was slid on the specimen with a test load of 15 N and speed of 10 mm/s, the wear length was 5 mm, and the test duration was 20 min. Each group of tests was repeated three times, and the micromorphology of the wear samples was characterized using a confocal microscope (KEYENCE, VK-X2500, Keens Japan Ltd., Osaka, Japan).

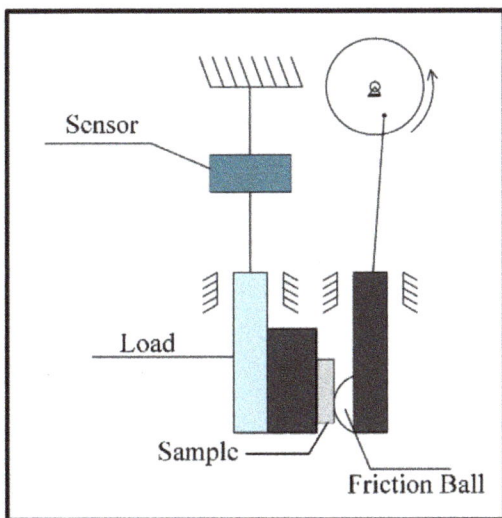

Figure 3. Equipment for the wear test.

3. Results

3.1. Microstructure

Figure 4 shows the macroscopic surface and cross-section of the W/Al composite layer with a powder feeding rate of 16 g/min. The XRD results in Figure 5 show that W, Al, and Al_4W are the constituent phases in the W/Al composite layer. The peaks from the aluminum alloy phases are very weak, and the main peak from aluminum is strong in the W/Al composite layer. Figure 6 shows the scanning electron microscopy (SEM) images of the W/Al composite layer. As shown in Figure 6, all of the W/Al composite layers were composed of white particles, dark blocks, and a black matrix. The EPMA results of the W/Al composite layers with powder feeding rates of 7 g/min, 10 g/min, 13 g/min, and 16 g/min are given in Figure 7. The EPMA results show that the composition of the white particles was 100W (at. %), that of the dark block was 79.3Al-20.7W (at. %), and that of the black matrix was 96.5Al-1.3Mg-1.7Zn-0.5Cu (at. %). Based on the EPMA and XRD results, it can be concluded that the white particles are W, the dark blocks are Al_4W, and the black matrix represents aluminum alloys. The fraction of the reinforcing phase is an important factor that affects the performance of the composites layer. Here, the area fraction of W and Al_4W in the W/Al composite layer was measured using Imaging-plus 6.0 software (Pro Plus 6.0, American Media Cybernetics image technology company, Rockville, MD, USA), as shown in Figure 8, and the area fraction of W and Al_4W increased with the increase in the powder feeding rate. When the powder feeding rate was 7 g/min, the area fraction of W particles and Al_4W in the W/Al composite layer was only 6.3% and 14.6%, respectively. As the powder feeding rate increased to 16 g/min, the area fraction of W particles and Al_4W increased to 46.2% and 35.9%, respectively.

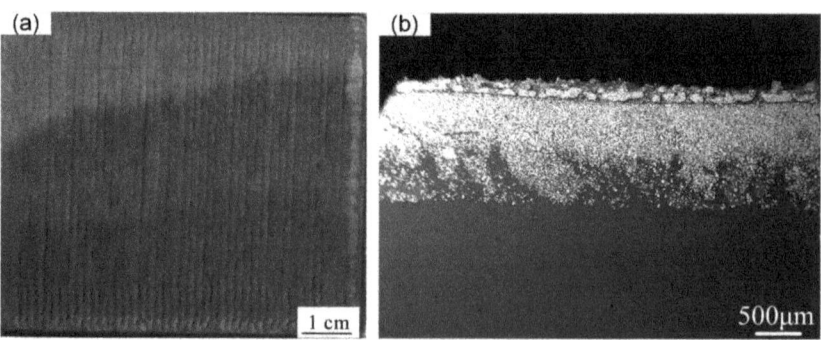

Figure 4. Macroscopic surface (**a**) and cross-section (**b**) of the W/Al composite layer with a powder feeding rate of 16 g/min.

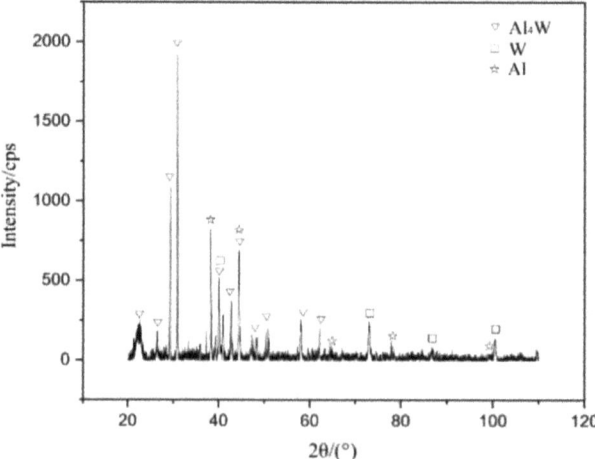

Figure 5. X-ray diffraction spectrum of the W/Al composite layer.

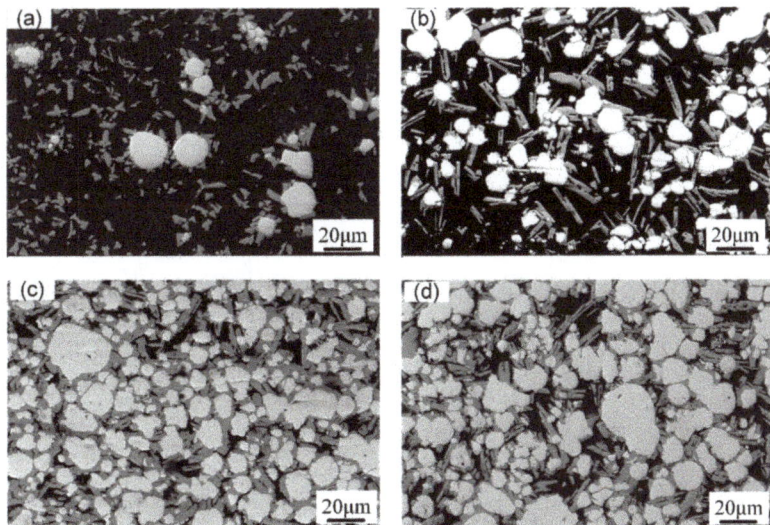

Figure 6. Microstructure of W/Al composite layers with powder feeding rates of (**a**) 7 g/min, (**b**) 10 g/min, (**c**) 13 g/min, and (**d**) 16 g/min.

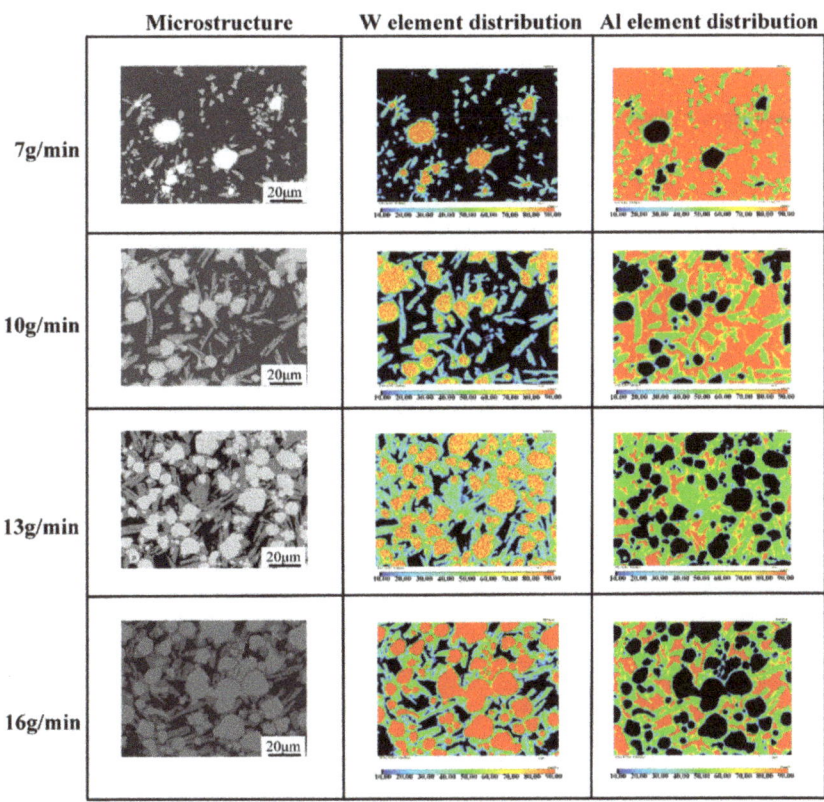

Figure 7. Microstructure and elemental distribution of the W/Al composite layers with powder feeding rates of 7 g/min, 10 g/min, 13 g/min, and 16 g/min.

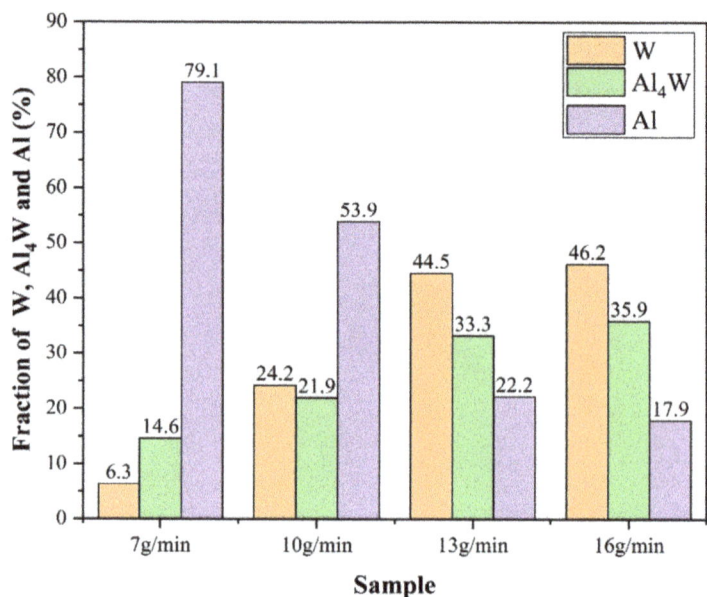

Figure 8. Area fraction of W, Al$_4$W, and Al alloy in the W/Al composite layer.

3.2. Hardness

As shown in Figure 9, the hardness of the W/Al layer increased with the increase in the powder feeding rate. When the powder feeding rate was 7 g/min, the hardness of the W/Al composite layer was almost the same as that of the 7075 Al substrate. As the powder feeding rate increased to 16 g/min, the hardness of the W/Al composite layer could reach up to 350 HV, which is 2.5 times higher than that of the 7075 Al substrate (142.3 HV).

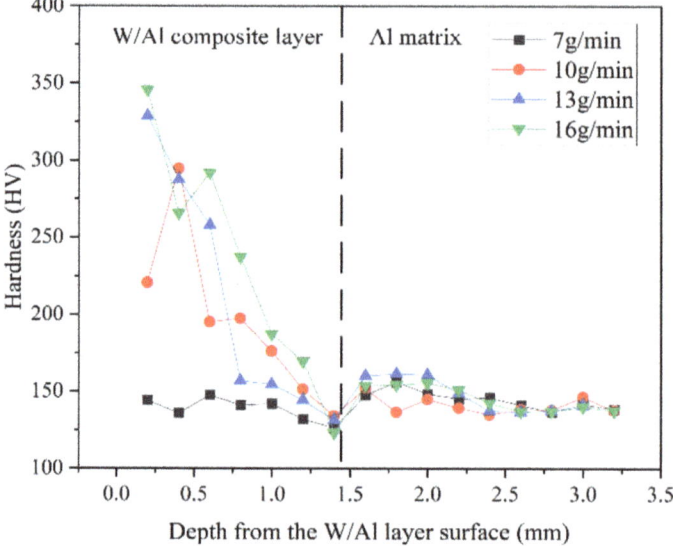

Figure 9. Hardness distribution of the W/Al composite layer.

3.3. Wear

As shown in Figure 10, all of the W/Al composite layers exhibited lower friction coefficients than that of the 7075 Al substrate. The average friction coefficient of the 7075 Al alloy substrate was about 0.442; with the increase in the W powder feeding rate from 7 g/min to 16 g/min, the average friction coefficient decreased from 0.404 to 0.367.

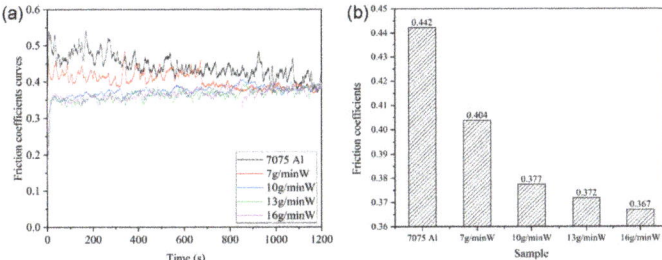

Figure 10. (a) Friction coefficient curves and (b) average friction coefficients of the W/Al composite layers and 7075 Al substrate.

Figure 11 shows the wear surface of all of the samples; as shown in Figure 11a, the abrasion width and depth of the 7075 Al substrate were 1368.4 μm and 114.7 μm, respectively, while all of the W/Al composite layers exhibited lower abrasion width and depth than those of the 7075 Al substrate. With the increase in the W powder feeding rate from 7 g/min to 16 g/min, the average abrasion width decreased from 1102.2 μm to 617.3 μm, and the average abrasion depth decreased from 50.7 μm to 20.7 μm. According to wear rate, $\varepsilon = V/(G \cdot L)$. The wear volume is V, the test load is G, and the wear scar length is L. As shown in Figure 12, all of the W/Al composite layers exhibited better wear resistance than that of the 7075 Al substrate. The wear rate of the 7075 Al alloy substrate was 4.74 mm^3/N m; with the increase in the W powder feeding rate from 7 g/min to 16 g/min, the wear rate decreased from 1.64 mm^3/N m to 0.40 mm^3/N m.

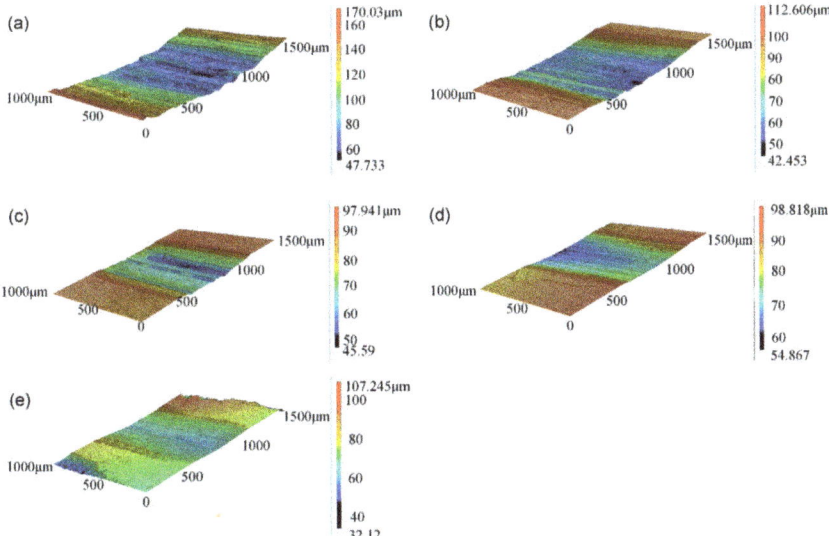

Figure 11. Wear surface morphology of (**a**) 7075 Al alloy and W/Al composite layers with W powder feeding rates of (**b**) 7 g/min, (**c**) 10 g/min, (**d**) 13 g/min, and (**e**) 16 g/min.

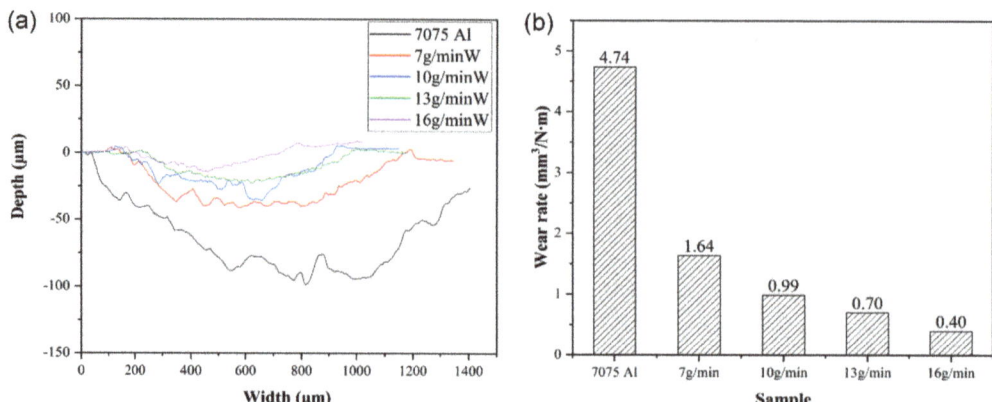

Figure 12. (a) Wear scar distribution curves and (b) wear rates of 7075 Al alloy and W/Al composite layers.

4. Discussion

During the laser melt injection, the W particles enter the high-temperature melt pool, and W atoms diffuse into the laser melt pool. According to the Al–W binary phase diagram, during the cooling process of the melt pool, W particles react with Al solution to form intermetallic compounds. Khoshhal, Niu, and Wang pointed out that Al_4W was first formed due to its low generation enthalpy, and further calculations show that the low generation enthalpy can be attributed to the fact that Al_4W has a smaller n(Ef) (the Fermi level) than $Al_{12}W$ [18–20]. According to the solid–liquid reaction mechanism, Al_4W is formed by a peritectic reaction between W and aluminum at 1327 °C. At the beginning of the laser melting, the liquid will quickly adhere to the surface of the W, forming an adherent layer with a certain concentration gradient, and the concentration of aluminum gradually decreases from the outside to the inside [21,22]. As the Al concentration in the inside layer of the diffusion layer increases, the solute atom W reacts with the solvent atom Al to form an Al_4W intermetallic compound enveloping the W particles [23]. There are also partially escaped W and Al reactions to form free Al_4W intermetallic compounds in the matrix between the W particles. During the process of LMI, the cooling rate is very fast (about 2.8×10^3 °C/s), and there is not enough time for the Al_4W to react with the molten Al and form Al_5W and $Al_{12}W$ [24]. Therefore, the W/Al composite layer consists of W, Al, and Al_4W.

During the process of wear testing, the temperature of the wear sample is raised due to the friction heat. The 7075 Al alloy has low hardness, and strengthens at elevated temperature; when temperature of the Al alloy reaches its flashpoint, the 7075 Al alloy is welded with the Si_3N_4 ceramic ball, and tears under the action of shear force (Figure 13a–c). Thus, the friction coefficient and wear rate of 7075 Al are larger. Compared with the 7075 Al alloy, the W and Al_4W in the W/Al composite layer have higher hardness at elevated temperature, which can enable them to effectively resist the extrusion of the Si_3N_4 ceramic ball, and reduces the wear (Figure 13d–f). Compared with the 7075 Al substrate, the friction coefficient and wear rate of the W/Al composite layer are smaller. This shows that the W/Al composite layer has excellent wear resistance [25].

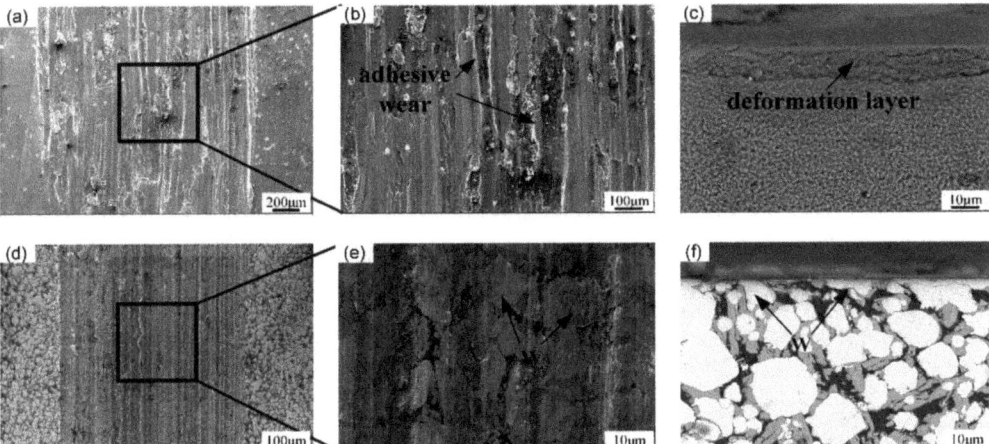

Figure 13. Wear surface (**a,b,d,e**) and cross-sectional view (**c,f**) of 7075 Al alloys (**a–c**) and W/Al layer with a powder feeding rate of 16 g/min (**d–f**).

5. Conclusions

(1) A W-particle-reinforced Al matrix composite layer without visible metallurgic defects was prepared via laser melt injection on a 7075 Al alloy substrate, and the composite layer consisted of W, Al$_4$W, and Al alloy. The reinforcing phases W and Al$_4$W endowed the composite layer with high hardness and excellent wear resistance.

(2) The SEM results show that the W and Al$_4$W contents in the W/Al composite layer increased with the increase in the W powder feeding rate; the contents of W particles and Al$_4$W were the highest in the W/Al composite layer with a W powder feeding rate of 16 g/min.

(3) With the increase in the W powder feeding rate, the hardness and wear resistance of the W/Al composite layer increased, and the friction coefficient decreased. The hardness of the W/Al composite layer was 1.5–2.5 times higher than that of the 7075 Al. The friction coefficient of the W/Al composite layer was 8.6–17% smaller than that of the 7075 Al, and the wear resistance of the W/Al composite layer was 2.9–11.8 times higher than that of the 7075 Al.

Author Contributions: Conceptualization, D.W.; methodology, Z.X. and D.W.; validation, Z.X. and W.S.; formal analysis, Z.X. and C.T.; investigation, Z.X., P.S. and J.Y.; writing—original draft preparation, Z.X.; writing—review and editing, D.W., Q.H. and X.Z.; supervision, D.W. and X.Z.; funding acquisition, X.Z. All authors have read and agreed to the published version of the manuscript.

Funding: This work was supported by the Key Projects of the National Natural Science Foundation of China (No. 92066201).

Acknowledgments: The authors would like to thank the State Key Laboratory of Material Processing, Die & Mould Technology in HUST, and the Analytical and Testing Centre of HUST for XRD, SEM, and wear tests.

Conflicts of Interest: The authors declare no conflict of interest.

References

1. Gabryelczyk, A.; Ivanov, S.; Bund, A.; Lota, G. Corrosion of aluminium current collector in lithium-ion batteries: A review. *J. Energy Storage* **2021**, *43*, 103226. [CrossRef]
2. Thakur, S.K.; Gupta, M. Improving mechanical performance of Al by using Ti as reinforcement. *Compos. Part A Appl. Sci. Manuf.* **2007**, *38*, 1010–1018. [CrossRef]

3. Freiße, H.; Bohlen, A.; Seefeld, T. Determination of the particle content in laser melt injected tracks. *J. Mater. Process. Technol.* **2019**, *267*, 177–185. [CrossRef]
4. Yin, J.; Zhang, W.; Ke, L.; Wei, H.; Zeng, X. Vaporization of alloying elements and explosion behavior during laser powder bed fusion of Cu–10Zn alloy. *Int. J. Mach. Tools Manuf.* **2021**, *161*, 103686. [CrossRef]
5. Yin, J.; Wang, D.; Yang, L.; Wei, H.; Zeng, X. Correlation between forming quality and spatter dynamics in laser powder bed fusion. *Addit. Manuf.* **2020**, *31*, 100958. [CrossRef]
6. Ayers, J.D.; Tucker, T.R. Particulate-TiC-hardened steel surfaces by laser melt injection. *Thin Solid Film.* **1980**, *73*, 201–207. [CrossRef]
7. Chen, Y.; Liu, D.; Li, F.; Li, L. WC p/Ti–6Al–4V graded metal matrix composites layer produced by laser melt injection. *Surf. Coat. Technol.* **2008**, *202*, 4780–4787. [CrossRef]
8. Ayers, J.D. Modification of metal surfaces by the laser melt-particle injection process. *Thin Solid Film.* **1981**, *84*, 323–331. [CrossRef]
9. Schaefer, R.J.; Tucker, T.R.; Ayers, J.D. Laser surface melting with carbide particle injection. In *Laser and Electron Beam Processing of Materials*; Academic Press: Cambridge, MA, USA, 1980.
10. Ayers, J.D.; Schaefer, R.J.; Robey, W.P. A Laser Processing Technique for Improving the Wear Resistance of Metals. *JOM* **1981**, *33*, 19–23. [CrossRef]
11. Ayers, J.D. Wear behavior of carbide-injected titanium and aluminum alloys. *Wear* **1984**, *97*, 249–266. [CrossRef]
12. Cooper, K.P.; Ayers, J.D. LASER Melt-Particle Injection Processing. *Surf. Eng.* **1985**, *1*, 263–272. [CrossRef]
13. Vreeling, J.A.; Ocelik, V.; Pei, Y.T. Laser melt injection in aluminum alloys: On the role of the oxide skin. *Acta Mater.* **2000**, *48*, 4225–4233. [CrossRef]
14. Wang, H.; Zhao, Q.; Wang, H.; Cui, W.; Yuan, X. Micromechanism characteristics of modified Al-Si coating by laser melt injection CeO_2 nano-particles. *Surf. Coat. Technol.* **2017**, *319*, 88–94. [CrossRef]
15. Rajamure, R.S.; Vora, H.D.; Srinivasan, S.G.; Dahotre, N.B. Laser alloyed Al-W coatings on aluminum for enhanced corrosion resistance. *Appl. Surf. Sci.* **2015**, *328*, 205–214. [CrossRef]
16. Ramakrishnan, A.; Dinda, G.P. Microstructural control of an Al–W aluminum matrix composite during direct laser metal deposition. *J. Alloy. Compd.* **2020**, *813*, 152208. [CrossRef]
17. Bauri, R.; Yadav, D.; Kumar, C.S.; Balaji, B. Tungsten particle reinforced Al 5083 composite with high strength and ductility. *Mater. Sci. Eng. A* **2015**, *620*, 67–75. [CrossRef]
18. Khoshhal, R.; Soltanieh, M.; Mirjalili, M. Formation and growth of titanium aluminide layer at the surface of titanium sheets immersed in molten aluminum. *Iran. J. Mater. Sci. Eng.* **2010**, *7*, 24–31.
19. Niu, H.; Chen, X.Q.; Liu, P.; Xing, W.; Li, Y. Extra-electron induced covalent strengthening and generalization of intrinsic ductile-to-brittle criterion. *Sci. Rep.* **2012**, *2*, 718. [CrossRef]
20. Chan, W.; Liang, S.; Jiang, Y. In-situ fabrication and characteristics of an $Al_4W/Al_{12}W$ composite using infiltration method. *Vacuum* **2018**, *160*, 95–101.
21. Tang, H.G.; Ma, X.F.; Zhao, W.; Yan, X.W.; Hong, R.J. Preparation of W–Al alloys by mechanical alloying. *J. Alloy. Compd.* **2002**, *347*, 228–230. [CrossRef]
22. Raskolenko, L.G.; Gerul'Skii, A.Y. Compounds WAl_4, WAl_3, W_3Al_7, and WAl_2 and Al-W-N combustion products. *Inorg. Mater.* **2008**, *44*, 30–39. [CrossRef]
23. Li, J.; Fei, L.; Hu, K. Preparation of Ni/Al_2O_3 nanocomposite powder by high-energy ball milling and subsequent heat treatment. *J. Mater. Process. Technol.* **2004**, *147*, 236–240. [CrossRef]
24. Li, L.; Wang, D.Z.; Song, W.; Gong, J.; Hu, Q.; Zeng, X. Microstructures and mechanical properties of WC_P/Ti-6Al-4V composite coatings by laser melt injection and laser-induction hybrid melt injection. *Surf. Coat. Technol.* **2020**, *385*, 125371. [CrossRef]
25. Liu, J.; Peng, X.; Liu, X.; Quan, Y. The Study Status of In Situ Aluminum Matrix Composites. *J. Chongqing Univ.* **2003**, *26*, 1–5.

Article

Fabrication of Titanium and Copper-Coated Diamond/Copper Composites via Selective Laser Melting

Lu Zhang [1], Yan Li [1,2], Simeng Li [1], Ping Gong [1], Qiaoyu Chen [1], Haoze Geng [1], Minxi Sun [1], Qinglei Sun [1,*] and Liang Hao [1,2,*]

1. Gemmological Institute, China University of Geosciences, Wuhan 430074, China; luzhang18468235771@163.com (L.Z.); yanli@cug.edu.cn (Y.L.); simengli@cug.edu.cn (S.L.); 2201710163@cug.edu.cn (P.G.); jojo_chen128@163.com (Q.C.); 13194594977@sina.cn (H.G.); smx8632@163.com (M.S.)
2. Hubei Gem & Jewelry Engineering Technology Research Center, Wuhan 430074, China
* Correspondence: sunqinglei@cug.edu.cn (Q.S.); haoliang@cug.edu.cn (L.H.)

Abstract: The poor wettability and weak interfacial bonding of diamond/copper composites are due to the incompatibility between diamond and copper which are inorganic nonmetallic and metallic material, respectively, which limit their further application in next-generation heat management materials. Coating copper and titanium on the diamond particle surface could effectively modify and improve the wettability of the diamond/copper interface via electroless plating and evaporation methods, respectively. Here, these dense and complex composites were successfully three-dimensionally printed via selective laser melting. A high thermal conductivity (TC, 336 W/mK) was produced by 3D printing 1 vol.% copper-coated diamond/copper mixed powders at an energy density of 300 J/mm^3 (laser power = 180 W and scanning rate = 200 mm/s). 1 and 3 vol.% copper-coated diamond/copper composites had lower coefficients of thermal expansions and higher TCs. They also had stronger bending strengths than the corresponding titanium-coated diamond/copper composites. The interface between copper matrix and diamond reinforcement was well bonded, and there was no cracking in the 1 vol.% copper-coated diamond/copper composite sample. The optimization of the printing parameters and strategy herein is beneficial to develop new approaches for the further construction of a wider range of micro-sized diamond particles reinforced metal matrix composites.

Keywords: selective laser melting; thermal management materials; titanium-coated diamond/copper composites; copper-coated diamond/copper composites

1. Introduction

Metal matrix composites (MMCs) are one of the most advanced potential materials in thermal management applications. The addition of nano/micro-sized fillers into metal matrix can reinforce the mechanical, thermal, and electrical performance of MMCs. To date, only relatively simple MMC designs with limited functionality have been produced by various solid (e.g., powder metallurgy) and liquid (e.g., stirring and squeeze casting) methods [1].

Diamond/copper composites are the excellent examples of MMCs. Diamond is a next-generation thermal management material, and the density of these composites is below that of pure copper. Many researchers employed diamond particles to tailor copper's coefficient of thermal expansion (CTE) and enhance the thermal conductivity (TC) [2]. Although these diamond-particle-reinforced MMCs have great prospects in heat dissipation, it's not easy to fabricate complex structure due to the complexity of processing diamond-based materials. With high energy density, small laser spot, and high cooling rate, selective laser melting (SLM) is a unique additive manufacturing (AM) technology that is used to construct complex designs [3], which has drawn the attention from industry and academia [4]. The method adopts a high-energy laser beam for melting metal powders layer by layer in

3D computer aided design (CAD) data [5,6], after which the micro-melted metal pool cools to form precise metal parts [7–11]. Thus, combining SLM's ability to create complex designs with an MMC's excellent performance could amplify the capabilities and reshape the application [12,13].

However, diamond and copper have extremely poor wettability, causing weak interfacial bonding and large interfacial thermal resistance [14,15]. There are two general solutions applied for this issue [16]. The first is matrix alloying, which leads the alloying element, for example, titanium [15], boron [17,18], zirconium [19,20], or chromium [21], into the copper matrix. However, it is difficult to precisely control the additive amount, thus resulting in excess elements residual in matrix, thereby decreasing the TC of MMC. The second is surface modification, which uses strong carbide-forming elements, like titanium [22], chromium [23,24], tungsten [25], or molybdenum [26], onto the diamond particle surface. The abovementioned four metal layers can react with diamond and partly dissolve in a copper matrix. Since the formation free energy of titanium carbide (TiC) is sufficiently low, it can easily form carbide in a short time and chemically bond with diamond. The interface layer formed serves as a bridge connecting copper and diamond, thereby increasing the composite's TC. Sun et al. [27] reported that the copper/diamond composites with titanium-coated diamond particle composites were synthesized by mechanical alloying, after annealing at 800 °C, the TC of a 40 vol.% diamond/copper composite reached 409 W/mK. The titanium-coating combination to the surface metallization of diamond particles helps to improve the copper/diamond interface and obtains a high TC within the composite material. Zhang et al. [28] reported that copper coated diamond powder in a variable mass ratio of diamond and copper was fabricated through an electroless plating process, before the coated powder was sintered through spark plasma sintering, the TC of a 70 vol.% diamond/copper composite reached 404 W/mK. In conclusion, they all have these disadvantages of the single sample shape and the relatively terrible interface bonding.

This research investigates the comparison for the thermal and mechanical performance between copper-coated diamond/copper combined materials manufactured by SLM and those with titanium-coated diamond/copper combined materials. In the current research, dense complex diamond/copper combined materials with titanium and copper-coated diamond particles were successfully 3D printed by implementing different forming processes and 3D printing strategies. A series of experiments were carried out via SLM single-line scanning to determine the appropriate processing parameters, and a cubic sample was prepared to characterize the composites' morphology and microstructure. The optimization of 3D printing parameters and strategy herein can be useful to develop new approaches for the further construction of a wider range of diamond-particle-reinforced MMCs [29]. In this work, the dense 1 vol.% copper-coated diamond/copper composite manufactured via SLM displays good interfacial bonding of the copper matrix and diamond reinforcement, and excellent thermal and mechanical performance were firstly revealed, which would serve as a promising candidate for thermal management material.

2. Materials and Methods

2.1. Materials

The micron-level pure gas atomized copper powders were purchased from China Metallurgical Research Institute (purity of 99.99%), the particles of which were primarily spherical, allowing them to improve the fluidity and bulk density in comparison with polyhedral particles [30]. The average powder particle size of 18.856 ± 15 μm was below that of the laser spot (30 μm). The diamond particles were purchased from Henan Yuxing Sino-crystal Micro-diamond Co., Ltd., with an average size of approximately 25 μm.

In this experiment, copper and titanium were directly deposited on the diamond particle surface via electroless plating (Figure 1a) and evaporation methods (Figure 1b), respectively. Table 1 lists the mix ratios of copper powder and coated diamond particles, combined in a ball mill at 100 rpm for 3 h, before which were dried for 3 h at 60 °C and then sifted through a 400 mesh.

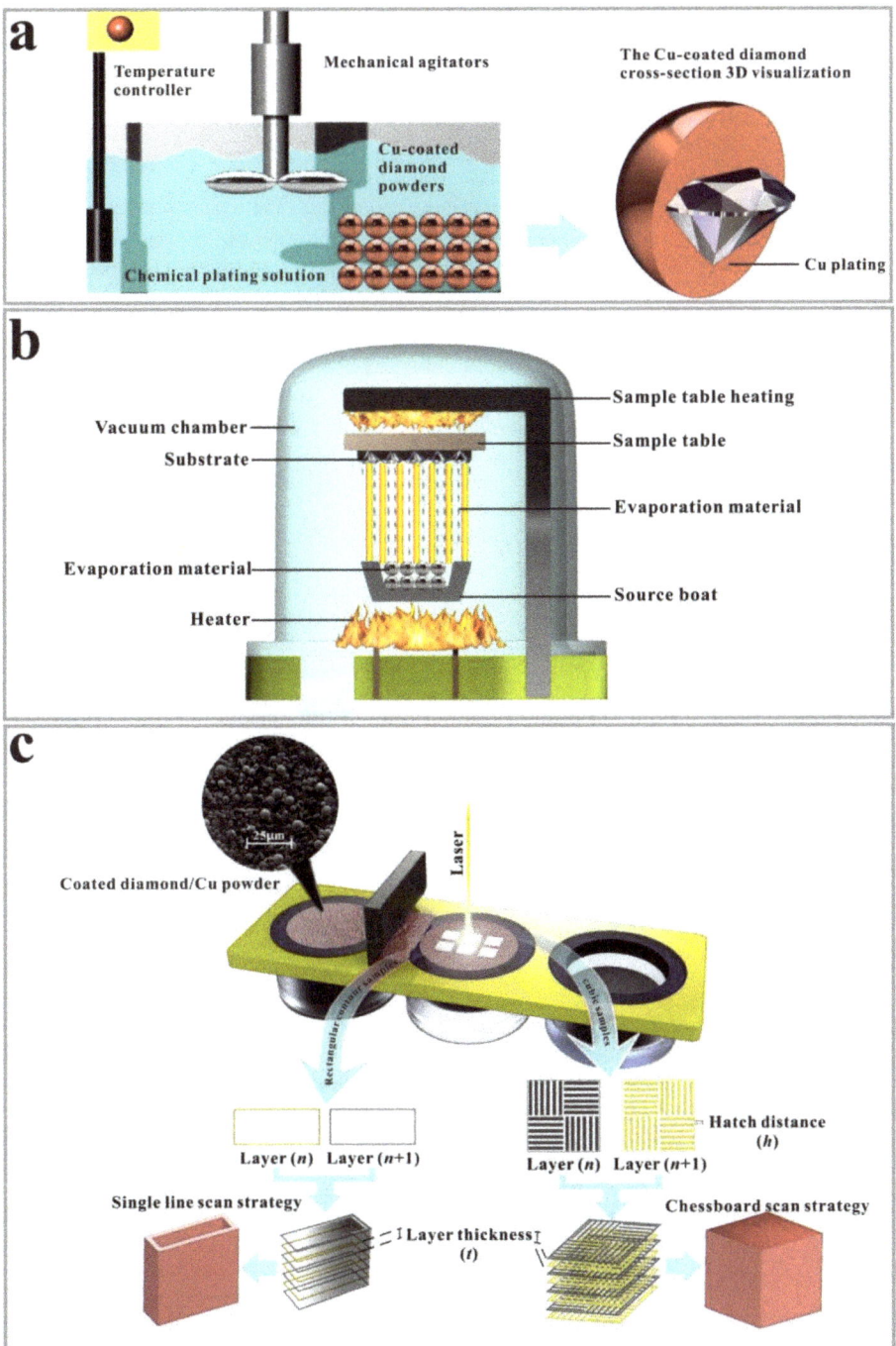

Figure 1. Schematic diagram of depositing copper and titanium on the diamond particle surface via (**a**) electroless plating and (**b**) evaporation process, respectively; (**c**) The preparation process for rectangular contour and cubic samples.

Table 1. The coated diamond/copper composite compositions.

Diamond vol.%	Diamond wt.%	Total Mass (g)	Coated Diamond Quality (g)	Copper Quality (g)
1	0.40	50	0.20	49.80
3	1.20	50	0.60	49.40
5	2.03	50	1.01	48.99

2.2. Preparation of the Titanium and Copper-Coated Diamond/Copper Components through SLM

In order to obtain the high-quality titanium and copper-coated diamond/copper samples, the SISMA MYSINT100 system with a neodymium-doped yttrium aluminum garnet fiber laser (wavelength: 1060 nm; maximal output laser power, 180 W; laser spot size, 30 μm) was used to investigate the detailed parameters from singlet to cubic formation in high-purity N_2 atmosphere (residual oxygen content < 0.5 vol.%). The titanium and copper-coated diamond/copper powders were protected from oxidation. Rectangular contour (1×3 mm^2) and cubic ($5 \times 5 \times 5$ mm^3) samples were used for the monorail and block experiments, separately (Figure 1c). The chessboard laser scanning strategy was used for the cubic samples, each layer was separated into four squares, and the scanning direction in each square was perpendicular to the adjacent square. The no-hatch laser scanning strategy was used for the rectangular contour samples. A single-line scan was performed via SLM to determine the appropriate processing parameters, which were then used to prepare the cubic samples for the morphology and microstructure characterization.

The hatch distance indicated the degree to which the titanium and copper-coated diamond/copper powders were repeatedly scanned by the laser. At the same laser power and scanning rate, the smaller the hatch distance, the greater the laser's influence on the composites. A variety of volumetric laser energy density (*D*) was adopted to determine the finished part parameters. *D* is computed through Equation (1):

$$D = \frac{P}{h \times t \times v} \qquad (1)$$

in which *P*, *v*, *h* and *t* refer to the laser power, scanning rate, hatch distance and layer thickness, respectively.

2.3. Characterization Techniques

The surface morphology and microstructure were observed via optical microscopy (OM, Leica A205, Wetzlar, Germany) and scan electron microscopy with energy dispersive spectroscopy (SEM-EDS, Hitachi-Su8010, Hitachi High-Tech, Clarksburg, MA, USA). Prior to the microscopic observation, the specimens were polished and etched (10 s within a mixed solution of 100 mL distilled water, 5 mL HCl and 5 g $FeCl_3$). The width of a single weld pool within the printed composites was assessed via image analysis with ImageJ. Titanium-coating and copper-coating thickness on the diamond particle surface were determined through focused ion beam (FIB) and SEM. The coated diamond cross-section specimens were prepared using FIB milling. X-ray diffraction (XRD, Bruker D8 Advance, Rheinstetten, Germany) employing Cu Kα radiation at 40 KV and 40 mA within the scope of $2\theta = 5°–90°$ was used to test the phase structure with a step size of 0.02°. The composite density was determined adopting Archimedes' law. A Netzsch LFA 427 Transient Laser Flash machine and the calorimetric technology were used for measuring the thermal diffusivity and specific heat, respectively. The TC was obtained by multiplying the composite density, thermal diffusivity, and specific heat. A carbon spray was used to coat the top and bottom surfaces of the specimens (Ø 12.7×3 mm) with graphite to improve their capacity for absorbing the applied energy. The mean TC of each specimen was determined by measuring three parallel positions. Finally, samples ($3 \times 4 \times 25$ mm^3) were used to test the bending strength and CTE. The bending strength test was performed applying an Instron 5569 Universal Testing machine, and a dilatometer (DIL 402C, Netzsch, Selb, Germany) was used to examine the CTE of the composite materials from room temperature to 400 °C. The roughness of the top surface was measured by a laser scanning confocal microscope (OLYMPUS OLS4100) with Gaussian filtering to evaluate the quality of 1 vol.% copper-coated diamond/copper combined materials surfaces, the OLS4100 can correctly identify a measuring position and easily perform roughness measurement of a target micro area, the accuracy of height measurement was less than 0.2 μm error per 100 μm.

3. Results and Discussion

3.1. Characterization and Analysis

The vacuum evaporation technique was used to coat the diamond particle surface with titanium [31]. Figure 2a displays the titanium-rich regions on the diamond sites via EDS element mapping, showing the preference of titanium for diffusion bonding with the diamond. The EDS elemental map of the titanium-coating layer is exhibited in Figure 2b, demonstrating the enrichment of Ti. The protective deposition on the surface edge caused the Pt signals. The titanium layer thickness on the diamond particle surface ranged between 93.04 and 122.8 nm. The coating layer was closely attached to the diamond particles, and the clear stepped surfaces illustrated that the titanium and diamond were strongly chemically bonded. Diamond particles were coated employing copper through electroless plating for enhancing its wettability with molten copper, the copper-coating layer was thick enough to melt with the copper powder that only copper region on the diamond site was displayed by EDS elements mapping (Figure 2c). And the copper layer thickness on the diamond particle surface ranged between 0.99 and 1.77 μm (Figure 2d).

The series of diffraction peaks marked in black plum blossom were indexed to the TiC (PDF#32-1383), and the peaks with rhombus were indexed to the diamond (PDF#06-0675). No impurities were characterized by the XRD (Figure 2e). As the natural non-wettability of diamond and copper made it difficult to form intermediate products and impossible to achieve perfect interface bonding [8], active element titanium was coated on the diamond particle surface for clearly generating carbide TiC at the interface. As a result, the metal matrix covered the diamond surface well, improving the poor interface bonding of the diamond and metal. Existing research confirmed these phenomena [15,32–36]. The series of diffraction peaks marked with heart symbols were indexed to copper (PDF#04-0836), and those peaks with rhombus were indexed to diamond (PDF#06-0675). No impurities were characterized by the XRD (Figure 2f). The copper plating on the diamond particle surface improved the poor interface adhesion between the diamond and copper.

3.2. Formation of the SLM Titanium and Copper-Coated Diamond/Copper Composites

3.2.1. SLM Manufacturing of Titanium-Coated Diamond/Copper Composites

The rectangular contour samples were printed in the single-track experiment, and their morphology was characterized and correlated with the process parameters. Due to scanning a single-track layer-by-layer along the Z-axis to form each rectangular contour sample, the width of a single wall was the width of a single weld pool. Samples with different process parameters were observed via OM to estimate the range of process parameters in the cubic experiment. The SLM laser parameters selected for the single-track formation test of the titanium-coated diamond/copper combined materials were as follows. The laser power was improved from 140 to 160 and 180 W, and the scanning rate was improved from 200 to 300 and 400 mm/s at a fixed powder layer thickness of 0.025 mm. It was important to observe the continuity of the molten pool, as any discontinuity would produce defects, for example, porosity, delamination and surface roughness. Figure 3a,b exhibited that the superior process parameters of the rectangular contour samples with 3 and 5 vol.% titanium-coated diamond/copper composites comprised a laser power of 140 W and a scanning rate of 200 mm/s, that with 1 vol.% titanium-coated diamond/copper composites comprised a laser power of 180 W and a scanning rate of 200 mm/s. In the single-track experiment, when the layer thickness was below the median powder particle size (0.025 mm), a significant amount of powder particles larger than the layer thickness would rub the previous layer in the melting region as the scraper moved, leading to failure of the print formation. Therefore, a layer thickness of 0.025 mm was optimal.

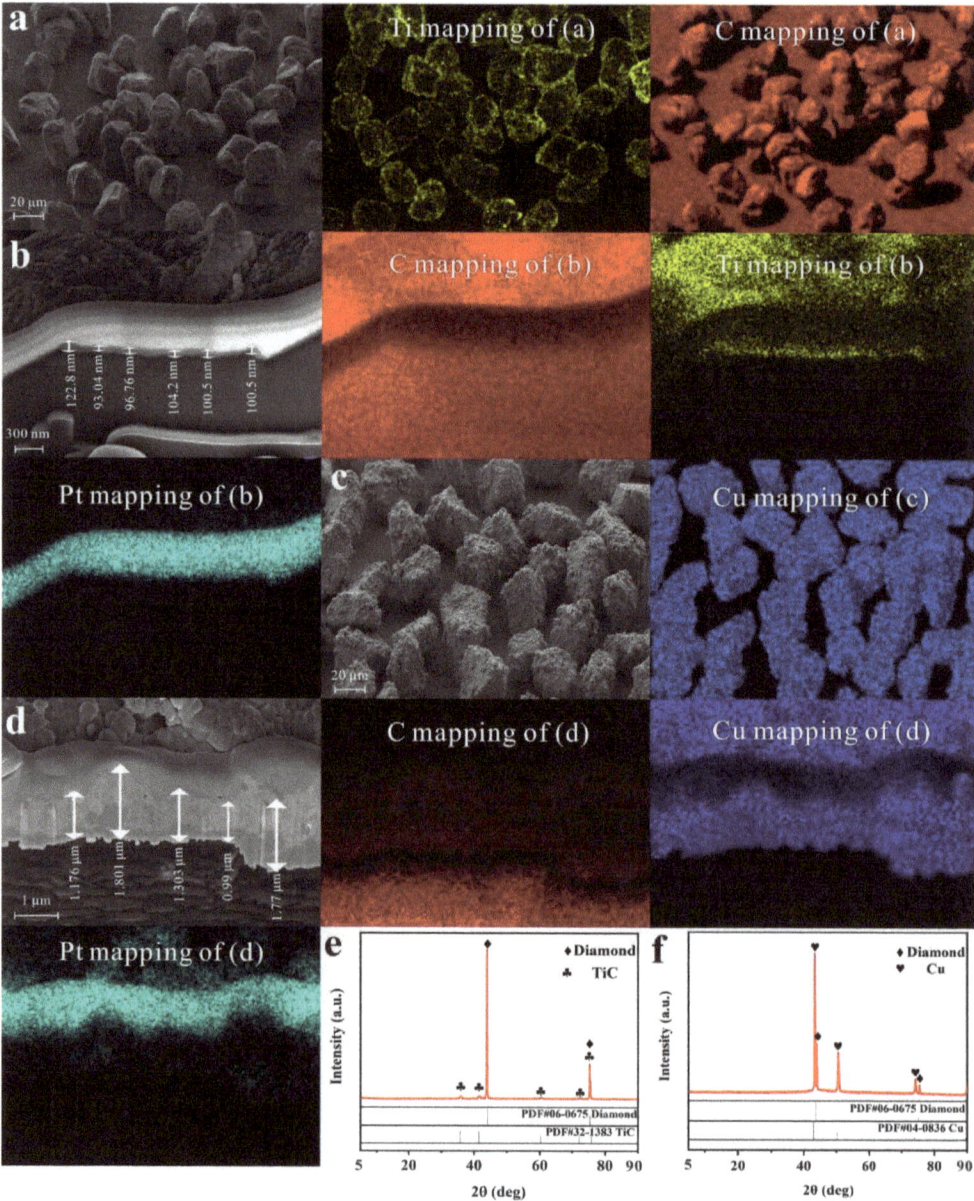

Figure 2. (a) The morphologies of the titanium-coated diamond particles and the corresponding EDS element mappings; (b) The thickness of the titanium-coating layer on the diamond particle surface and the corresponding EDS element mappings; (c) The morphologies of the copper-coated diamond particles and the corresponding EDS element mappings; (d) The thickness of the copper-coating layer on the diamond particle surface and the corresponding EDS element mappings; The XRD pattern of (e) the titanium-coated and (f) the copper-coated diamond particles.

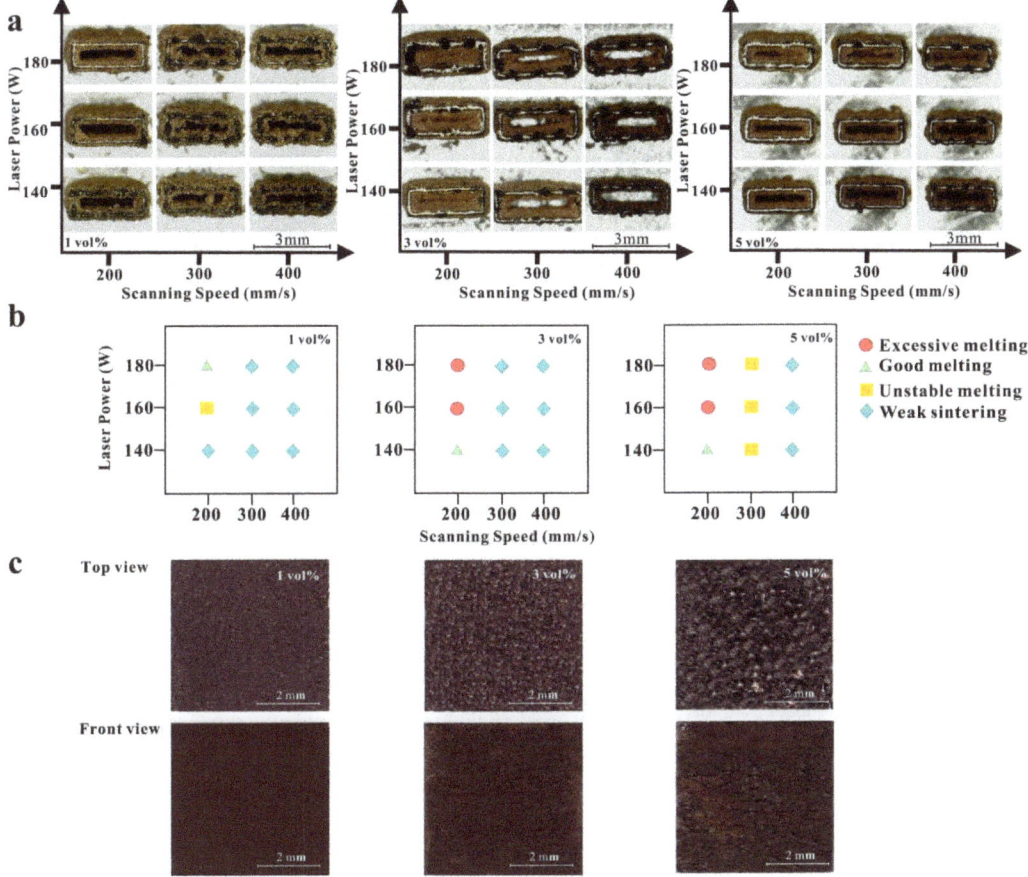

Figure 3. (**a**) Rectangular contour samples of the 1, 3 and 5 vol.% titanium-coated diamond/copper composites; (**b**) the corresponding processing window of the laser power and scanning rate; (**c**) The SLM manufactured morphology: top and front view of the 1, 3 and 5 vol.% titanium-coated diamond/copper composite, respectively.

Compared with the single-track experiment involving only three process parameters (layer thickness, scanning rate and laser power), the cubic experiment further considered the hatch distance and the scanning strategy. The hatch distance (h) was calculated as follows:

$$h = (1 - Hr) \times w \qquad (2)$$

where Hr and w indicate the overlap rate and melt pool width, respectively. The higher the overlap rate, the higher the density and the lower the porosity. The highest densities and lowest porosities were obtained for each parameter group when the melt pool overlap rate reached 60%. The center of the next scan track overlapped the edge of the adjacent single-track melt pool and was partially remelted to achieve good metallurgical bonding between the pools and reduce the porosity. However, when the overlap was greater than 60%, the porosity increased slightly. If the laser energy density increased further upon a rise in the laser power or a decrease in the hatch distance, the porosity increased slightly when the density reached its peak value, that is, when the porosity was at its lowest. Existing research confirmed these phenomena [37–39].

The data of the single-track formation test of the 1, 3 and 5 vol.% titanium-coated diamond/copper combined materials could be obtained through the ImageJ software, the melt pool width was found to be approximately 250 µm, and the h was calculated as approximately 100 µm. Figure 3c shows the unpolished samples of the SLM-printed 1, 3 and 5 vol.% titanium-coated diamond/copper combined materials. The 1 and 3 vol.% composites had higher relative density than that of the 5 vol.% composite, the relative density of 1, 3 and 5 vol.% titanium-coated diamond/copper composites were 96%, 90% and 81%, respectively. A higher relative density is related to better specimen performance [40]. Hence, 1 and 3 vol.% coated diamond/copper composites featuring high relative density were chosen for the investigation below.

Additionally, with the emergence of a metal vapor above the molten pool, a recoil pressure was induced onto the surface of pool. Meanwhile with the quick development of a thermal gradient inside the liquid, a flow of molten metal was produced from the hot region to the coldest one, referred to as the Marangoni role. Both roles brought particle ejection, known as recoil-induced ejection, as described in Figure 4 [41,42]. Besides, a denudation area was built on the sides of the molten track, where we could sweep powders under the flow of the metal vapor and the gas shield. This kind of particle ejections was known as entrainment particle (Figure 4) [43]. Metal vapor-induced entrainment caused powder-spattering behavior [44]. To be intuitive, micrometric particles changed the surface tension, molten pool rheology, and metal vapor density according to declaration [45–47]. Also, it was believed that the imbalance of the molten pool, hot spatter collision during flight and entrained particles gathered on the solidified area were among the major driving forces for big spatter production. A pronounced spattering situation was found while mixing 5 vol.% coated diamond with copper by comparing with a pure copper bed condition, thus determining the negative role of the coated diamond in the molten pool. The hot particles partially fused with the solid materials after falling back into the powder bed, cooled down after ejection [29].

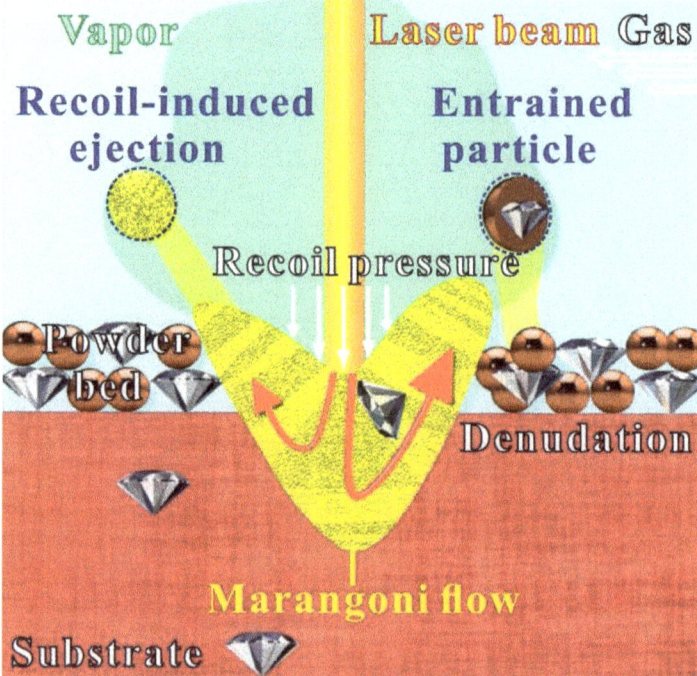

Figure 4. Spatter ejection phenomenon in SLM of the coated diamond/copper combined materials.

3.2.2. The Formation of SLM Copper-Coated Diamond/Copper Composites

The preparation of dense copper/diamond composite materials with a high TC required the shaping of a strong interphase layer between the diamond and copper due to their incompatibility [48,49]. For improving the wettability of metal matrix and diamond, many researchers adopted electroless plating for coating the copper layer on diamond powders [50]. The superior SLM process parameters of the rectangular contour samples with 1 vol.% copper-coated diamond/copper composites comprised a laser power of 180 W and a scanning rate of 200 mm/s (Figure 5a), that with 3 vol.% copper-coated diamond/copper composites comprised a laser power of 160 W and a scanning rate of 100 mm/s (Figure 5c,d). According to the quality of the melted rails, the processing window was separated into four different zones (Figure 5d,e), that is, a weak sintering zone (52.8%; A), an unstable melting zone (22.2%; B), a continuous track zone (2.8%; C), and an over-melting zone (22.2%; D), in reference to their different line-energy densities (LEDs, J/m). The less continuous track area suggested a formation difficulty under the constrained process parameters. It was not easy to form a scanning track due to the insufficient LED within zone A. The powder failed to form a stable width track within zone B, and a large amount of unmelted powder adhered to the surface due to insufficient energy. In zone C, the melt flow in the molten pool stabilized and had a sufficient penetration depth into the previous layer, thus obtaining a relatively smooth trajectory when the input LED was 1600 J/m. When the LED was too high (>1700 J/m) in zone D, a track featuring a width of approximately 517 μm occurred, and micro-cracks appeared due to the accumulation of excess heat related to the high power and low scanning rate caused by the high residual stress [51].

The printing parameters were optimized to form the dense copper/diamond composites. Scanning speeds ranging from 50 to 300 mm/s and laser power levels ranging between 130 and 180 W caused numerous printing defects (e.g., balling and pores). To obtain parts with minimal printing defects, the narrow processing window was determined, with a scanning rate of 100 mm/s and a high laser power (160 W). With a high laser power (170–180 W) and a low scanning rate (50 mm/s), the printed parts exhibited superfusion (Figure 5c,e). These parameters increased the molten pool size, thereby increasing the height and width of the powder tracks.

Additionally, the values of roughness gradually decreased with increasing laser power (Figure 6). When the laser power reached the maximum value of 180 W, the surface roughness value Sa reached a minimum value of 5.751 μm at the scanning rate of 200 mm/s. While the scanning rate was varied between 50 and 200 mm/s, the values of roughness gradually decreased with increasing scanning rate. When the scanning rate was 200 mm/s, the surface roughness value Sa reached a minimum. While the scanning rate was varied between 200 and 300 mm/s, the values of roughness gradually increased with increasing scanning rate. Laser power and scanning rate played important roles in the roughness of the composite. The lifetime of the molten pool is the key parameter that influence the flatness and surface roughness, which will be discussed in the future [52].

3.3. Comparison of the SLM Titanium and Copper-Coated Diamond/Copper Composites

Interfacial bonding holds the key to determining the thermal and mechanical performance of composites [53]. 1 vol.% copper-coated diamond/copper composite sample showed relatively better interface bonding of the copper matrix and diamond reinforcement (Figure 7c), no remarkable defects like flaws or cracks were seen at the interface. The pull-out of diamond particle was merely discovered in the polished surface, implying strong interfacial bonding between the copper matrix and diamond particles. However, 1 vol.% titanium-coated diamond/copper combined material sample showed the pull-out of diamond particle that could be discovered in the polished surface (Figure 7a). For the 3 vol.% titanium-coated diamond/copper combined material sample, the copper matrix and diamond reinforcement bonding were extremely poor and showed obvious cracking (Figure 7b). Resulting from poor interface bonding between diamond and copper, 3 vol.% titanium-coated diamond/copper composite showed a low TC of 57 W/mK at an energy density of 280 J/mm^3 (140 W, 200 mm/s). There were small cracks in the edge area between copper matrix and diamond reinforcement for the 3 vol.% copper-coated diamond/copper composite sample (Figure 7d). Good interfacial bonding was exhibited in the 3 vol.% copper-coated diamond/copper composite sample for comparison with the 3 vol.% titanium-coated diamond/copper composite sample. The reason why the interfacial bonding of titanium-coated diamond/copper composite was worse than that of copper-coated diamond/copper composite was that introducing electroless copper plating process could avoid essentially the particles gathering and it could improve the relative density, the interfacial bonding and the TC of the diamond/copper composites [28].

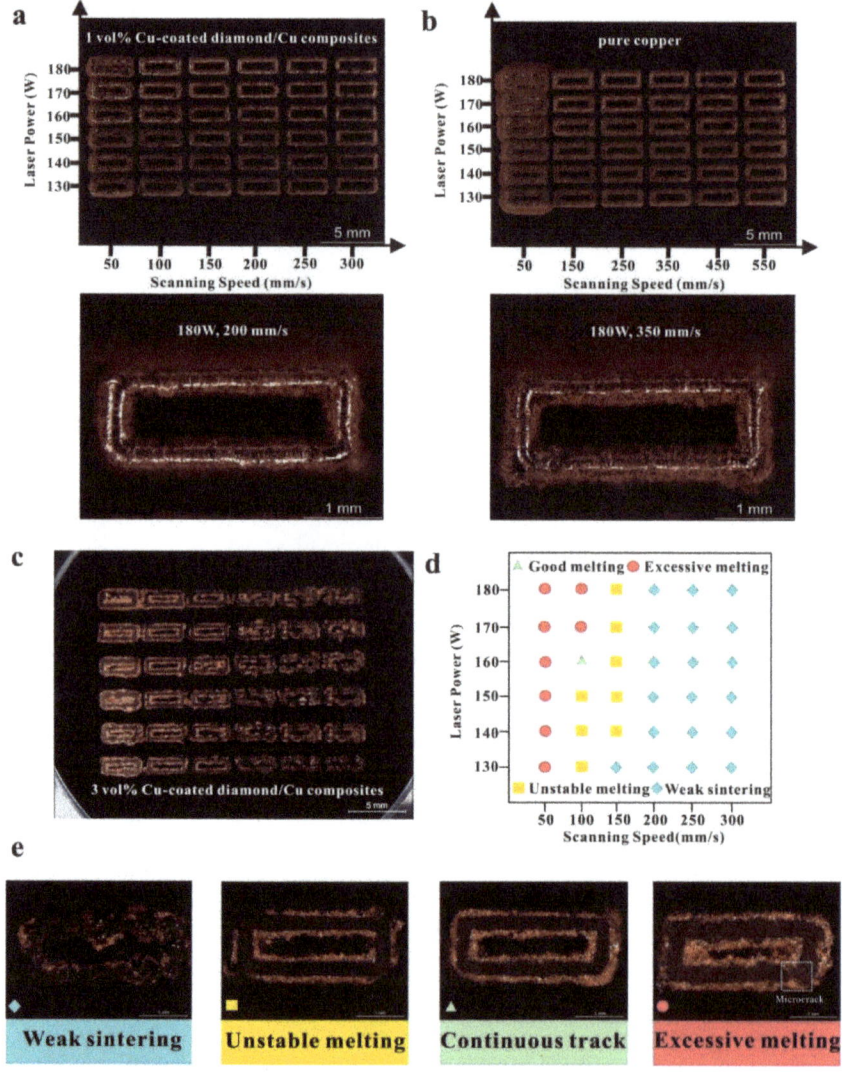

Figure 5. 1, 3 vol.% copper-coated diamond/copper combined materials and pure copper featuring various process parameters within the XY plane and surface morphologies: (**a**) 1 vol.% copper-coated diamond/copper composites; (**b**) Pure copper; (**c**,**d**) 3 vol.% copper-coated diamond composites and process window of laser power and scanning rate; (**e**) Typical track types of zones A, B, C, and D.

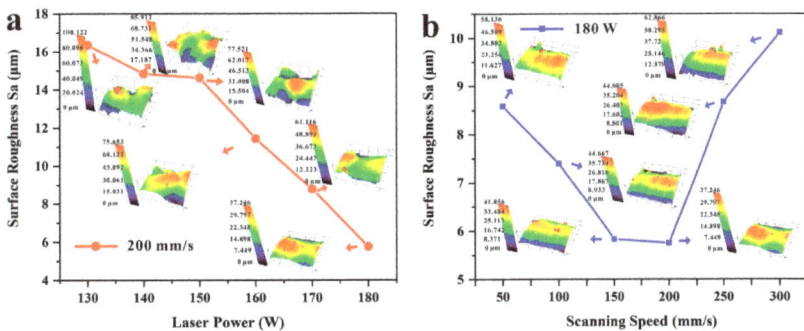

Figure 6. 1 vol.% copper-coated diamond/copper combined materials relationship between the surface roughness and (**a**) laser power and (**b**) scanning rate.

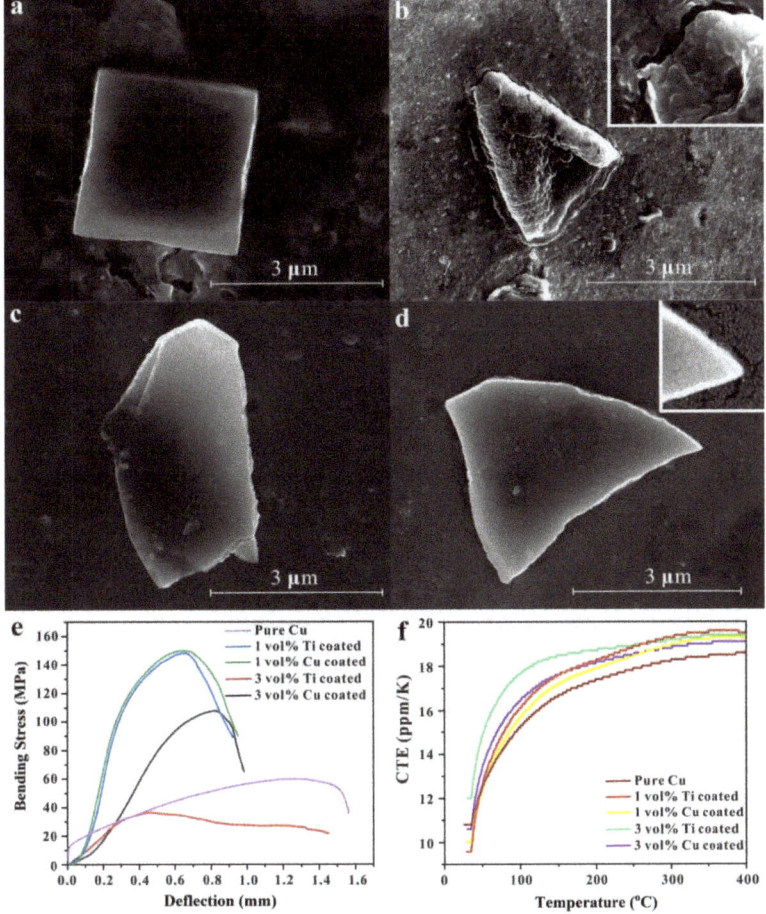

Figure 7. SEM images of the copper matrix and diamond bonding of (**a**) 1 vol.% and (**b**) 3 vol.% titanium-coated diamond/copper combined materials; (**c**) 1 vol.% and (**d**) 3 vol.% copper-coated diamond/copper combined materials; (**e**) The bending stress and (**f**) CTE values of titanium and copper-coated diamond/copper combined materials and pure copper.

The bending strength of 1 and 3 vol.% copper-coated diamond/copper composites significantly exceeded that of corresponding titanium-coated diamond/copper composites. The maximum bending strength of 3 vol.% copper-coated combined materials was 108 MPa, while that of the 3 vol.% titanium-coated combined materials was only 36 MPa. The maximum bending strength of the 1 vol.% copper-coated combined materials was 150 MPa, that of the 1 vol.% titanium-coated composites was 148 MPa. And the printed composites with 1 vol.% copper-coated diamond were approximately three times stronger than the printed copper ($\leq$58 MPa) for the bending strength. When the diamond concentration rose from 1 to 3 vol.%, the bending strength decreased as the relative density decreased (Figure 7e), the viscosity of melt increases obviously as the diamond particle content increases at a constant size, resulting in the decrease in the fluidity and deterioration in the sample surface quality, leading to the decrease in relative density [54]. These experiments indicated that a moderate TC (174 W/mK) was produced by printing 1 vol.% titanium-coated diamond/copper mixed powders at an energy density of 360 J/mm^3 (180 W, 200 mm/s), a maximum TC (336 W/mK) was produced by printing 1 vol.% copper-coated diamond/copper mixed powders at an energy density of 300 J/mm^3 (180 W, 200 mm/s) and a moderate TC (162 W/mK) was produced by printing 3 vol.% copper-coated diamond/copper mixed powders at an energy density of 533 J/mm^3 (160 W, 100 mm/s). Additionally, the printed composites with 3 vol.% copper-coated diamond were approximately three times larger than those with 3 vol.% titanium-coated diamond for the TC. A moderate TC (183 W/mK) was produced by printing the copper powders at an energy density of 171 J/mm^3 (180 W, 350 mm/s) as shown in Figure 5b. This difference was likely caused by the dissimilarity of those interfacial bonding between the copper matrix and diamond reinforcement. The higher energy density required to print diamond/copper composites compared to pure copper was caused by solid coated diamond particles into the molten copper pool. The solid coated diamond particles improved the molten metal viscosity and restricted its ability to flow and fuse. And as the coated diamond particle content further increased, the porosity and the laser absorptivity of the mixed powder further increased, the powder fluidity and the thermal conductivity further decreased [6].

Figure 7f shows the CTE curves of the 1 and 3 vol.% titanium and copper-coated diamond/copper composites, as well as copper upon raising the temperature from 30 to 400 °C. The CTE of 1 and 3 vol.% copper-coated diamond/copper composites was significantly below that of corresponding titanium-coated diamond/copper composites, the minimum CTE of 1 vol.% copper-coated diamond/copper combined materials was very close to that of the copper. The shear stress had little effect on the interior of the copper-coated diamond/copper composite during heating, demonstrating the interfacial bonding of the copper matrix and diamond was better in the 1 vol.% copper-coated diamond/copper composites. During the heating process, the shear stress along the interface of the copper matrix and diamond had little effect on the CTE and led to a better thermal stability. This highlighted the advantages of copper plating on diamond particle surfaces, while the copper-coated diamond/copper composite properties reached high levels in comparison.

4. Conclusions

SLM technology was used to form titanium and copper-coated diamond/copper composites. The microstructure, roughness, interface bonding, thermal and mechanical performance were studied.

(1) The values of roughness gradually decreased with increasing laser power. When the laser power reached the maximum value of 180 W, the surface roughness (Sa) reached a minimum value of 5.751 μm. The surface roughness Sa reached a minimum at the scanning rate of 200 mm/s.

(2) 1 vol.% copper-coated diamond/copper composite sample showed relatively best interface bonding of the copper matrix and diamond reinforcement, corresponding the lowest CTE and the strongest bending strength.

(3) 1 vol.% copper-coated diamond/copper composites had the highest TC (336 W/mK) at an energy density of 300 J/mm^3 (180 W, 200 mm/s). 3 vol.% copper-coated diamond/copper composites had the moderate TC (162 W/mK, 533 J/mm^3, 160 W, 100 mm/s). 1 vol.% titanium-coated diamond/copper composites had the moderate TC (174 W/mK, 360 J/mm^3, 180 W, 200 mm/s). 3 vol.% titanium-coated diamond/copper composites had the lowest TC (57 W/mK, 280 J/mm^3, 140 W, 200 mm/s). The copper powders had the moderate TC (183 W/mK, 171 J/mm^3, 180 W, 350 mm/s).

The article offered electroless plating and evaporation methods for SLM to coat copper and titanium on the diamond particle surface for modifying and improving the wettability of diamond/copper interface, which opened up a new way for laser 3D printing technology to print a broad range of diamond-particle-reinforced MMCs. Thereby, unleashing their full potential for electronic package and thermal management applications.

Author Contributions: L.Z. and Q.S. designed the experiments and wrote manuscript; L.H. provided the initial idea of this paper and financial support; Y.L. revised the manuscript; M.S. and H.G. performed the experiments; S.L. improved the language; Q.C. and P.G. analyzed the data. All authors have read and agreed to the published version of the manuscript.

Funding: This research is funded by Wuhan Applied Foundational Frontier Project from Wuhan Science and Technology Bureau Project, China (No. 2020010601012172), the National Natural Science Foundation of China (No. 61805095, No. 51675496, No. 51902295), and the Fundamental Research Funds for the Central Universities, China University of Geosciences (Wuhan) (No. CUG2021234).

Data Availability Statement: Not applicable.

Conflicts of Interest: The authors declare no conflict of interest.

References

1. Sharma, D.K.; Mahant, D.; Upadhyay, G. Manufacturing of metal matrix composites: A state of review. *Mater. Today Proc.* **2020**, *26*, 506–519. [CrossRef]
2. Silvain, J.F.; Heintz, J.M.; Veillere, A.; Constantin, L.; Lu, Y. A review of processing of Cu/C base plate composites for interfacial control and improved properties. *Int. J. Extrem. Manuf.* **2020**, *2*, 012002. [CrossRef]
3. Hojjatzadeh, S.M.H.; Parab, N.D.; Yan, W.; Guo, Q.; Xiong, L.; Zhao, C.; Qu, M.; Escano, L.I.; Xiao, X.; Fezzaa, K.; et al. Pore elimination mechanisms during 3D printing of metals. *Nat. Commun.* **2019**, *10*, 3088. [CrossRef] [PubMed]
4. Li, R.; Shi, Y.; Liu, J.; Xie, Z.; Wang, Z. Selective laser melting W–10 wt% Cu composite powders. *Int. J. Adv. Manuf. Technol.* **2010**, *48*, 597–605. [CrossRef]
5. Aversa, A.; Marchese, G.; Lorusso, M.; Calignano, F.; Biamino, S.; Ambrosio, E.P.; Manfredi, D.; Fino, P.; Lombardi, M.; Pavese, M. Microstructural and mechanical characterization of aluminum matrix composites produced by laser powder bed fusion. *Adv. Eng. Mater.* **2017**, *19*, 1700180. [CrossRef]
6. Gu, D.; Hagedorn, Y.C.; Meiners, W.; Wissenbach, K.; Poprawe, R. Nanocrystalline TiC reinforced Ti matrix bulk-form nanocomposites by selective laser melting (SLM): Densification, growth mechanism and wear behavior. *Compos. Sci. Technol.* **2011**, *71*, 1612–1620. [CrossRef]
7. Gao, C.; Wang, Z.; Xiao, Z.; You, D.; Wong, K.; Akbarzadeh, A.H. Selective laser melting of TiN nanoparticle-reinforced AlSi10Mg composite: Microstructural, interfacial, and mechanical properties. *J. Mater. Process. Technol.* **2020**, *281*, 116618. [CrossRef]
8. Gu, D.; Wang, H.; Dai, D.; Chang, F.; Meiners, W.; Hagedorn, Y.C.; Wissenbach, K.; Kelbassa, I.; Poprawe, R. Densification behavior, microstructure evolution, and wear property of TiC nanoparticle reinforced AlSi10Mg bulk-form nanocomposites prepared by selective laser melting. *J. Laser Appl.* **2014**, *27*, S17003. [CrossRef]
9. Leong, C.C.; Lu, L.; Fuh, J.Y.H.; Wong, Y.S. In-situ formation of copper matrix composites by laser sintering. *Mater. Sci. Eng.* **2002**, *338*, 81–88. [CrossRef]
10. Slocombe, A.; Li, L. Selective laser sintering of TiC–Al$_2$O$_3$ composite with selfpropagating high-temperature synthesis. *J. Mater. Process. Technol.* **2001**, *118*, 173–178. [CrossRef]
11. Kumar, S.; Kruth, J.P. Composites by rapid prototyping technology. *Mater. Des.* **2010**, *31*, 850–856. [CrossRef]
12. Neugebauer, R.; Müller, B.; Gebauer, M.; Toppel, T. Additive manufacturing boosts efficiency of heat transfer components. *Assem. Autom.* **2011**, *31*, 344–347. [CrossRef]
13. Constantin, L.; Fan, L.; Pontoreau, M.; Wang, F.; Cui, B.; Battaglia, J.L.; Silvain, J.F.; Lu, Y.F. Additive manufacturing of copper/diamond composites for thermal management applications. *Manuf. Lett.* **2020**, *24*, 61–66. [CrossRef]
14. He, J.; Wang, X.; Zhang, Y.; Zhao, Y.; Zhang, H. Thermal conductivity of Cu–Zr/ diamond composites produced by high temperature–high pressure method. *Compos. B Eng.* **2015**, *68*, 22–26. [CrossRef]

15. Li, J.; Zhang, H.; Wang, L.; Che, Z.; Zhang, Y.; Wang, J.; Kim, M.J.; Wang, X. Optimized thermal properties in diamond particles reinforced copper–titanium matrix composites produced by gas pressure infiltration. *Compos. Part A Appl. Sci. Manuf.* **2016**, *91*, 189–194. [CrossRef]
16. Dai, S.; Li, J.; Lu, N. Research progress of diamond/copper composites with high thermal conductivity. *Diam. Relat. Mater.* **2020**, *108*, 107993. [CrossRef]
17. Bai, G.; Li, N.; Wang, X.; Wang, J.; Kim, M.J.; Zhang, H. High thermal conductivity of Cu–B/diamond composites prepared by gas pressure infiltration. *J. Alloys Compd.* **2018**, *735*, 1648–1653. [CrossRef]
18. Bai, G.; Wang, L.; Zhang, Y.; Wang, X.; Wang, J.; Kim, M.J.; Zhang, H. Tailoring interface structure and enhancing thermal conductivity of Cu/diamond composites by alloying boron to the Cu matrix. *Mater. Charact.* **2019**, *152*, 265–275. [CrossRef]
19. Wang, L.; Li, J.; Bai, G.; Li, N.; Wang, X.; Zhang, H.; Wang, J.; Kim, M.J. Interfacial structure evolution and thermal conductivity of Cu–Zr/diamond composites prepared by gas pressure infiltration. *J. Alloys Compd.* **2019**, *781*, 800–809. [CrossRef]
20. Chu, K.; Jia, C.; Guo, H.; Li, W. On the thermal conductivity of Cu–Zr/diamond composites. *Mater. Des.* **2013**, *45*, 36–42. [CrossRef]
21. Prokhorov, V.; Bagramov, R.; Gerasimov, V.; Zhuravlev, V. Copper and its alloys thermal conductivity controlling with diamond and Ti or Cr addition. *Mater. Today* **2018**, *5*, 20104–26107. [CrossRef]
22. Che, Q.; Chen, X.; Ji, Y.; Li, Y.; Wang, L.; Cao, S.; Jiang, Y.; Wang, Z. The influence of minor titanium addition on thermal properties of diamond/copper composites made in situ reactive sintering. *Mater. Sci. Semicond. Process.* **2015**, *30*, 104–111. [CrossRef]
23. Chu, K.; Liu, Z.; Jia, C.; Chen, H.; Liang, X.; Gao, W.; Tian, W.; Guo, H. Thermal conductivity of SPS consolidated Cu/diamond composites with Cr–coated diamond particles. *J. Alloys Compd.* **2010**, *490*, 453–458. [CrossRef]
24. Ren, S.; Shen, X.; Guo, C.; Liu, N.; Zang, J.; He, X.; Qu, X. Effect of coating on the microstructure and thermal conductivities of diamond–Cu composites prepared by powder metallurgy. *Compos. Sci. Technol.* **2011**, *71*, 1550–1555. [CrossRef]
25. Abyzov, A.; Kidalov, S.; Shakhov, F. High thermal conductivity composites consisting of diamond filler with tungsten coating and copper (silver) matrix. *J. Mater. Sci.* **2011**, *46*, 1424–1438. [CrossRef]
26. Shen, X.; He, X.; Ren, S.; Zhang, H.; Qu, X. Effect of molybdenum as interfacial element on the thermal conductivity of diamond/Cu composites. *J. Alloys Compd.* **2012**, *529*, 134–139. [CrossRef]
27. Sun, J.; Zang, J.; Li, H.; Feng, X.; Shen, Y. Influence of diamond content and milling duration on microstructure and thermal conductivity of Ti-coated diamond/copper composite coating on copper substrate. *Mater. Chem. Phys.* **2021**, *259*, 124017. [CrossRef]
28. Zhang, Y.; Cai, H.; Shen, Z. Preparation of Cu-Coated Diamond Particles and its Influence on the Performances of Diamond/Cu Composites. *Adv. Mater. Res.* **2012**, *602*, 66–70. [CrossRef]
29. Constantin, L.; Kraiem, N.; Wu, Z.; Cui, B.; Battaglia, J.; Garnier, C.; Silvain, J.; Lu, Y.F. Manufacturing of complex diamond-based composite structures via laser powder-bed fusion. *Addit. Manuf.* **2021**, *40*, 101927. [CrossRef]
30. Xiong, W.; Hao, L.; Li, Y.; Tang, D.; Cui, Q.; Feng, Z.; Yan, C. Effect of selective laser melting parameters on morphology, microstructure, densification and mechanical properties of supersaturated silver alloy. *Mater. Des.* **2019**, *170*, 107697–107708. [CrossRef]
31. Abhilash, S.R.; Saini, S.K.; Kabiraj, D. Methods adopted for improving the collection efficiency in vacuum evaporation technique. *J. Radioanal. Nucl. Chem.* **2014**, *299*, 1137–1139. [CrossRef]
32. Weber, L.; Tavangar, R. On the influence of active element content on the thermal conductivity and thermal expansion of Cu-X (X = Cr, B) diamond composites. *Scr. Mater.* **2007**, *57*, 988–991. [CrossRef]
33. Li, J.; Wang, X.; Qiao, Y.; Zhang, Y.; He, Z.; Zhang, H. High thermal conductivity through interfacial layer optimization in diamond particles dispersed Zralloyed Cu matrix composites. *Scr. Mater.* **2015**, *109*, 72–75. [CrossRef]
34. Guo, C.; He, X.; Ren, S.; Qu, X. Effect of (0–40) wt.% Si addition to Al on the thermal conductivity and thermal expansion of diamond/Al composites by pressure infiltration. *J. Alloys Compd.* **2016**, *664*, 777–783. [CrossRef]
35. Ma, S.; Zhao, N.; Shi, C.; Liu, E.; He, C.; Ma, L. Mo2C coating on diamond: Different effects on thermal conductivity of diamond/Al and diamond/Cu composites. *Appl. Surf. Sci.* **2017**, *402*, 372–383. [CrossRef]
36. Pan, Y.; He, X.; Ren, S.; Wu, M.; Qu, X. Optimized thermal conductivity of diamond/Cu composite prepared with tungsten-copper-coated diamond particles by vacuum sintering technique. *Vacuum* **2018**, *153*, 74–81. [CrossRef]
37. Gorsse, S.; Hutchinson, C.; Gouné, M.; Banerjee, R. Additive manufacturing of metals: A brief review of the characteristic microstructures and properties of steels, Ti-6Al-4V and high-entropy alloys. *Sci. Technol. Adv. Mater.* **2017**, *18*, 585. [CrossRef]
38. Rao, H.; Giet, S.; Yang, K.; Wu, X.; Davies, C. The influence of processing parameters on aluminium alloy A357 manufactured by Selective Laser Melting. *Mater. Des.* **2016**, *109*, 334–346. [CrossRef]
39. Xiong, W. Multi-scale Synergistic Mechanical Optimization of Silver Alloy by Selective Laser Melting. Ph.D. Thesis, China University of Geosciences, Wuhan, China, 2021.
40. Tan, Q.; Liu, Y.; Fan, Z.; Zhang, J.; Yin, Y.; Zhang, M. Effect of processing parameters on the densification of an additively manufactured 2024 Al alloy. *J. Mater. Sci. Technol.* **2020**, *58*, 34–45. [CrossRef]
41. Yin, J.; Wang, D.; Yang, L.; Wei, H.; Dong, P.; Ke, L.; Wang, G.; Zhu, H.; Zeng, X. Correlation between forming quality and spatter dynamics in laser powder bed fusion. *Addit. Manuf.* **2020**, *31*, 100958.
42. Yin, J.; Yang, L.; Yang, X.; Zhu, H.; Wang, D.; Ke, L.; Wang, Z.; Wang, G.; Zeng, X. High-power laser-matter interaction during laser powder bed fusion. *Addit. Manuf.* **2019**, *29*, 100778.

43. Ly, S.; Rubenchik, A.M.; Khairallah, S.A.; Guss, G.; Matthews, M.J. Metal vapor microjet controls material redistribution in laser powder bed fusion additive manufacturing. *Sci. Rep.* **2017**, *7*, 4085. [CrossRef] [PubMed]
44. Yin, J.; Hao, L.; Yang, L.; Li, Y.; Li, Z.; Sun, Q.; Shi, B. Investigation of interaction between vapor plume and spatter during selective laser melting additive manufacturing. *Chin. J. Lasers* **2022**, *49*, 1402202.
45. Xi, L.; Gu, D.; Lin, K.; Guo, S.; Liu, Y.; Li, Y.; Guo, M. Effect of ceramic particle size on densification behavior, microstructure formation, and performance of TiB_2-reinforced Al-based composites prepared by selective laser melting. *J. Mater. Res.* **2020**, *35*, 559–570. [CrossRef]
46. Sitek, R.; Szustecki, M.; Zrodowski, L.; Wysocki, B.; Jaroszewicz, J.; Wisniewski, P.; Mizera, J. Analysis of microstructure and properties of a Ti-AlN composite produced by selective laser melting. *Materials* **2020**, *13*, 2218. [CrossRef] [PubMed]
47. Li, Y.; Gu, D.; Zhang, H.; Xi, L. Effect of trace addition of ceramic on microstructure development and mechanical properties of selective laser melted AlSi10Mg alloy. *Chin. J. Mech. Eng.* **2020**, *33*, 33. [CrossRef]
48. Silvain, J.-F.; Veillère, A.; Lu, Y. Copper-carbon and aluminum-carbon composites fabricated by powder metallurgy processes. *J. Phys. Conf. Ser.* **2014**, *525*, 012015. [CrossRef]
49. Kang, Q.; He, X.; Ren, S.; Zhang, L.; Wu, M.; Guo, C.; Cui, W.; Qu, X. Preparation of copper-diamond composites with chromium carbide coatings on diamond particles for heat sink applications. *Appl. Therm. Eng.* **2013**, *60*, 423–429. [CrossRef]
50. Yao, H.; Zhang, N.; Wang, L.; Ding, L. Study on Electroplating of Cu on Diamond Surface. *J. Synth. Cryst.* **2014**, *43*, 987–990.
51. Liverani, E.; Toschi, S.; Ceschini, L.; Fortunato, A. Effect of selective laser melting (SLM) process parameters on microstructure and mechanical properties of 316L austenitic stainless steel. *J. Mater. Process. Technol.* **2017**, *249*, 255–263. [CrossRef]
52. Yin, J.; Zhang, W.; Ke, L.; Wei, H.; Wang, D.; Yang, L.; Zhu, H.; Dong, P.; Wang, G.; Zeng, X. Vaporization of alloying elements and explosion behavior during laser powder bed fusion of Cu–10Zn alloy. *Int. J. Mach. Tools Manuf.* **2021**, *161*, 103686. [CrossRef]
53. Stournara, M.; Xiao, X.; Qi, Y.; Johari, P.; Lu, P.; Sheldon, B.; Gao, H.; Shenoy, V.B. Li segregation induces structure and strength changes at the amorphous Si/Cuinterface. *Nano Lett.* **2013**, *13*, 4759–4768. [CrossRef]
54. Xi, L.; Gu, D.; Guo, S.; Wang, R.; Ding, K.; Prashanth, K. Grain refinement in laser manufactured Al-based composites with TiB_2 ceramic. *J. Mater. Res. Technol.* **2020**, *9*, 2611–2622. [CrossRef]

Article

Microstructure Transformation in Laser Additive Manufactured NiTi Alloy with Quasi-In-Situ Compression

Xiao Yang [1,*], Shuo Wang [1], Hengpei Pan [1], Congyi Zhang [1], Jieming Chen [1], Xinyao Zhang [1,2] and Lingqing Gao [1,2]

1 Luoyang Ship Material Research Institute, Luoyang 471023, China
2 Henan Key Laboratory of Technology and Application of Structural Materials for Ships and Marine Equipments, Luoyang 471023, China
* Correspondence: y19850419h@126.com; Tel.: +86-0379-67256734

Abstract: For NiTi alloys, different additive manufacturing processes may have different compressive recovery capabilities. In particular, there are relatively few studies on the compressive recovery ability of NiTi alloys by the laser-directed energy deposition (LDED) process. In this paper, the compression recovery properties of NiTi alloys with the LDED process were investigated quasi-in-situ by means of transmission electron microscopy, an electron backscatter diffractometer, and focused ion beam–fixed-point sample preparation. The results showed that the material can be completely recovered under 4% deformation and the B19' martensite phase content and dislocation density are basically unchanged. However, the recovery rate was only 90% and the unrecoverable strain was 0.86% at 8% deformation. Meanwhile, the B19' martensite phase content and dislocation density of the material increased. Furthermore, with the increase in deformation, the relative dislocation pinning effect of the Ti_2Ni precipitated phase in the alloy was enhanced, which reduced the compressive strain recovery to a certain extent.

Keywords: laser additive manufacturing; compression; microstructure transformation; dislocation pinning; recovery ability

1. Introduction

NiTi alloy, with a nearly equal atomic ratio, has the most excellent performance, which is the most common application among many known shape memory alloys. It has many advantages, such as superelasticity, the shape memory effect, fatigue resistance, a low elastic modulus, and biocompatibility [1–4]. As we know, the most widely used commercial methods for producing NiTi alloy parts are vacuum arc melting and vacuum induction melting, followed by hot working or cold working. It is likely that casting would lead to segregation defects [5]. Meanwhile, vacuum induction melting has the drawback of crucible contamination [6].However, when NiTi components undergo cold working, they encounter springback and make the overall dimension difficult to be shaped, hindering the application of nickel-titanium alloys.Additive manufacturing (AM), which has emerged in the past decade, is a new technology that can realize the integrated molding of complex components, and a lot of research results have been obtained [7–10]. Among them, selective laser melting (SLM) technology [11–14] and laser-directed energy deposition (LDED) technology [15–17] are typical metal additive manufacturing technologies, which could achievethe rapid formation of metal parts.

In the recent years, laser additive manufacturing has become an ideal preparation method for complex NiTi alloy components, and related technologies have developed rapidly, especially SLM technology [18–21].Dadbakhsh et al. [22] showed that SLM parameters have a great influence on the phase transition temperature and mechanical response of dense porous NiTi alloys. Meier et al. [23] studied the effect of deposition orientation on the compressive properties of SLM Ti-rich $Ni_{50.2}Ti_{49.8}$ (at.%) and found that crystal orientation had no significant effect on the compressive properties of these samples. Yang et al. [24] investigated the additivemanufacturing process of gradient NiTi alloys and obtained the gradient martensite phase by adjusting the process parameters. Bormann et al. [25] focused on the microstructure and texture of NiTi alloys fabricated by SLM and considered the effects of different processing parameters and the scanning rate. Haberland et al. [26] researched the superelasticity and cyclic response of NiTi alloys fabricated by SLM. Lu et al. [27] learned the simultaneous improvement of mechanical properties and shape memory properties by proper precipitation of the Ti_2Ni phase and its mechanism of action. It can be found that a lot of research has been carried out on NiTi alloys with SLM technology, from process parameters and structure to properties.

Compared toSLM technology, LDED technology has lower cost, faster formation, and the ability to form large components and has received extensive attention and research in the industry. Bimber et al. [28] studied the spatial anisotropy of NiTi alloys prepared by LDED and explored the differences of microstructures with different deposition heights. Wan et al. [29] studied the phase transformationbehavior, microstructure evolution, and elastocaloric properties of NiTi alloys prepared by LDED. It is confirmed that NiTi alloys prepared by the LDED process haveexcellent properties and arenot inferior to as-cast NiTi alloys. Research on the compressive properties of NiTi alloys prepared by AM technology has also been reported recently, but the research results are relatively few. Marattukalam [30] prepared NiTi alloys by means of LDED technology; 8% strain was recovered under a pre-compression of 10%, and the recovery rate was further improved after heat treatment. Andani et al. [31] fabricated and designed NiTi shape memory alloys with porous forms by selective laser melting, which exhibited a good shape memory effect, with a recoverable strain of about 5% and functional stability after eight cycles of compression. In addition, the stiffness and residual plastic strain of porous NiTi alloys were found to depend highly on the pore shape and the level of porosity. Moghaddam et al. [32] fabricated Ni-rich NiTi components by using the additive manufacturing process with 250 W laser power, 1250 mm/s scanning speed, 80 μm hatch spacing and without any post-process heat treatments. The results showed superelasticity with 5.62% strain recovery and a 98% recovery ratio.Chen et al. [33] successfully fabricated uniform and graded gyroid cellular structures of NiTi alloys by laser powder bed fusion additive manufacturing. The results showed that all laser powder bed fusion NiTi structures exhibited similar nominal compressive elastic moduli (5–7 GPa) ashuman bones. The resultsof Zhang et al. [34] showed that the energy input balances against the energy output during cyclic loading of porous NiTi alloys after performing several compression cycles as 'training' and the porous NiTi alloys exhibit reliable linear superelasticity and a stable elastic modulus, with strain as high as 4%.

Most of the research on NiTi alloys with AM technology has mainly focused on their functional properties and process parameters. However, there is little systematic in-depth study on the microstructure transformation of the material after compression, especially the microstructure transformation and recovery ability after compression under the LDED process. In this paper, an in-situ compression test was carried out on LDED NiTi samples, and the microstructure transformation and recovery ability of shape memory alloyswere researched in detail.

2. Materials and Methods
2.1. Material Preparation Process

The spherical near-equiatomic $Ni_{50}Ti_{50}$ alloy powder used in this experiment was purchased from China Shenzhen Micro-Nano Additive Technology Co., Ltd. The powder particle size range was 60–150 μm, and the particle size distribution was uniform and exhibited good sphericity. In this paper, LDED technology was used to realize the preparation of samples. The samples were fabricated in LDED equipment consisting of a 4 kW semiconductor laser, a five-axis numerical control working table, a coaxial powder feeder nozzle, and a chamber for circulating inert gas. The preparation process is shown in

Figure 1 The samples were deposited using abidirectional scanning strategy, alaser power of 1800 W, a scanning speed of 600 mm/min, a powder feeding rate of 15 g/min, and a layer thickness of 0.5 mm. Before the LDED process, the mixed powders were dried in a vacuum oven for 2 h at 100 ± 5 °C to eliminate moisture absorption and ensure good flow ability. The forged NiTi plate, with a dimension of 150 × 50 × 10 mm^3, was used as the substrate during the LDED process. Since the oxygen content would have a significant impact on the formation of NiTi alloys, the forming chamber was evacuated before fabrication and high-purity argon (>99.999%) was used to reduce the introduction of oxygen and to ensure that the oxygen content in the chamber was less than 100 ppm during the forming process.

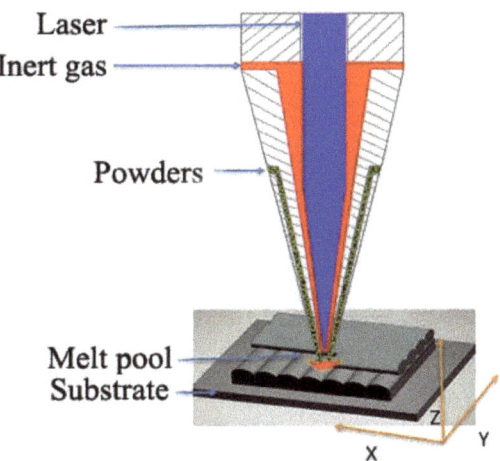

Figure 1. Basic structure diagram of LDED.

During the LDED process, the NiTi alloy powder is exposed to a laser beam with high energy density. The powder is rapidly heated to a temperature above the melting point or even the boiling point. When the laser beam leaves, the melt solidifies quickly (depending on the LDED process parameters and materials). The previously solidified material undergoes a cyclic heating/cooling process, which could promote the continuous epitaxial growth of grain sand evolved to form columnar grain morphologies [35].

2.2. Samples and Test Preparation

The Φ10*20 mm mechanical compression samples were cut from the LDED sample by wire cutting, and to minimize the error of the compression test, the compressed upper and lower surfaces weresanded with sandpaper and polished with flannel to ensure sufficient smoothness and parallelism. Next, the quasi-in-situ [36,37] observation area (the light-blue box in Figure 2) of the sample was marked by an American Wilson VH3100 microhardness tester (made by Buehler Corporation of America) with aforce value of 50 gf, and the distance between the hardness points was 1.5 mm.

The samples with 0% deformation, 4% deformation, and 8% deformation were observed by electron backscatter diffraction (EBSD) and a transmission electron microscope (TEM) to achieve a comparative analysis of the microstructure and phasecomposition. EBSD analysis was performed with a medium-speed and high-resolution electron backscatter diffractometer (American EDAX Co., Ltd., Mahwah, NJ, USA), and TEM analysis was performed with a JEOL-2100 microscope (Japan electronics Co., Ltd., Tokyo, Japan).

EBSD samples needed to be prepared before analysis. As pecific sample preparation process was followed. First, the sample surface was polished to a particle size of 2.5 μm using silicon carbide grinding papers from 180 to 1200 grit. Second, the sample surface was subsequently electro-polished (electro-polishing refers to the process in which metal is subjected to special anodic treatment in a certain composition of polishing liquid to obtain a smooth and bright surface)—in a solution of HNO$_3$:CH$_3$OH (1:10 volume fraction) under 20 V for 15 s.

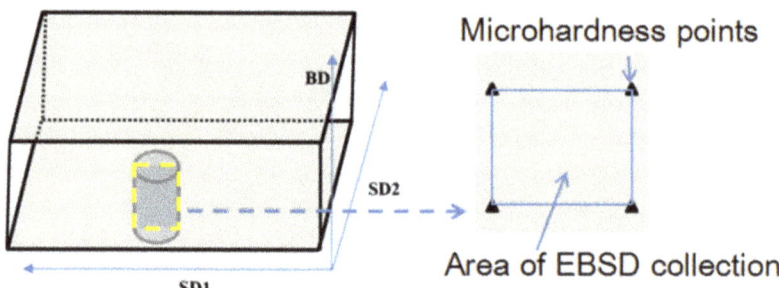

Figure 2. Schematic diagram of insitu region interception and preparation.

TEM samples were prepared by a dual-beam microscope system (American Thermo Electron Corporation) equipped with FIB and SEM at the same time, which can realize the precise preparation of TEM specimens in a fixed-point area. The details are as follows: First, a layer of Pt with a thickness of about 0.5 µm was deposited on the surface of the sample by an electron beam, which could avoid damage to the surface because the electron beam was small and the energy was low. Second, a 2 µm layer of Pt was deposited on the surface of a 0.5 µm Pt layer by ion beam deposition, which was used to eliminate the damage to the sample surface in the process of cutting and thinning in the later stage. Third, the area protected by Pt was processed by ion-beam-cutting technology, and then, the micro-nano-processed sample was transferred to as pecial copper mesh by a nano-manipulator. Lastly, the thickness of the sample was reduced to about 200 nm with a small current ion beam by the tilt function of the sample stage, and the surface deformation layer was also removed. Finally, the sample was transferred to the TEM for analysis.

3. Results and Discussion

3.1. Material Microstructure and Thermal Analysis

The morphology of the shape memory alloy prepared by the LDED method under anoptical microscope (OM; equipment model Leica DMI5000M, made by Leica Geosystems GmbH Vertrieb) is shown in Figure 3a. The sample was polished using silicon carbide grinding papers from 180 to 1200 grit and then polished with flannel to remove surface scratches and deformed layers. The result showed that the NiTi alloy prepared by LDED has fewer macro-defects, no microcrack defects, and a small number of pore defects. The small numbers of pore defects can be attributed to the unstable molten-pool-induced spatter [38,39] or the air flow introduced into the melt pool, but the overall forming quality was good. The microstructure of the alloy was dominated by columnar grains, and a few equiaxed grains were scattered in the interior. The transformation from columnar grains to equiaxed grains occurred. The lifting amount of each layer of the technology was high, and the diameter and expansion range of the laser spot were also large. The deposition size of the single layer of the single melting path was 1 order of magnitude larger than that of SLM technology. The spot diameter of the laser three-dimensional formationreachedseveral millimeters, which made the microstructure of the Ni$_{50.8}$Ti$_{49.2}$ alloy produced by laser additive change greatly in the temperature field (temperature gradient and direction) between different molten pools and less in a single molten pool. The grain hada larger expansion range between single cladding layers, so its grain size was larger. The growth morphology of grains depends on the ratio of temperature gradient (G) to solidification rate (R). The larger the G/R, the easier formation of columnar grains. The smaller the G/R, the easier the formation of equiaxed grains [40].

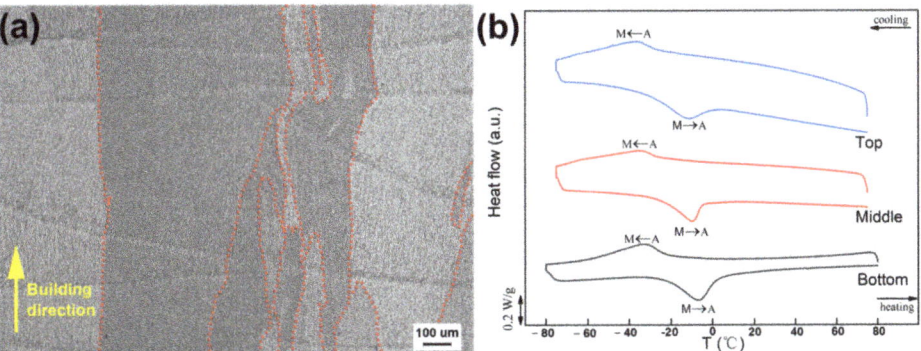

Figure 3. (**a**) Metallographic photos and (**b**) DSC curves of the bottom, middle, and top positions along the deposition direction.

In NiTi alloys with a near-equiatomic ratio, the Ni/Ti atomic ratio significantly affects the phase transformation temperature and an increase inNi content sharply reduces the phase transformation temperature, ranging from 50 to 51 at.%, and there is a temperature change of about 100 K/at.% [41]. Some studies have shown that a high-energy input causes serious vaporization and ablation of Ni during deposition, resulting in a decrease inthe Ni content of the as-built sample matrix and an increase in the phase transformation temperature. Figure 3b shows the differential scanning calorimetry (DSC) curves of different positions of the sample. It can be seen that the start temperature of martensitic transformation (Ms) and the end temperature of reverse transformation (Af) of the sample were both lower than room temperature, so the main phase composition of the sample was the B2 parent phase at room temperature. Based on the fact that Ms and Af have great influence on superelasticity at room temperature, the phase transformation temperature indicates that the deformation of the sample at room temperature is superelasticity.

3.2. Phase Transition Behavior under Compressive Strain

The LDED sample was compressed on anMTS mechanical testing machine according to 4% and 8% deformation of the original size. The stress–strain curve of compression is shown in Figure 4. When the sample was at 4% deformation, the recovery rate was 100%. However, it had 10% plastic deformation, with 8% compression deformation. It is noteworthy that in the compression deformation at 4%, as shown in Figure 4a, the critical stress for stress-induced martensitic transformation was about 360 MPa and the critical strain was about 3% (determinedby the tangent method, and point E is the end point of 4% deformation). The difference in the critical strain is due to the compression of the sample through a smaller strain, which activates the deformation path of more martensitic variants [42], and stress-induced martensitic transformation is more likely to occur under a large strain.

When a load is applied, the parent phase (A) experiences elastic loads (A,B). At a specific loading level, the loading path intersects the onset surface of the martensitic transformation on the phase diagram, which marks the beginning of the transformation to martensite. It is worth mentioning that the stress-induced transformation from austenite to martensite is accompanied by the generation of a large amount of inelastic strain. In the transformation process (B,C), when the stress level reaches Mf, it means the end of the phase transformation. When the slope of the stress–strain curve changes significantly, the martensitic transformation is complete. When we continue to increase the force, only the elastic deformation (C,D) of the self-cooperative martensite occurs and there is no further phasetransformation. When the stress is gradually unloaded, the phase transformation causes the recovery of the strain. The end of the transformation to austenite is indicated by the point at which the stress–strain unloading curve re-enters the elastic region of austenite, and the material then undergoes elastic deformation back to A. The length of the blue line in Figure 4b is 0.86%, which is the amount of irreversible strain caused by plastic deformation.

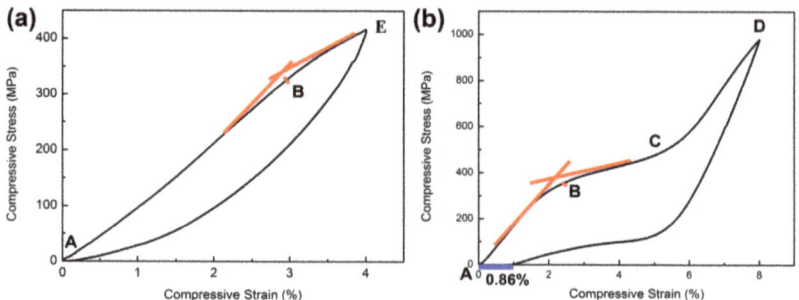

Figure 4. Stress–strain curve of compression: (**a**) 4% deformation and (**b**) 8% deformation.

3.3. Hardness Analysis after Different Compression

The microhardness test was carried out using American Wilson VH3100 (made by Buehler Corporation of America), with a force of 100 gf, and was completed within 10 min after compression. As shown in Figure 5, with the increase indeformation, the hardness value of the sample also increased, which indicates that the amount of deformation has a positive correlation with microhardness. In addition, the microhardness increased significantly at 8% deformation, reaching 16.9%. It is well known that the main mechanism of deformation strength is based on dislocation movement. With an increase in deformation in the LDED sample, the dislocation density of the sample increased, and then, the strength and hardness of the surface increased accordingly. At 4% deformation, the recovery rate of the sample was 100%. Although no obvious martensite phase was identified, the dislocation density still increased during the deformation process. In addition, at 8% strain, the deformation of the sample was not fully recovered, which significantly introduced plastic deformation. At the same time, as shown in Figure 4, the appearance of the martensite phase may have also promoted an increase in the microhardness value [43].

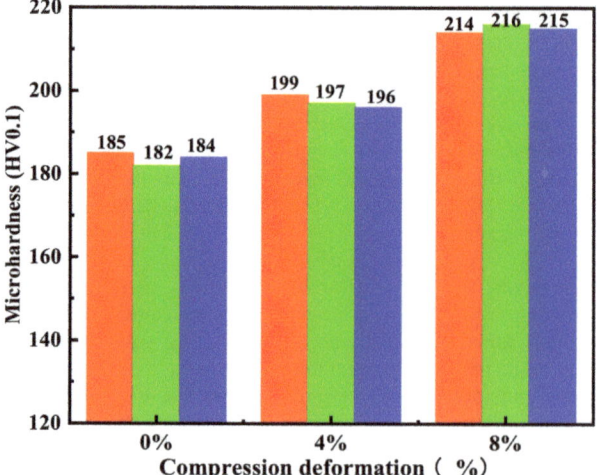

Figure 5. Microhardness values of samples at 0%, 4%, and 8% compressive deformation.

3.4. EBSD Analysis

Figure 6 shows the quasi-in-situ EBSD morphologies of the 0%, 4%, and 8% deformation.

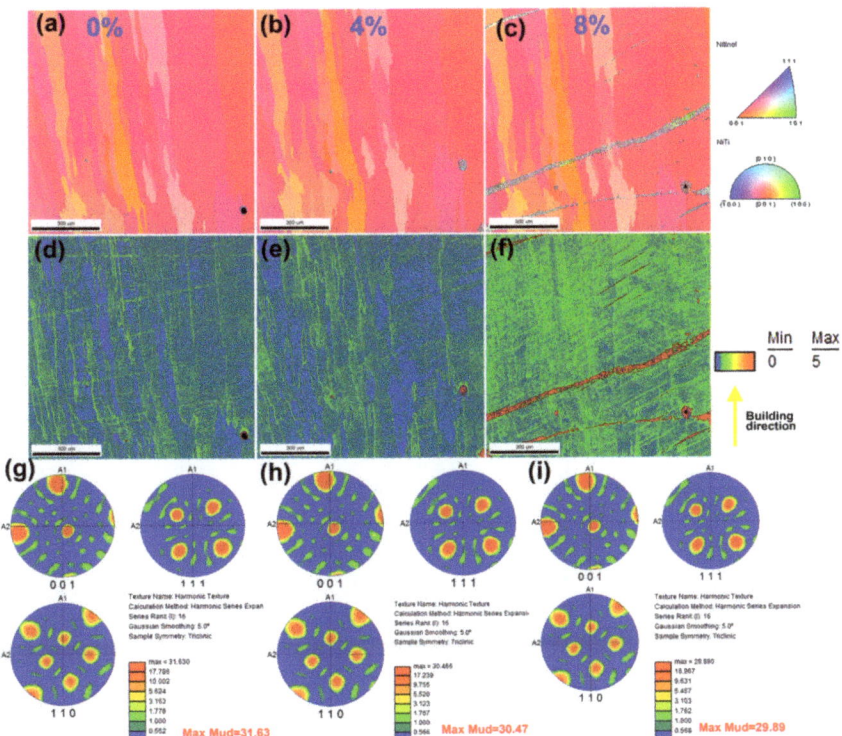

Figure 6. EBSD analysis of different samples: (**a**–**c**) inverse pole figure orientation contrast maps of the original state, 4% deformation, and 8% deformation samples, respectively; (**d**–**f**) KAM images of the original state, 4% deformation, and 8% deformation samples, respectively; and (**g**–**i**) pole figures of the 0% deformation, 4% deformation, and 8% deformation samples in {001}, {110}, and {111}, respectively.

The inverse pole figure orientation contrast maps of the original state, 4% deformation, and 8% deformation samples are shown in Figure 6a–c, respectively. The results showed that the 0% deformation sample was a single-parent phase with a B2 crystalstructure and hada strong texture of <100>∥BD (deposition direction). The sample with 4% deformation did not exhibit obvious martensite and dislocation defects, which are caused by deformation. Thisshows that the sample with 4% compression deformation completely recovered and there wasbasically no structural deformation and no obvious accumulation of dislocation density. However, when the amount of compression deformation increased to 8%, the content of the deformed martensite phase increased suddenly and reached 4.5%. Meanwhile, the kernel average misorientation (KAM) diagramsof the original state, 4% deformation, and 8% deformation samples are exhibited in Figure 6d–f, respectively. KAM is the most commonly used method in local misfit angle analysis. It is generally used to describe the local strain distribution of crystalline materials and is especially suitable for describing the strain distribution at the grain and phase boundaries of crystalline materials after deformation.It can be seen from the KAM diagram that as the amount of deformation increased, the color of the quasi-in-situ region of the material became darker. Therefore, it can be concluded that the stress distribution in the quasi-in situ region also increasedsignificantly when the deformation increasedto 8%.

The compression with 8% deformation caused a certain irreversible plastic deformation, and the stress-induced martensite was elongated and distributed at a certain angle (30–40°) to the deposition direction (BD). It is worth noting that with an increase in deformation, the strength of the preferred orientation slightly decreased. The decrease in the texture in the 8% deformation sample may be related to the presence of the B19′ martensite phase, leading to a decrease in the B2 parent phase.

3.5. TEM Analysis

The quasi-in-situ TEM samples with different deformations were cut by an FIB. The phase morphology of the original sample is shown in Figure 7a. We concluded that there was no obvious dislocation aggregation phenomenon in the original sample and there were two different phases in the original sample, which are marked as regions b and c. The selected area electron diffraction (SAED) of regions b and c is shown in Figure 7b and Figure 7c, respectively. Region b is the B2 parent phase. Region c was the Ti_2Ni phase, which is the main precipitation phase of the material.

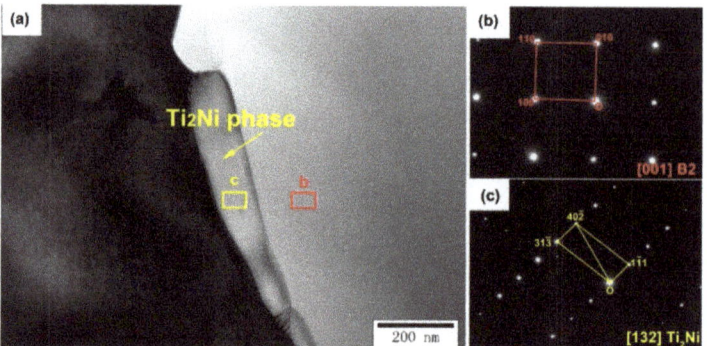

Figure 7. (a) is TEM morphology analysis of the 0% compressive deformation sample, (b) is SAED of the B2 parent phase (red box in (a)) and (c) is the Ti_2Ni precipitated phase (yellow box in (a)).

When the sample was subjected to 4% deformation, the microstructure of the material changed significantly. As shown in Figure 8, there was obvious dislocation aggregation in the quasi-in-situ area of the sample. Meanwhile, the phase of the material did not change significantly and the whole quasi-in-situ area of the sample was still mainly the B2 parent phase. However, it is worth noting that a small amount of the B19′ martensite phase had begun to exist in the individual positions of the quasi-in situ region. The morphology of dislocation aggregation and SAED of the B19′ martensite phase are shown in Figure 8.

The morphology of dislocation aggregation and SAED of the B19′ martensite phase with 8% deformation are shown in Figure 9. The results showed that the dislocation aggregation phenomenon in the quasi-in situ region was more obvious and the dislocation density increased significantly. Furthermore, there was more B19′ martensite phase in the whole quasi-in-situ region.

To further determine the relationship between the Ti_2Ni precipitated phase and dislocation aggregation, we performed TEM analysis on the original sample, the 4% deformation sample, and the 8% deformation sample, and the results are shown in Figure 10. It can be seen that there were no obvious dislocations near the Ti_2Ni precipitated phase of the original sample. However, when the sample was subjected to 4% deformation, there was a certain degree of dislocation aggregation near the Ti_2Ni precipitated phase. Moreover, the dislocation density around the Ti_2Ni precipitated phase obviously increased; after 8% deformation, which means the hindering effect of the Ti_2Ni precipitated phase on the dislocation was more obvious. The accumulation of dislocations leads to local stress concentration, so the stress-induced martensite is difficult to recover and the strain is retained.

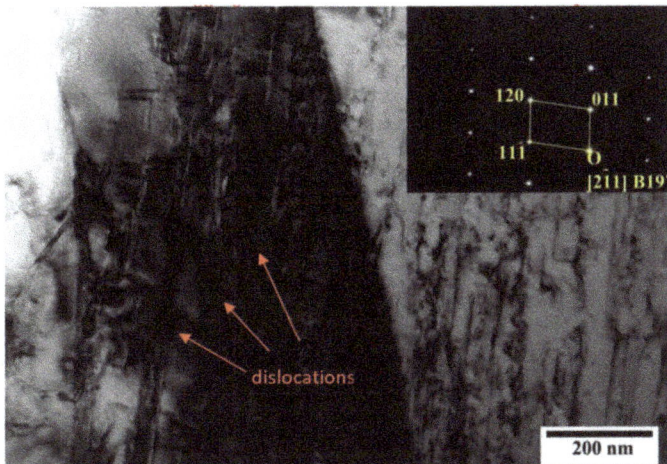

Figure 8. TEM analysis of the 4% compression sample and SAED of the B19′ phase.

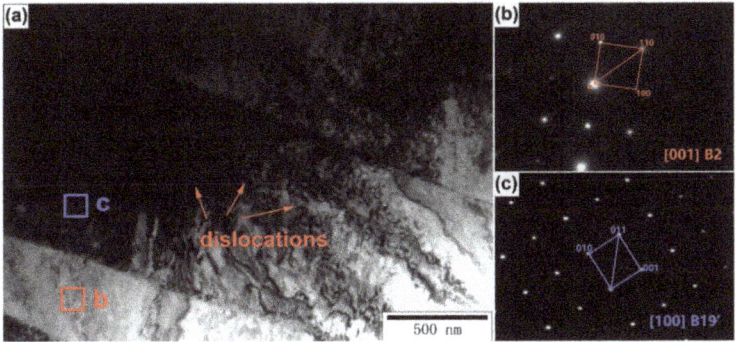

Figure 9. (a) is the TEM morphologyanalysis of the 8% deformation sample, (b) is the SAED of the B2 parent phase (red box in (a)) and (c) is the B19′ phase (blue box in (a)).

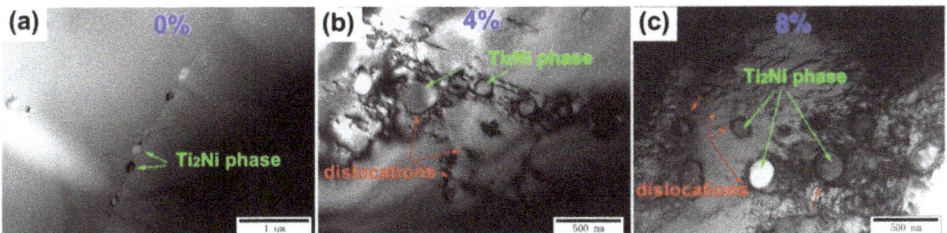

Figure 10. TEM bright-field images of (a) 0% compressive deformation, (b) 4% compressive deformation, and (c) 8% compressive deformation samples.

4. Conclusions

The quasi-in situ analysis of LDED-prepared samples with 0%, 4%, and 8% deformation showed compression behavior can reflect the strength and plasticity of the sample, and it is a common method to characterize the mechanical properties of metal materials. According to the compression test, the microhardness of the material increases with an increase in the deformation amount, and the increase in microhardness can reach about 16.9%

under 8% deformation. The increase in material strength is mainly due to the formation of deformed martensite and an increase in dislocation density.

Shape memory alloy materials have good superelastic properties, which can be fully recovered under 4% compressive strain, and the recovery rate can also be as high as 90% under 8% compressive strain.

In terms of microstructure transmission, under a compressive deformation of 4%, there is basically no B19' martensite phase and the dislocation density does not change significantly. However, when the sample issubjected to 8% compressive deformation, the content of the B19' martensite phase and the dislocation density in the material increasessignificantly.

With the increase incompressive strain, the dislocation density near the Ti_2Ni phase increases and its dislocation pinning effect also increases. The dislocation pinning effect of the Ti_2Ni precipitated phase reduces the deformation recovery performance of shape memory alloys toa certain extent.

Author Contributions: X.Y. conceived and designed the experiments; X.Y., C.Z. and S.W. performed the experiments; X.Y., S.W., J.C. and H.P. analyzed the data; X.Y., X.Z. and L.G. contributed reagents/materials/analysis tools; X.Y. wrote the paper. All authors have read and agreed to the published version of the manuscript.

Funding: This research received no external funding.

Institutional Review Board Statement: Not applicable.

Informed Consent Statement: Not applicable.

Data Availability Statement: The data presented in this study are available on request from the corresponding author. The data are not publicly available due to privacy.

Conflicts of Interest: The authors declare no conflict of interest.

References

1. Elahinia, M.; Shayesteh-Moghaddam, N.; Taheri Andani, A.; Amerinatanzi, A.; Bimber, B.A.; Hamilton, R.F. Fabrication of NiTi through additive manufacturing: A review. *Prog. Mater. Sci.* **2016**, *83*, 630–663. [CrossRef]
2. Ou, S.F.; Peng, B.Y.; Chen, Y.C.; Meng-Hsiu, T. Manufacturing and Characterization of NiTi Alloy with Functional Properties by Selective Laser Melting. *Metals* **2018**, *8*, 342. [CrossRef]
3. Sam, J.; Franco, B.; Ma, J.; Karaman, I.; Elwany, A.; Mabe, J.H. Tensile actuation response of additively manufactured nickel-titanium shape memory alloys. *Scripta Mater.* **2018**, *146*, 164–168. [CrossRef]
4. Mohd Jani, J.; Leary, M.; Subic, A.; Gibson, A. A review of shape memory alloyresearch, applications and opportunities. *Mater. Des.* **2014**, *56*, 1078–1113. [CrossRef]
5. Hey, J.; Jardine, A. Shape memory TiNi synthesis from elemental powders. *Mater. Sci. Eng. A* **1994**, *188*, 291–300. [CrossRef]
6. Shin, Y.; Halani, P. In-Situ Synthesis and Micro-Structural Characterization of Shape Memory Alloy-Nitinol by Laser Direct Deposition. In Proceedings of the Aeromat 22 Conference and Exposition American Society for Metals, Long Beach, CA, USA, 23–26 May 2011.
7. Herzog, D.; Seyda, V.; Wycisk, E.; Emmelmann, C. Additive manufacturing of metals. *Acta Mater.* **2016**, *117*, 371–392. [CrossRef]
8. Qi, T.; Zhu, H.; Zhang, H.; Yin, J.; Ke, L.; Zeng, X. Selective laser melting of Al7050 powder: Melting mode transition and comparison of the characteristics between the keyhole and conduction mode. *Mater. Des.* **2017**, *135*, 257–266. [CrossRef]
9. Li, Z.; Li, H.; Yin, J.; Li, Y.; Nie, Z.; Li, X.; You, D.; Guan, K.; Duan, W.; Cao, L.; et al. A Review of Spatter in Laser Powder Bed Fusion Additive Manufacturing: In Situ Detection, Generation, Effects, and Countermeasures. *Micromachines* **2022**, *13*, 1366. [CrossRef]
10. Zhou, Y.; Xu, L.; Yang, Y.; Wang, J.; Wang, D.; Shen, L. Microstructure and Corrosion Behavior of Iron Based Biocomposites Prepared by Laser Additive Manufacturing. *Micromachines* **2022**, *13*, 712. [CrossRef]
11. Liu, Y.; Meng, J.; Zhu, L.; Chen, H.; Li, Z.; Li, S.; Wang, D.; Wang, Y.; Kosiba, K. Dynamic compressive properties and underlying failure mechanisms of selective laser melted Ti-6Al-4V alloy under high temperature and strain rate conditions. *Addit. Manuf.* **2022**, *54*, 102772. [CrossRef]
12. Aboulkhair, N.T.; Simonelli, M.; Parry, L.; Ashcroft, I.; Tuck, C.; Hague, R. 3D printing of Aluminium alloys: Additive Manufacturing of Aluminium alloys using selective laser melting. *Prog. Mater. Sci.* **2019**, *106*, 100578. [CrossRef]
13. Kusano, M.; Kitano, H.; Watanabe, M. Novel Calibration Strategy for Validation of Finite Element Thermal Analysis of Selective Laser Melting Process Using Bayesian Optimization. *Materials* **2021**, *14*, 4948. [CrossRef] [PubMed]
14. Zhang, Y.; Hu, X.; Jiang, Y. Study on the Microstructure and Fatigue Behavior of a Laser-Welded Ni-Based Alloy Manufactured by Selective Laser Melting Method. *J. Mater. Enge. Perform.* **2020**, *29*, 2957–2968. [CrossRef]

15. Jinoop, A.N.; Paul, C.P.; Nayak, S.K.; Kumar, J.G.; Bindra, K.S. Effect of laser energy per unit powder feed on Hastelloy-X walls built by laser directed energy deposition based additive manufacturing. *Opt. Laser Technol.* **2021**, *138*, 106845. [CrossRef]
16. Radhakrishnan, M.; Hassan, M.M.; Long, B.E.; Otazu, D.; Lienert, T.J.; Anderoglu, O. Microstructures and properties of Ti/TiC composites fabricated by laser-directed energy deposition. *Addit. Manuf.* **2021**, *46*, 102198. [CrossRef]
17. Pan, Q.; Kapoor, M.; Mileski, S.; Carsley, J.; Lou, X. Technical basis of using laser direct energy deposition as a high-throughput combinatorial method for DC-cast Al-Mn alloy development. *Mater. Des.* **2021**, *212*, 110290. [CrossRef]
18. Saedi, S.; Turabi, A.S.; Andani, M.T.; Moghaddam, N.S.; Elahinia, M.; Karaca, H.E. Texture, aging, and superelasticity of selective laser melting fabricated Ni-rich NiTi alloys. *Mater. Sci. Eng. A* **2017**, *686*, 1–10. [CrossRef]
19. Qiu, P.; Gao, P.; Wang, S.; Li, Z.; Yang, Y.; Zhang, Q.; Xiong, Z.; Hao, S. Study on corrosion behavior of the selective laser melted NiTi alloy with superior tensile property and shape memory effect. *Corros. Sci.* **2020**, *175*, 108891. [CrossRef]
20. Li, S.; Hassanin, H.; Attallah, M.; Adkins, N.J.; Essa, K. The development of TiNi-based negative Poisson's ratio structure using selective laser melting. *Acta Mater.* **2016**, *105*, 75–83. [CrossRef]
21. Saedi, S.; Moghaddam, N.; Amerinatanzi, A.; Elahinia, M.; Karaca, H.E. On the effects of selective laser melting process parameters on microstructure and thermomechanical response of Ni-rich NiTi. *Acta Mater.* **2018**, *144*, 552–560. [CrossRef]
22. Dadbakhsh, S.; Speirs, M.; Kruth, J.P.; Schrooten, J.; Luyten, J.; Van Humbeeck, J. Effect of SLM Parameters on Transformation Temperatures of Shape Memory Nickel Titanium Parts. *Adv. Eng. Mater.* **2014**, *16*, 1140–1146. [CrossRef]
23. Meier, H.; Haberland, C.; Frenzel, J. Structural and functional Properties of NiTi Shape Memory Alloys produced by Selective Laser Melting. In Proceedings of the 5th International Conference on Advanced Research and Rapid Proto Typing, Leiria, Portugal, 28 September–1 October 2011.
24. Yang, Y.; Zhan, J.; Sui, J.; Li, C.; Yang, K.; Castany, P.; Gloriant, T. Functionally graded NiTi alloy with exceptional strain-hardening effect fabricated by SLM method. *ScriptaMaterialia* **2020**, *188*, 130–134. [CrossRef]
25. Bormann, T.; Schumacher, R.; Müller, B.; Mertmann, M. Tailoring Selective Laser Melting Process Parameters for NiTi Implants. *J Mater Enge Perform.* **2012**, *21*, 2519–2524. [CrossRef]
26. Haberland, C.; Elahinia, M.; Walker, J.; Meier, H.; Frenzel, J. On the development of high quality NiTi shape memory and pseudoelastic parts by additive manufacturing. *Smart Mater. Struct.* **2014**, *23*, 104002. [CrossRef]
27. Lu, H.; Liu, L.; Yang, C.; Luo, X.; Song, C.; Wang, Z.; Wang, J.; Su, Y.; Ding, Y.; Zhang, L.; et al. Simultaneous enhancement of mechanical and shape memory properties by heat-treatment homogenization of Ti2Ni precipitates in TiNi shape memory alloy fabricated by selective laser melting. *J. Mater. Sci. Technol.* **2022**, *101*, 205–216. [CrossRef]
28. Bimber, B.; Hamilton, R.F.; Keist, J.; Palmer, T.A. Anisotropic microstructure and superelasticity of additive manufactured NiTi alloy bulk builds using laser directed energy deposition. *Mater. Sci. Eng. A* **2016**, *674*, 125–134. [CrossRef]
29. Wan, X.; Feng, Y.; Lin, X.; Tan, H. Large superelastic recovery and elastocaloric effect in as-deposited additive manufactured Ni50.8Ti49.2 alloy. *Appl. Phys. Lett.* **2019**, *114*, 221903. [CrossRef]
30. Marattukalam, J.; Balla, V.; Das, M.; Bontha, S.; Kalpathy, S.K. Effect of heat treatment on microstructure, corrosion, and shape memory characteristics of laser deposited NiTi alloy. *J. Alloy. Compd.* **2018**, *744*, 337–346. [CrossRef]
31. Taheri Andani, M.; Saedi, S.; Turabi, A.S.; Karamooz, R.; Haberland, C.; Karac, E.; Elahinia, M. Mechanical and shape memory properties of porous Ni50.1Ti49.9 alloys manufactured by selective laser melting. *J. Mech. Behav. Biomed. Mater.* **2017**, *68*, 224–231. [CrossRef]
32. Hayesteh Moghaddam, N.; Saedi, S.; Amerinatanzi, A.; Hinojos, A.; Ramazani, A.; Kundin, J.; Mills, M.J.; Karaca, H.; Elahinia, M. Achieving superelasticity in additively manufactured NiTi in compression without post-process heat treatment. *Sci. Rep.* **2019**, *9*, 41. [CrossRef]
33. Chen, W.; Yang, Q.; Huang, S.; Kruzic, J.J.; Li, X. Compression Behavior of Graded NiTi Gyroid-Structures Fabricated by Laser Powder Bed Fusion Additive Manufacturing Under Monotonic and Cyclic Loading. *JOM* **2021**, *73*, 4154–4165. [CrossRef]
34. Zhang, Y.; Zhao, S.; Xiao, M.; Zhang, X. Compression mechanical behavior of porous NiTi alloys exhibiting high linear superelasticity. *Chin. J. Nonferrous Met.* **2009**, *19*, 2167–2172. [CrossRef]
35. Li, X.; Wang, T. Numerical investigation of effects of nucleation mechanisms on grain structure in metal additive manufacturing. *Comput. Mater. Sci.* **2018**, *153*, 159–169. [CrossRef]
36. Wang, Y.; Yao, Y.; Wang, Z.; Jin, Y.; Zhang, X.; Liu, J. Thermal ageing on the deformation and fracture mechanisms of a duplex stainless steel by quasi in-situ tensile test under OM and SEM. *Mater. Sci. Eng. A* **2016**, *666*, 184–190. [CrossRef]
37. Xu, H.; Xu, Y.; He, Y.; Jiao, H.; Yue, S.; Li, J. A quasi in-situ EBSD study of the nucleation and growth of Goss grains during primary and secondary recrystallization of a strip-cast Fe-6.5 wt% Si alloy. *J. Alloy. Compd.* **2020**, *861*, 158550. [CrossRef]
38. Yin, J.; Wang, D.; Yang, L.; Wei, H.; Dong, P.; Ke, L.; Wang, G.; Zhu, H.; Zeng, X. Correlation between forming quality and spatter dynamics in laser powder bed fusion. *Addit. Manuf.* **2020**, *31*, 100958. [CrossRef]
39. Yin, J.; Zhang, W.; Ke, L.; Wei, H.; Wang, D.; Yang, L.; Zhu, H.; Dong, P.; Wang, G.; Zeng, X. Vaporization of alloying elements and explosion behavior during laser powder bed fusion of Cu–10Zn alloy. *Int. J. Mach. Tools Manuf.* **2021**, *161*, 103686. [CrossRef]
40. Froend, A.M.; Ventzke, V.; Dorn, F.; Kashaev, N.; Klusemann, B.; Enz, J. Microstructure by design: An approach of grain refinement and isotropy improvement in multi-layer wire-based laser metal deposition. *Mater. Sci. Eng. A* **2020**, *772*, 138635. [CrossRef]
41. Frenzel, J.; George, E.; Dlouhy, A.; Somsen, C.; Wagner, M.; Eggeler, G. Influence of Ni on martensitic phase transformations in NiTi shape memory alloys. *Acta Mater.* **2010**, *58*, 3444–3458. [CrossRef]

42. Sehitoglu, H.; Ikaraman, I.; Anderson, R.; Zhang, X.; Gall, K.; Maier, H.; Chumlyakov, Y. Compressive response of NiTi single crystals. *Acta Mater.* **2000**, *48*, 3311–3326. [CrossRef]
43. Saedi, S.; Turabi, A.; Andani, M.; Haberland, C.; Karaca, H.; Elahinia, M. The influence of heat treatment on the thermomechanical response of Ni-rich NiTi alloys manufactured by selective laser melting. *J. Alloy. Compd.* **2016**, *677*, 204–210. [CrossRef]

Review

A Review of Spatter in Laser Powder Bed Fusion Additive Manufacturing: In Situ Detection, Generation, Effects, and Countermeasures

Zheng Li [1], Hao Li [1], Jie Yin [1,*], Yan Li [1], Zhenguo Nie [2], Xiangyou Li [3], Deyong You [4], Kai Guan [5], Wei Duan [6], Longchao Cao [7], Dengzhi Wang [3], Linda Ke [8], Yang Liu [9], Ping Zhao [10], Lin Wang [11], Kunpeng Zhu [6], Zhengwen Zhang [12], Liang Gao [13] and Liang Hao [1]

1. Gemological Institute, China University of Geosciences, Wuhan 430074, China
2. Department of Mechanical Engineering, Tsinghua University, Beijing 100084, China
3. Wuhan National Laboratory for Optoelectronics, Huazhong University of Science and Technology, Wuhan 430074, China
4. Diligine Photonics Co., Ltd., Guangzhou 510000, China
5. TSC Laser Technology Development (Beijing) Co., Ltd., Beijing 100076, China
6. School of Machinery and Automation, Wuhan University of Science and Technology, Wuhan 430081, China
7. School of Aerospace Engineering, Huazhong University of Science & Technology, Wuhan 430074, China
8. Shanghai Engineering Technology Research Center of Near-Net-Shape Forming for Metallic Materials, Shanghai Spaceflight Precision Machinery Institute, Shanghai 201600, China
9. Faculty of Mechanical Engineering & Mechanics, Ningbo University, Ningbo 315211, China
10. Department of Microtechnology and Nanoscience, Chalmers University of Technology, 41296 Gothenburg, Sweden
11. Nanjing Chamlion Laser Technology Co., Ltd., Nanjing 210039, China
12. The State Key Laboratory of Mechanical Transmissions, Chongqing University, Chongqing 400044, China
13. State Key Laboratory of Digital Manufacturing Equipment and Technology, School of Mechanical Science and Engineering, Huazhong University of Science and Technology, Wuhan 430074, China
* Correspondence: yinjie@cug.edu.cn

Abstract: Spatter is an inherent, unpreventable, and undesired phenomenon in laser powder bed fusion (L-PBF) additive manufacturing. Spatter behavior has an intrinsic correlation with the forming quality in L-PBF because it leads to metallurgical defects and the degradation of mechanical properties. This impact becomes more severe in the fabrication of large-sized parts during the multi-laser L-PBF process. Therefore, investigations of spatter generation and countermeasures have become more urgent. Although much research has provided insights into the melt pool, microstructure, and mechanical property, reviews of spatter in L-PBF are still limited. This work reviews the literature on the in situ detection, generation, effects, and countermeasures of spatter in L-PBF. It is expected to pave the way towards a novel generation of highly efficient and intelligent L-PBF systems.

Keywords: spatter; laser powder bed fusion; in situ detection; generation mechanism; detrimental effects; counter-measures; additive manufacturing

1. Introduction

Additive manufacturing (AM) is widely used in aerospace, medicine, jewelry, and other industries because of its rapid fabrication [1,2], low cost, and the ability to print parts with complex geometries [3,4]. Today, many developed and developing countries regard AM technology as a fifth industrial revolution and make many efforts in the development of AM. The United States Department of Defense (DoD) released the Department of Defense Additive Manufacturing Strategy [5] to stimulate the development of AM applications in national defense. Meanwhile, the Office of the Under Secretary of Defense released the first policy paper, DoD 5000.93 Directive Use of Additive Manufacturing in the Department of Defense [6], which promoted the implementation of the AM strategy. The Ministry of

Science and Technology of the People's Republic of China released the 2022 annual project application guide for the key projects of additive manufacturing and laser manufacturing under the 14th Five-Year National Key R&D Program [7] to establish a new standard system for AM that is consistent with international standards. Additionally, AM and laser manufacturing are two of the important tasks of the National Program for Medium-to-Long-Term Scientific and Technological Development and Made in China 2025. The EU began funding projects on AM technology as early as the first Framework Program for Research and Technological Development. Under these conditions, AM technology has advanced significantly and rapidly in developing standard systems, key technologies, and multi-industry applications.

AM technology emerged in the 1990s and has been under development for approximately three decades [8]. Unlike "subtractive manufacturing" (e.g., cutting, drilling, and milling) and "equal-material manufacturing" (e.g., welding, casting, and forging), AM is built on 3D models [9], relies on layer by layer printing-extrusion, sintering [10,11], melting, light curing, and jetting to form solids from metallic or non-metallic materials [12,13].

Metal AM is one of the most difficult and cutting-edge AM technologies. As shown in Figure 1, metal AM technologies can be divided into two categories, direct energy deposition (DED) and powder bed fusion (PBF) [14,15]. PBF is one of the AM technologies used to fabricate metal objects from powder feedstocks with two kinds of input energy: laser and electron [16–18]. In the printing process, the metal powder bed is melted by the high energy source with a designed pattern using a layer by layer printing strategy [19–21].

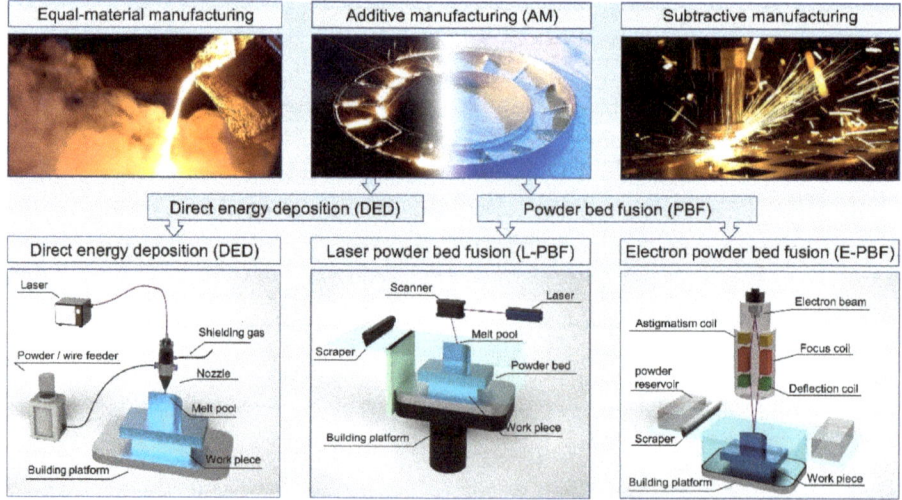

Figure 1. Classification of metal manufacturing processes: equal-material manufacturing, additive manufacturing [22], subtractive manufacturing.

Figure 1 also illustrates the forming principle of laser powder bed fusion (L-PBF), which is widely used today to rapidly manufacture parts with complicated shapes, a fine grain size, high densities, and superior mechanical properties [23,24]. Although it can currently fabricate complicated metal parts [25,26], the reliability and stability of the printing process remain inadequate [27]. There are still defects in L-PBF processing that decrease the density and affect the mechanical characteristics of the part or even result in fabrication failure. The many unresolved problems with L-PBF become a barrier to the expansion of L-PBF applications.Spatter is generated in conventional laser welding and cutting, DED, and L-PBF. Spatters are the particles ejected from a melt pool during the laser–metal interaction [28]. In conventional laser welding and cutting, the laser scanning path is relatively simple, with few overlap regions between the scanning paths, and DED has a lower scanning velocity and a larger spot than L-PBF. However, L-PBF is a powder-bed-based technology, and the printing process is more complicated than that of the three technologies mentioned above, which results in a more complex spatter behavior. Furthermore, during multi-laser L-PBF, the thermal and stress cycling, melt pool characteristics, spatter behavior, and metal vapor evolution will be definitely different from that of the single-laser PBF. The detection of spatter under multi-laser L-PBF is more difficult.

For this reason, studies on L-PBF spatter are becoming very urgent. Spatter as a by-product of L-PBF is unpreventable [29,30]. It is a detriment to the forming process, and the part and the redeposited spatters can destroy the original well-built powder layer, resulting in non-fusion defects [31,32]. Due to the uniqueness of L-PBF, the undesired effects of spatter are amplified during the layer-by-layer process. Spatter affects the subsequent re-coating and melting of the powder, resulting in internal defects in the produced part or the part failing to form.

As spatter has a significant effect on L-PBF, it can be used to represent the L-PBF machining state. Spatter contains a plethora of information and can be used in various ways to analyze the manufacturing processing of L-PBF. By observing and quantifying the spatter, it is possible to establish an intrinsic correlation between spatter and the part quality, enabling a more comprehensive understanding of the L-PBF process to solve the problems of insufficient stability and reliability, allowing this technology to be popularized and applied more widely.

Recently, the research concerning the spatter during L-PBF has received more and more extensive attention. In this work, we review academic publications concerning L-PBF spatter in the Web of Science database from 2015 to date (Topic: ["laser-powder bed fusion" and "spatter"] or ["selective laser melting" and "spatter"]). Figure 2 shows the trend in the number of articles on this topic over the last several years.

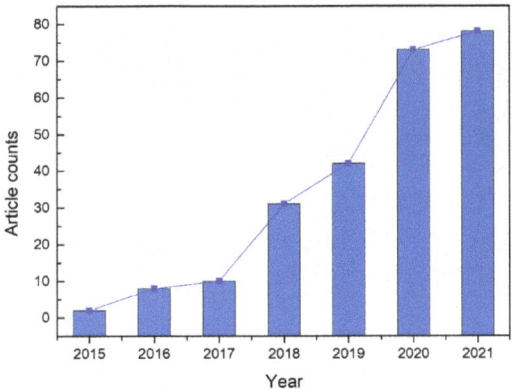

Figure 2. Number of articles about L-PBF spattering since 2016 (Topic: ["laser-powder bed fusion" and "spatter"] or ["selective laser melting" and "spatter"]) Database: Web of Science.

This article builds on previous research by reviewing a synthesis of in situ spatter detection systems, spatter detection equipment, the generation of spatter and its associated disadvantages, and current approaches for the suppression and removal of spatter. Finally, the future of research on L-PBF spatter is discussed.

2. Laser Powder Bed Fusion Spatter In Situ Detection Device

The L-PBF detection system can be categorized as: static detection (imaging of spreading powder and deformation) and dynamic detection (characterization of melt pool, spatter, and vapor plume).

The spatter generated by conventional laser welding, cutting, and DED is similar to that produced by L-PBF and is caused by the interaction between the laser and the metal material. However, L-PBF has a smaller spot (~10^1 to 10^2 μm), a smaller melt pool (up to 100 μm), a shorter lifetime (~10 ms), and a higher scanning velocity (~10^2 to 10^3 mm/s) compared to laser welding, cutting, and DED [33]. Furthermore, in L-PBF, the laser interacts with the powder bed and the metal part more than once, resulting in a greater number and variety of spatters and complicating in situ spatter detection.

The laser–powder bed interaction produces the melt pool, spatter, and vapor plume (even plasma). The trajectory of the melt pool is in the plane of the laser path and can be predicted according to the strategy path, whereas the motion of the spatter is in a 3D space, and its trajectory is complex and difficult to predict. So, the detection of spatter is more difficult. Spatter can be divided into hot droplet spatter (mainly from the instability of the melt pool) and cold powder spatter (mainly driven by the vapor-induced entrainment of the protective gas). Both of them can be detected with the visible-light camera equipped with an illumination source, and the relevant collected information can be used to analyze them.

According to various studies, the following methods are currently available for L-PBF spatter detection: (1) a visible-light high-speed camera, (2) X-ray video imaging, (3) infrared video imaging, and (4) schlieren video imaging. These detection techniques can detect different characteristics, as shown in Figure 3 and Table 1.

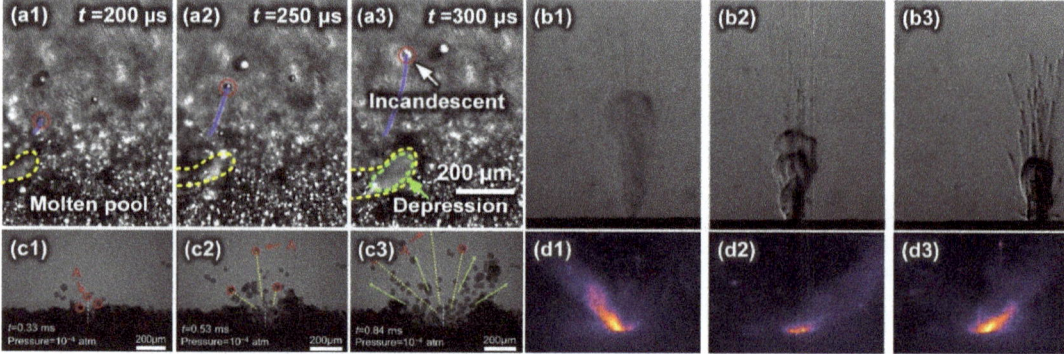

Figure 3. Characteristics obtained from different in situ detection techniques: (**a1–a3**) time series snapshots taken by visible light high-speed camera (Reprinted with permission from Ref. [34]. Copyright 2019 Elsevier B.V.); (**b1–b3**) high-speed schlieren images during single track scans (Reprinted with permission from Ref. [35]. Copyright 2018 Springer Nature.); (**c1–c3**) dynamic X-ray images showing powder motion, A is the ejected powder (Reprinted with permission from Ref. [36]. Copyright 2018 Elsevier B.V.); (**d1–d3**) three consecutive frames of an infrared video acquired during L-PBF (Reprinted with permission from Ref. [37]. Copyright 2018 Elsevier B.V.).

Table 1. Characteristics obtained from different in situ detection techniques.

In Situ Detection Technology	Obtained Characteristics
Visible-light high-speed camera	Surface characteristics
X-ray video imaging	Internal structure Flow behavior of melt inside the melt pool
Infrared video imaging	Temperature distribution Flow behavior of gas
Schlieren video imaging	Gas flow propagation and distribution

2.1. Visible-Light High-Speed Detector

There are two main methods for observing L-PBF with a high-speed visible-light camera: coaxial and off-axis. In Figure 4a, the camera shares the same optical path with the laser in a coaxial solution. In Figure 4b, the camera is placed at an angle to the optical path of the laser for viewing in Figure 4a, an off-axis solution.

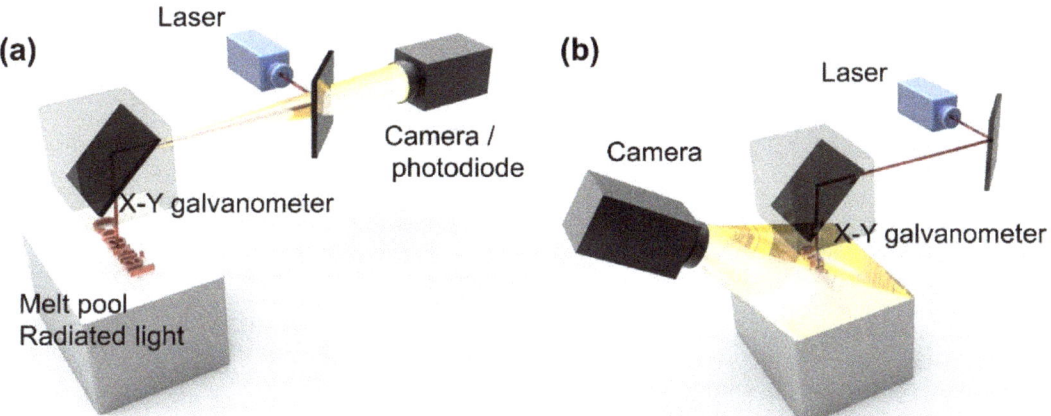

Figure 4. L-PBF in situ detection system: (**a**) coaxial (sharing the optical path with the laser); (**b**) off-axial (at a slight angle to the laser optical path).

Coaxial in situ detection of a commercial L-PBF machine requires extensive modification of the machine, and it is still difficult to obtain clear images because of the distance between the optical path system and the powder bed in the L-PBF machine. Another hindrance is the small optical aperture of the scanner and F-theta lens, which results in low magnification. In addition, the low reflectivity of the scanner and the low transmittance of the F-theta lens also reduce the temporal and spatial resolution of imaging, and these two characters are vital for the analyzing the trajectory and behavior of spatters. To overcome the disadvantages of coaxial in situ detection, Zhang et al. [38] improved the optical path, built segmentation algorithms, and demonstrated the algorithms' efficiency in dealing with defocused and distorted spatter images.

Unlike the coaxial solution, the off-axis solution, which places the detection device at an angle to the powder bed, enables spatter detection without altering the existing L-PBF equipment, as shown in Figure 5. The system is more adaptable and simpler to alter, and because the detection system does not share the optical path of the laser, it is not constrained by the laser's original optical path and can be used to detect spatter at higher magnification and frame rates than those of the coaxial system. Due to these factors, off-axial in situ detection system is becoming increasingly popular.

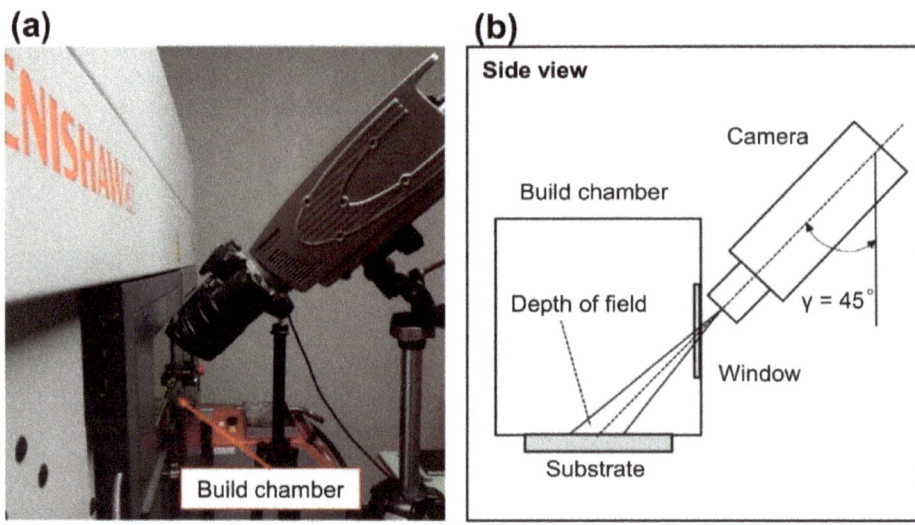

Figure 5. Off-axial detection system: (**a**) off-axial mounting of the high-speed camera outside the build chamber; (**b**) off-axial high-speed camera is at an angle of 45° to the plane of the observed powder bed. (Reprinted with permission from Ref. [39]. Copyright 2017 Elsevier B.V.).

In the case of coaxial detection, the detection equipment and external light source affect the final detection findings. Yang et al. installed a high-speed camera (pco. Dimax HS4, 3000 fps) outside the L-PBF machine at a 65° angle to the working platform to detect the spatter. Due to the little difference in brightness between the powder spatter and power bed within the view field of the high-speed camera, only the droplet spatters were detected, but not the nonmolten powder particles. Tan et al. [40] used a computational technique to analyze the obtained images, segmenting each block to extract the spatter. In the same year, Yin et al. [41] introduced an external light source (a CAVILUX® pulsed high-power diode laser light source) and a high-speed camera (Phantom V2012) to detect the spatter and obtain clearer images. After that, this in situ detection system was used to investigate the correlation between ex situ melt track properties and in situ high-speed, high-resolution characterizations [34].

The above studies were based on the monocular camera, and the picture information collected was in a 2D space. By combining multiple cameras and using image processing arithmetic, 3D information of spatter and its mobility can be gathered. Based on the use of monocular sensors, Luo et al. [42] innovatively proposed the use of acoustic signals combined with deep learning for spatter detection, demonstrating the feasibility of the acoustic signal detection of spatter behavior. Due to the dimensional limitation of the 2D image (acquired by the monocular sensor), it is difficult to accurately calculate the behavioral information of the spatter and obtain accurate spatter trajectory, velocity, and other information. A binocular stereo detector can obtain the spatter information in two viewing angles. By using the multi-directional information, its algorithm can present the 3D trajectory and velocity of a single spatter, and the obtained information is more accurate than those of a monocular sensor. Barret et al. [43] established a stereo vision spatter detection system for spatter tracking analysis at a cost of less than USD 1000 using two slow-motion cameras (FPS1000 by The Slow Motion Camera Company), as illustrated in Figure 6. Later, Eschner et al. [44] combined two ultra-high-speed cameras with algorithms to create a 3D tracking system for measuring spatter in L-PBF. Visible in situ detection systems for L-PBF in recent years are summarized in Table 2.

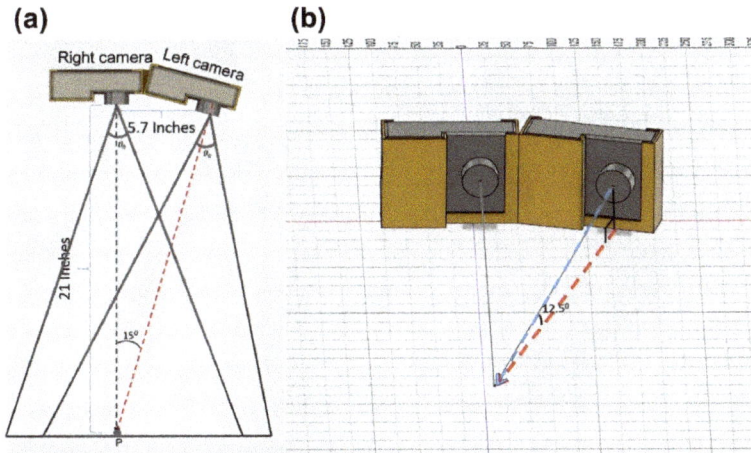

Figure 6. Spatter detection system for stereo vision: (**a**) the horizontal angle between the two sensors is 15°; (**b**) the vertical direction of the sensor is 12.5° from the observation object. (Reprinted with permission from Ref. [43]. Copyright 2018 University of Texas at Austin).

Table 2. In situ detection system for L-PBF.

System	Sensors	Spatial Resolution (μm/Pixel)	Temporal Resolution (Hz)	Light Source	Object of Detection	Materials	References
Coaxial	Phantom V2512 by Vision Research Inc.	14.6	23,077 (Max. 1,000,000)	—	Hot spatter	316L	Zhang et al. (2022) [38]
Three-dimensional off-axis	FPS1000 by The Slow Motion Camera Company	18–24	1000	—	Spatter and ejecta	—	Barrett et al. (2018) [43]
	Phantom v1210 by Vision Research Inc.	40	60,000	CAVILUX HF	Spatter	316L	Eschner et al. (2019) [44]
	Asler aca640–750 μm USB3	200	750	—	Spatter	316L	Eschner et al. (2022) [45]
Two-dimensional off-axis without light source	Photron Fastcam Mini AX200	—	5000		Denudation and vapor plume	316L	Chen et al. (2022) [46]
	I-SPEED high-speed CMOS camera	—	50,000		Plume	Ti-6Al-4V	Zheng et al. (2021) [47]
	Qianyanlang 5KF10	14	9800		Spatter and powder	316L	Wang et al. (2021) [48]
	Pco. dimaX HS4	11	3000		Spatter	316L	Yang et al. (2020) [49]
	—	11.7	2000		Melt pool and spatter	316L	Zhang et al. (2019) [50]
	I-SPEED 716	—	20,000		Vapor plume and spatter	304	Zheng et al. (2018) [51]
	Fastcam 1024 PCI	—	6000		Plume and spatter	Al-Si10-Mg	Andani et al. (2018) [52]
	FASTCAM Mini UX50/100	—	5000		Plume and spatter	304 L	Ye et al. (2018) [53]
Two-dimensional off-axis with light source	Phantom V2012 by Vision Research Inc.	3.92–5.70	100,000	CAVILUX® pulsed high-power diode laser light source	Droplet and melt pool	Inconel 718	Yin et al. (2020) [34]
	Phantom V1212 by Vision Research Inc.	—	37,500	Diode laser	Ejecta	Inconel625	Nasser et al. (2019) [54]
	Phantom V2512 by Vision Research Inc.	1.5–11	8000	Lumencor SOLA SM white light source	Spatter and denudation	316L	Biadre et al. (2018) [35]

Table 2. Cont.

System	Sensors	Spatial Resolution (μm/Pixel)	Temporal Resolution (Hz)	Light Source	Object of Detection	Materials	References
X-ray	Argonne National Laboratory, USA	—	50,000	—	Melt pool and spatter	Ti-6Al-4V	Zhao et al. (2017) [28]
		1	54,310		Powder spatter	316L/Al-Si10-Mg	Guo et al. (2018) [36]
		2	400,000		Keyhole *	Ti-6Al-4V	Cunningham et al. (2019) [55]
		—	45,259–135,776		Spatter	Al-Si10-Mg/Ti-6Al-4V	Young et al. (2020) [56]
	55 keV monochromatic X-rays	6.6	5100		Melt pool	Invar 36	Leung et al. (2019) [57]

* Keyhole: also known as the depression zone, is wrapped by the gas–liquid interface and penetrates through the melt pool.

2.2. Invisible-Light In Situ Detection

For the invisible-light in situ detection of L-PBF, the imaging technologies mainly include X-ray imaging, schlieren video imaging, infrared imaging, and thermal imaging.

X-rays have a short wavelength, high energy, and high penetration ability. High-strength X-rays can penetrate a certain thickness of metal with high temporal and spatial resolution, which is the preferred method for many L-PBF spatter studies [35]. A schematic diagram of an X-ray system is shown in Figure 7. As one of the most productive X-ray sources globally, the Advanced Photon Source (APS) in the Argonne National Laboratory provides experimental conditions for many researchers. More than 5500 researchers per year use X-rays produced by APS to do experiments. Many of those researchers use those X-rays to detect L-PBF spatter. For example, Zhao et al. [28] pioneered the use of high-speed X-rays (harmonic energy 24.4 keV) for in situ characterizations of L-PBF progress. Guo et al. [36] found transient spatter dynamics in L-PBF using a high-speed, high-resolution, and high-energy X-ray imaging technique. Ross Cunningham et al. quantified the keyhole in Ti-6Al-4V powder during laser melting based on X-ray image information [55]. Leung et al. raised the X-ray power (monochromatic X-ray power: 55 keV) and studied stainless steel (316L) and 13–93 bioactive glass. They found that melt pool wetting and vapor-driven powder entrainment are key track growth mechanisms for L-PBF [57]. A summary of X-ray in situ detection is shown in Table 2.

Due to the Schlieren video imaging and infrared imaging to picture previously invisible light or materials, these two technologies are also used for the in situ detection of spatter. Schlieren video imaging, used to detect the plume in L-PBF, can visualize the invisible substance by measuring its refractive index. Bidare et al. [58] used a combination of a high-speed camera and schlieren video imaging to capture images of the denuded region, laser plume, and argon atmosphere, and explained the relation between the powder-bed denuded region and spatter. An infrared camera can collect the light emitted by an infrared light source. Ye et al. [53] used infrared cameras to detect the properties of the original plume and spatter. Grasso et al. used the plume as the information source and examined it with an infrared camera to rapidly discover processing defects and unstable states [59,60].

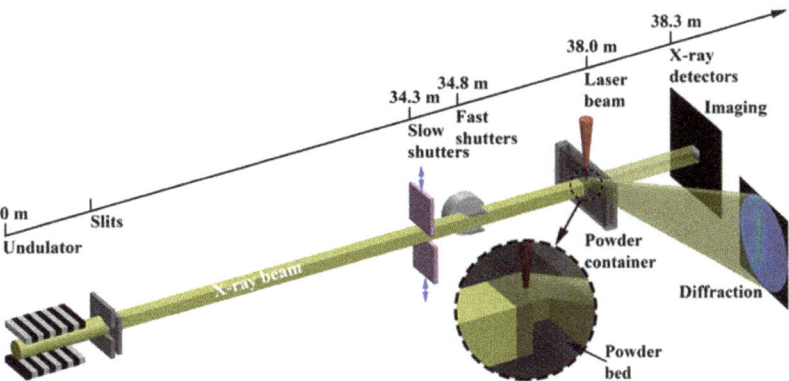

Figure 7. Schematic of the high-speed X-ray imaging and diffraction experiments on laser powder bed fusion process at the 32-ID-B beamline of the Advanced Photon Source. A pseudo-pink beam with a first harmonic energy of 24.4 keV ($\lambda = 0.508$Å) is generated by a short-period undulator. The laser irradiates the micro-powder bed sample from the top, the X-rays penetrate from the side of the sample. The imaging and diffraction detectors are placed approximately 300 mm downstream from the sample. The inset surrounded by the dashed circle enlarges the view of the laser-sample and X-ray-sample interaction. The distance of each component from the source is labeled on top. (Reprinted with permission from Ref. [28]. Copyright 2017 Springer Nature).

2.3. Data Processing during Spatter Detection

Spatter image obtained from in situ detection requires post-processing to enable the extraction and analysis of spatter behaviors.

2.3.1. Spatter 2D Image Processing Algorithm

Algorithms for 2D image processing are less complex than those for 3D image processing. Tan et al. [40] captured spatter images using Kalman filter tracking, segmented the images with grayscale and edge information, and obtained spatter information using fully convolutional networks and Mask R-CNN. Yin et al. [61] projected the 3D spatter trajectory into a 2D plane with image processing, used a filtering technique to improve the sharpness of the spatter image, and tracked the spatter motion information frame by frame using ImageJ.

2.3.2. Spatter 3D Image Processing Algorithm

Barrett et al. used a low-cost binocular sensor for spatter detection, laying a foundation for future analysis of the data [43]. Eschner et al. [44] used algorithms in a binocular sensor system to carry out many processes on the images, including (1) identifying particle positions and calibrating the camera system, (2) matching particles between multi-camera images, (3) determining the 3D coordinates, (4) using a priori knowledge of processes and particles to distinguish ghost particles from real particles, (5) tracking particles, and (6) processing the 3D data. Those processes require more complex algorithms to complete. Currently, they have enabled the construction of a quadruple-eye sensor system, which uses a third camera to achieve the recognition of ghost particles. However, relative to the binocular sensor detection system, the quadruple-eye sensor detection system must process a larger amount of information that is more difficult to process [45].

2.4. Full-Cycle Detection of Spatter in L-PBF

During L-PBF process, the full cycle of the spatter can be divided into three stages: the initial stage (generation), the flight stage (ejection), and the fall-back stage (re-deposition). The detection of the spatter in these three stages is conductive to the deep understanding of the origin of the spatter, the correlation of the spatter and defect, and the influence of the spatter on the part.

- **Initial stage (generation, adjacent to the melt pool):** The positions of the generation of both the cold spatters and hot spatters are adjacent to the melt pool. The ultra-high-frame-rate in situ detection using a high-temporal-spatial-resolution off-axis camera combined with the illumination light source can obtain a clear morphology of spatters, which helps to reveal the mechanism of the spatter generation.
- **Flight stage (ejection, away from the powder bed):** The amount of spatter and the ejection angle significantly affect the internal defect of the part. The spatter trajectory, ejection velocity, ejection angle, and spatter size of the spatter should be obtained to investigate the intrinsic correlation between the spatter and the defect. A long monitoring time, high-frame-rate in situ detection system, along with the laser path using multi-sensors, is applied to capture the spatter flight (even with 3D information). The high-throughput data during L-PBF process can be used for the statistics analysis of spatter characterization. In general, only hot spatters are detected in this stage to reduce the processing pressure of the monitoring system.
- **Fall-back stage (re-deposition, close to the powder bed):** The spatter eventually redeposits on the powder bed and parts, which affect re-coating and part quality. A layer-by-layer in situ detection with a wide field-of-view and high-spatial-resolution camera can obtain high quality images of the powder and parts. The image data employing algorithms extract and confirm the size and location of the redeposited spatter, which helps in predicting the forming quality of the parts and the location of the defect.

2.5. Differences In Situ Detection between Spatter and Melt Pool

Due to the complexity of spatters, algorithmic requirements are higher than for melt pool detection. Generally speaking, the melt pool goes along with the laser spot and the melt pool movement is in the 2D trajectory, but the spatter movement is in the 3D trajectory, so the detection of the spatter must be extended to 3D, which requires more in situ sensors and more information needs to be processed.

(1) Compared with the detection of the melt pool, the spatter, with a micro size and extensive range of motion in the 3D space, is much more difficult to be detected, which requires multiple sensors, up to four sensors, with micron spatial resolution.
(2) Additionally, the melt pool is generated by the action of the laser in the metal powder bed, and its trajectory can be predicted according to the pre-defined laser path. In contrast, the trajectory of spatter is hard to be predicted due to the high-speed random motion in the 3D space, which requires sensors with a higher temporal resolution up to microseconds to detect the whole process of motion trajectory deflection.
(3) The data of spatter collected using sensors with high spatial resolution and high temporal resolution are several orders larger than the data of melt pool detection. Therefore, the data processing of spatter detection is more complex, which puts higher demands on the algorithm.

As a result, the observation of the spatter and data processing, is much more challenging than the detection of the melt pool. The complexity of the spatter detection algorithms is further increased by 3D detection systems with multiple sensors.

3. Mechanism of Spatter Generation

Under the interaction with a high-energy laser in L-PBF, metal powders are melted to form a melt pool when the temperature attains the melting point, then vaporized to form metal vapor or even a plasma plume when the surface temperature of the melt pool surpasses the boiling point. The different phases (solid, liquid, and vapor) significantly interact with each other during L-PBF process, among which the vapor–solid interaction and vapor–liquid interaction are the main mechanism of spatter generation. Therefore, it is necessary to investigate the mechanism of spatter generation.

3.1. Spatter Classification

The spatters generated in L-PBF are in a different morphology, and a variety of parameters affect spatter generation. Until now, there has been no common definition of spatter categorization. Liu et al. [62] performed L-PBF single-pass scanning experiments with 316L stainless steel powder, reflecting the dynamic behavior of spatter perpendicular to the single-track scanning direction by the high-speed imaging technology. They divided the spatter into two categories: droplet spatter and powder spatter. It is known that the spatter formation mechanism can be demonstrated as the hot spatter ejection, mainly driven by the instability of the melt pool due to the vapor-induced recoil pressure, and the cold spatter ejection, mainly driven by the vapor-induced entrainment of the protective gas. Wang et al. [63] used a high-speed camera to record the dynamic spattering process of Co–Cr alloys during L-PBF manufacturing and investigated the spatter generation mechanism in further detail. As shown in Figure 8, they recognized three major sources of spattering: recoil pressure, the Marangoni effect, and the heat effect in the melt pool. These three different sources of spattering led to three types of spattering morphologies.

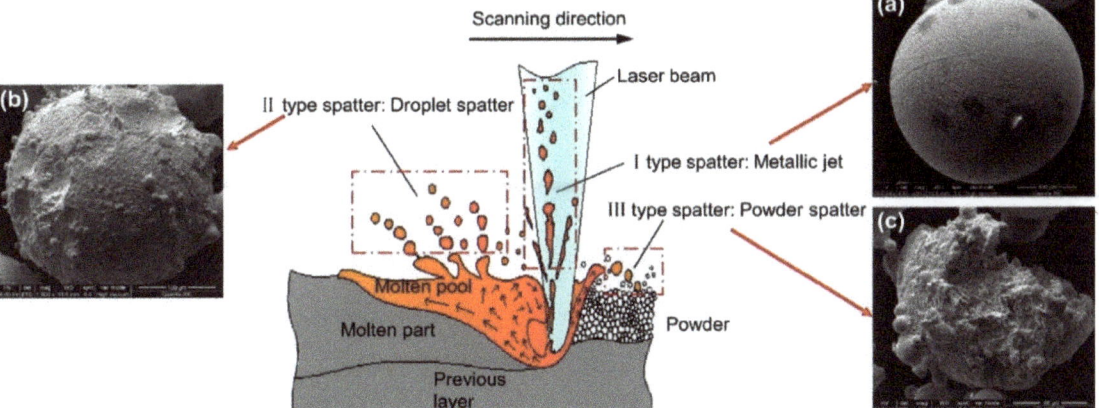

Figure 8. Formation mechanisms of different types of spatter during L-PBF: (**a**) morphology of spherical spatter (Type-I spatter); (**b**) morphology of coarse spherical morphology (Type-II spatter); (**c**) morphology of irregular spatter (Type-III spatter). (Reprinted with permission from Ref. [63]. Copyright 2016 Elsevier B.V.).

According to Ref. [63], there are three types of spatters: (i) The Type I spatters are associated with the extreme expansion of the gas phase. The spontaneous metal liquid flowing will occur from the high-temperature bottom of the excavation to the low-temperature sidewall and edge at the back under the Marangoni effect. (ii) Then, in this process, the recoil pressure can induce the jet of low-viscosity metal liquid, and this jetted liquid metal will divide into small drops in the flight process to minimize the surface tension; therefore, the Type II spatter is formed. (iii) In the printing process, some metal liquid accumulates near the spot laser, and it can be easily squeezed by the blast wave and then interrupt these non-melted particles in the front-end area; then the Type III spatter will occur at the front of the melt pool.

Ly et al. [64] used a high-speed camera to explore the influence of gas flow entrainment on spatter during L-PBF. They described the entrainment phenomena of 316L stainless steel powder and Ti-6Al-4V powder layers and divided spatter into three categories. As shown in Figure 9, 60% of the ejection was due to hot entrainment ejection at velocities ranging from 6 m/s to 20 m/s: 25% was cold entrainment ejection, which occurred at a velocity of 2 m/s to 4 m/s, and 15% was droplet breakup ejection from the melt pool as a result of the recoil pressure applied at a velocity of 3 to 8 m/s. Raza et al. [65] also found that spatter from the melt pool was less than that due to vapor-induced entrainment.

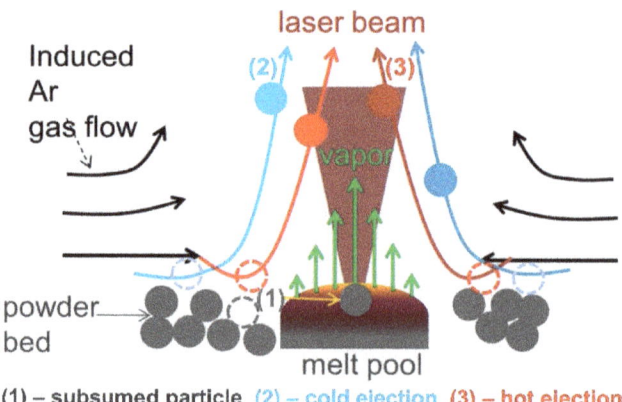

(1) – subsumed particle (2) – cold ejection (3) – hot ejection

Figure 9. Schematic representation of the entrainment effect of metal-vapor-driven airflow on fine particles in the presence of a fixed laser beam. A vapor jet creates a zone of low pressure, which results in three different trajectories of entrained particles: (1) Particles with low vertical momentum are swept into the melt pool; (2) Particles with higher vertical momentum but originating > 2 melt pool widths away are swept into the trailing portion of the vapor jet, and ejected as cold particles; (3) particles with roughly the same vertical momentum as (2) but originating closer to the point of laser irradiation (<2 melt pool widths) are swept into or near the laser beam itself rapidly heat, and are ejected as incandescent, hot particles. (Reprinted with permission from Ref. [64]. Copyright 2017 Springer Nature).

Young et al. [56] showed the characteristics and generation mechanisms of five unique types of spatter during L-PBF by in situ high-speed, high-energy X-ray video imaging: solid spatter, metallic ejected spatter, agglomeration spatter, entrainment melting spatter, and defect-induced spatter. They quantified the speed, size, and direction of metallic ejected spatter, powder agglomeration spatter, and entrainment melting spatter. The results showed that the metallic ejected spatter speed was the highest, and the size of the powder agglomeration spatter was the largest. The spatter direction was highly dependent on the characteristics of the depression zone, which was impacted directly by the metal vapor recoil pressure.

Whereas the above researches had classified spatter using an in-process analysis, the following is a study that classified spatter using a post-mortem analysis. Gasper et al. [66] divided the spatter into seven categories according to the size, morphology, and other descriptors, such as oxides and agglomeration derived from SEM analysis, namely: (1) particles similar to virgin gas-atomized particles, (2) particles morphologically different from those gas-atomized, (3) larger singular particles with different morphologies, (4) particles with oxide spots, (5) particles covered with oxide, (6) small particles, and (7) agglomerates. Yang et al. [67] studied the influence of the L-PBF parameters on the pore characteristics and mechanical properties of Al-Si10-Mg parts. Three distinct types of solidified droplets were detected: hollow droplets, semi-hollow droplets, and solid droplets. Hollow droplets and semi-hollow droplets were a major source of pores inside the sample. Table 3 summarizes current studies on the categorization of spatter generation during L-PBF.

Table 3. Summary of spatter classification studies.

Classification according to the "In-Process Analysis"			
Classification Principle	Materials	Spatter Categories	References
Vapor recoil pressure, Marangoni effect	316L, CoCr; 316L, Ti-6Al-4V; Al-Si10-Mg, Ti-6Al-4V	Metallic ejected spatter	Liu et al. (2015) [62]; Wang et al. (2017) [63]; Ly et al. (2017) [64] Young et al. (2020) [56]
Vapor recoil pressure	316L; Al-Si10-Mg, Ti-6Al-4V	Powder spatter	Liu et al. (2015) [62]; Young et al. (2020) [56]
Entrainment effect	316L, Ti-6Al-4V; Al-Si10-Mg, Ti-6Al-4V	Powder spatter; Entrainment melting spatter	Ly et al. (2017) [64]; Young et al. (2020) [56]
Instability during laser–pore interaction	Al-Si-10Mg, Ti-6Al-4V	Defect-induced spatter	Young et al. (2020) [56]
Agglomeration	Al-Si-10Mg, Ti-6Al-4V	Agglomeration spatter	Young et al. (2020) [56]
Classification According to the Post-Mortem Analysis			
Classification Principle	Materials	Spatter Categories	References
Appearance and Composition	Inconel 718	(i) Particles similar to virgin gas-atomized particles; (ii) Particles with morphology different to gas-atomized; (iii) Larger singular particles with different morphologies; (iv) Particles with oxide spots; (v) Particles covered with oxide; (vi) Small particles; (vii) agglomerates	Gasper et al. (2018) [66]
	Al-Si10-Mg	Hollow droplets, semi-hollow droplets, solid droplets	Yang et al. (2020) [67]

3.2. Study of Droplet Spatter Ejected from "Liquid Base" of Melt Pool

The melt pool is a critical feature of L-PBF. Numerous studies on the spattering from the melt pool have been done using a numerical simulation, which avoided the high cost and inefficiency of repeated experiments. Khairallah et al. [68] studied the mechanism of spatter generation at the powder scale using a 3D high-precision model. The metal vapor exerted pressure on the melt pool during L-PBF, causing the emission of liquid metal. When the liquid metal was stretched, the column grew thinner and decomposed into tiny droplets because the surface tension tended to minimize the surface energy. Additionally, it was discovered that at the start of the scanning, it was rather easy to generate large-sized back-ejected spatters [69]. They assumed that the laser scanning velocity could not be kept constant at the beginning and end of the trajectory due to inertia, resulting in a deposition of a nonuniform energy density and causing such spatters. They proposed a stability criterion to eliminate back-ejected spatter effectively. Altmeppen et al. [70] proposed a method to simulate time-dependent particles and heat ejection from the moving melt pool. This model can predict the direction and velocity of spatter emission and determine the size and temperature of a single particle by evaluating the direction and velocity of local laser scanning.

In order to verify the intrinsic mechanism of the spatter generation, experiments were applied to detect the spatter using X-ray imaging and high-speed imaging. The explosion caused by the instability of the front wall of the keyhole, which resulted from the vaporization of the L-PBF volatile element, induced much droplet spatter. Zhao et al. used X-ray imaging to study the spatter behavior of Ti-6Al-4V powder during L-PBF. As illustrated in Figure 10, they demonstrated how the bulk-explosion induced by the instability of the front wall of the keyhole in the melt pool resulted in a considerable amount of droplet spatter [71]. Using in situ high-speed high-resolution imaging and thermodynamic analysis, Yin et al. investigated the vaporization and explosion behavior of alloy components in a Cu-10Zn alloy during L-PBF [72]. It was found that the explosion caused by the violent vaporization of a low boiling point also induced much droplet spatter and defects in the melt track.

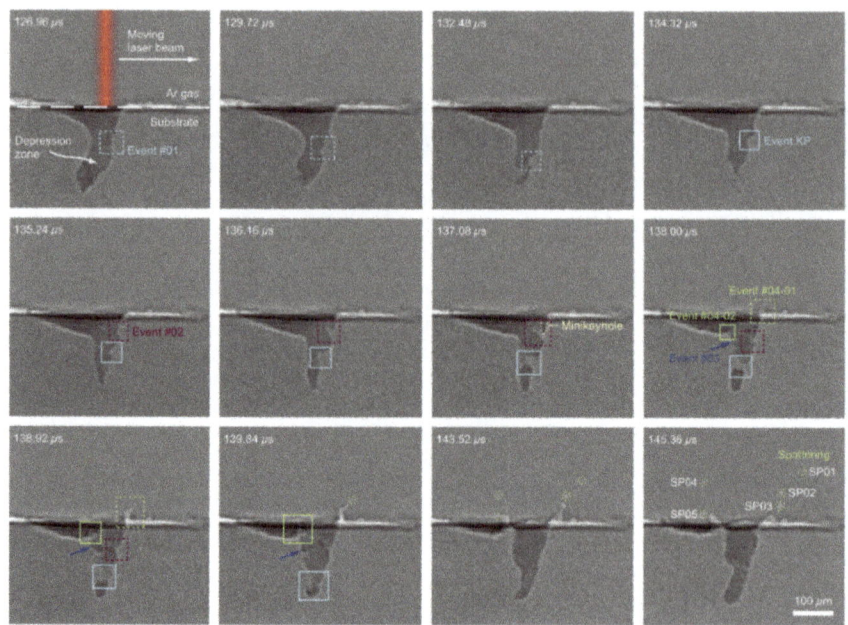

Figure 10. MHz X-ray images of metal spattering of Ti-6Al-4V during laser processing. **Event No. 01 (sky blue dashed rectangles):** A protrusion forms at the top surface and runs down along the front keyhole wall, accompanied by the keyhole morphology changing from a J-like shape to a reverse-triangle-like shape. **Event No. 02 (purple dashed rectangles):** A following protrusion appears, grows, and collapses around the horizontal center of the keyhole. A mini keyhole on top of the protrusion is outlined by a light yellow dashed curve. **Event No. 03 (dark blue arrows):** The local curvature on the rear keyhole wall changes. **Event No. 04 (light green dashed and solid rectangles):** Melt ligaments form, elongate, and break up into spatters (light green dashed circles numbered SP01–SP05). **Event KP (sky blue solid rectangles):** describes the formation and vanishing of a keyhole pore (Reprinted with permission from Ref. [71]. Copyright 2019 APS Physics).

Using high-speed and high-resolution imaging technologies, Yin et al. [41] investigated the spatter behavior of Inconel 718 powder during L-PBF. The subthreshold ejection phenomenon was detected in which droplets emitted from the droplet column fell back to the melt pool. Later, the authors also studied the correlation between the ex situ melt track characteristics and the in situ high-speed and high-resolution characterization. They showed that the protrusion of the head of the melt trajectory was caused by the combined action of the backward flowing melt and the droplet ejection behavior in the melt pool [34]. Moreover, as illustrated in Figure 11, the melt pool first forms a depression under the action of the recoil pressure of the vapor; a high-energy laser beam impinges on the front wall of the depression, causing the surface of the front wall to quickly vaporize and generate a metal vapor that is perpendicular to this surface; the metal vapor expands and impacts the rear wall of the depression; finally, the spatter is formed and ejected backwards. The vertical metal vapor plume was identified as the principal reason for the melt pool spattering.

Through in situ measurements of a typical forward spatter ejection angle, the vapor recoil pressure (approximately 0.46 atm) was quantified.

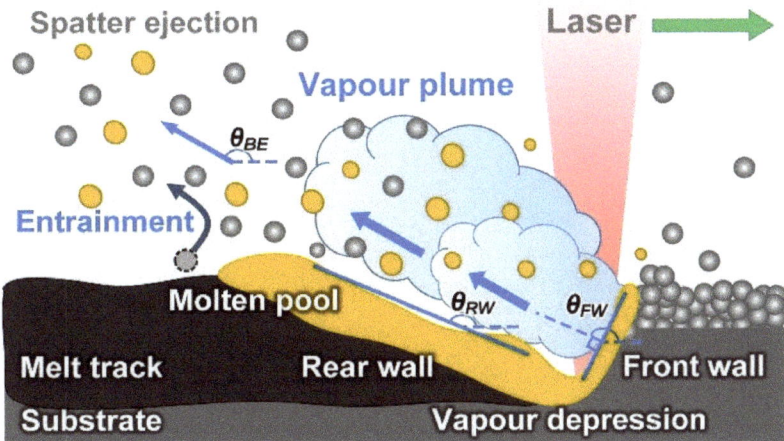

Figure 11. Schematic of the correlation between the depression zone in melt pool and the backward-ejected spatter during L-PBF. The inclined angles for the normal direction of the front depression wall θ_{FW} and the inclination angle of the rear depression wall θ_{RW} had the same trends with the average angle of the backward-ejected spatter (θ_{BE}). (Reprinted with permission from Ref. [34]. Copyright 2019 Elsevier B.V.).

The development of various advanced in situ characterization methods provides new directions for spatter research. Wang et al. [48] used a high-speed camera to investigate the characteristics of the droplet spatter of 316L stainless steel powder during L-PBF process. Gould et al. [73] reported an in situ method to analyze the L-PBF process of Ti-6Al-4V and W powders by using high-speed X-ray and high-speed infrared imaging simultaneously. Combining both imaging of high-speed X-rays and high-speed infrared imaging, various phenomena can be identified including 3D dynamics of melt pools, vapor plume dynamics, and spatter generation.

Surface tension and evaporation both have a noticeable effect on the melt pool. Dai et al. [74] studied the process parameters of the thermal behavior, fluid dynamics, and surface morphology in a melt pool using a mesoscopic simulation model. The results indicated that the evolution of the melt pool was highly sensitive to the melt viscosity, surface tension, and recoil pressure during L-PBF. Bärtl et al. [75] investigated the ability of the aluminum alloy powder materials Al-Cr-Zr-Mn, Al-Cr-Sc-Zr, and Al-Mg-Sc-Mn-Zr to produce lightweight and high-performance structures by L-PBF. They regarded that both the surface tension and evaporation were potentially crucial factors dominating the melt dynamics, and the melt dynamics of materials with a lower surface tension and less evaporation were the most unstable. Table 4 summarizes the research on droplet spatter ejected from the "liquid" base of the melt pool.

Table 4. Summary of research on droplet spatter ejected from the "liquid base" of the melt pool.

Generation Mechanism	Materials	References
Surface tension	Ti-6Al-4V, TiC	Dai et al. (2020) [74]
	Al-Cr-Zr-Mn, Al-Cr-Sc-Zr & Al-Mg-Sc-Mn-Zr	Bärtl et al. (2022) [75]
Vapor recoil pressure	316L	Khairallah et al. (2016) [68]
	Inconel 718	Yin et al. (2019) [41]
		Yin et al. (2020) [34]
Explosion	Ti-6Al-4V	Zhao et al. (2019) [71]
	Cu-10Zn	Yin et al. (2021) [72]
Laser energy uneven deposition	316, Ti-6Al-4V	Khairallah et al. (2020) [69]
Movement process of melt and powder	316L	Wang et al.(2021) [48]

3.3. Study of Powder Spatter Ejected from "Solid Base" of Substrate

Due to the entrainment effect of the gas flow, powder particles close to the laser zone of action are ejected and spattered. Ly et al. [64] performed an experimental comparison of the melt pool hydrodynamics of laser welding and L-PBF processes. In contrast to laser welding, the primary cause of spatter in L-PBF was not the laser-induced recoil pressure, but the entrainment effect of the ambient gas flow driven by the metal vapor on the microparticles. The high-speed X-ray video imaging of the defects and melt pool performed by Leung et al. [76] supported the Ly et al. hypothesis about the generation of cold and hot entrainment spatter during L-PBF. Chen et al. [77] built a multi-phase flow model to investigate the spatter generation during L-PBF. The spatter phenomena were shown to be the result of metal vapor- and ambient gas-induced entrainment, which supported the findings of Ly et al. [64].

Gunenthiram et al. [78] used high-speed camera techniques to investigate the dynamic behavior of 316L stainless steel powder and 4047 aluminum–silicon alloy powder during the generation of spatter in L-PBF. As shown in Figure 12 [61], due to the heat transfer from the surrounding powder bed, the powder particles in close contact with the front and sides of the melt pool tended to agglomerate to form larger droplets. Some of the agglomerates were subject to an entrainment gas flow, which in turn were ejected as spatter. To establish the correlation between the scanning velocity and spatter generation, Zheng et al. [51] used a high-speed camera technique to investigate the effect of the scanning velocity on the generation and evolution of the metal vapor plumes during L-PBF of 304 stainless steel powder. The results indicated that the powder spatter generations are more closely related with the stability/evolution of the vapor plume and resulting melt-track, rather than the changing of the volumetric energy density (VED). The trend of an increasing number of spatters with an increasing VED was reported by Gunenthiram et al. [78]. The droplet spatter generated at the commencement of the scan trajectory was found to be the consequence of coupling between the melt pool and the inclined metal vapor plume. Table 5 summarizes the studies of the spatter from the solid substrate ejection.

Table 5. A summary of the studies on spatter from solid substrate ejection.

Generation Mechanism	Material	References
Metal vapor-induced entrainment	316L, Ti-6Al-4V	Ly et al. (2017) [64]
	316L, 4047 aluminum–silicon	Gunenthiram et al. (2018) [78]
	316L	Chen et al. (2020) [77]
	GH4169	Yin et al. (2022) [61]
Metal vapor recoil pressure	304	Zheng et al. (2018) [51]

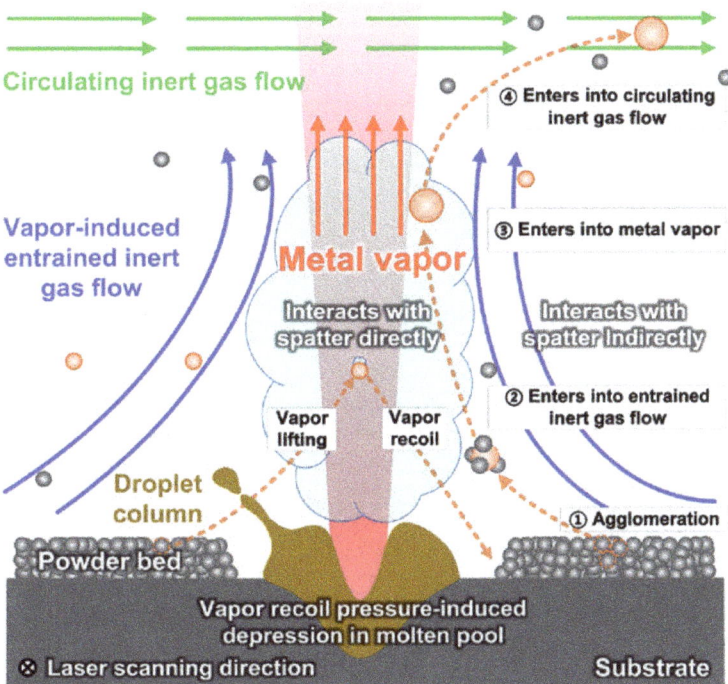

Figure 12. Schematic of spatter ejection process and interaction between vapor plume and spatter behavior in L-PBF. (Reprinted with permission from Ref. [61]. Copyright 2022 Chinese laser press).

3.4. Study of Spatter Generation Mechanism in Multi-Laser-PBF Fabrication Process

Recently, a multi-laser beam based on L-PBF has been applied to fulfil the growing demand for large-sized part manufacturing in aerospace and energy fields. Andani et al. [79] investigated the spatter behavior of Al-Si10-Mg powder during dual-beam L-PBF using a high-speed camera technique. They showed that the number of operating laser beams significantly influences the spatter creation mechanisms during the SLM process. A higher number of working laser beams induces a greater recoil pressure above the melting pools and ejects a larger amount of metallic material from the melt pools. However, there was no description of the interaction between the dual-beam laser and the material in the overlap region.

The mechanism by which a dual-beam laser generates spatter is distinct from that of a single-beam laser. Yin et al. [80] investigated the interaction between dual-beam lasers and the material in the overlap region during the dual-beam L-PBF of Inconel 718 alloy powder using a high-speed, high-resolution video imaging system. They proposed to use the spatter growth rate (rs) to quantitatively characterize the spatter behavior in multi-laser powder bed fusion (ML-PBF).

According to experimental observations, Yin et al. [80] believe that most of the spatter in multi-laser L-PBF is due to metal vapor-induced entrainment (ejected from the "solid baes" of the substrate) rather than the metal vapor recoil pressure (ejected from the "liquid baes" of the melt pool). In fact, the rs in the vapor entrainment dominant stages is one order of magnitude higher than that in the unstable melt pool dominant stage disturbed by the recoil pressure and the collision of the two melt pools. This proves that the entrainment effect is dominant in the cause of the multi-laser-PBF spatter, as shown in Figure 13. A summary of the studies on the mechanism of the spatter generation during an ML-PBF process is shown in Table 6.

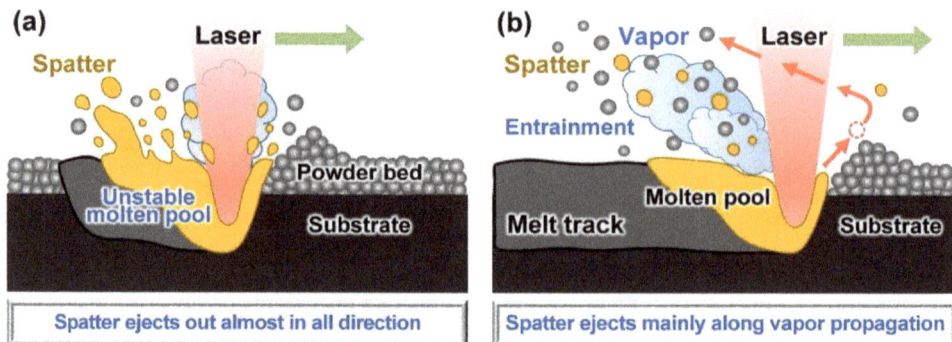

Figure 13. Schematic diagram of the transformation of the main mechanisms of spatter generation, which changes from (**a**) the vapor-induced recoil pressure with an almost homogeneous distribution of spatter ejection angle, into (**b**) the vapor-induced entrainment that majority of spatters eject along the direction of the metal vapor propagation. (Reprinted with permission from Ref. [80]. Copyright 2021 Elsevier B.V.).

Table 6. A summary of the studies on the mechanism of spatter generation during ML-PBF process.

Dominant Mechanism	Material	Research Content	References
Vapor-induced recoil pressure	Al-Si10-Mg	Number of laser beams ↑, Recoil pressure ↑, Number of spatters ↑.	Andani et al. (2017) [79]
Vapor-entrainment effect	Inconel 718	Spatter growth rate (*rs*) in vapor entrainment dominant stages is one order of magnitude higher than that in unstable melt pool dominant stage	Yin et al. (2021) [80]

4. Disadvantage of Spatter

Spatter is an unpreventable by-product of the complex heat transfer process between the laser and the metal powder in L-PBF [20,30,54]. Spatter brings a negative influence to the process stability and the efficiency of the energy, which reduces the quality of the manufactured object and can potentially damage the machine [68]. In accordance with the current research, the disadvantages posed by spatter in L-PBF can be classified into three categories: (1) The effect of spatter on the printing processing: spatter can affect the powder re-coating in the next layer, and reduce the energy input efficiency of the laser and the operation stability of the powder re-coating device [63,81] as well as the optical lens. (2) The effect of spatter on structure and performance: spatter is not conducive to controlling the structure (e.g., voids, roughness) and performance (e.g., tensile properties, oxygen contents) of printed parts. (3) The effect of spatter on powder recycling: recycled powder can entrain spatter particles, resulting in a significant deterioration of powder quality. The use of recycled powder for forming parts can lead to a reduction in part performance.

4.1. Effect of Spatter on Printing Processing

According to the generation mechanism of spatter, it can be found that spatter has a negative influence on powder re-coating and energy absorption during L-PBF processing.

4.1.1. Effect of Spatter on Powder Re-Coating

Spatter particles that redeposit onto the powder bed hinder the powder re-coating, and voids between the spatter particles and powder can induce part defects. Figure 14 shows how spatter generated during L-PBF introduces voids and internal defects in the printed part. Wang et al. [63] discovered that the re-coating powders were influenced by the spatter particles due to a small amount of spatter attached to the surface of the printed parts during stacking, and the spatter particles caused the deformation of the scraper (Figure 14a). When the redeposited spatter particles are smaller than the layer thickness, after laser scanning, the spatter particles melted completely and were metallurgically bonded to the powder and the underlying part. If the redeposited spatter particles' size exceeded the layer thickness, they did not melt completely, which induced voids between the powder and the spatter particles, as illustrated in Figure 14b. The voids remained after the scanning of the next layer, creating metallurgical defects, as illustrated in Figure 14c. Schwerz et al. [82] found the presence of spatter particles of approximately 136 μm in the cross-section of the part, illustrating how particles significantly larger than the nominal layer thickness were incorporated into the material despite recoating, and in the process, large spatter bumps of particles can cause damage to the scraper, as shown in Figure 14d.

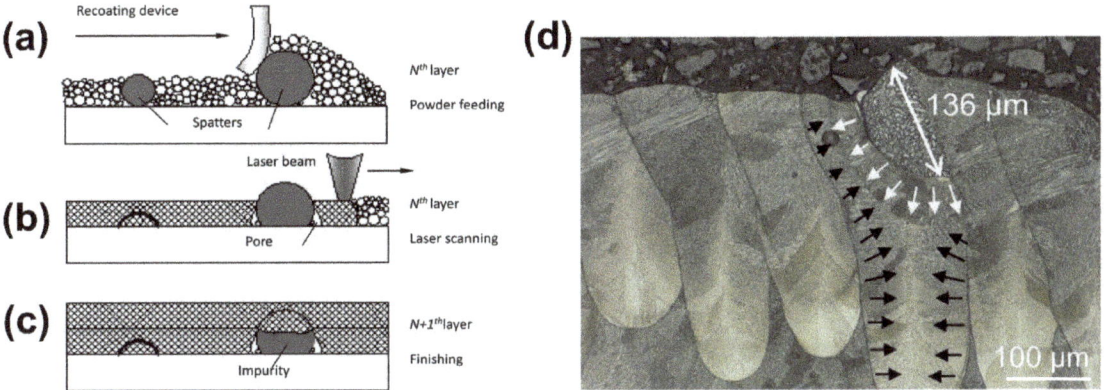

Figure 14. The effect of spatter on re-coating powder. (**a**) Pre-placing powders will be blocked when the next powder layer spreads; (**b**) spattering particles impede circulation of powders and cause voids nearby (before laser melting); (**c**) laser scanning can completely melt small spatter to achieve metallurgical bonding, while large spatter can only melt some of them. (Reprinted with permission from Ref. [63]. Copyright 2016 Elsevier B.V.). (**d**) A spatter particle of cross-section ~136 μm incites a solidification front (schematized with white arrows) that competes with the solidification fronts in the melt pool (schematized with black arrows). (Reprinted with permission from Ref. [82]. Copyright 2021 Elsevier B.V.).

In order to detect the distribution of the re-deposition of the spatters on the build area, a long-exposure near-infrared in situ monitoring associated with image analysis was employed to determine the exact locations using the EOS EOSTATE Exposure OT system [82]. This system consists of a 5-megapixel sCMOS (scientific complementary metal-oxide-semiconductor) camera positioned on top of the build chamber and comprises the entire build platform area in its field of view. A bandpass filter of 900 nm ± 12.5 nm is placed on the camera to filter the detection of the reflected laser to avoid the detection of the environmental noise. A sample image representative of a single layer can be observed in Figure 15a, samples near the gas inlet (Figure 15b) and gas outlet (Figure 15c) are shown separately. The long-exposure images revealed deviations in the form of high-intensity spots preferentially distributed towards the gas outlet, as in Figure 15c, the re-deposition spatter can be extracted by algorithms (Figure 15d). The spatter deposited near the gas outlet has been identified as one of the factors responsible for the rise of internal defects, which will be discussed in Section 4.2.

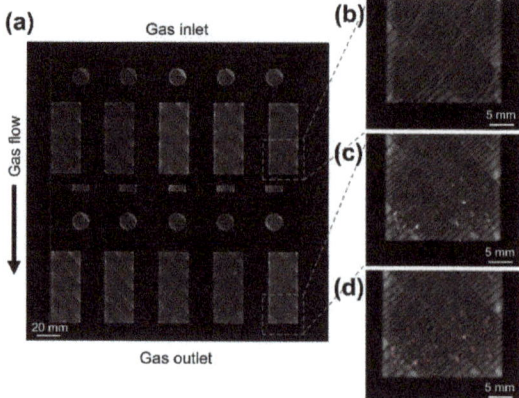

Figure 15. The results obtained by the monitoring system in conjunction with the spatter detection algorithm. (**a**) Sample long-exposure image consisting of the signals emitted during the exposure of a single layer on the entire build area. (**b**) A sample area near the gas inlet without any identified disturbances is highlighted for comparison. (**c**) Areas with disturbances are observed preferentially near the gas outlet. (**d**) A sample output from the spatter detection algorithm, in which the region shown in (**c**) is overlayed with detections. (Reprinted with permission from Ref. [82]. Copyright 2021 Elsevier B.V.).

4.1.2. Effect of Spatter on Energy Absorption

If spatter occurs in the laser path, it might result in an inefficient use of laser energy. Several studies have been done on the influence of spatter on the energy required to melt the powder. Ferrar et al. [83] first reported on the influence of gas flow on L-PBF in 2012. They demonstrated that by-products of processing in the laser path could absorb and scatter the laser beam, inducing laser beam attenuation and the generation of a lack of fusion. Anwar et al. [84] came to a similar conclusion in the selective laser melting of Al-Si10-Mg, implying that laser energy might be squandered on spatter, as shown in Figure 16. The laser beam irradiated the spatter particles that entered the beam path and consumed a significant amount of energy, which induced the incomplete melting of the powder and defects [85]. The accumulated spatter in the powder bed inevitably consumed the energy required to melt the fresh powder [86].

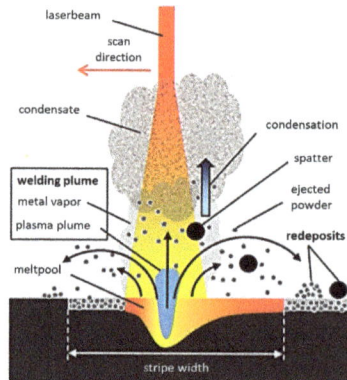

Figure 16. Spatter and other by-products pass through the laser stream and squander laser energy, condensate is the product of vaporized metal that quickly cools and condenses. (Reprinted with permission from Ref. [87]. Copyright 2016 Elsevier B.V.).

4.2. Effect of Spatter on Structure and Performance

Spatter causes a loss of laser energy, moreover, spatter re-deposition and oxidation also have an effect on the quality and structure of parts. A coating of oxide is generated on the spatter surface after L-PBF and the oxide layer greatly reduces the humidity of the liquid metal, which induces spheroidization [88,89]. The particles with an oxidized surface require more energy for melting and incorporation in the melt pool and in the bulk material, resulting in a lack of fusion [82]. The seriously oxidized spatter particles redeposit into the high-temperature melt pool, reversing the Marangoni convection flow direction [90,91]. Additionally, the oxidized spatter particles in the melt pool induce holes and defects [88,92]. The oxide composition of Inconel 718 spatter particles was evaluated by SEM-EDS by Gasper et al., as shown in Figure 17. In order to determine the extent of the oxidation of the spatter particles, a particle with oxide spots and fully oxidized particles were also analyzed by SEM-EDS with an in situ Focused Ion Beam (FIB), as shown in Figure 18.

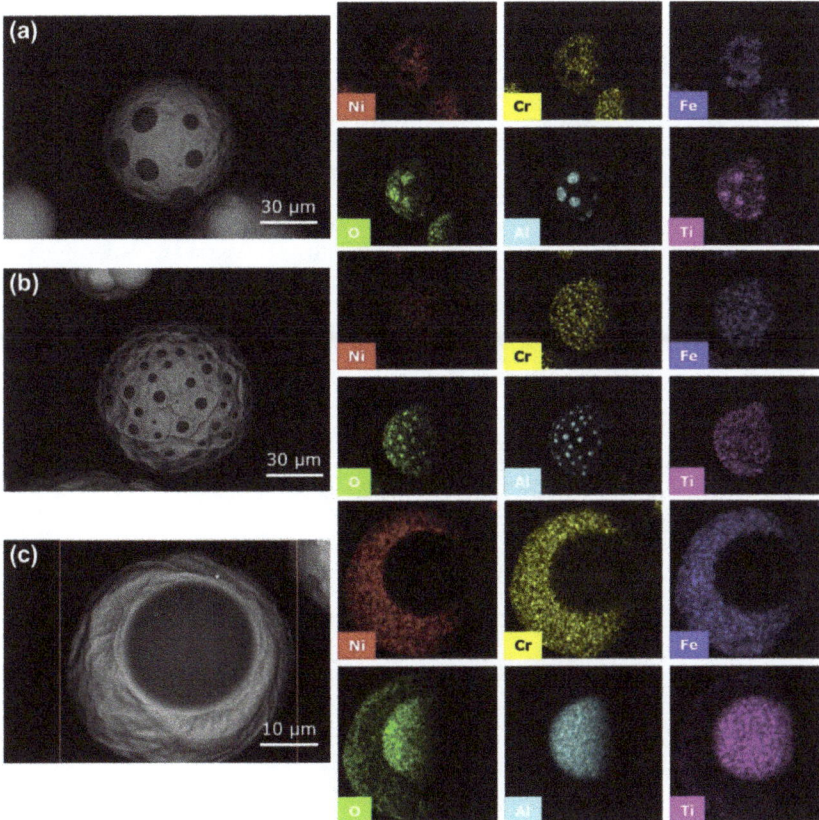

Figure 17. Back-scattered electron micrograph, and electron X-ray dispersive spectroscopy mapping of elements of Inconel 718 spatter collected from the ReaLizer SLM50. (**a**–**c**) shows that the dark spots mostly contain Al and O, and that the larger dark spots also contain Ti. EDS quantification results indicated that the oxides were a combination of Al_2O_3 and TiO_2. (Reprinted with permission from Ref. [66]. Copyright 2018 Elsevier B.V.).

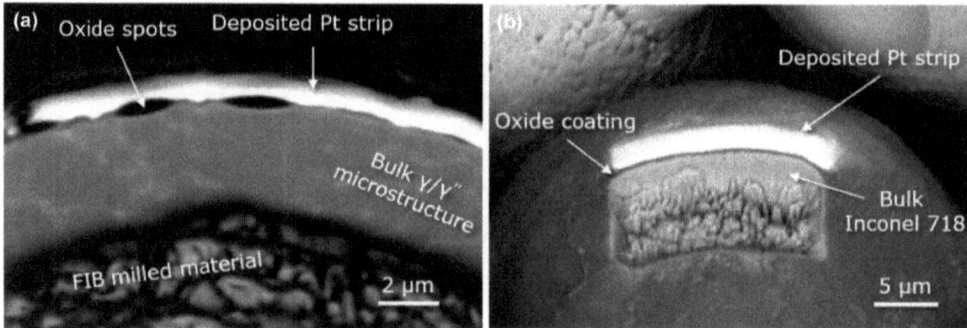

Figure 18. Back-scattered electron micrograph of particle with FIB sectioning to reveal microstructure and surface oxides (darker material) for particle (**a**) with oxide spots and (**b**) with oxide coating. The bright section is the sacrificial platinum strip deposited prior to ion milling. (Reprinted with permission from Ref. [66]. Copyright 2018 Elsevier B.V.).

Schwerz et al. [82] investigated the effect of spatter on parts using destructive (metallographic analysis) and non-destructive (ultrasonic inspection) methods. It was discovered that the spatter redeposits zone included numerous internal defects. Based on the results of the redeposited spatters (Figure 19a,c), the cross-section metallography of samples with high and low rates of re-deposition spatters were analyzed. No obvious internal defects were found in the area with a low spatter re-deposition rate, as shown in Figure 19b. Numerous internal defects were found in the area with a high spatter deposition rate, as shown in Figure 19d. These internal defects are observed in conjunction with round particles with a dendritic structure, indicated by white arrows in Figure 19e,f, located with inter-melt pool boundaries, i.e., lack of fusion defects. Multiple internal defects larger than 500 μm were verified by the ultrasonic inspection as the layer thickness increased.

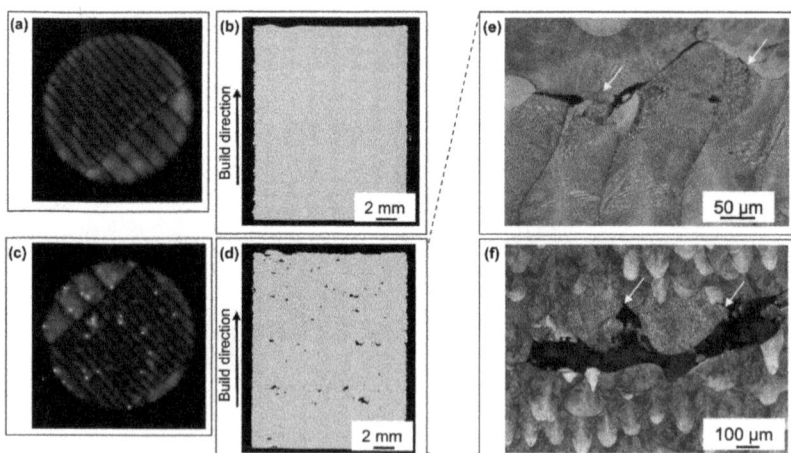

Figure 19. Cross section metallography of damaged testing [82]. (**a**) A low number of spatter redeposits are detected in specimens manufactured in the proximity of the gas inlet. (**b**) Metallographic analysis of these specimens reveals no major internal defects. (**c**) Detections of spatter redeposits can be abundant in specimens manufactured in the proximity of the gas outlet, (**d**) and these specimens present large internal defects. (**e**,**f**) are round particles with dendritic structure neighbor and lack of fusion defects, indicated by white arrows. (Reprinted with permission from Ref. [82]. Copyright 2021 Elsevier B.V.).

Spatter can cause a reduction in the tensile properties of the parts. Liu et al. [62] conducted tensile testing from fresh and contaminated 316L stainless steel powder, and the results showed that the mechanical properties of the specimens manufactured with contaminated powder are far inferior to those manufactured with fresh powder, as shown in Figure 20. Specimens with contaminated powder show considerably more voids in the fracture compared to specimens with fresh powder. These voids cause cracks and accelerate crack propagation during tensile testing, resulting in a dramatic reduction of mechanical properties in the specimens.

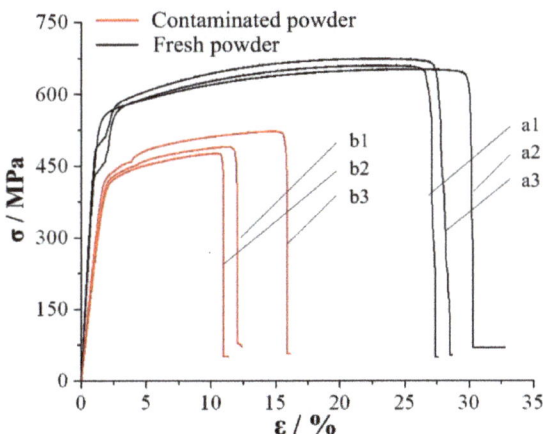

Figure 20. The stress–strain curves of tensile test pieces (fabricated from fresh and contaminated). (Reprinted with permission from Ref. [62]. Copyright 2015 Elsevier B.V.).

4.3. Effect of Spatter on Powder Recycling

Only 2 wt.% to 3 wt.% of the powder is selected for laser melting to metal pieces during L-PBF. Therefore, powder recycling is an efficient method of extending powder use [93]. However, recycled powder contains L-PBF by-products, which causes difficulties in powder recycling. Spatter particles are distributed in various sizes, a sieving mesh can easily remove most of the particles, but a small percentage of spatters smaller than the size of the original powders still remain. The powder recycling shows a distinct impact on the L-PBF process for powders of different components. (1) The 316L stainless steel powder is unique with an inherent SiO_2 oxide layer on its surface that prevents the variable valence of metallic elements. It can be used up to 15 times in L-PBF without much affecting the mechanical properties of parts, but the oxygen content of the print increases with the number of recycles, and the part density decreases after 5 to 6 recycles [94]. (2) Ti-6Al-4V also contains an oxide layer on the surface; the elemental content of the powder remains nearly the same after 31 recycles, and the tensile strength, yield strength, and elongation are also almost unchanged [95]. (3) The recyclability of Al-Si10-Mg is poor, and its oxygen content doubles after 6 recycles [96]. (4) The steel alloy 17-4 PH showed a narrowing of the particle size distribution and a loss of tensile strength after 5 recycles [97]. (5) Hastelloy X is easy to be oxidized because it contains oxygenophilic elements such as Si, Cr, and Ni. Due to the wettability of Hastelloy X powder, it produces more spatters, which affects the re-cycling of the powder. He et al. [98] found that after 6 cycles of Hastelloy, the average particle size increased by 22% and the oxygen content increased by 48%, and the part porosity increased, resulting in a reduced part quality. The following Table 7 summarizes the number of re-cycle times available for different powders.

Table 7. Summary of the re-cycle times available for different powders.

Material	Powder Parameters	Re-Cycle Times	References
316L	20~45 μm	10–15	Gorji et al. (2019) [99] Delacroix et al. (2022) [94]
Ti-6Al-4V	<63 μm	21–31	Tang et al. (2015) [100] Quintana et al. (2018) [95]
Al-Si10-Mg	20~63 μm	6–30	Cordova et al. (2019) [96] Mohd et al. (2020) [101]
17-4 PH	15~45 μm	5–11	Nezhadfar et al. (2018) [97] Jacob et al. (2017) [102]
Hastelloy X	20~60 μm	6	He et al. (2022) [98]

According to a study done by Marco Simonelli et al. [103], when powders are used for an extended period of time without sieving, numerous impurities mix with the powder and eventually become embedded in the surface of the manufactured part. Most of those impurities are spatter particles with the same composition as the slag produced during the conventional steel manufacturing process; the impurity consists primarily of SiO_2 and other oxides, which can lead to impurity in the composition of the powder. Even after sieving, some spatter particles remain, and printing using powders containing spatter particles easily results in defects inside the part. Wang et al. [104] discovered that during L-PBF formation of a porous structure, the spatter particles in the recycled powder became inclusions in the part, influencing the part quality. Santecchia et al. [105] found that the environmental conditions in the build chamber can lead to the rapid condensation of vaporized material, and large amounts of condensate and spatter deposited together on the powder bed can affect the reuse of the powder. High concentrations of condensate and condensate on spatter particles were found by Sutton et al. [90] by SEM imaging, as shown in Figure 21.

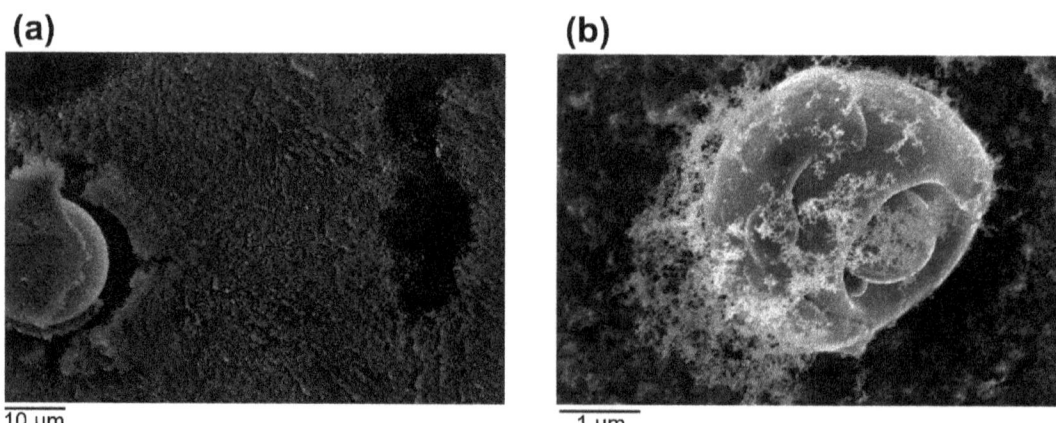

Figure 21. SEM images of condensate. (a) A heavy concentration of condensate. (b) Condensate on a captured laser spatter particle. (Reprinted with permission from Ref. [90]. Copyright 2019 Elsevier B.V.).

The spatter has a negative effect on the whole process of L-PBF including the equipment (e.g., laser beam, scraper), current L-PBF manufacturing (e.g., structure and mechanical property), and subsequent L-PBF manufacturing (e.g., powder recycling). The generation of spatter will prevent the laser from directly irradiating on the powder bed, resulting in the loss of laser energy. The redeposited spatters will damage the scraper and become inclusions in the parts, which will reduce the structure and mechanical properties of the parts. Furthermore, spattering has an influence on the whole life cycle of powder. In current manufacturing, the spatters redeposit into the powder bed, and irregularly shaped spatter particles will become inclusions in the powder, increasing the powder's oxygen concentration. These powders can result in inferior quality parts in subsequent manufacturing, leading to a decrease in the amount of powder recycling. Metal powders are more expensive than ingot metal, therefore, increasing the number of recycles of the powder is critical to making it more efficient to utilize. Spatter reduces powder quality and re-cycle times, and its removal can effectively improve powder usage efficiency, thus it is essential to research spatter countermeasures. The disadvantages of spatter are summarized in Table 8.

Table 8. Summary of studies on the disadvantages of spatter.

	Disadvantage	Material	References
Printing processing	Laser energy loss	316L	Liu et al. (2015) [62]
		Ti-6Al-4V	Pal et al. (2020) [106]
	Abrasion of scraper	CoCr	Wang et al. [63]
		Hastelloy X	Schwerz et al. [82]
Structure and mechanical property (current L-PBF manufacturing)	Spatter oxidation (oxygen content of part increases due to redeposited spatters)	316L	Hatami et al. (2021) [107]
		Al-Si10-Mg	Lutter et al. (2018) [108]
		CoCrMo	Darvish et al. (2016) [109]
	Lack of fusion	Al-Si10-Mg; Ti-6Al-4V	Young et al. (2020) [56]
		Ti-6Al-4V	Pal et al. (2020) [106]
		316L	Obeidi et al. (2020) [110]
		Inconel 718	Ladewig et al. (2016) [87]
		CoCr	Wang et al. (2017) [63]
	Increase in surface roughness	17-4 PH	Ali et al. (2019) [111]
		Hastelloy-X	Esmaeilizadeh et al. (2019) [112]
Powder recycling (subsequent L-PBF manufacturing)	Porosity increase	Ti-6Al-4V	Strondl et al. (2015) [113]
	Mixing of spatter particles	Al-Si10-Mg	Lutter et al. (2018) [108]
		304 L	Obeidi et al. (2020) [110]
	High oxygen content (oxidized spatter in recycled powder increases)	Hastelloy X	Esmaeilizadeh et al. (2019) [112]
		316L	Lu et al. (2022) [114]

5. Spatter Countermeasures

The disadvantages of spatter include the equipment, components, and powders. Effective spatter countermeasures would extend equipment life, improve the parts' quality, and enhance powder use. The full cycle of the spatter can be divided into three parts: generation, ejection, and re-deposition. In the generation stage, the generation of spatter can be suppressed by optimizing the laser volumetric energy density (VED), laser beam mode, and pressure of the building chamber. During the ejection and re-deposition stages, the protective gas flow is applied to remove the spatters which are in motion above the powder bed.

5.1. Process Parameters

In practice, regulating process parameters has emerged as a critical topic of study in reducing spatter effects during L-PBF. Process parameters such as (VED), scanning strategy, and build chamber pressures can affect the generation of spatter as follows: (1) Adopting a large spot combined with a low volume energy density can increase the depth of the melt pool and effectively suppress spatter. (2) The Bessel beam can be employed to stabilize the melt pool and reduce the generation of spatter. (3) The pre-sintering and re-coating printing strategy can reduce spatter generation. (4) Adding helium to the protective gas, reducing its oxygen content, and increasing the build chamber pressure can reduce spatter generation. A summary of studies on the control of L-PBF process parameters to reduce spatter generation during processing is shown in Table 9.

Table 9. Summary of studies on the regulation of process parameters.

Process Parameters	Spatter Countermeasures	Materials	References
Laser VED	Decrease laser power	316L, TC4	Liu et al. (2015) [62] Shi et al. (2021) [115] Luo et al. (2021) [42] Chen et al. (2022) [46]
	Increase laser scanning velocity	Al-Si10-Mg	Andani et al. (2018) [52]
	Increase laser spot	316L, 4047 Al-Si alloy; Inconel 625; Ti-6Al-4V	Gunenthiram et al. (2018) [78] Sow et al. (2020) [116] Young et al. (2022) [117]
	Reduce layer thickness	316L	Zhang et al. (2022) [38]
Laser beam modes	Bessel beams	316L	Nguyen et al. (2021) [118]
	Flat-top beam	Co-Cr	Okunkova et al. (2014) [119]
Printing Strategy	Pre-sintering	316L, Al-Si10-Mg, Ti-6Al-4V	Simonelli et al. (2015) [103]
		Ti-6Al-4V, 316L	Khairallah et al. (2020) [69]
	Scan in the opposite direction to the gas flow	Al-Si10-Mg	Andani et al. (2017) [79] Anwar et al. (2018) [85] Anwar et al. (2019) [120]
Ambient pressure	Increasing the ambient pressure	316L	Bidare et al. (2018) [121]
		Pure (CP) titanium grade 2, Maraging steel 1.2709	Kaserer et al. (2020) [122]
		316L	Guo et al. (2018) [36] Li et al. (2021) [123]
Protective Gas	Reducing the oxygen content of atmosphere	316L	Wu et al. (2016) [124]
	Increase gas flow velocity (without blowing away the powder bed)	Inconel 718	Ladewig et al. (2016) [87]
	Adding helium to protective gas	Ti-6Al-4V	Pauzon et al. (2021) [125]
	Printing in the central area of the powder bed	Ti-6Al-4V	Wang et al. (2021) [126]

5.1.1. Laser VED

The laser VED affects the number and volume of spatters. The formula for calculating laser VED is $E_V = \frac{P}{V d_l h_p}$. In the formula, P is the laser power, V is the scanning velocity, d_l is the laser diameter, and h_p is the layer thickness of the powder [127]. Gunenthiram et al. [78] demonstrated that the volume of spatter increased with increasing the VED, as seen in Figure 22. Mumtaz et al. [128] used pulse shaping techniques to precisely regulate the energy of the laser–material interaction zone, minimizing the generated spatter during L-PBF, which improved the top surface roughness of the parts and minimized the melt pool width. Shi et al. [115] demonstrated that by adjusting the energy density during single-layer formation, the spatter defects can be successfully reduced. The sample with the smoothest surface was produced when the linear energy density and the surface energy density was applied to 0.4 J/mm to 0.6 J/mm and 4 J/mm^2 to 6 J/mm^2, respectively.

- **Laser power:** The laser power applied affects the number and volume of spatters, in most situations, studies have shown that the higher the laser power input, the more severe the spatter behavior. Andani et al. [52] concluded that decreasing the laser power would reduce spatter in L-PBF, and the laser power dominates the effect on spatter generation. Chen et al. [46] demonstrated that adjusting the power intensity and distribution of the laser beam to maintain the melt pool temperature between the melting and boiling points can significantly reduce spatter generation.

- **Scanning velocity:** The velocity of the laser scanning will affect the generation of spatter. Andani et al. [52] considered that increasing the laser scanning velocity would reduce spatter in L-PBF. Gunenthiram et al. [78] studied the number of spatters at different scanning velocities ($V = 0.33 \sim 0.75$ m/s) and found that the higher the scanning velocity, the less the number of hot spatters, as shown in Figure 22. However, a high scanning velocity leads to a longer scanning path, which increases the cold spatter caused by entrainment.
- **Laser diameter:** The laser spot size during L-PBF can significantly affect the melt dynamics and droplet spatter generation [117]. There are two reasons for the variation of the spot size: passive variation and active variation. For passive changes, the lens could be deformed due to thermal expansion and contraction induced by the incident high-energy laser, so that the spot size varies during laser conduction. The active variation is to adjust the spot size of the laser artificially. Gunenthiram et al. [78] demonstrated a possible way to entirely suppress the spatter by using a large spot when the melt pool is sufficiently deep. Sow et al. [116] investigated the influence of a large laser spot on L-PBF and concluded that combining a large spot with a low VED significantly improved the L-PBF in terms of the process stability, spatter reduction, and component density.
- **Layer thickness:** A high layer thickness results in a large amount of spatter. Schwerz et al. conducted experiments with layer thicknesses of 80 µm, 120 µm, and 150 µm, and found that the number of redeposited spatters increased with the layer thickness [82]. The heat of the melt pool cannot be conducted quickly by the surrounding powder as the layer thickness rises, which leads to the instability of the melt pool, and the number of spatters increases accordingly. However, due to the limited area of laser irradiation, the increase in the spatter will slow down when the layer thickness reaches a certain thickness. Zhang et al. [38] found that spatter generation slows down when the layer thickness exceeds twice the size of the powder particles.

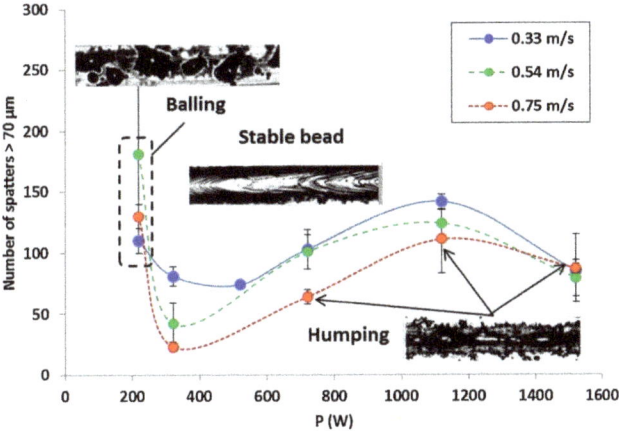

Figure 22. On a 316L stainless steel powder bed, the effect of laser power and scanning velocity on large-sized spatter, For low laser powers ($P = 220$ W) and resulting VED values severe balling occurs, that generates important spattering. The lower amount of spatters is obtained for P values just above the balling threshold ($P = 320$ W, $V = 0.54$ m/s and 0.75 m/s). (Reprinted with permission from Ref. [78]. Copyright 2018 Elsevier B.V.).

5.1.2. Laser Mode

The generation of spatter is influenced by the mode of the laser beam used in L-PBF. The main modes of lasers currently used in L-PBF are: the Gaussian beam, inverse Gaussian (annular) beams, flat-top beam, and Bessel beam. Several studies have shown that Bessel beams are significantly better than Gaussian beams in L-PBF.

- **Gaussian beam:** Less spatter would be produced while printing with L-PBF equipment that uses Bessel beams. The Gaussian beam produces more spatter and the spatter is ejected at a higher velocity, this is due to the higher recoil forces generated by the Gaussian-like thermal distribution of the laser beam on the melt pool [129].
- **Inverse Gaussian (annular) beams:** Compared to the Gaussian beam, the inverse Gaussian (annular) can reduce the creation of spatter and increase the geometric tolerance of the 3D parts [119].
- **Flat-top beam:** L-PBF with a flat-top beam generates less and slower spatter than Gaussian beam and inverse Gaussian (annular) beams, as stated by Okunkova et al. [119].
- **Bessel beam:** The Bessel beam helps stabilize the melt pool to reduce spatter. Nguyen et al. [118] investigated the possibility of using Bessel beams for ultrafast laser processing in AM, indicating that Bessel beams might alleviate the negative impacts of spatter in L-PBF. Tumkur et al. [129], utilizing high-speed imaging to detect the dynamics of melt pool, found that Bessel beams stabilize the melt pool's turbulence, increase their solidification times, and reduce spatter generation (Figure 23).

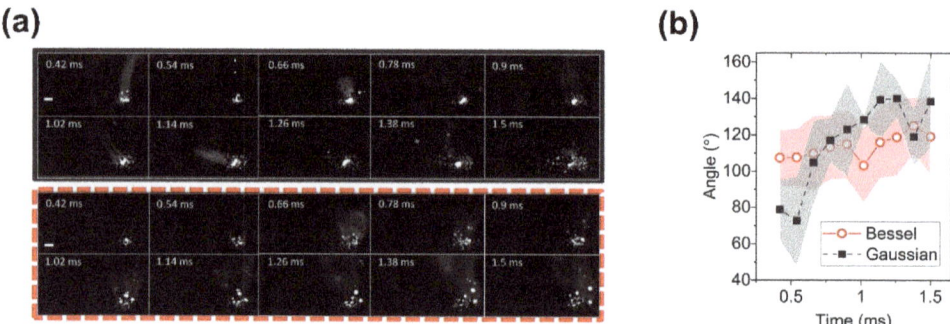

Figure 23. (**a**) Side views of melt pool captured using Gaussian (top, gray border) and Bessel (bottom, dashed red border) lasers; (**b**) angle of melt pool steam relative to horizontal level as a function of time. (Reprinted with permission from Ref. [129]. Copyright 2021 AAAS).

5.1.3. Printing Strategy

The scanning strategy can be divided into two categories: scanning path and pre-sintering method. The checkerboard scanning path can reduce the generation of spatter, and when the scanning direction is consistent with the gas flow direction, the spatter can be effectively removed. Pre-sintering with a low-energy density can also effectively suppress the generation of spatter.

- **Generation of spatter:** Rivalta et al. [130] found that the hexagonal (outside-in verse) scanning strategy would produce more spatter. It is speculated that when hexagonal patterns are used for component manufacturing, the time between adjacent scan tracks rises, the temperature range becomes too wide, so more energy is required to heat the surrounding environment, resulting in increased spatter. A checkerboard scan approach can help to reduce the generation of spatter.
- **Removal of spatter:** The trajectory of the spatter is dependent on the direction of the laser scan. The movement trajectory of most spatters is opposite to the scanning direction. The spatter can be effectively removed if the direction of the spatter movement is consistent with the protective gas flow. However, the gas flow direction is determined

by the design of the equipment, and the optimizing of the laser scanning direction can be performed. Effective spatter removal can be achieved by changing the direction of the laser scanning so that the trajectory of the spatter is consistent with the direction of the protecting gas flow. Anwar et al. [84] found that spatters re-depositioned near the outlet of the build chamber were greatly decreased when the laser scans were against the direction of the protective gas flow, but large particle spatters were still difficult to be removed [85,120].

Pre-sintering can form necks between powder particles, which is often used in electron powder bed fusion (E-PBF) to prevent powder redistribution. Similarly, pre-sintering can be introduced into L-PBF to reduce the generation of spatters. Metal powder has a significantly higher thermal absorption rate than solid bulk metal, the amount of spatter generated during L-PBF can be reduced by using a scanning strategy of a low-energy-density laser pre-sintering [103]. Khairallah et al. [69] demonstrated that combining high laser power with pre-sintering can significantly suppress spatter generation, particularly oversized (~200 mm) back-ejected spatter (spatter in the backward direction) at the start of the scanning trajectory. Achee et al. [131] used pre-sintering to prevent spatter and denudation, and they found that the control of spatter and denudation was most effective when the pre-sintered VED was 1–4 J/mm^3. Moreover, Annovazzi et al. [132] indicated that pre-sintering powder could help prevent spattering. Constantin et al. [133] demonstrated that adding a re-coating step can increase the part quality compared to the conventional L-PBF process.

5.1.4. Pressure of Build Chamber

The environmental pressure within the build chamber affects spatter generation. As the environmental pressure increased, the total amount of spatter dropped gradually, but the hot spatter generated by argon gas flow entrainment increased [36], and the smoothness and continuity of the built layers was degraded [35], as illustrated in Figure 24. Kaserer et al. [122] investigated the effect of pressure variation on L-PBF. They discovered that the amount of spatter produced by the pure titanium and maraging steel 1.2709 used in the study did not change considerably when the process pressure was varied between 200 mbar and atmospheric pressure.

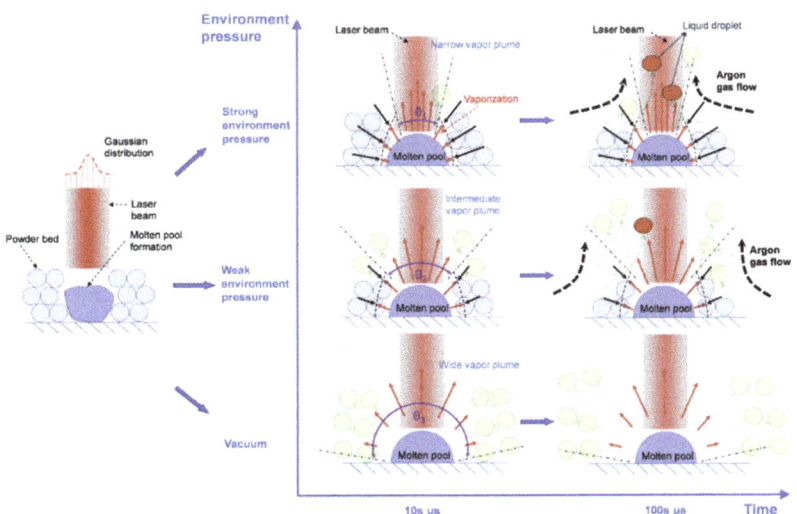

Figure 24. Schematic of powder spattering behavior as a function of time and environment pressure during L-PBF.(Reprinted with permission from Ref. [36]. Copyright 2018 Elsevier B.V.).

Based on research of the laser–powder bed interaction at sub-atmospheric pressures, Bidare et al. [121] demonstrated that while the ambient pressure decreased as gas entrainment rose, the expanding laser plume prevented the powder particles from reaching the melt pool. Li et al. [123] investigated the flow of gas, the gas–solid interaction, and the powder behavior in L-PBF at various ambient pressures. It was noted that as ambient pressure decreased, powder spatter particle and divergence angles increased, which is consistent with the Guo et al. [36] experiment results. They considered that as the ambient pressure decreased, the number of spatters grew monotonically. Spatter movement was suppressed by increasing the ambient pressure during L-PBF. Annovazzi et al. [132] demonstrated that vacuum conditions and a high laser velocity are detrimental to the stability of the powder layer, which induced more spatter.

5.1.5. Protective Gas

The influence of inert gas on spatter is due to two factors: the primary component of the gas (Ar, He, N_2, 50% Ar–50% He mixture) and the secondary component of the gas (O). The inert gas' protective effect is due to its major component. Helium, which has a positive influence on spatter suppression, has a high thermal conductivity (ten times that of Argon). As a result of this high thermal conductivity, the temperature of the melt pool is lower and the back punch is smaller, resulting in less spatter generated. However, the rarity of Helium is the reason for its high price, in the range of about 3 to 6 times per cylinder compared to argon, so, taking this into account, there is more use of argon gas for production. Oxygen, being a tiny component of the inert gas, can cause spatter to increase and oxidize; therefore, lowering the oxygen level in the inert gas helps to suppress spatter generation.

- **Primary components of inert gases:** Pauzon et al. [125] studied the effect of protective gas on L-PBF of Ti-6Al-4V powder in three different conditions: pure argon, pure helium, and a helium and argon mix (oxygen content was controlled at 100 ppm). In comparison to the common use of argon, studies have indicated that using pure helium or a mixture of helium and argon can reduce hot spatter by at least 60% and ~30%, respectively, as shown in Figure 25. No influence of different protective gases on the number of cold spatters was detected. The study also found that adding helium to the gas can help cool spatter more quickly, which is important for limiting powder-bed degradation throughout L-PBF.

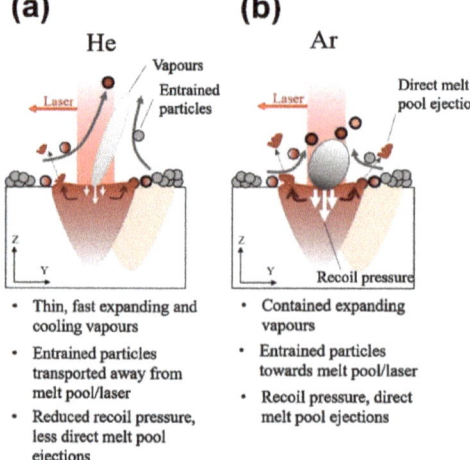

Figure 25. The interaction of the laser–powder bed with (**a**) Helium and (**b**) Argon in the L-PBF protective gas. (Reprinted with permission from Ref. [125]. Copyright 2021 CIRP).

- **Secondary component of the inert gas:** According to Wu et al. [124], the oxygen concentration in the protective environment increased considerably, resulting in the generation of spatter and an increase in the oxygen content of spatter during flight. By decreasing the oxygen level of the build chamber, the spatter generation can be reduced.

Reducing the oxygen content in the build chamber is an efficient approach to prevent spatters from generating. Through multiple gas circulations, the equipment can decrease the oxygen level in the build chamber as much as feasible. Furthermore, keeping the build chamber at slightly above the atmospheric pressure can prevent the entry of oxygen from outside the equipment and, at the same time, the flowing inert gas can eliminate the generated spatter.

5.1.6. Gas Flow Strategies

Most modern L-PBF equipment using gas flow removes process by-products from the process zone to enable an undisturbed process. Ladewig et al. [87] examined the influence of the protective gas flow uniformity and rate on single-laser tracks and the hatching process during the building procedure of bulk material. The efficiency of spatter removal decreased as the velocity of the protective gas flow reduced. Chien et al. [134] proposed to optimize and calibrate the inert purge airflow in an L-PBF build chamber using simulation framework methods such as coupled computational fluid dynamics (CFD) and the discrete element method (DEM). Wang et al. [126] created a full-scale geometric model to explore the interaction between the protective gas flow and the laser-induced spatter particles. The flow field was found to be steady up to a height of 30 mm above the surface of the powder bed. It was discovered that printing in this region could improve the final quality due to the consistent high-velocity flow of the protective airflow in the center of the powder bed, which removed by-products such as spatter.

5.2. Equipment and Materials for L-PBF

In addition to regulating process parameters, research on L-PBF equipment and materials has become a major focus for mitigating the effect of spatter. These two research areas will also contribute to the future commercialization of L-PBF technology. A summary of the research on L-PBF equipment and materials is shown in Table 10.

Table 10. A summary of the research on L-PBF equipment and materials.

	Materials	Spatter Countermeasures	References
L-PBF equipment	316L, Aluminum	Uniformity of flow field	Philo et al. (2018) [135] Xiao et al. (2021) [136]
	316L	Prevent powder from blowing away	Zhang et al. (2020) [137]
	316L	High gravity powder bed	Koike et al. (2021) [138,139]
Powder materials	316L, 13-93 bioactive glass	Increasing the viscosity of melt	Leung et al. (2018) [140]
	AISI 4130; 316L	Reducing the oxygen content of powder	Heiden et al. (2019) [141] Fedina et al. (2020) [142] Fedina et al. (2021) [143]

5.2.1. Research on L-PBF Equipment

Spatter generation can be reduced by optimizing L-PBF equipment. Koike et al. [138,139] developed a high-gravity L-PBF system that generated a strong gravitational field by centrifugal acceleration. At a high gravity acceleration of more than 10 G, the spatters were greatly suppressed. As illustrated in Figure 26, the height of the spatter trajectory was inversely related to the increased gravitational acceleration. They noted that when a suitably strong gravitational acceleration was applied, spatter generation was dramatically suppressed.

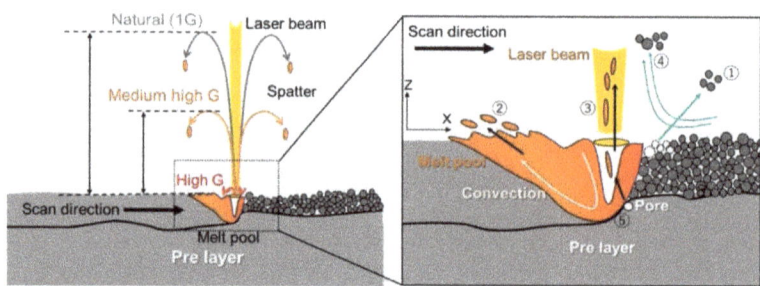

Figure 26. Classification and suppression of spatter under high gravitational acceleration: ① solid spatter; ② metallic ejected spatter; ③ powder agglomeration spatter; ④ entrainment melting spatter; and ⑤ defect induced spatter. (Reprinted with permission from Ref. [139]. Copyright 2021 Elsevier B.V.).

Philo et al. [135] used numerical simulations to investigate the interaction between the gas flow and spatter. They discovered that the parameters of the protective gas inlet and outlet in the build chamber (e.g., the radius of the inlet nozzles, the heights of the inlet and outlet) significantly affect the flow velocity, uniformity, and spatter concentration. Xiao et al. [136] simulated the flow field in an L-PBF build chamber to optimize the flow-field structure. The flow-field state was evaluated using the particle tracer method. It was shown that the flow-field distribution was made more uniform by structural optimization, which can improve the ability of the gas flow to entrain spatter.

To increase the capability for spatter removal, Zhang et al. [137] proposed a novel design for the gas flow system in the build chamber, as illustrated in Figure 27. The effect of the gas flow on the solid particles was obtained using the fully coupled CFD-DPM fluid–particle interaction model. The new design increased the spatter removal rate by reducing the Coanda effect, which substantially affected the spatter removal process. In addition, another row of nozzles was added directly under the primary inlet nozzles.

Current novel L-PBF machines generally use multi-laser beams to print simultaneously to increase efficiency, which generates more spatter. Optimizing the equipment, especially the build chamber, to remove spatter has become a major concern for many L-PBF machine manufacturers. SLM Solutions GmbH (Lubeck, Germany) has introduced adopting the building chamber to a high pressure in order to minimize the spatter activity, which hence has lowered spatter generation [144]. Through the streamlined special-shaped design of the flow channel, Bright Co. Ltd. (Xi'an, China) [145] reduced the vortex current at the outlet of the protective gas, and the steam plume and spatters are ensured to be blown away and not redeposit on the forming surface during forming, which solves the quality problem of the forming surface during printing. General Electric Co. invented a gas flow system for an additive manufacturing machine that uses a gas flow parallel to the powder bed to remove by-products (including spatter) from the L-PBF manufacturing process [146]. The MYSINT 100 3D printer from SISMA [147], Italy, has a stable and uniform flow field to ensure spatter removal efficiency.

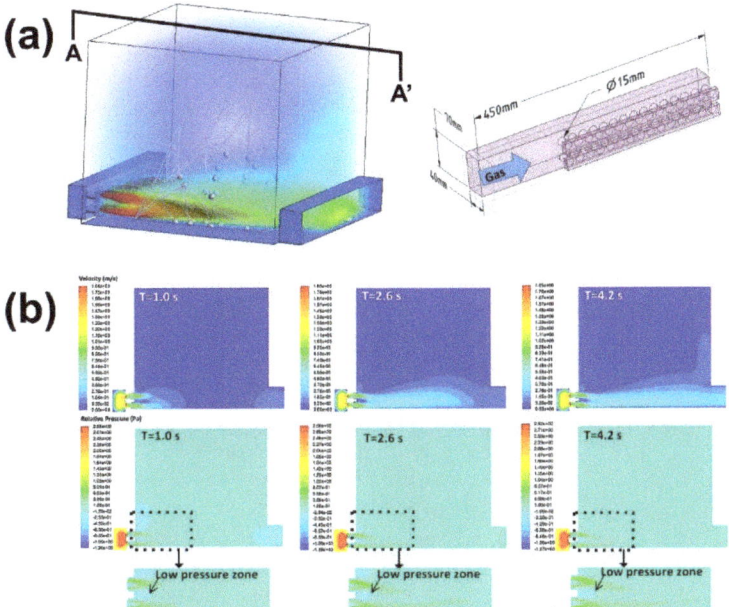

Figure 27. CAD model of counter-Coanda effect in L-PBF build chamber: (**a**) the counter-Coanda effect design that employs another row of nozzles directly under the primary nozzles; (**b**) A-A' plane: transient velocity and pressure field. (Reprinted with permission from Ref. [137]. Copyright 2020 Elsevier B.V.).

5.2.2. Research on Powder Material

The physical properties and oxygen content of the powder can also contribute to differences in spatter behaviors, which can be reduced by a high viscosity, high thermal conductivity, and high density. Powders with a low oxygen content caused significantly less spatter in L-PBF.

- **Physical properties:** High thermal conductivity and densification have a positive effect on spatter suppression. Due to the higher thermal conductivity of aluminum in the liquid state 316L, the laser energy can be rapidly dissipated into the substrate, limiting the vaporization of the aluminum alloy and the resulting spattering [78]. Gunenthiram et al. [78] pointed out that due to the densification effect, the melt pool will be located below the surface of the powder bed, which will inhibit the generation of spatter. The melt pools formed by the laser irradiation of different powder particles have varying viscosities which influence the generation of spatter. Leung et al. [140] investigated the laser–material interaction of 316L stainless steel powder and 13–93 bioactive glass powder during L-PBF at short time scales. The results indicate that droplet spatters are easily generated in a low-viscosity melt (e.g., 316L) because of the strong Marangoni-driven flow. By contrast, a high-viscosity melt (e.g., 13–93 bioactive glass) reduces spatter generation by dampening the Marangoni-driven flow.
- **Oxygen content:** For the raw powder used in L-PBF, the higher the oxygen content, the greater the melt pool instability and the greater the probability of spattering. Fedina et al. [143] found that with the oxygen content of the powder rose, the number of spatters increased, whereas the other chemical elements remained relatively constant. They suggested that the increase in oxygen might have affected the powder spattering. Additionally, an increase in the powder oxygen content led to an increase in the oxygen content of the melt pool, which in turn affected the flow behavior of

the fluid in the melt pool, leading to spattering as the melt pool broke into molten droplets [148]. Fedina et al. [142] investigated L-PBF dynamics and powder behavior by comparing water-atomized and gas-atomized powders. They discovered that the water-atomized powder had more frequent spatter ejection and speculated that the higher oxygen level in the powder caused the melt pool to become unstable, resulting in an excessive number of spatters.

Manufacturers are also concentrating their efforts on developing powder materials suitable for L-PBF, offering a wide variety of powder materials such as various titanium alloys, nickel alloys, aluminum alloys, and cobalt–chromium alloy powder materials for the aerospace, automotive, and biomedical fields.

6. Conclusions

This paper reviews the literature on the in situ detection, generation, effects, and countermeasures against spatter in L-PBF. The main points of this review are summarized as the following:

(1) **In situ detection system for spatter during L-PBF:** The detection methods are based on the physical properties (trajectory and brightness) of the spatter and melt pool. The variances in the trajectory and brightness lead to differences in the sensors and light sources of the detection system.

- **Sensor:** Due to the complex and unpredictable trajectories of the spatters in the 3D space compared to the melt pool, detection requires multiple sensors and sophisticated algorithms. A 3D detection solution with a quadruple-eye sensor combined with algorithms has been applied in a visible-light detection system. The emergence of 3D detection solutions provides more information in three dimensions, which improves the accuracy of the spatter detection.
- **Light source:** Compared to the bright high-temperature melt pool, the spatters consist of both bright hot droplet spatters and dark cold powder spatters. The motion of dark cold powder spatter can hardly be captured without an external light source. Therefore, a visible light source must be applied to enable the detecting of two types of spatters.

(2) **Mechanism of spatter generation in L-PBF:** spatter can be divided into droplet spatter from the "liquid base" of the melt pool and powder spatter from the "solid base" of the substrate.

- **Droplet spatter from the "Liquid base" of the melt pool:** The droplet spatter originates from the instability of the melt pool. The Marangoni effect and the metal vapor recoil pressure generated on the surface of the melt pool lead to the spatter ejection from "liquid base" of the melt pool.
- **Powder spatter from the "Solid base" of the substrate:** Powder spatter is induced by the entrainment effect of the ambient gas flow driven by the metal vapor. A low-pressure area is generated near the high-speed moving metal vapor, and the surrounding inert protective gas will be "entrained" to the vicinity of the melt pool, driving the powder spatter to be ejected from the "solid base" of the substrate.

(3) **Spatter effects during L-PBF:** Spatter has negative effects not only on the equipment and quality of parts, but also on the whole life cycle of the powder. Therefore, spatter significantly affects both the current L-PBF manufacturing and the subsequent L-PBF manufacturing.

- **Equipment:** the laser light path will be obstructed by the ejected spatter, and the scraper will be damaged by the redeposited spatter.
- **Current L-PBF manufacturing:** redeposited spatter can cause deterioration in the part structure and mechanical property.

- **Subsequent L-PBF manufacturing:** the spatters redeposit into the powder bed to be inclusions, resulting in a decrease in the quality of the re-cycle powder and affecting the subsequent L-PBF manufacturing.

(4) **Countermeasures for spatter in L-PBF:** for the full cycle of spatter (generation–ejection–redeposition), the countermeasures for spatter are divided into spatter generation suppression and spatter removal.

- **Spatter generation suppression:** the generation of spatter can be suppressed by optimizing the laser volumetric energy density (e.g., raising the scanning velocity, lowering the laser power, decreasing the layer thickness, and increasing the laser spot), laser beam mode (Bessel beams), and pressure of the building chamber.
- **Spatter removal efficiency:** The gas flow removes process by-products from the process zone to enable an undisturbed process. Simulation framework methods (CFD and DEM) and a full-scale geometric model are employed to optimize the flow filed structure. A high-velocity gas flow under a certain value (counter-Coanda effect) applied in the center of the powder bed greatly improves the efficiency of spatter removal.

7. Future Research Directions

As the main technology in metal AM, L-PBF is evolving toward a greater efficiency, precision, speed, and fabrication of large-sized parts. However, spattering has caused negative influence on the product quality during L-PBF. The following trends characterize the directions of research on L-PBF spatter behavior:

(1) **Study of spatter behavior under multiple lasers:** Multi-laser synergy has been the main solution to achieve more efficient fabrication of large-sized parts. However, the mechanism of spatter becomes more complicated due to the enhancement of metal vapor, the Marangoni effect, and entrainment under the multi-laser interaction. Additionally, each laser induces both "liquid-based" and "solid-based" ejected spatters, and the amount of spatter increases dramatically using multiple lasers. The spatter is more difficult to be removed by gas flow due to the large-scaled build chamber. Therefore, the research of spatter in multi-beam manufacturing has become more urgent.

(2) **Improving the quality of in situ spatter detection:** The combination of a visible-light high-speed camera and X-ray imaging technology in spatter detection coincides with the development trend of spatter detection [149]. The combination of the two methods enables us to study spatter behaviors from the inside (melt pool) to the outside (powder bed), and gain more information on the behaviors of the spatter. The multi-sensor system is indispensable in the research of spatter and the number of sensors can be expanded based on the existing quadruple-eye sensor.

(3) **Information processing using artificial intelligence:** The data volume of the multi-sensor system could exponentially increase with the addition of data sources such as temperature, radiant intensity, light intensity information, acoustic signals, and images of melt pools and spatters. Therefore, machine learning (supervised, semi-supervised, unsupervised) is necessary for the efficient processing of the multi-source and heterogeneous data.

(4) **Countermeasures for spatter:** At present, simulations are commonly used to study the countermeasures of spatter, and the raw data used in the simulations come from their detection. Improving the comprehensiveness and accuracy of detection information is conducive to the actual application of the simulation of spatter countermeasures.

(5) **Commercial L-PBF equipment:** Several companies (e.g., Concept laser, EOS, SLM solutions) have developed systems for detecting melt pools during L-PBF manufacturing, but there is still a lack of spatter detection in the equipment. As a result of the complex spatter behaviors and serious negative impact in L-PBF, it is necessary to remove as much of the spatter as possible by using dynamical control of the pro-

tective gas flow field. The addition of an in situ spatter detection system enables the dynamical feedback of the control of the gas flow field.

Author Contributions: Conceptualization, J.Y. and Z.L.; methodology, J.Y. and L.H.; investigation, Y.L. (Yang Liu), Z.N. and W.D.; resources, J.Y. and Z.L.; writing—original draft preparation, Z.L. and H.L.; writing—review and editing, J.Y., L.C., L.K., D.W., P.Z. and Y.L. (Yan Li); supervision, J.Y., L.W., K.Z., Z.Z., L.G. and L.H.; Project administration, L.H., J.Y., X.L., D.Y. and K.G.; Funding acquisition, L.H., J.Y., Z.L. and Y.L. (Yan Li). All authors have read and agreed to the published version of the manuscript.

Funding: This work was financially supported by the National Natural Science Foundation of China (61805095, 51675496, 51902295, 52175359, 51905279, 52175237), the Science and Technology Project of the Hubei Province (2021BEC010), the Wuhan Applied Foundational Frontier Project (2020010601012172), the Hubei Province Natural Science Foundation grant (2020 CFB170), and the Fundamental Research Funds for the Central Universities, China University of Geosciences (Wuhan).

Acknowledgments: The authors gratefully appreciate Cang Zhao from Tsinghua University and Zhenyu Yan from China Academy of Launch Vehicle Technology for fruitful discussions.

Conflicts of Interest: The authors declare no conflict of interest.

References

1. DebRoy, T.; Mukherjee, T.; Wei, H.L.; Elmer, J.W.; Milewski, J.O. Metallurgy, mechanistic models and machine learning in metal printing. *Nat. Rev. Mater.* **2020**, *6*, 48–68. [CrossRef]
2. Gu, D.; Shi, X.; Poprawe, R.; Bourell, D.L.; Setchi, R.; Zhu, J. Material-structure-performance integrated laser-metal additive manufacturing. *Science* **2021**, *372*, eabg1487. [CrossRef] [PubMed]
3. MacDonald, E.; Wicker, R. Multiprocess 3D printing for increasing component functionality. *Science* **2016**, *353*, aaf2093. [CrossRef]
4. Wei, H.; Mukherjee, T.; Zhang, W.; Zuback, J.; Knapp, G.; De, A.; DebRoy, T. Mechanistic models for additive manufacturing of metallic components. *Prog. Mater. Sci.* **2020**, *116*, 100703. [CrossRef]
5. Office of the Under Secretary of Defense, Research and Engineering (USD(R&E)). Department of Defense Additive Manufacturing Strategy. Available online: https://www.cto.mil/dod-additive-manufacturing-strategy/ (accessed on 3 May 2022).
6. U.S. Department of Defense. DoD Instruction 5000.93, "Use of Additive Manufacturing in the DoD". Available online: https://www.defense.gov/News/News-Stories/Article/Article/2712969/dod-promotes-additive-manufacturing-expansion-standardization-training-through/ (accessed on 3 May 2022).
7. National Science and Technology Information System, Public Service Platform. The 2022 Annual Project Application Guide for the Key Projects of Additive Manufacturing and Laser Manufacturing Under the 14th Five-Year National Key R&D Program. Available online: https://service.most.gov.cn/kjjh_tztg_all/20220427/4894.html (accessed on 3 May 2022).
8. Yang, Y. Analysis of Classifications and Characteristic of Additive Manufacturing (3D Print). *Adv. Aeronaut. Sci. Eng.* **2019**, *10*, 309–318. (In Chinese)
9. Lu, B.H.; Li, D.C. Development of the additive manufacturing (3D printing) technology. *Mach. Build. Autom.* **2013**, *42*, 1–4. (In Chinese)
10. Ian Gibson, D.R. Brent Stucker. *Additive Manufacturing Technologies 3D Printing, Rapid Prototyping, and Direct Digital Manufacturing*; Springer: New York, NY, USA, 2015.
11. Frazier, W.E. Metal additive manufacturing: A review. *J. Mater. Eng. Perform.* **2014**, *23*, 1917–1928. [CrossRef]
12. Mellor, S.; Hao, L.; Zhang, D. Additive manufacturing: A framework for implementation. *Int. J. Prod. Econ.* **2014**, *149*, 194–201. [CrossRef]
13. Zhang, L.; Li, Y.; Li, S.; Gong, P.; Chen, Q.; Geng, H.; Sun, M.; Sun, Q.; Hao, L. Fabrication of Titanium and Copper-Coated Diamond/Copper Composites via Selective Laser Melting. *Micromachines* **2022**, *13*, 724. [CrossRef]
14. Wang, X.; Jiang, J.; Tian, Y. A Review on Macroscopic and Microstructural Features of Metallic Coating Created by Pulsed Laser Material Deposition. *Micromachines* **2022**, *13*, 659. [CrossRef]
15. Xu, Z.; Wang, D.; Song, W.; Tang, C.; Sun, P.; Yang, J.; Hu, Q.; Zeng, X. Microstructure and Wear of W-Particle-Reinforced Al Alloys Prepared by Laser Melt Injection. *Micromachines* **2022**, *13*, 699. [CrossRef] [PubMed]
16. Cardon, A.; Mareau, C.; Ayed, Y.; Van Der Veen, S.; Giraud, E.; Santo, P.D. Heat treatment simulation of Ti-6Al-4V parts produced by selective laser melting. *Addit. Manuf.* **2020**, *39*, 101766. [CrossRef]
17. Bartlett, J.L.; Li, X. An overview of residual stresses in metal powder bed fusion. *Addit. Manuf.* **2019**, *27*, 131–149. [CrossRef]
18. Grasso, M. In Situ Monitoring of Powder Bed Fusion Homogeneity in Electron Beam Melting. *Materials* **2021**, *14*, 7015. [CrossRef]
19. Sun, S.; Brandt, M.; Easton, M. Powder bed fusion processes: An overview. *Laser Addit. Manuf.* **2017**, 55–77.
20. King, W.E.; Anderson, A.T.; Ferencz, R.M.; Hodge, N.E.; Kamath, C.; Khairallah, S.A.; Rubenchik, A.M. Laser powder bed fusion additive manufacturing of metals; physics, computational, and materials challenges. *Appl. Phys. Rev.* **2015**, *2*, 041304. [CrossRef]

21. Ji, H.R.; Zhao, M.C.; Xie, B.; Zhao, Y.C.; Yin, D.F.; Gao, C.D.; Shuai, C.J.; Atrens, A. Corrosion and antibacterial performance of novel selective-laser-melted (SLMed) Ti-xCu biomedical alloys. *J. Alloy. Compd.* **2021**, *864*, 158415. [CrossRef]
22. Aachen Center for Additive Manufacturing. Seminar 3D Printing with SLM – Challenges for Prediction of Deformation and Integration in Industrial Process Chains on 16 May 2017. Available online: https://acam.rwth-campus.com/news/seminar-3d-printing-with-slm-on-may-16-2017/ (accessed on 3 May 2022).
23. Liu, Y.; Meng, J.; Zhu, L.; Chen, H.; Li, Z.; Li, S.; Wang, D.; Wang, Y.; Kosiba, K. Dynamic compressive properties and underlying failure mechanisms of selective laser melted Ti-6Al-4V alloy under high temperature and strain rate conditions. *Addit. Manuf.* **2022**, *54*, 102772. [CrossRef]
24. Wang, W.; Takata, N.; Suzuki, A.; Kobashi, M.; Kato, M. Microstructural Variations in Laser Powder Bed Fused Al–15%Fe Alloy at Intermediate Temperatures. *Materials* **2022**, *15*, 4497. [CrossRef]
25. Zhang, X.; Chueh, Y.-H.; Wei, C.; Sun, Z.; Yan, J.; Li, L. Additive manufacturing of three-dimensional metal-glass functionally gradient material components by laser powder bed fusion with in situ powder mixing. *Addit. Manuf.* **2020**, *33*, 101113. [CrossRef]
26. Song, C.; Hu, Z.; Xiao, Y.; Li, Y.; Yang, Y. Study on Interfacial Bonding Properties of NiTi/CuSn10 Dissimilar Materials by Selective Laser Melting. *Micromachines* **2022**, *13*, 494. [CrossRef] [PubMed]
27. Grasso, M.; Colosimo, B.M. Process defects and in situ monitoring methods in metal powder bed fusion: A review. *Meas. Sci. Technol.* **2017**, *28*, 044005. [CrossRef]
28. Zhao, C.; Fezzaa, K.; Cunningham, R.W.; Wen, H.; De Carlo, F.; Chen, L.; Rollett, A.D.; Sun, T. Real-time monitoring of laser powder bed fusion process using high-speed X-ray imaging and diffraction. *Sci. Rep.* **2017**, *7*, 3602. [CrossRef]
29. Fabbro, R. Melt pool and keyhole behaviour analysis for deep penetration laser welding. *J. Phys. D Appl. Phys.* **2010**, *43*, 445501. [CrossRef]
30. Sames, W.J.; List, F.A.; Pannala, S.; Dehoff, R.R.; Babu, S.S. The metallurgy and processing science of metal additive manufacturing. *Int. Mater. Rev.* **2016**, *61*, 315–360. [CrossRef]
31. Matthews, M.J.; Guss, G.; Khairallah, S.A.; Rubenchik, A.M.; Depond, P.J.; King, W.E. Denudation of metal powder layers in laser powder bed fusion processes. *Acta Mater.* **2016**, *114*, 33–42. [CrossRef]
32. Yadroitsev, I.; Gusarov, A.; Yadroitsava, I.; Smurov, I. Single track formation in selective laser melting of metal powders. *J. Mater. Process. Technol.* **2010**, *210*, 1624–1631. [CrossRef]
33. Riedlbauer, D.; Scharowsky, T.; Singer, R.F.; Steinmann, P.; Körner, C.; Mergheim, J. Macroscopic simulation and experimental measurement of melt pool characteristics in selective electron beam melting of Ti-6Al-4V. *Int. J. Adv. Manuf. Technol.* **2016**, *88*, 1309–1317. [CrossRef]
34. Yin, J.; Wang, D.; Yang, L.; Wei, H.; Dong, P.; Ke, L.; Wang, G.; Zhu, H.; Zeng, X. Correlation between forming quality and spatter dynamics in laser powder bed fusion. *Addit. Manuf.* **2019**, *31*, 100958. [CrossRef]
35. Bidare, P.; Bitharas, I.; Ward, R.; Attallah, M.; Moore, A.J. Laser powder bed fusion in high-pressure atmospheres. *Int. J. Adv. Manuf. Technol.* **2018**, *99*, 543–555. [CrossRef]
36. Guo, Q.; Zhao, C.; Escano, L.I.; Young, Z.; Xiong, L.; Fezzaa, K.; Everhart, W.; Brown, B.; Sun, T.; Chen, L. Transient dynamics of powder spattering in laser powder bed fusion additive manufacturing process revealed by in-situ high-speed high-energy x-ray imaging. *Acta Mater.* **2018**, *151*, 169–180. [CrossRef]
37. Grasso, M.; Colosimo, B. A statistical learning method for image-based monitoring of the plume signature in laser powder bed fusion. *Robot. Comput. Manuf.* **2018**, *57*, 103–115. [CrossRef]
38. Zhang, W.; Ma, H.; Zhang, Q.; Fan, S. Prediction of powder bed thickness by spatter detection from coaxial optical images in selective laser melting of 316L stainless steel. *Mater. Des.* **2021**, *213*, 110301. [CrossRef]
39. Repossini, G.; Laguzza, V.; Grasso, M.L.G.; Colosimo, B.M. On the use of spatter signature for in-situ monitoring of Laser Powder Bed Fusion. *Addit. Manuf.* **2017**, *16*, 35–48. [CrossRef]
40. Tan, Z.; Fang, Q.; Li, H.; Liu, S.; Zhu, W.; Yang, D. Neural network based image segmentation for spatter extraction during laser-based powder bed fusion processing. *Opt. Laser Technol.* **2020**, *130*, 106347. [CrossRef]
41. Yin, J.; Wang, L.; Yang, X.; Zhu, H.; Wang, D.; Ke, L.; Wang, Z.; Wang, G.; Zeng, X. High-power laser-matter interaction during laser powder bed fusion. *Addit. Manuf.* **2019**, *29*, 100778. [CrossRef]
42. Luo, S.; Ma, X.; Xu, J.; Li, M.; Cao, L. Deep Learning Based Monitoring of Spatter Behavior by the Acoustic Signal in Selective Laser Melting. *Sensors* **2021**, *21*, 7179. [CrossRef]
43. Barrett, C.; Carradero, C.; Harris, E.; McKnight, J.; Walker, J.; MacDonald, E.; Conner, B. Low cost, high speed stereovision for spatter tracking in laser powder bed fusion. In Proceedings of the 2018 International Solid Freeform Fabrication Symposium, Austin, TX, USA, 13–15 August 2018; pp. 2122–2134.
44. Eschner, E.; Staudt, T.; Schmidt, M. 3D particle tracking velocimetry for the determination of temporally resolved particle trajectories within laser powder bed fusion of metals. *Int. J. Extreme Manuf.* **2019**, *1*, 035002. [CrossRef]
45. Eschner, E.; Staudt, T.; Schmidt, M. Sensing approach for the in-situ determination of spatter motion within PBF-LB/M. *CIRP Ann.* **2022**, *71*, 149–152. [CrossRef]
46. Chen, H.; Zhang, Y.; Giam, A.; Yan, W. Experimental and computational study on thermal and fluid behaviours of powder layer during selective laser melting additive manufacturing. *Addit. Manuf.* **2022**, *52*, 102645. [CrossRef]
47. Zheng, H.; Wang, Y.; Xie, Y.; Yang, S.; Hou, R.; Ge, Y.; Lang, L.; Gong, S.; Li, H. Observation of Vapor Plume Behavior and Process Stability at Single-Track and Multi-Track Levels in Laser Powder Bed Fusion Regime. *Metals* **2021**, *11*, 937. [CrossRef]

48. Wang, D.; Dou, W.; Ou, Y.; Yang, Y.; Tan, C.; Zhang, Y. Characteristics of droplet spatter behavior and process-correlated mapping model in laser powder bed fusion. *J. Mater. Res. Technol.* **2021**, *12*, 1051–1064. [CrossRef]
49. Yang, D.; Li, H.; Liu, S.; Song, C.; Yang, Y.; Shen, S.; Lu, J.; Liu, Z.; Zhu, Y. In situ capture of spatter signature of SLM process using maximum entropy double threshold image processing method based on genetic algorithm. *Opt. Laser Technol.* **2020**, *131*, 106371. [CrossRef]
50. Zhang, Y.; Soon, H.G.; Ye, D.; Fuh, J.Y.H.; Zhu, K. Powder-Bed Fusion Process Monitoring by Machine Vision With Hybrid Convolutional Neural Networks. *IEEE Trans. Ind. Inform.* **2019**, *16*, 5769–5779. [CrossRef]
51. Zheng, H.; Li, H.; Lang, L.; Gong, S.; Ge, Y. Effects of scan speed on vapor plume behavior and spatter generation in laser powder bed fusion additive manufacturing. *J. Manuf. Process.* **2018**, *36*, 60–67. [CrossRef]
52. Andani, M.T.; Dehghani, R.; Karamooz-Ravari, M.R.; Mirzaeifar, R.; Ni, J. A study on the effect of energy input on spatter particles creation during selective laser melting process. *Addit. Manuf.* **2018**, *20*, 33–43. [CrossRef]
53. Ye, D.; Fuh, J.Y.H.; Zhang, Y.; Hong, G.S.; Zhu, K. In situ monitoring of selective laser melting using plume and spatter signatures by deep belief networks. *ISA Trans.* **2018**, *81*, 96–104. [CrossRef]
54. Nassar, A.R.; Gundermann, M.A.; Reutzel, E.; Guerrier, P.; Krane, M.H.; Weldon, M.J. Formation processes for large ejecta and interactions with melt pool formation in powder bed fusion additive manufacturing. *Sci. Rep.* **2019**, *9*, 5038. [CrossRef]
55. Cunningham, R.; Zhao, C.; Parab, N.; Kantzos, C.; Pauza, J.; Fezzaa, K.; Sun, T.; Rollett, A.D. Keyhole threshold and morphology in laser melting revealed by ultrahigh-speed x-ray imaging. *Science* **2019**, *363*, 849–852. [CrossRef]
56. Young, Z.A.; Guo, Q.; Parab, N.D.; Zhao, C.; Qu, M.; Escano, L.I.; Fezzaa, K.; Everhart, W.; Sun, T.; Chen, L. Types of spatter and their features and formation mechanisms in laser powder bed fusion additive manufacturing process. *Addit. Manuf.* **2020**, *36*, 101438. [CrossRef]
57. Leung, C.L.A.; Marussi, S.; Towrie, M.; Atwood, R.C.; Withers, P.J.; Lee, P.D. The effect of powder oxidation on defect formation in laser additive manufacturing. *Acta Mater.* **2018**, *166*, 294–305. [CrossRef]
58. Bidare, P.; Bitharas, I.; Ward, R.M.; Attallah, M.M.; Moore, A.J. Fluid and particle dynamics in laser powder bed fusion. *Acta Mater.* **2018**, *142*, 107–120. [CrossRef]
59. Grasso, M.L.G.; Demir, A.; Previtali, B.; Colosimo, B. In situ monitoring of selective laser melting of zinc powder via infrared imaging of the process plume. *Robot. Comput. Manuf.* **2018**, *49*, 229–239. [CrossRef]
60. Grasso, M.; Laguzza, V.; Semeraro, Q.; Colosimo, B.M. In-Process Monitoring of Selective Laser Melting: Spatial Detection of Defects Via Image Data Analysis. *J. Manuf. Sci. Eng.* **2016**, *139*, 051001. [CrossRef]
61. Yin, J.; Hao, L.; Yang, L.; Li, Y.; Li, Z.; Sun, Q.; Shi, B. Investigation of Interaction between Vapor Plume and Spatter Behavior during Selective Laser Melting Additive Manufacturing. *Chin. J. Lasers* **2022**, *49*, 1402010. (In Chinese)
62. Liu, Y.; Yang, Y.; Mai, S.; Wang, D.; Song, C. Investigation into spatter behavior during selective laser melting of AISI 316L stainless steel powder. *Mater. Des.* **2015**, *87*, 797–806. [CrossRef]
63. Wang, D.; Wu, S.; Fu, F.; Mai, S.; Yang, Y.; Liu, Y.; Song, C. Mechanisms and characteristics of spatter generation in SLM processing and its effect on the properties. *Mater. Des.* **2017**, *117*, 121–130. [CrossRef]
64. Ly, S.; Rubenchik, A.M.; Khairallah, S.A.; Guss, G.; Matthews, M.J. Metal vapor micro-jet controls material redistribution in laser powder bed fusion additive manufacturing. *Sci. Rep.* **2017**, *7*, 4085. [CrossRef]
65. Raza, A.; Pauzon, C.; Hryha, E.; Markström, A.; Forêt, P. Spatter oxidation during laser powder bed fusion of Alloy 718: Dependence on oxygen content in the process atmosphere. *Addit. Manuf.* **2021**, *48*, 102369. [CrossRef]
66. Gasper, A.; Szost, B.; Wang, X.; Johns, D.; Sharma, S.; Clare, A.; Ashcroft, I. Spatter and oxide formation in laser powder bed fusion of Inconel 718. *Addit. Manuf.* **2018**, *24*, 446–456. [CrossRef]
67. Yang, T.; Liu, T.; Liao, W.; MacDonald, E.; Wei, H.; Zhang, C.; Chen, X.; Zhang, K. Laser powder bed fusion of AlSi10Mg: Influence of energy intensities on spatter and porosity evolution, microstructure and mechanical properties. *J. Alloy. Compd.* **2020**, *849*, 156300. [CrossRef]
68. Khairallah, S.A.; Anderson, A.T.; Rubenchik, A.; King, W.E. Laser powder-bed fusion additive manufacturing: Physics of complex melt flow and formation mechanisms of pores, spatter, and denudation zones. *Acta Mater.* **2016**, *108*, 36–45. [CrossRef]
69. Khairallah, S.A.; Martin, A.A.; Lee, J.R.I.; Guss, G.; Calta, N.P.; Hammons, J.A.; Nielsen, M.H.; Chaput, K.; Schwalbach, E.; Shah, M.N.; et al. Controlling interdependent meso-nanosecond dynamics and defect generation in metal 3D printing. *Science* **2020**, *368*, 660–665. [CrossRef]
70. Altmeppen, J.; Nekic, R.; Wagenblast, P.; Staudacher, S. Transient simulation of particle transport and deposition in the laser powder bed fusion process: A new approach to model particle and heat ejection from the melt pool. *Addit. Manuf.* **2021**, *46*, 102135. [CrossRef]
71. Zhao, C.; Guo, Q.; Li, X.; Parab, N.; Fezzaa, K.; Tan, W.; Chen, L.; Sun, T. Bulk-Explosion-Induced Metal Spattering During Laser Processing. *Phys. Rev. X* **2019**, *9*, 021052. [CrossRef]
72. Yin, J.; Zhang, W.; Ke, L.; Wei, H.; Wang, D.; Yang, L.; Zhu, H.; Dong, P.; Wang, G.; Zeng, X. Vaporization of alloying elements and explosion behavior during laser powder bed fusion of Cu–10Zn alloy. *Int. J. Mach. Tools Manuf.* **2020**, *161*, 103686. [CrossRef]
73. Gould, B.; Wolff, S.; Parab, N.; Zhao, C.; Lorenzo-Martin, M.C.; Fezzaa, K.; Greco, A.; Sun, T. In Situ Analysis of Laser Powder Bed Fusion Using Simultaneous High-Speed Infrared and X-ray Imaging. *JOM* **2020**, *73*, 201–211. [CrossRef]
74. Dai, D.; Gu, D.; Ge, Q.; Li, Y.; Shi, X.; Sun, Y.; Li, S. Mesoscopic study of thermal behavior, fluid dynamics and surface morphology during selective laser melting of Ti-based composites. *Comput. Mater. Sci.* **2020**, *177*, 109598. [CrossRef]

75. Bärtl, M.; Xiao, X.; Brillo, J.; Palm, F. Influence of Surface Tension and Evaporation on Melt Dynamics of Aluminum Alloys for Laser Powder Bed Fusion. *J. Mater. Eng. Perform.* **2022**, 1–13. [CrossRef]
76. Leung, C.L.A.; Marussi, S.; Atwood, R.C.; Towrie, M.; Withers, P.; Lee, P.D. In situ X-ray imaging of defect and molten pool dynamics in laser additive manufacturing. *Nat. Commun.* **2018**, *9*, 1355. [CrossRef]
77. Chen, H.; Yan, W. Spattering and denudation in laser powder bed fusion process: Multiphase flow modelling. *Acta Mater.* **2020**, *196*, 154–167. [CrossRef]
78. Gunenthiram, V.; Peyre, P.; Schneider, M.; Dal, M.; Coste, F.; Koutiri, I.; Fabbro, R. Experimental analysis of spatter generation and melt-pool behavior during the powder bed laser beam melting process. *J. Mater. Process. Technol.* **2018**, *251*, 376–386. [CrossRef]
79. Andani, M.T.; Dehghani, R.; Karamooz-Ravari, M.R.; Mirzaeifar, R.; Ni, J. Spatter formation in selective laser melting process using multi-laser technology. *Mater. Des.* **2017**, *131*, 460–469. [CrossRef]
80. Yin, J.; Wang, D.; Wei, H.; Yang, L.; Ke, L.; Hu, M.; Xiong, W.; Wang, G.; Zhu, H.; Zeng, X. Dual-beam laser-matter interaction at overlap region during multi-laser powder bed fusion manufacturing. *Addit. Manuf.* **2021**, *46*, 102178. [CrossRef]
81. Spierings, A.; Herres, N.; Levy, G. Influence of the particle size distribution on surface quality and mechanical properties in AM steel parts. *Rapid Prototyp. J.* **2011**, *17*, 195–202. [CrossRef]
82. Schwerz, C.; Raza, A.; Lei, X.; Nyborg, L.; Hryha, E.; Wirdelius, H. In-situ detection of redeposited spatter and its influence on the formation of internal flaws in laser powder bed fusion. *Addit. Manuf.* **2021**, *47*, 102370. [CrossRef]
83. Ferrar, B.; Mullen, L.; Jones, E.; Stamp, R.; Sutcliffe, C.J. Gas flow effects on selective laser melting (SLM) manufacturing performance. *J. Mater. Process. Technol.* **2012**, *212*, 355–364. [CrossRef]
84. Anwar, A.B.; Pham, Q.C. Selective laser melting of AlSi10Mg: Effects of scan direction, part placement and inert gas flow velocity on tensile strength. *J. Mater. Processing Technol.* **2017**, *240*, 388–396. [CrossRef]
85. Anwar, A.B.; Pham, Q.C. Study of the spatter distribution on the powder bed during selective laser melting. *Addit. Manuf.* **2018**, *22*, 86–97. [CrossRef]
86. Anwar, A.B.; Pham, Q. Spattering in selective laser melting: A review of spatter formation, effects and countermeasures. In Proceedings of the International Conference on Progress in Additive Manufacturing, Singapore, 14–17 May 2018; pp. 541–546.
87. Ladewig, A.; Schlick, G.; Fisser, M.; Schulze, V.; Glatzel, U. Influence of the shielding gas flow on the removal of process by-products in the selective laser melting process. *Addit. Manuf.* **2016**, *10*, 1–9. [CrossRef]
88. Li, R.; Shi, Y.; Wang, Z.; Wang, L.; Liu, J.; Jiang, W. Densification behavior of gas and water atomized 316L stainless steel powder during selective laser melting. *Appl. Surf. Sci.* **2010**, *256*, 4350–4356. [CrossRef]
89. Kruth, J.P.; Froyen, L.; Van Vaerenbergh, J.; Mercelis, P.; Rombouts, M.; Lauwers, B. Selective laser melting of iron-based powder. *J. Mater. Processing Technol.* **2004**, *149*, 616–622. [CrossRef]
90. Sutton, A.T.; Kriewall, C.S.; Leu, M.C.; Newkirk, J.W.; Brown, B. Characterization of laser spatter and condensate generated during the selective laser melting of 304L stainless steel powder. *Addit. Manuf.* **2019**, *31*, 100904. [CrossRef]
91. Aucott, L.; Dong, H.; Mirihanage, W.; Atwood, R.; Kidess, A.; Gao, S.; Wen, S.; Marsden, J.; Feng, S.; Tong, M.; et al. Revealing internal flow behaviour in arc welding and additive manufacturing of metals. *Nat. Commun.* **2018**, *9*, 1–7. [CrossRef]
92. Wang, D.; Ye, G.; Dou, W.; Zhang, M.; Yang, Y.; Mai, S.; Liu, Y. Influence of spatter particles contamination on densification behavior and tensile properties of CoCrW manufactured by selective laser melting. *Opt. Laser Technol.* **2019**, *121*, 105678. [CrossRef]
93. Sartin, B.; Pond, T.; Griffith, B.; Everhart, W.; Elder, L.; Wenski, E.; Cook, C.; Wieliczka, D.; King, W.; Rubenchik, A. 316L powder reuse for metal additive manufacturing. In Proceedings of the 2017 International Solid Freeform Fabrication Symposium, Austin, TX, USA, 7–9 August 2017; pp. 351–364.
94. Delacroix, T.; Lomello, F.; Schuster, F.; Maskrot, H.; Garandet, J.-P. Influence of powder recycling on 316L stainless steel feedstocks and printed parts in laser powder bed fusion. *Addit. Manuf.* **2021**, *50*, 102553. [CrossRef]
95. Quintana, O.A.; Alvarez, J.; Mcmillan, R.; Tong, W.; Tomonto, C. Effects of Reusing Ti-6Al-4V Powder in a Selective Laser Melting Additive System Operated in an Industrial Setting. *JOM* **2018**, *70*, 1863–1869. [CrossRef]
96. Cordova, L.; Campos, M.; Tinga, T. Revealing the Effects of Powder Reuse for Selective Laser Melting by Powder Characterization. *JOM* **2019**, *71*, 1062–1072. [CrossRef]
97. Nezhadfar, P.D.; Soltani-Tehrani, A.; Sterling, A.; Tsolas, N.; Shamsaei, N. The effects of powder recycling on the mechanical properties of additively manufactured 17-4 PH stainless steel. In Proceedings of the 2018 International Solid Freeform Fabrication Symposium, Austin, TX, USA, 13–15 August 2018; pp. 1292–1300.
98. He, X.; Kong, D.; Zhou, Y.; Wang, L.; Ni, X.; Zhang, L.; Wu, W.; Li, R.; Li, X.; Dong, C. Powder recycling effects on porosity development and mechanical properties of Hastelloy X alloy during laser powder bed fusion process. *Addit. Manuf.* **2022**, *55*, 102840. [CrossRef]
99. Gorji, N.E.; O'Connor, R.; Mussatto, A.; Snelgrove, M.; González, P.G.M.; Brabazon, D. Recyclability of stainless steel (316L) powder within the additive manufacturing process. *Materialia* **2019**, *8*, 100489. [CrossRef]
100. Tang, H.P.; Qian, M.; Liu, N.; Zhang, X.Z.; Yang, G.Y.; Wang, J. Effect of Powder Reuse Times on Additive Manufacturing of Ti-6Al-4V by Selective Electron Beam Melting. *JOM* **2015**, *67*, 555–563. [CrossRef]
101. Yusuf, S.M.; Choo, E.; Gao, N. Comparison between Virgin and Recycled 316L SS and AlSi10Mg Powders Used for Laser Powder Bed Fusion Additive Manufacturing. *Metals* **2020**, *10*, 1625. [CrossRef]

102. Jacob, G.; Brown, C.U.; Donmez, M.A.; Watson, S.S.; Slotwinski, J. *Effects of Powder Recycling on Stainless Steel Powder and Built Material Properties in Metal Powder Bed Fusion Processes*; National Institute of Standards and Technology: Gaithersburg, MD, USA, 2017; p. 46.
103. Simonelli, M.; Tuck, C.; Aboulkhair, N.T.; Maskery, I.; Ashcroft, I.; Wildman, R.D.; Hague, R. A Study on the Laser Spatter and the Oxidation Reactions During Selective Laser Melting of 316L Stainless Steel, Al-Si10-Mg, and Ti-6Al-4V. *Met. Mater. Trans. A* **2015**, *46*, 3842–3851. [CrossRef]
104. Wang, D.; Yang, Y.; Liu, R.; Xiao, D.; Sun, J. Study on the designing rules and processability of porous structure based on selective laser melting (SLM). *J. Mater. Process. Technol.* **2013**, *213*, 1734–1742. [CrossRef]
105. Santecchia, E.; Spigarelli, S.; Cabibbo, M. Material Reuse in Laser Powder Bed Fusion: Side Effects of the Laser—Metal Powder Interaction. *Metals* **2020**, *10*, 341. [CrossRef]
106. Pal, S.; Lojen, G.; Hudak, R.; Rajtukova, V.; Brajlih, T.; Kokol, V.; Drstvenšek, I. As-fabricated surface morphologies of Ti-6Al-4V samples fabricated by different laser processing parameters in selective laser melting. *Addit. Manuf.* **2020**, *33*, 101147. [CrossRef]
107. Hatami, S. Variation of fatigue strength of parts manufactured by laser powder bed fusion. *Powder Met.* **2021**, *65*, 259–264. [CrossRef]
108. Lutter-Günther, M.; Bröker, M.; Mayer, T.; Lizak, S.; Seidel, C.; Reinhart, G. Spatter formation during laser beam melting of AlSi10Mg and effects on powder quality. *Procedia CIRP* **2018**, *74*, 33–38. [CrossRef]
109. Darvish, K.; Chen, Z.; Pasang, T. Reducing lack of fusion during selective laser melting of CoCrMo alloy: Effect of laser power on geometrical features of tracks. *Mater. Des.* **2016**, *112*, 357–366. [CrossRef]
110. Obeidi, M.A.; Mussatto, A.; Groarke, R.; Vijayaraghavan, R.K.; Conway, A.; Kaschel, F.R.; McCarthy, E.; Clarkin, O.; O'Connor, R.; Brabazon, D. Comprehensive assessment of spatter material generated during selective laser melting of stainless steel. *Mater. Today Commun.* **2020**, *25*, 101294. [CrossRef]
111. Ali, U.; Esmaeilizadeh, R.; Ahmed, F.; Sarker, D.; Muhammad, W.; Keshavarzkermani, A.; Mahmoodkhani, Y.; Marzbanrad, E.; Toyserkani, E. Identification and characterization of spatter particles and their effect on surface roughness, density and mechanical response of 17-4 PH stainless steel laser powder-bed fusion parts. *Mater. Sci. Eng. A* **2019**, *756*, 98–107. [CrossRef]
112. Esmaeilizadeh, R.; Ali, U.; Keshavarzkermani, A.; Mahmoodkhani, Y.; Marzbanrad, E.; Toyserkani, E. On the effect of spatter particles distribution on the quality of Hastelloy X parts made by laser powder-bed fusion additive manufacturing. *J. Manuf. Process.* **2018**, *37*, 11–20. [CrossRef]
113. Strondl, A.; Lyckfeldt, O.; Brodin, H.; Ackelid, U. Characterization and Control of Powder Properties for Additive Manufacturing. *JOM* **2015**, *67*, 549–554. [CrossRef]
114. Lu, C.; Zhang, R.; Wei, X.; Xiao, M.; Yin, Y.; Qu, Y.; Li, H.; Liu, P.; Qiu, X.; Guo, T. An investigation on the oxidation behavior of spatters generated during the laser powder bed fusion of 316L stainless steel. *Appl. Surf. Sci.* **2022**, *586*, 152796. [CrossRef]
115. Shi, W.; Han, Y.; Liu, Y.; Jing, Y.; Ren, B. Mechanism and Experimental Study of TC4 Spheroidization and Splash in Selective Laser Melting. *Surf. Technol.* **2021**, *50*, 75–82. (In Chinese)
116. Sow, M.; De Terris, T.; Castelnau, O.; Hamouche, Z.; Coste, F.; Fabbro, R.; Peyre, P. Influence of beam diameter on Laser Powder Bed Fusion (L-PBF) process. *Addit. Manuf.* **2020**, *36*, 101532. [CrossRef]
117. Young, Z.A.; Coday, M.M.; Guo, Q.; Qu, M.; Hojjatzadeh, S.M.H.; Escano, L.I.; Fezzaa, K.; Sun, T.; Chen, L. Uncertainties Induced by Processing Parameter Variation in Selective Laser Melting of Ti6Al4V Revealed by In-Situ X-ray Imaging. *Materials* **2022**, *15*, 530. [CrossRef]
118. Nguyen, H.D.; Sedao, X.; Mauclair, C.; Bidron, G.; Faure, N.; Moreno, E.; Colombier, J.-P.; Stoian, R. Non-Diffractive Bessel Beams for Ultrafast Laser Scanning Platform and Proof-of-Concept Side-Wall Polishing of Additively Manufactured Parts. *Micromachines* **2020**, *11*, 974. [CrossRef]
119. Okunkova, A.; Volosova, M.; Peretyagin, P.; Vladimirov, Y.; Zhirnov, I.; Gusarov, A. Experimental Approbation of Selective Laser Melting of Powders by the Use of Non-Gaussian Power Density Distributions. *Phys. Procedia* **2014**, *56*, 48–57. [CrossRef]
120. Bin Anwar, A.; Ibrahim, I.H.; Pham, Q.-C. Spatter transport by inert gas flow in selective laser melting: A simulation study. *Powder Technol.* **2019**, *352*, 103–116. [CrossRef]
121. Bidare, P.; Bitharas, I.; Ward, R.; Attallah, M.; Moore, A.J. Laser powder bed fusion at sub-atmospheric pressures. *International J. Mach. Tools Manuf.* **2018**, *130–131*, 65–72. [CrossRef]
122. Kaserer, L.; Bergmueller, S.; Braun, J.; Leichtfried, G. Vacuum laser powder bed fusion—Track consolidation, powder denudation, and future potential. *Int. J. Adv. Manuf. Technol.* **2020**, *110*, 3339–3346. [CrossRef]
123. Li, X.; Guo, Q.; Chen, L.; Tan, W. Quantitative investigation of gas flow, powder-gas interaction, and powder behavior under different ambient pressure levels in laser powder bed fusion. *Int. J. Mach. Tools Manuf.* **2021**, *170*, 103797. [CrossRef]
124. Wu, W.; Yang, Y.; Mao, X.; Li, Y. Precision Optimization Process for Metal Part Manufactured by Selective Laser Melting. *Foundry Technol.* **2016**, *37*, 2636–2640. (In Chinese)
125. Pauzon, C.; Hoppe, B.; Pichler, T.; Goff, S.D.-L.; Forêt, P.; Nguyen, T.; Hryha, E. Reduction of incandescent spatter with helium addition to the process gas during laser powder bed fusion of Ti-6Al-4V. *CIRP J. Manuf. Sci. Technol.* **2021**, *35*, 371–378. [CrossRef]
126. Wang, J.; Zhu, Y.; Li, H.; Liu, S.; Shen, S.; Wang, L.; Wen, S. Numerical Study of the Flow Field and Spatter Particles in Laser-based Powder Bed Fusion Manufacturing. *Int. J. Precis. Eng. Manuf. Technol.* **2021**, *9*, 1009–1020. [CrossRef]

127. Pérez-Ruiz, J.D.; de Lacalle, L.N.L.; Urbikain, G.; Pereira, O.; Martínez, S.; Bris, J. On the relationship between cutting forces and anisotropy features in the milling of LPBF Inconel 718 for near net shape parts. *Int. J. Mach. Tools Manuf.* **2021**, *170*, 103801. [CrossRef]
128. Mumtaz, K.; Hopkinson, N. Selective Laser Melting of thin wall parts using pulse shaping. *J. Mater. Process. Technol.* **2010**, *210*, 279–287. [CrossRef]
129. Tumkur, T.U.; Voisin, T.; Shi, R.; Depond, P.J.; Roehling, T.T.; Wu, S.; Crumb, M.F.; Roehling, J.D.; Guss, G.; Khairallah, S.A.; et al. Nondiffractive beam shaping for enhanced optothermal control in metal additive manufacturing. *Sci. Adv.* **2021**, *7*, eabg9358. [CrossRef]
130. Rivalta, F.; Ceschini, L.; Jarfors, A.; Stolt, R. Effect of Scanning Strategy in the L-PBF Process of 18Ni300 Maraging Steel. *Metals* **2021**, *11*, 826. [CrossRef]
131. Achee, T.; Guss, G.; Elwany, A.; Matthews, M. Laser pre-sintering for denudation reduction in the laser powder bed fusion additive manufacturing of Ti-6Al-4V alloy. *Addit. Manuf.* **2021**, *42*, 101985. [CrossRef]
132. Annovazzi, A.; Dembinski, L.; Blanchet, E.; Vayre, B.; Fenineche, N.; Walrand, G. Influence of residual pressure on the melting of a powder bed induced by a laser beam. *J. Manuf. Process.* **2021**, *73*, 715–724. [CrossRef]
133. Constantin, L.; Kraiem, N.; Wu, Z.; Cui, B.; Battaglia, J.-L.; Garnier, C.; Silvain, J.-F.; Lu, Y.F. Manufacturing of complex diamond-based composite structures via laser powder-bed fusion. *Addit. Manuf.* **2021**, *40*, 101927. [CrossRef]
134. Chien, C.-Y.; Le, T.-N.; Lin, Z.-H.; Lo, Y.-L. Numerical and Experimental Investigation into Gas Flow Field and Spattering Phenomena in Laser Powder Bed Fusion Processing of Inconel 718. *Mater. Des.* **2021**, *210*, 110107. [CrossRef]
135. Philo, A.M.; Butcher, D.; Sillars, S.; Sutcliffe, C.J.; Sienz, J.; Brown, S.G.R.; Lavery, N.P. A Multiphase CFD Model for the Prediction of Particulate Accumulation in a Laser Powder Bed Fusion Process. In *Proceedings of the CFD Modeling and Simulation in Materials Processing 2018*; Springer: Cham, Switzerland, 2018; pp. 65–76. [CrossRef]
136. Xiao, J.; Xie, Y. Wind field simulation and optimization of 3D metal printing device with SLM. *Mag. Equip. Mach.* **2021**, *2*, 34–39. (In Chinese)
137. Zhang, X.; Cheng, B.; Tuffile, C. Simulation study of the spatter removal process and optimization design of gas flow system in laser powder bed fusion. *Addit. Manuf.* **2020**, *32*, 101049. [CrossRef]
138. Koike, R.; Sugiura, Y. Metal powder bed fusion in high gravity. *CIRP Ann.* **2021**, *70*, 191–194. [CrossRef]
139. Sugiura, Y.; Koike, R. High-gravitational effect on process stabilization for metal powder bed fusion. *Addit. Manuf.* **2021**, *46*, 102153. [CrossRef]
140. Leung, C.L.A.; Marussi, S.; Towrie, M.; Garcia, J.D.V.; Atwood, R.C.; Bodey, A.J.; Jones, J.R.; Withers, P.J.; Lee, P.D. Laser-matter interactions in additive manufacturing of stainless steel SS316L and 13–93 bioactive glass revealed by in situ X-ray imaging. *Addit. Manuf.* **2018**, *24*, 647–657. [CrossRef]
141. Heiden, M.J.; Deibler, L.A.; Rodelas, J.M.; Koepke, J.R.; Tung, D.J.; Saiz, D.J.; Jared, B.H. Evolution of 316L stainless steel feedstock due to laser powder bed fusion process. *Addit. Manuf.* **2018**, *25*, 84–103. [CrossRef]
142. Fedina, T.; Sundqvist, J.; Powell, J.; Kaplan, A.F. A comparative study of water and gas atomized low alloy steel powders for additive manufacturing. *Addit. Manuf.* **2020**, *36*, 101675. [CrossRef]
143. Fedina, T.; Sundqvist, J.; Kaplan, A.F.H. Spattering and oxidation phenomena during recycling of low alloy steel powder in Laser Powder Bed Fusion. *Mater. Today Commun.* **2021**, *27*, 102241. [CrossRef]
144. Andreas Wiesner, B.H. Apparatus for Producing Work Pieces under Elevated Pressure. EP2774703A1, 10 September 2014.
145. Zhao, Y. Metal 3D Printer Blast Apparatus. CN112024879A, 4 December 2020. (In Chinese).
146. Justin Manrak, M.R.R. Airflow System of Additive Manufacturing Machine. CN111315511A, 19 June 2020. (In Chinese).
147. Fausto Riva, S.C. Gas Flow within Additive Manufacturing Device. EP3023228B1, 8 August 2018.
148. Tan, J.H.; Wong, W.L.E.; Dalgarno, K.W. An overview of powder granulometry on feedstock and part performance in the selective laser melting process. *Addit. Manuf.* **2017**, *18*, 228–255. [CrossRef]
149. Bitharas, I.; Parab, N.; Zhao, C.; Sun, T.; Rollett, A.D.; Moore, A.J. The interplay between vapour, liquid, and solid phases in laser powder bed fusion. *Nat. Commun.* **2022**, *13*, 2959. [CrossRef]

MDPI
St. Alban-Anlage 66
4052 Basel
Switzerland
Tel. +41 61 683 77 34
Fax +41 61 302 89 18
www.mdpi.com

Micromachines Editorial Office
E-mail: micromachines@mdpi.com
www.mdpi.com/journal/micromachines

www.ingramcontent.com/pod-product-compliance
Lightning Source LLC
LaVergne TN
LVHW070503100526
838202LV00014B/1778